MICROSOFT
POWERPOINT 7
COMPLETE CONCEPTS AND TECHNIQUES

MICROSOFT **POWERPOINT 7**
COMPLETE CONCEPTS AND TECHNIQUES

Gary B. Shelly
Thomas J. Cashman
Marvin M. Boetcher
Sherry L. Green

COURSE
TECHNOLOGY

SHELLY
CASHMAN
SERIES®

boyd & fraser

A DIVISION OF COURSE TECHNOLOGY
ONE MAIN STREET
CAMBRIDGE MA 02412

an International Thomson Publishing company   I T P°

CAMBRIDGE • ALBANY • BONN • CINCINNATI • LONDON • MADRID • MELBOURNE

MEXICO CITY • NEW YORK • PARIS • SAN FRANCISCO • TOKYO • TORONTO • WASHINGTON

© 1997 boyd & fraser publishing company
A Division of Course Technology
One Main Street
Cambridge, Massachusetts 02142

 International Thomson Publishing
boyd & fraser publishing company is an ITP company.
The ITP logo is a registered trademark of International Thomson Publishing.

Printed in the United States of America

For more information, contact boyd & fraser publishing company:

boyd & fraser publishing company
A Division of Course Technology
One Main Street
Cambridge, Massachusetts 02142, USA

International Thomson Editores
Campos Eliseos 385, Piso 7
Colonia Polanco
11560 Mexico D.F. Mexico

International Thomson Publishing Europe
Berkshire House
168-173 High Holborn
London, WC1V 7AA, United Kingdom

International Thomson Publishing GmbH
Konigswinterer Strasse 418
53227 Bonn, Germany

Thomas Nelson Australia
102 Dodds Street
South Melbourne
Victoria 3205 Australia

International Thomson Publishing Asia
Block 211, Henderson Road #08-03
Henderson Industrial Park
Singapore 0315

Nelson Canada
1120 Birchmont Road
Scarborough, Ontario
Canada M1K 5G4

International Thomson Publishing Japan
Hirakawa-cho Kyowa Building, 3F
2-2-1 Hirakawa-cho, Chiyoda-ku
Tokyo 102, Japan

ISBN 0-7895-0715-3

PHOTO CREDITS: *Project 1, page PP 1.4*, SoftKey International Inc.; *Project 2, page PP 2.2*, Planes and chart, Courtesy of Corel
Professional Photos CD-ROM Image usage; *Project 3, page PP 3.4*, Speaker image provided by PhotoDisc Inc. © 1996; Demosthenes
provided by North Wind Picture Archive; *page PP 3.5*, Pie chart, Courtesy of Corel Professional Photos CD-ROM Image usage;
Project 4, page PP 4.2, Film strip image provided by PhotoDisc Inc. © 1996; Mona Lisa and velociraptors, Courtesy of Corel
Professional Photos CD-ROM Image usage; *page PP 4.3*, Golf, top hat and baseball images, © Metatools, created by PhotoSpin

1 2 3 4 5 6 7 8 9 10 BC 10 9 8 7

MICROSOFT POWERPOINT 7
COMPLETE CONCEPTS AND TECHNIQUES

C O N T E N T S

Microsoft PowerPoint 7   **PP 1.1**

▶ **PROJECT ONE**

USING A DESIGN TEMPLATE AND STYLE CHECKER TO CREATE A PRESENTATION

Objectives	**PP 1.3**
What Is PowerPoint?	**PP 1.6**
Project One – College Survival	**PP 1.8**
Mouse Usage	PP 1.8
Slide Preparation Steps	PP 1.9
Starting a Presentation as a New Office Document	**PP 1.9**
The PowerPoint Window	PP 1.13
PowerPoint Views	**PP 1.13**
PowerPoint Window in Slide View	PP 1.13
Creating a Title Slide	**PP 1.16**
Entering the Presentation Title	PP 1.16
Correcting a Mistake When Typing	PP 1.17
Entering the Presentation Subtitle	PP 1.18
Text Attributes	**PP 1.19**
Changing the Font Size	PP 1.19
Changing the Style of Text to Italic	PP 1.21
Saving a Presentation to a Floppy Disk	**PP 1.22**
Adding a New Slide to a Presentation	**PP 1.24**
Creating a Bulleted List Slide	**PP 1.26**
Entering a Slide Title	PP 1.26
Selecting a Text Placeholder	PP 1.27
Typing a Multi-level Bulleted List	PP 1.28
Adding a New Slide with the Same AutoLayout	PP 1.30
Saving a Presentation with the Same Filename	**PP 1.32**
Moving to Another Slide in Slide View	**PP 1.33**
Using the Vertical Scroll Bar to Move to Another Slide	PP 1.33
Viewing the Presentation Using Slide Show	**PP 1.34**
Starting Slide Show View	PP 1.34
Advancing through a Slide Show Manually	PP 1.35
Displaying the Popup Menu in Slide Show View	PP 1.35
Using the Popup Menu to End a Slide Show	PP 1.36
Closing PowerPoint	**PP 1.37**
Opening a Presentation	**PP 1.38**
Opening an Existing Presentation	PP 1.38
Checking a Presentation for Visual Clarity, Consistency, and Style	**PP 1.40**
Starting Style Checker	PP 1.41
Correcting Errors	**PP 1.44**

Types of Corrections Made to Presentations	PP 1.44
Deleting Text	PP 1.44
Replacing Text into an Existing Slide	PP 1.45
Changing Line Spacing	**PP 1.45**
Displaying the Slide Master	PP 1.46
Changing Line Spacing on the Slide Master	PP 1.47
Displaying a Presentation in Black and White	**PP 1.49**
Printing a Presentation	**PP 1.50**
Saving Before Printing	PP 1.51
Printing the Presentation	PP 1.51
Making a Transparency	PP 1.53
PowerPoint Help	**PP 1.53**
Using the Contents Sheet to Obtain Help	PP 1.53
Using the Index Sheet to Obtain Help	PP 1.55
Using the Find Sheet to Obtain Help	PP 1.56
Using the Answer Wizard Sheet to Obtain Help	PP 1.58
Using the Help Button	PP 1.60
Using the Question Mark Button	PP 1.61
Closing PowerPoint	PP 1.61
Project Summary	**PP 1.62**
What You Should Know	**PP 1.62**
Test Your Knowledge	**PP 1.63**
Use Help	**PP 1.66**
Apply Your Knowledge	**PP 1.67**
In the Lab	**PP 1.68**
Cases and Places	**PP 1.72**

▶ **PROJECT TWO**

USING OUTLINE VIEW AND CLIP ART TO CREATE AN ELECTRONIC SLIDE SHOW

Objectives	**PP 2.1**
Creating a Presentation from an Outline	**PP 2.4**
Project Two – Spring Break Specials	**PP 2.5**
Presentation Preparation Steps	PP 2.6
Starting a New Presentation	**PP 2.7**
Using Outline View	**PP 2.7**
The PowerPoint Window in Outline View	PP 2.9
Creating a Presentation in Outline View	**PP 2.10**
Creating a Title Slide in Outline View	PP 2.10
Adding a Slide in Outline View	PP 2.12
Creating Multi-level Bulleted List Slides in Outline View	PP 2.13
Creating a Subordinate Slide	PP 2.15
Creating a Second Subordinate Slide	PP 2.16
Creating a Slide with Multiple Text Objects in Outline View	**PP 2.16**

Creating a Closing Slide in Outline View — PP 2.17
Saving the Presentation — **PP 2.18**
Reviewing a Presentation in Slide Sorter View — **PP 2.19**
Adding a Blank Line — PP 2.20
Adding a Blank Line to Slide 2 — PP 2.22
Changing Slide Layout — **PP 2.23**
Moving Text — PP 2.25
Adding Clip Art to a Slide — **PP 2.26**
Using AutoLayouts to Add Clip Art — PP 2.27
Changing Slide Layout to Clip Art & Text — PP 2.27
Inserting Clip Art into a Clip Art Placeholder — PP 2.28
Inserting Clip Art on a Slide without a
Clip Art Placeholder — PP 2.32
Moving Clip Art — PP 2.33
Changing the Size of Clip Art Using the Scale
Command — PP 2.33
Saving the Presentation — PP 2.36
Adding a Header and a Footer to Outline Pages — **PP 2.36**
Using the Notes and Handouts Sheet to
Add Headers and Footers — PP 2.36
**Checking the Presentation for Spelling
and Style Errors** — **PP 2.38**
Adding Animation Effects — **PP 2.39**
Adding Slide Transitions to a Slide Show — PP 2.39
Slide Sorter Toolbar — PP 2.43
Applying Text Build Effects to Bulleted Slides — PP 2.43
Saving the Presentation Again — PP 2.45
Running a Slide Show with Animation Effects — **PP 2.46**
Printing in Outline View — **PP 2.47**
Printing an Outline — PP 2.48
Printing Presentation Slides in Outline View — PP 2.49
Editing a Presentation — **PP 2.53**
Displaying Slide Titles in Outline View — PP 2.53
Changing Slide Order in Outline View — PP 2.54
Displaying All Text in Outline View — PP 2.56
Changing Slide Order in Slide Sorter View — PP 2.56
Copying a Slide — PP 2.58
Pasting a Slide into a Presentation — PP 2.59
Using the Undo Button to Reverse the
Last Edit — PP 2.60
Saving and Closing PowerPoint — PP 2.60
Project Summary — **PP 2.61**
What You Should Know — **PP 2.61**
Test Your Knowledge — **PP 2.62**
Use Help — **PP 2.65**
Apply Your Knowledge — **PP 2.66**
In the Lab — **PP 2.68**
Cases and Places — **PP 2.75**

▶ **INTEGRATION FEATURE**
**LINKING AN EXCEL CHART TO A
POWERPOINT PRESENTATION**

Introduction — **PPI 1.1**
Opening an Existing Presentation and
Saving It with a New Filename — PPI 1.2
Creating a Chart Slide — **PPI 1.3**
Inserting a New Slide Between Two Slides — PPI 1.3
Typing a Slide Title — PPI 1.4

Linking an Excel Chart to a Presentation — **PPI 1.4**
Scaling a Linked Object — PPI 1.6
Saving and Printing a Linked Presentation — PPI 1.6
Summary — **PPI 1.7**
What You Should Know — **PPI 1.7**
In the Lab — **PPI 1.7**

▶ **PROJECT THREE**
EMBEDDED VISUALS

Objectives — **PP 3.3**
**Creating Exciting Presentations Using
Embedded Visuals** — **PP 3.6**
Project Three – Microsoft Office 95 Workshop — **PP 3.6**
Slide Preparation Steps — PP 3.7
Importing Outlines Created in Another Application — **PP 3.8**
Opening an Existing Outline Created in
Another Application — PP 3.8
Changing Presentation Design Templates — **PP 3.11**
Saving the Presentation — **PP 3.14**
Creating a Custom Background — **PP 3.14**
Changing the Slide Layout to Title Slide — PP 3.14
Inserting a Picture to Create a Custom
Background — PP 3.15
Embedding an Organization Chart — **PP 3.20**
Changing Slide Layouts — PP 3.21
Opening the Organization Chart Application — PP 3.21
Maximizing the Organization Chart Window — PP 3.22
Creating the Title for the Root Manager Box — PP 3.23
Deleting Subordinate Boxes — PP 3.24
Titling the Subordinate Box — PP 3.25
Adding Subordinate Boxes — PP 3.25
Adding Another Level of Subordinate Boxes — PP 3.27
Adding Names to the Subordinate Boxes — PP 3.27
Changing Organization Chart Styles — PP 3.28
Copying a Branch of an Organization Chart — PP 3.30
Pasting a Branch of an Organization Chart — PP 3.31
Editing an Organization Chart — PP 3.32
Formatting an Organization Chart — PP 3.33
Adding Shadow Effects to Boxes in an
Organization Chart — PP 3.34
Adding Shadow Effects to Boxes in an
Organization Chart — PP 3.34
Changing Border Styles in an Organization Chart — PP 3.35
Closing Organization Chart and Returning to
PowerPoint — PP 3.36
Scaling an Organization Chart Object — PP 3.37
Creating a PowerPoint Clip Art Object — **PP 3.38**
Inserting Clip Art — PP 3.39
Scaling Clip Art — PP 3.39
Using the View Menu to Display the
Drawing+ Toolbar — PP 3.40
Disassembling Clip Art — PP 3.41
Deselecting Clip Art Objects — PP 3.43
Embedding an Existing Excel Chart — PP 3.44
Moving a PowerPoint Object — PP 3.44
Embedding an Excel Chart — PP 3.45
Scaling an Embedded Object — PP 3.47
Grouping Objects — **PP 3.48**
Overlaying Objects — PP 3.49

Grouping the Two Layered Objects into
One Modified Screen Object PP 3.50
Dragging a Modified Object PP 3.51
Sending an Object to the Background PP 3.51
Selecting Objects PP 3.52
Grouping Selected Objects PP 3.53
Embedding a Picture into a Slide **PP 3.54**
Inserting a Picture PP 3.54
Resizing a Picture PP 3.55
Adding a Border to the Picture PP 3.57
Changing the Fill Color of the Border PP 3.58
Creating a Blank Closing Slide **PP 3.60**
Adding Slide Transition and Text Build Effects PP 3.60
Printing Slides as Handouts PP 3.61
Project Summary **PP 3.63**
What You Should Know **PP 3.63**
Test Your Knowledge **PP 3.64**
Use Help **PP 3.68**
Apply Your Knowledge **PP 3.69**
In the Lab **PP 3.71**
Cases and Places **PP 3.75**

▶ **PROJECT FOUR**

CREATING A PRESENTATION CONTAINING
INTERACTIVE OLE DOCUMENTS

Objectives **PP 4.1**
Introduction **PP 4.4**
Slide Preparation Steps PP 4.5
Project Four – Customizing an Existing Presentation **PP 4.6**
Opening a Presentation and Saving It with a
New Filename PP 4.7
Editing Text PP 4.7
Changing Design Template PP 4.8
Displaying Background Graphics on the Masters PP 4.9
Selecting a New Color Scheme **PP 4.10**
Selecting a Color Scheme PP 4.10
Modifying a Color Scheme PP 4.12
Creating a Logo **PP 4.15**
Opening a New Presentation PP 4.16
Drawing a Logo PP 4.16
Displaying Rulers PP 4.17
Displaying Guides PP 4.17
Increasing Zoom Control PP 4.18
Drawing a Circle PP 4.19
Adding a Border to a Logo PP 4.20
Creating a Graphic Object with Text **PP 4.21**
Opening WordArt PP 4.21
Entering WordArt Text PP 4.23
Shaping WordArt Text PP 4.23
Changing the WordArt Font Color PP 4.24
Adding a Border to WordArt Text PP 4.26
Exiting WordArt PP 4.28
Scaling an Object **PP 4.30**
Grouping Objects **PP 4.30**
Adding an Object to the Slide Master **PP 4.31**
Adjusting the Size and Placement of an Object PP 4.33
Pasting an Object on a Slide PP 4.34
Creating an Interactive Document **PP 4.36**

Adding a New Slide PP 4.37
Inserting and Linking a Word Document to a
PowerPoint Presentation PP 4.38
Linking a PowerPoint Presentation to
Another PowerPoint Presentation PP 4.39
Linking a Worksheet and Chart to a
PowerPoint Presentation PP 4.39
Embedding an Access Database to a PowerPoint
Presentation PP 4.40
Scaling Objects PP 4.40
Adding Fill Color to an Object PP 4.41
Adding Shadow to an Object PP 4.41
Adding a Border to an Object PP 4.42
Setting Up an Application to Open During a
Slide Show PP 4.43
Replacing a Picture **PP 4.45**
Deleting an Object PP 4.45
Editing a Bulleted List PP 4.46
Inserting a Picture PP 4.47
Scaling an Object PP 4.48
Displaying and Positioning Guides PP 4.48
Positioning and Resizing an Object PP 4.49
Adding a Border PP 4.51
Ending a Presentation with a Black Slide **PP 4.52**
Ending with a Black Slide PP 4.53
Applying Slide Transition Effects PP 4.53
Hiding Slides **PP 4.54**
Hiding a Slide PP 4.54
Animating an Object **PP 4.55**
Animating Text PP 4.57
Spell Check and Save the Presentation PP 4.57
**Running a Slide Show with a Hidden Slide and
Interactive Documents** **PP 4.58**
Project Summary **PP 4.59**
What You Should Know **PP 4.59**
Test Your Knowledge **PP 4.60**
Use Help **PP 4.62**
Apply Your Knowledge **PP 4.63**
In the Lab **PP 4.64**
Cases and Places **PP 4.71**

▶ **INTEGRATION FEATURE**

EMBEDDING A WORD TABLE INTO
A POWERPOINT PRESENTATION

Introduction **PPI 2.1**
Opening an Existing Presentation and Saving It
with a New FIlename PPI 2.2
Adding a Word Table to a PowerPoint Presentation **PPI 2.2**
Inserting a New Slide with the Table AutoLayout PPI 2.3
Opening Word and Inserting a Table PPI 2.3
Adding Column Headings PPI 2.4
Entering Data into Rows in a Table PPI 2.5
Formatting a Word Table in PowerPoint **PPI 2.6**
Saving and Printing an Embedded Presentation **PPI 2.7**
Summary **PPI 2.8**
In the Lab **PPI 2.8**

Index **PP I.2**

Preface

Shelly Cashman Series® Microsoft Windows 95 Books

The Shelly Cashman Series Microsoft Windows 95 books reinforce the fact that you made the right choice when you use a Shelly Cashman Series book. The Shelly Cashman Series Microsoft Windows 3.1 books were used by more schools and more students than any other series in textbook publishing. Yet the Shelly Cashman Series team wanted to produce even better books for Windows 95, so the books were thoroughly redesigned to present material in an even easier to understand format and with more project-ending activities. Features such as Other Ways and More Abouts were added to give in-depth knowledge to the student. The opening of each project provides a fascinating perspective of the subject covered in the project. Completely redesigned student assignments include the unique Cases and Places. This book provides the finest educational experience for a student learning about computer software.

Objectives of This Textbook

Microsoft PowerPoint 7: Complete Concepts and Techniques is intended for a one-unit course that presents Microsoft PowerPoint 7. The objectives of this book are:

- ▶ To teach the fundamentals of PowerPoint 7
- ▶ To foster an appreciation of presentations as a useful tool in the workplace
- ▶ To give students an in-depth understanding of designing presentations, including outlining, inserting clip art, and OLE
- ▶ To provide a knowledge base of Microsoft PowerPoint 7 on which students can build
- ▶ To help students who are working on their own

When students complete the course using this textbook, they will have a firm knowledge and understanding of PowerPoint 7.

The Shelly Cashman Approach

Features of the Shelly Cashman Series Windows 95 books include:

- ▶ **Project Orientation:** Each project in the book uses the unique Shelly Cashman Series screen-by-screen, step-by-step approach.
- ▶ **Screen-by-Screen, Step-by-Step Instructions:** Each of the tasks required to complete a project is identified throughout the development of the project. Then, steps to accomplish the task are specified. The steps are accompanied by screens. The student is not told to perform a step without seeing the result of the step on a color screen. Hence, students learn from this book the same as if they were using a computer.

▶ **Thoroughly Tested Projects:** The computer screens in the Shelly Cashman Series Windows 95 books are shot directly from the author's computer. The screen is shot immediately after the author performs the step specified in the text. Therefore, every screen in the book is correct because it is produced only after performing a specific step, resulting in unprecedented quality in a computer textbook.

▶ **Multiple Ways to Use the Book:** The book can be used in a variety of ways, including: (a) Lecture and textbook approach – The instructor lectures on the material in the book. The student reads and studies the material and then applies the knowledge to an application on the computer; (b) Tutorial approach – The student performs each specified step on a computer. At the end of the project, the student has solved the problem and is ready to solve comparable student assignments; (c) Other approaches – Many teachers lecture on the material and then require their students to perform each step in the project, reinforcing the material lectured. The students then complete one or more of the In the Lab exercises; and (d) Reference – Each task in a project is clearly identified. Therefore, the material serves as a complete reference.

▶ **Windows/Graphical User Interface Approach:** Windows 95 provides a graphical user interface and all the examples in this book use this interface. Thus, the mouse is the preferred user communication tool. The secondary, or right, mouse button is used extensively.

▶ **Other Ways Boxes for Reference:** Windows 95 provides a wide variety of ways to carry out a given task. The Other Ways boxes displayed at the end of most of the step-by-step sequences specify the other ways to do the task completed in the steps. Thus, the steps and the Other Ways box make a comprehensive reference unit. You no longer have to reference tables at the end of a chapter or the end of a book.

Organization of This Textbook

Microsoft PowerPoint 7: Complete Concepts and Techniques consists of four projects on Microsoft PowerPoint 7 and two Integration features. A short description of each follows.

Project 1 – Using a Design Template and Style Checker to Create a Presentation In Project 1, students are introduced to PowerPoint terminology, the PowerPoint window, and the basics of creating a multiple-level bulleted list presentation. Topics include starting PowerPoint; establishing the design of the presentation by selecting a Design Template; displaying information on every slide; changing text style; decreasing font size; saving a presentation; displaying slides in an electronic slide show; closing a presentation; opening an existing presentation; checking a presentation for spelling errors; identifying design inconsistencies using Style Checker, editing a presentation to correct errors; adjusting line spacing; displaying and printing a presentation in black and white; and obtaining online Help.

Project 2 – Using Outline View and Clip Art to Create an Electronic Slide Show In Project 2, students create a presentation in Outline view and learn how to insert clip art. Topics include creating a slide presentation by promoting and demoting text in Outline view; changing slide layouts; inserting clip art; adding slide transition effects and text build effects; running an animated electronic slide show; printing a presentation outline; printing presentation slides in Outline view; rearranging slide order; copying and pasting slides; and using the Undo button to reverse the last edit.

More *About* **Presentation Design**

Use pictures and graphics to convey a message. An audience can scan a graphic faster than text, thereby allowing the audience to focus on what the presenter is saying.

Other Ways

1. Double-click name of current Design Template on status bar
2. On Format menu click Apply Design Template
3. Press ALT+O, press M

Integration Feature 1 – Linking an Excel Chart to a PowerPoint Presentation   In this section, students are introduced to the linking feature of OLE by showing them how to link an Excel pie chart to a PowerPoint slide using the insert object method. Topics include linking a chart object to a slide; scaling a linked object; and saving a linked presentation.

Project 3 – Embedded Visuals   In Project 3, students create a presentation from a Microsoft Word outline and then enhance it with embedded visuals. Topics include creating a special slide background using a picture; embedding an organization chart; scaling an object; disassembling clip art; embedding a Microsoft Excel chart; grouping objects: layering objects; stacking objects; resizing objects; adding a border to a picture; and creating a closing slide.

Project 4 – Creating a Presentation Containing Interactive OLE Documents   In Project 4, students customize the presentation created in Project 3 by inserting a company logo, selecting a new color scheme, and then modifying the color scheme. Topics include: drawing a company logo; creating a graphic image from text using Microsoft WordArt; grouping the logo and graphic image into a logo object; embedding an object on the Slide Master; using object linking and embedding to create a slide containing interactive documents; using guides to position and size objects; modifying PowerPoint options to end a presentation with a black slide; hiding a slide; animating an object; and running a slide show to display a hidden slide in an active interactive document.

Integration Feature 2 – Embedding a Word Table into a PowerPoint Presentation   This section uses the Object Linking and Embedding (OLE) feature of Microsoft Office to insert a Word table into a PowerPoint slide. Topics include: opening an existing presentation and saving it with a new filename; opening Word and inserting a table; adding column headings; formatting a table; and saving and printing an embedded presentation.

End-of-Project Student Activities

A notable strength of the Shelly Cashman Series Windows 95 books is the extensive student activities at the end of each project. Well-structured student activities can make the difference between students merely participating in a class and students retaining the information they learn. These activities include all of the following sections.

▷ **What You Should Know**   A listing of the tasks completed within a project together with the pages where the step-by-step, screen-by-screen explanations appear. This section provides a perfect study review for the student.

▷ **Test Your Knowledge**   Four pencil-and-paper activities designed to determine the student's understanding of the material in the project. Included are true/false questions, multiple-choice questions, and two short-answer exercises.

▷ **Use Help**   Any user of Windows 95 applications must know how to use Help. Therefore, this book contains two Help exercises per project. These exercises alone distinguish the Shelly Cashman Series from any other set of Windows 95 instructional materials.

▷ **Apply Your Knowledge**   This exercise requires the student to open and manipulate a file from the Student Floppy Disk that accompanies the book.

▷ **In the Lab**   Three in-depth assignments per project that require the student to apply the knowledge gained in the project to solve problems on a computer.

▷ **Cases and Places**   Seven unique case studies allow students to apply their knowledge to real-world situations.

Instructor's Resource Kit

A comprehensive Instructor's Resource Kit (IRK) accompanies this textbook in the form of a CD-ROM. The CD-ROM includes an electronic Instructor's Manual (called ElecMan) and teaching and testing aids. The CD-ROM (ISBN 0-7895-1179-7) is available through your Course Technology representative or by calling 1-800-648-7450. The contents of the CD-ROM are listed below.

▶ **ElecMan** (*Electronic Instructor's Man*ual)   ElecMan is made up of Microsoft Word files. The files include lecture notes, solutions to laboratory assignments, and a large test bank. The files allow you to modify the lecture notes or generate quizzes and exams from the test bank using your own word processor. Where appropriate, solutions to laboratory assignments are embedded as icons in the files. When an icon appears, double-click it and the application will start and the solution will display on the screen. ElecMan includes the following for each project: project objectives; project overview; detailed lesson plans with page number references; teacher notes and activities; answers to the end-of-project exercises; test bank of 110 questions for every project (50 true/false, 25 multiple-choice, and 35 fill-in-the blank) with page number references; and transparency references. The transparencies are available through the Figures on CD-ROM described below. The test bank questions are numbered the same as in Course Test Manager. Thus, you can print out a copy of the project and use the printed test bank to select your questions in Course Test Manager.

▶ **Figures on CD-ROM**   Illustrations for every screen in the textbook are available. Use this ancillary to create a slide show from the illustrations for lecture or to print transparencies for use in lecture with an overhead.

▶ **Course Test Manager**   This cutting edge Windows-based testing software helps instructors design and administer tests and pre-tests. The full-featured online program permits students to take tests at the computer where their grades are computed immediately following completion of the exam. Automatic statistics collection, student guides customized to the student's performance, and printed tests are only a few of the features.

▶ **Lecture Success System**   Lecture Success System files are for use with the application software, a personal computer, and projection device to explain and illustrate the step-by-step, screen-by-screen development of a project in the textbook without entering large amounts of data.

▶ **Lab Tests**   Tests that parallel the In the Lab assignments are supplied for the purpose of testing students in the laboratory on the material covered in the project. You also can use these assignments as supplementary exercises.

▶ **Instructor's Lab Solutions**   Solutions and required files for all the In the Lab assignments at the end of each project are available.

▶ **Student Files**   All the files that are required by the student to complete the Apply Your Knowledge exercises and some of the later projects in the Office 95 textbook are included.

▶ **Interactive Labs**   Fourteen hands-on interactive labs that take the student from ten to fifteen minutes to step through help solidify and reinforce computer concepts. Student assessment is available in each interactive lab by means of a Print button. The assessment requires the student to answer questions about the contents of the interactive lab.

Shelly Cashman Online

Shelly Cashman Online is a World Wide Web service available to instructors and students of computer education. Visit Shelly Cashman Online at http://www.bf.com/scseries.html. Shelly Cashman Online is divided into four areas:

▶ **Series Information** Information on the Shelly Cashman Series products.

▶ **The Community** Opportunities to discuss your course and your ideas with instructors in your field and with the Shelly Cashman Series team.

▶ **Teaching Resources** This area includes password-protected data from Instructor's Floppy Disks that can be downloaded, course outlines, teaching tips, and ancillaries such as ElecMan.

▶ **Student Center** Dedicated to students learning about computers with Shelly Cashman Series textbooks and software. This area includes cool links, data from Student Floppy Disks that can be downloaded, and much more.

Most of the instructor aids just described also are available to registered instructors on the Shelly Cashman Online home page (http://www.bf.com/scseries.html).

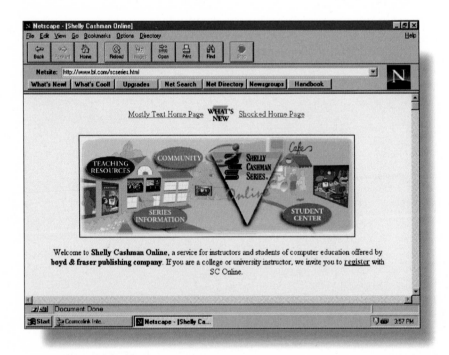

Acknowledgments

The Shelly Cashman Series would not be the leading computer education series without the contributions of outstanding publishing professionals. First, and foremost, among them is Becky Herrington, director of production and designer. She is the heart and soul of the Shelly Cashman Series, and it is only through her leadership, dedication, and tireless efforts that superior products are made possible. Becky created and produced the award-winning Windows 95 series of books.

Under Becky's direction, the following individuals made significant contributions to these books: Peter Schiller, production manager; Ginny Harvey, series administrator and manuscript editor; Marilyn Martin, copy editor; Nancy Lamm and Cherilyn King, proofreaders; Tim Walker and Peggy Wyman and Jerry Orton, contributing writers; Ken Russo, senior illustrator and cover artist; Mike Bodnar, Stephanie Nance, Greg Herrington, and Dave Bonnewitz, Quark artists and illustrators; Patti Garbarino and Lora Wade, editorial assistants; Bill Lisowski, marketing director; Jeanne Black, Quark expert; Cristina Haley, indexer; Sarah Evertson of Image Quest, photo researcher; Henry Blackham, cover photographer; and Kent Lauer, cover glass work. Special mention must go to Suzanne Biron, Becky Herrington, and Michael Gregson for the outstanding book design, to Ken Russo for the cover design; and to Jim Quasney, series editor.

Gary B. Shelly
Thomas J. Cashman
Marvin M. Boetcher
Sherry L. Green

Visit Shelly Cashman Online at
http://www.bf.com/scseries.html

Shelly Cashman Series - Traditionally Bound Textbooks

The Shelly Cashman Series presents computer textbooks across the entire spectrum including both Windows- and DOS-based personal computer applications in a variety of traditionally bound textbooks, as shown in the table below. For more information, see your Course Technology representative or call 1-800-648-7450.

COMPUTERS	
Computers	Using Computers: A Gateway to Information, World Wide Web Edition
	Using Computers: A Gateway to Information, World Wide Web Brief Edition
	Using Computers: A Gateway to Information, World Wide Web Edition and Exploring Computers: A Record of Discovery with CD-ROM
	Using Computers: A Gateway to Information
	Using Computers: A Gateway to Information, Brief Edition
	Exploring Computers: A Record of Discovery with CD-ROM
	A Record of Discovery for Exploring Computers
	Study Guide for Using Computers: A Gateway to Information, World Wide Web Edition
	Study Guide for Using Computers: A Gateway to Information
and Windows Apps	Using Computers: A Gateway to Information and Microsoft Office (also in spiral bound)
	Using Computers: A Gateway to Information and Microsoft Works 3.0 (also in spiral bound)
and Programming	Using Computers: A Gateway to Information and Programming in QBasic

WINDOWS APPLICATIONS	
Integrated Packages	Microsoft Office 95: Introductory Concepts and Techniques (also in spiral bound)
	Microsoft Office 95: Advanced Concepts and Techniques (also in spiral bound)
	Microsoft Office 4.3 running under Windows 95: Introductory Concepts and Techniques (also in spiral bound)
	Microsoft Office: Introductory Concepts and Techniques (also in spiral bound)
	Microsoft Office: Advanced Concepts and Techniques (also in spiral bound)
	Microsoft Works 4 for Windows 95*
	Microsoft Works 3.0 (also in spiral bound)* • Microsoft Works 2.0 (also in spiral bound)
	Microsoft Works 3.0—Short Course
Windows	Microsoft Windows 95: Introductory Concepts and Techniques (96-page)
	Introduction to Microsoft Windows 95 (224-page)
	Microsoft Windows 95: Complete Concepts and Techniques
	Microsoft Windows 3.1 Introductory Concepts and Techniques
	Microsoft Windows 3.1 Complete Concepts and Techniques
Windows Applications	Microsoft Word 2.0, Microsoft Excel 4, and Paradox 1.0 (also in spiral bound)
Word Processing	Microsoft Word 7* • Microsoft Word 6* • Microsoft Word 2.0
	WordPerfect 6.1* • WordPerfect 6* • WordPerfect 5.2
Spreadsheets	Microsoft Excel 7* • Microsoft Excel 5* • Microsoft Excel 4
	Lotus 1-2-3 Release 5* • Lotus 1-2-3 Release 4* • Quattro Pro 6 • Quattro Pro 5
Database Management	Microsoft Access 7* • Microsoft Access 2
	Paradox 5 • Paradox 4.5 • Paradox 1.0 • Visual dBASE 5/5.5
Presentation Graphics	Microsoft PowerPoint 7* • Microsoft PowerPoint 4*

DOS APPLICATIONS	
Operating Systems	DOS 6 Introductory Concepts and Techniques
	DOS 6 and Microsoft Windows 3.1 Introductory Concepts and Techniques
Integrated Package	Microsoft Works 3.0 (also in spiral bound)
Word Processing	WordPerfect 6.1 • WordPerfect 6.0
	WordPerfect 5.1 Step-by-Step Function Key Edition • WordPerfect 5.1 Function Key Edition
Spreadsheets	Lotus 1-2-3 Release 4 • Lotus 1-2-3 Release 2.4 • Lotus 1-2-3 Release 2.3
	Lotus 1-2-3 Release 2.2 • Lotus 1-2-3 Release 2.01
	Quattro Pro 3.0 • Quattro with 1-2-3 Menus (with Educational Software)
Database Management	dBASE 5 • dBASE IV Version 1.1 • dBASE III PLUS (with Educational Software)
	Paradox 4.5 • Paradox 3.5 (with Educational Software)

PROGRAMMING AND NETWORKING	
Programming	Introduction to Microsoft Visual Basic 4* (available with Student version of Visual Basic 4)
	Microsoft Visual Basic 3.0 for Windows*
	QBasic • QBasic: An Introduction to Programming • Microsoft BASIC
	Structured COBOL Programming
Networking	Novell NetWare for Users
	Business Data Communications: Introductory Concepts and Techniques
Internet	The Internet: Introductory Concepts and Techniques (UNIX)
	Netscape Navigator 3: An Introduction • Netscape Navigator 2 running under Windows 3.1
	Netscape Navigator: An Introduction (Version 1.1)
	Netscape Navigator Gold: Creating Web Pages

SYSTEMS ANALYSIS	
Systems Analysis	Systems Analysis and Design, Second Edition

*Also available as a Double Diamond Edition, which is a shortened version of the complete book

Shelly Cashman Series - **Custom Edition**® Program

If you do not find a Shelly Cashman Series traditionally bound textbook to fit your needs, the Shelly Cashman Series' unique **Custom Edition** program allows you to choose from a number of options and create a textbook perfectly suited to your course. Features of the **Custom Edition** program are:

▶ Textbooks that match the content of your course

▶ Windows- and DOS-based materials for the latest versions of personal computer applications software

▶ Shelly Cashman Series quality, with the same full-color materials and Shelly Cashman Series pedagogy found in the traditionally bound books

▶ Affordable pricing so your students receive the **Custom Edition** at a cost similar to that of traditionally bound books

The table on the right summarizes the available materials.

For more information, see your Course Technology representative or call 1-800-648-7450.

For Shelly Cashman Series information, visit Shelly Cashman Online at http://www.bf.com/scseries.html

COMPUTERS	
Computers	Using Computers: A Gateway to Information, World Wide Web Edition
	Using Computers: A Gateway to Information, World Wide Web Brief Edition
	Using Computers: A Gateway to Information
	Using Computers: A Gateway to Information, Brief Edition
	A Record of Discovery for Exploring Computers (available with CD-ROM)
	Study Guide for Using Computers: A Gateway to Information, World Wide Web Edition
	Study Guide for Using Computers: A Gateway to Information
	Introduction to Computers (32-page)

OPERATING SYSTEMS	
Windows	Microsoft Windows 95: Introductory Concepts and Techniques (96-page)
	Introduction to Microsoft Windows 95 (224-page)
	Microsoft Windows 95: Complete Concepts and Techniques
	Microsoft Windows 3.1 Introductory Concepts and Techniques
	Microsoft Windows 3.1 Complete Concepts and Techniques
DOS	Introduction to DOS 6 (using DOS prompt)
	Introduction to DOS 5.0 or earlier (using DOS prompt)

WINDOWS APPLICATIONS	
Integrated Packages	Microsoft Works 4 for Windows 95*
	Microsoft Works 3.0*
	Microsoft Works 3.0—Short Course
	Microsoft Works 2.0
Microsoft Office	Using Microsoft Office (16-page)
	Object Linking and Embedding (OLE) (32-page)
	Schedule+ 7
Word Processing	Microsoft Word 7* • Microsoft Word 6* • Microsoft Word 2.0
	WordPerfect 6.1* • WordPerfect 6* • WordPerfect 5.2
Spreadsheets	Microsoft Excel 7* • Microsoft Excel 5* • Microsoft Excel 4
	Lotus 1-2-3 Release 5* • Lotus 1-2-3 Release 4*
	Quattro Pro 6 • Quattro Pro 5
Database Management	Microsoft Access 7* • Microsoft Access 2*
	Paradox 5 • Paradox 4.5 • Paradox 1.0 • Visual dBASE 5/5.5
Presentation Graphics	Microsoft PowerPoint 7* • Microsoft PowerPoint 4*

DOS APPLICATIONS	
Integrated Package	Microsoft Works 3.0
Word Processing	WordPerfect 6.1 • WordPerfect 6.0
	WordPerfect 5.1 Step-by-Step Function Key Edition
	WordPerfect 5.1 Function Key Edition
	Microsoft Word 5.0
Spreadsheets	Lotus 1-2-3 Release 4 • Lotus 1-2-3 Release 2.4 • Lotus 1-2-3 Release 2.3
	Lotus 1-2-3 Release 2.2 • Lotus 1-2-3 Release 2.01
	Quattro Pro 3.0 • Quattro with 1-2-3 Menus
Database Management	dBASE 5 • dBASE IV Version 1.1 • dBASE III PLUS
	Paradox 4.5 • Paradox 3.5

PROGRAMMING AND NETWORKING	
Programming	Introduction to Microsoft Visual Basic 4* (available with Student version of Visual Basic 4) • Microsoft Visual Basic 3.0 for Windows*
	Microsoft BASIC
	QBasic
Networking Internet	Novell NetWare for Users
	The Internet: Introductory Concepts and Techniques (UNIX)
	Netscape Navigator 3: An Introduction
	Netscape Navigator 2 running under Windows 3.1
	Netscape Navigator: An Introduction (Version 1.1)
	Netscape Navigator Gold: Creating Web Pages

* Also available as a mini-module

▶ **PROJECT ONE**

USING A DESIGN TEMPLATE AND STYLE CHECKER TO CREATE A PRESENTATION

Objectives   PP 1.3
What Is PowerPoint?   PP 1.6
Project One – College Survival   PP 1.8
Starting a Presentation as a New Office
    Document   PP 1.9
PowerPoint Views   PP 1.13
Creating a Title Slide   PP 1.16
Text Attributes   PP 1.19
Saving a Presentation to a Floppy Disk
    PP 1.22
Adding a New Slide to a Presentation
    PP 1.24
Creating a Bulleted List Slide   PP 1.26
Saving a Presentation with the Same
    Filename   PP 1.32
Moving to Another Slide in Slide View
    PP 1.33
Viewing the Presentation Using Slide Show
    PP 1.34
Closing PowerPoint   PP 1.37
Opening a Presentation   PP 1.38
Checking a Presentation for Visual Clarity,
    Consistency, and Style   PP 1.40
Correcting Errors   PP 1.44
Changing Line Spacing   PP 1.45
Displaying a Presentation in Black and White
    PP 1.49
Printing a Presentation   PP 1.50
PowerPoint Help   PP 1.52
Project Summary   PP 1.62
What You Should Know   PP 1.62
Test Your Knowledge   PP 1.63
Use Help   PP 1.66
Apply Your Knowledge   PP 1.67
In the Lab   PP 1.68
Cases and Places   PP 1.72

▶ **PROJECT TWO**

USING OUTLINE VIEW AND CLIP ART TO CREATE AN ELECTRONIC SLIDE SHOW

Objectives   PP 2.1
Creating Presentation from an Outline   PP 2.4
Project Two — Spring Break Specials   PP 2.5
Starting a New Presentation   PP 2.7
Using Outline View   PP 2.7
Creating a Presentation in Outline View
    PP 2.10
Creating a Slide with Multiple Text Objects
    in Outline View   PP 2.16
Saving the Presentation   PP 2.18
Reviewing a Presentation in Slide Sorter View
    PP 2.19
Changing Slide Layout   PP 2.23
Adding Clip Art to a Slide   PP 2.26
Adding a Header and a Footer to Outline
    Pages   PP 2.36
Checking the Presentation for Spelling
    and Style Errors   PP 2.38
Adding Animation Effects   PP 2.39
Running a Slide Show with Animation Effects
    PP 2.46
Printing in Outline View   PP 2.47
Editing a Presentation   PP 2.53
Project Summary   PP 2.61
What You Should Know   PP 2.61
Test Your Knowledge   PP 2.62
Use Help   PP 2.65
Apply Your Knowledge   PP 2.66
In the Lab   PP 2.68
Cases and Places   PP 2.75

▶ **INTEGRATION FEATURE**

LINKING AN EXCEL CHART TO A POWERPOINT PRESENTATION

Introduction   PPI 1.1
Creating a Chart Slide   PPI 1.3
Linking an Excel Chart to a
    Presentation   PPI 1.4
Summary   PPI 1.7
What You Should Know   PPI 1.7
In the Lab   PPI 1.7

Microsoft PowerPoint 7 Windows 95

Windows 95

Using A Design Template And Style Checker To Create A Presentation

Objectives:

You will have mastered the material in this project when you can:

▶ Start a new PowerPoint document

▶ Describe the PowerPoint window

▶ Select a Design Template

▶ Create a title slide

▶ Change the font size of selected text

▶ Italicize selected text

▶ Save a presentation

▶ Add a new slide

▶ Demote a bulleted paragraph

▶ Promote a bulleted paragraph

▶ View a presentation in Slide Show view

▶ Close PowerPoint

▶ Open a presentation

▶ Use Style Checker to identify spelling, visual clarity, case, and end punctuation inconsistencies

▶ Edit a presentation

▶ Change line spacing on the Slide Master

▶ Display a presentation in black and white

▶ Print a presentation in black and white

▶ Use online help

Picture This!

A Story without Words

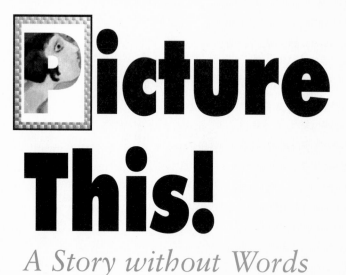

A modern movie without dialogue? The 1981 movie, *Quest for Fire*, contained no dialogue yet told a clear, compelling story about prehistoric humans who had no language to speak. Since the dawn of mankind, humans have relied on graphic images to communicate, even after the advent of spoken language. In today's global village, images play a vital role in promoting understanding between peoples of different languages.

People have long used pictures, or graphics, as guides for building structures involving complex spatial relationships. Imagine trying to build the Pharaoh's pyramids without a plan drawn out on papyrus or a Boeing 767 without engineering drawings.

Yet, in recent years, graphics have assumed an even greater role in the *art of persuasion*. People

Persuasion

understand arguments far more easily when pictures are used; pictures help establish credibility, which is the first step in persuasion. From sales presentations to the perennial debate over the U.S. federal budget to Presidential addresses, people turn to images to persuade others to adopt their points of view. Human beings grasp information more quickly and remember it longer when images augment words.

It has not always been so easy to create winning graphics. In the past, teams of artists often required days, even weeks, using special equipment many times more expensive than personal computers to lay out slide presentations. Corrections or changes were costly and time-consuming, whereas now, changes can be made inexpensively, in seconds.

Microsoft PowerPoint is an outstanding example of the marriage of pictures and text to help people present persuasive arguments or simply to inform or entertain. Bar graphs, pie charts, scatter diagrams, Gantt charts, and other visuals can be created quickly and easily within PowerPoint or imported from other applications such as Microsoft Excel or Microsoft Works.

For people who need help, Wizards simplify the job of getting started. Wizards provide more than 100 predesigned *looks* and can guide the user through a series of steps to create a unique presentation within one of several popular formats. And it is easy to modify the style, color, and content of all images created with PowerPoint.

PowerPoint can be a boon to students by helping to organize and format papers, prepare overhead slides, and lay out storyboards. Especially where numbers are involved, papers can be enhanced by the inclusion of a graphic from PowerPoint.

In a world increasingly dependent on images as well as language to communicate and persuade, the capability to create those images becomes essential. Who knows what improvements in gradepoint averages may result — with the right graphics presented to the right professor?

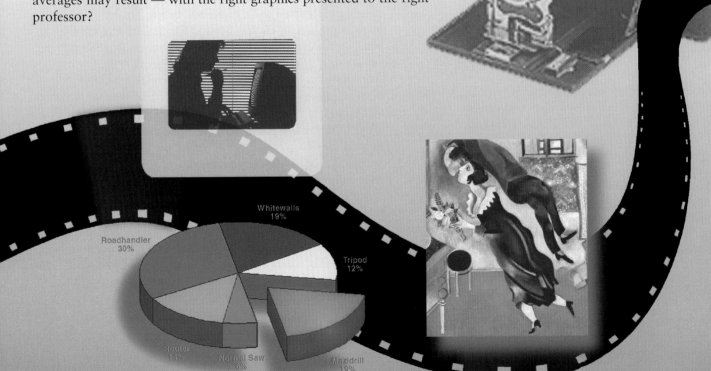

Project 1

Microsoft
PowerPoint 7
Windows 95

Using a Design Template and Style Checker to Create a Presentation

Case Perspective

Each summer, Hammond University conducts an orientation seminar for all students new to the campus. As a new part of the orientation process, the Office of Student Services is conducting a short presentation on how to survive on campus. Ms. Margaret Ray, Director of Student Services, provides you with data and assigns you the task of designing the presentation. Because the location of the orientation session is uncertain, you also must create overhead transparencies.

The data is an accumulation of responses collected each spring from student surveys. The survey focuses on three areas of campus life: dormitory, classroom, and social. Students completing the survey suggest survival tips for each of these three areas. Ms. Ray analyzes the survey responses and identifies the four tips most frequently submitted in each category.

You and Ms. Ray decide the presentation will consist of a title slide and three bulleted list slides.

What is PowerPoint?

Microsoft PowerPoint is a complete presentation graphics program that allows you to produce professional-looking presentations. PowerPoint gives you the flexibility to make informal presentations using overhead transparencies (top of Figure 1-1), make electronic presentations using a projection device attached to a personal computer (middle of Figure 1-1), or make formal presentations using 35mm slides (bottom of Figure 1-1). Additionally, PowerPoint can create paper printouts, outlines, speaker notes and audience handouts.

PowerPoint contains several features to simplify creating a presentation. For example, you can instruct PowerPoint to create a predesigned presentation, and then you can modify the presentation to fulfill your requirements. You quickly can format a presentation using one of the professionally designed presentation Design Templates. To make your presentation more impressive, you can add tables, graphs, pictures, video, and sound; and you can be certain your presentation meets specific design criteria by using Style Checker to locate inconsistencies in spelling, visual clarity, uppercase and lowercase usage, and end punctuation. For example,

FIGURE 1-1

you can instruct PowerPoint to restrict the number of bulleted items on a slide or limit the number of words in each paragraph. Additional PowerPoint features include the following:

- **Word Processing** — **Word Processing** allows you to create bulleted lists, combine words and images, find and replace text, and use multiple fonts and type sizes. Using its IntelliSense features, PowerPoint can perform tasks such as checking spelling and formatting text – *all while you are typing.*
- **Outlining** — **Outlining** allows you quickly to create your presentation using an outline format. You also can import outlines from Microsoft Word or other word processors.
- **Graphing** — **Graphing** allows you to create and insert charts into your presentations. Graph formats include two-dimensional (2D) graphs: area, bar, column, combination, line, pie, xy (scatter); and three-dimensional (3D) graphs: area, bar, column, line, and pie.

More *About* **Overhead Transparencies**

Overhead transparencies are best when you want audience interaction in a lighted room, for groups less than 40 people, or when other equipment is not available.

More *About*
Electronic
Presentations

Use an electronic presentation for any size audience. The choice of projection device depends on the number of people in the audience. Be certain you test the system before you deliver the presentation.

More *About*
35mm Slides

35mm slides are best for formal presentations made to any size audience and are highly recommended when audience size exceeds 50 people. 35mm slide presentations are best-suited for a non-interactive presentation because the room is dark.

More *About*
Presentation
Graphics

Presentation graphics help people see what they hear. People remember:
10% of what they *read*
20% of what they *hear*
30% of what they *see*
70% of what they *see and hear*

More *About*
Presentation
Design

Identify the purpose of the presentation. Is it to sell an idea or product, report results of a study, or educate the audience? Whatever the purpose, your goal is to capture the attention of the audience and to explain the data or concept in a manner that is easy to understand.

▶ **Drawing** — **Drawing** allows you to create diagrams using shapes such as arcs, arrows, cubes, rectangles, stars, and triangles. Drawing also allows you to modify shapes without redrawing.

▶ **Clip Art** — **ClipArt** allows you to insert artwork into your presentation without creating it yourself. You can find hundreds of graphic images in the Microsoft ClipArt Gallery, or you can import art from other applications. With the **AutoClipArt feature**, PowerPoint can suggest a clip art image appropriate for your presentation.

▶ **Multimedia Effects** — To add interest and keep your audience attentive, **multimedia effects**, such as sound and video, can be added to your presentations.

▶ **Presentation Management** — **Presentation management** allows you to control the design and arrangement of your presentation, as well as add special presentation effects, such as flying bullets.

▶ **Wizards** — A **wizard** is a tutorial approach for quickly and efficiently creating a presentation. PowerPoint wizards make it easy to create quality presentations by prompting you for specific content criteria. For example, the **AutoContent Wizard** asks you what are you going to talk about and the type of presentation you are going to give, such as recommending a strategy or selling a product. The **Answer Wizard** allows you to ask questions in your own words and then displays step-by-step instructions and visual examples showing how to complete the task. When giving a presentation away from the computer on which you created your presentation, it is important you take all the necessary files. The **Pack And Go Wizard** helps you bundle everything you need, including any objects associated with that presentation.

Project One – College Survival

This book presents a series of projects using PowerPoint to produce slides similar to those you would develop in an academic or business environment. Project 1 uses PowerPoint to create the presentation shown in Figure 1-2. The objective is to produce a presentation, called College Survival, to be presented using an overhead projector. As an introduction to PowerPoint, this project steps you through the most common type of presentation, a bulleted list. A **bulleted list** is a list of paragraphs, each preceded by a bullet. A **bullet** is a symbol (usually a heavy dot (•)) that precedes text when the text warrants special emphasis. The first of the four slides is called the title slide. The **title slide** introduces the presentation to the audience.

Mouse Usage

In this book, the mouse is used as the primary way to communicate with Microsoft PowerPoint. You can perform seven operations with a mouse: point, click, right-click, double-click, triple-click, drag, and right-drag.

Point means you move the mouse across a flat surface until the mouse pointer rests on the item of choice on the screen. As you move the mouse, the mouse pointer moves across the screen in the same direction.

Click means you press and release the left mouse button. The terminology used in this book to direct you to point to a particular item and then click is, Click the particular item. For example, Click the Bold button, means point to the Bold button and then click.

Right-click means you press and release the right mouse button. As with the left mouse button, you normally will point to an item on the screen before right-clicking.

Double-click means you quickly press and release the left mouse button twice without moving the mouse. In most cases, you must point to an item before double-clicking. In this book, **triple-clicking** in a text object selects the entire paragraph.

Drag means you point to an item, hold down the left mouse button, move the item to the desired location on the screen, and then release the left mouse button. **Right-drag** means you point to an item, hold down the right mouse button, move the item to the desired location, and then release the right mouse button.

The use of the mouse is an important skill when working with PowerPoint 7 for Windows 95.

Slide Preparation Steps

The preparation steps summarize how the slide presentation shown in Figure 1-2 will be developed in Project 1. The following tasks will be completed in this project:

1. Start a new Office document.
2. Select a Design Template.
3. Create a title slide.
4. Save the presentation on a floppy disk.
5. Create three multi-level bulleted lists.
6. Save the presentation again.
7. Close PowerPoint.
8. Open the presentation as a Microsoft Office document.
9. Style check the presentation.
10. Edit the presentation.
11. Print the presentation.
12. Close PowerPoint.

The following pages contain a detailed explanation of these tasks.

Starting a Presentation as a New Office Document

A PowerPoint document is called a **presentation**. The quickest way to begin a new presentation is to use the **Start button** on the **taskbar** at the bottom of your screen. When you click the Start button, the **Start menu** displays several commands for simplifying tasks in Windows 95. When Microsoft Office 95 is installed, the Start menu displays two commands: New Office Document and Open Office Document. You use the **New Office Document** command to designate the type of Office document you are creating. Then, you specify the Design Template or wizard on which you wish to base your document. A **Design Template** provides consistency in design and color throughout the entire presentation. The Design Template determines the color scheme, font face and size, and layout of your presentation. Then PowerPoint starts and the specified template or wizard displays. The Open Office Document command is discussed later in this project. Perform the steps on the following pages to start a new presentation, or ask your instructor how to start PowerPoint on your system.

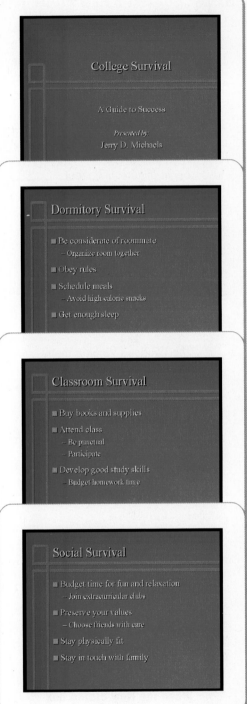

FIGURE 1-2

Steps To Start a New Presentation

---

1 **Point to the Start button on the taskbar at the lower left corner of the desktop.**

When you position the mouse pointer on the Start button, a ToolTip displays, Click here to begin (Figure 1-3). Your computer system displays the time on the clock at the right end of the taskbar.

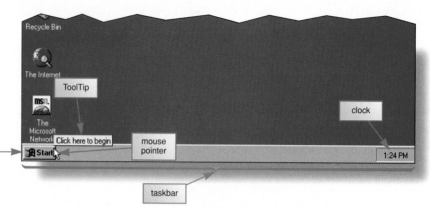

FIGURE 1-3

---

2 **Click the Start button. When the Windows 95 Start menu displays, point to New Office Document.**

The Windows 95 Start menu displays the names of several programs. The mouse pointer points to New Office Document (Figure 1-4). When the mouse pointer points to a name on the menu, the name is highlighted.

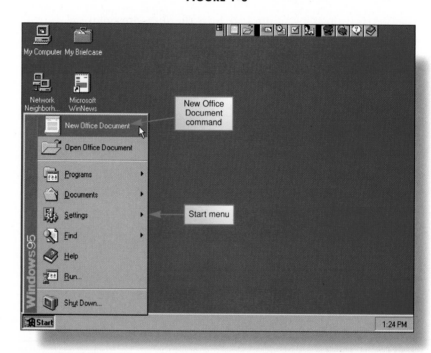

FIGURE 1-4

---

3 **Click New Office Document. When the New dialog box displays, point to the Presentation Designs tab.**

The New dialog box displays on the desktop and the mouse pointer points to the Presentation Designs tab (Figure 1-5). Depending on your installation, your computer may display a Design tab.

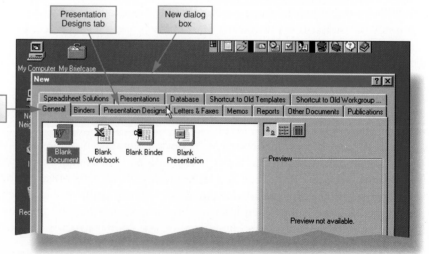

FIGURE 1-5

4 Click the Presentation Designs tab. When the Presentation Designs sheet displays, point to Embossed.

The Presentation Designs sheet displays (Figure 1-6). The Presentation Designs sheet displays the names and icons for several Design Templates. The Preview box displays a message about how to see a preview of a presentation Design Template. The OK button currently is dimmed, which means it is not available, because a Design Template icon has not been selected. The Cancel button is available, however, as indicated by the black text on the button. The Cancel button is used to close the New dialog box and return to the desktop or return to the window from which you started.

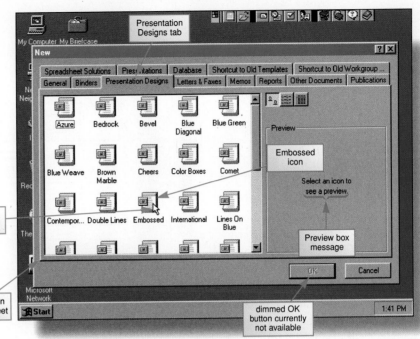

FIGURE 1-6

5 Click Embossed.

The Embossed Design Template icon is highlighted and a thumbnail view of the Design Template displays in the Preview box (Figure 1-7). The OK button now is available as indicated by the black text on the button.

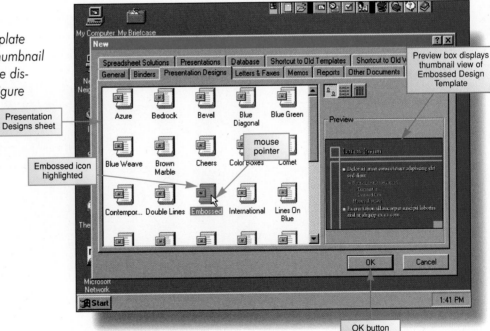

FIGURE 1-7

6 Select the Embossed Design Template by double-clicking Embossed. When the New Slide dialog box displays, point to the OK button.

Double-clicking the Embossed Design Template icon indicates that you are using a PowerPoint template. As a result, PowerPoint starts and the New Slide dialog box displays (Figure 1-8). In the New Slide dialog box, a frame displays around the Title Slide AutoLayout to indicate it is selected. At the bottom of the screen, Microsoft PowerPoint displays as a button on the taskbar.

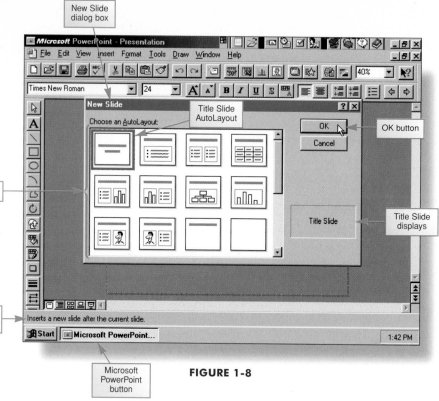

FIGURE 1-8

7 Click the OK button. Maximize the screen if it does not display maximized.

PowerPoint displays the maximized Title Slide AutoLayout and the Embossed Design Template on Slide 1 (Figure 1-9). The title bar identifies this as a Microsoft PowerPoint presentation currently titled Presentation. The status bar displays information about the current slide, such as the slide number and the current Design Template.

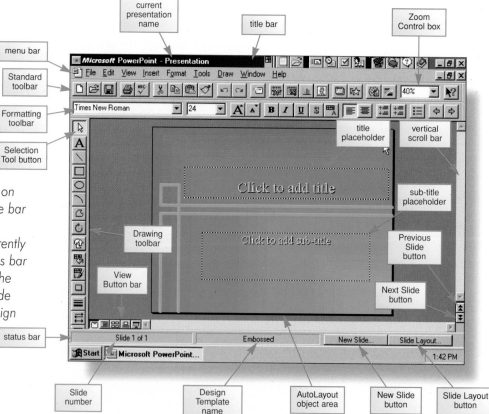

FIGURE 1-9

As an alternative to double-clicking the Embossed Design Template in Step 6, you can click the OK button to apply the selected Design Template.

The PowerPoint Window

The basic unit of a PowerPoint presentation is a **slide. Objects** are the building blocks for a PowerPoint slide. A slide contains one or many objects, such as a title, text, graphics, tables, charts, and drawings. In PowerPoint, you have the option of using the PowerPoint default settings or establishing your own. A **default setting** is a particular value for a variable that is assigned initially by PowerPoint and remains in effect unless canceled or overridden by the user. These settings control the placement of objects, the color scheme, the transition between slides, and other slide attributes. **Attributes** are the properties or characteristics of an object. For example, if you underline the title of a slide, the title is the object and the underline is the attribute. When you start PowerPoint, the default **slide layout** is **landscape orientation**, in which the slide width is greater than its height. In landscape orientation, the slide size is preset to 10 inches wide and 7.5 inches high. The slide layout can be changed to **portrait orientation,** so that the slide height is greater than its width, by clicking Slide Setup on the File menu. In portrait orientation, the slide height is 10 inches and its width is 7.5 inches.

> ◆ **More** *About*
> **Design Templates**
>
> When deciding on a Design Template, choose one designed to display light colored text on a medium to dark background. Light text on a dark background provides a stronger contrast than light text on a light background.

PowerPoint Views

PowerPoint has five views: Slide view, Outline view, Slide Sorter view, Notes Pages view, and Slide Show view. A **view** is the mode in which the presentation displays on the screen. You may use any or all views when creating your presentation, but you can use only one at a time. Change views by clicking one of the view buttons found on the **View Button bar** at the bottom of the PowerPoint screen (see Figure 1-9). The PowerPoint window display is dependent on the view. Some views are graphical while others are textual.

Table 1-1 identifies the view buttons and provides an explanation of each view.

Table 1-1

VIEW BUTTON	VIEW	EXPLANATION
	Slide view	Displays a single slide as it appears in your presentation. Use Slide view to create or edit a presentation. Slide view also is used to incorporate text and graphic objects and to create line-by-line progressive disclosure, called build effects.
	Outline view	Displays a presentation in an outline format showing slide titles and text. It is best used for organizing and developing the content of your presentation.
	Slide Sorter view	Displays miniatures of the slides in your presentation. You can then copy, cut, paste, or otherwise change slide position to modify your presentation. Slide Sorter view also is used to add slide transitions.
	Notes Pages view	Displays the current notes page. Notes Pages view allows you to create speaker's notes to use when you give your presentation. Each notes page corresponds to a slide and includes a reduced slide image.
	Slide Show view	Displays your slides as an electronic presentation on the full screen of your computer's monitor. Looking much like a slide projector display, you can see the effect of transitions, build effects, and slide timings.

PowerPoint Window in Slide View

The PowerPoint window in Slide view contains the title bar; the menu bar; the status bar; the toolbars: Standard, Formatting, and Drawing; the AutoLayout object area; the mouse pointer; the scroll bars; and the view buttons.

More *About*
**Presentation
Design**

The audience determines the
level of detail you place on one
slide. Before you create your
presentation, determine who is
likely to attend. Design your
presentation around the amount
of detail the audience wants to
see. Remember, you want to
keep their attention, not bore
them with details.

TITLE BAR   The **title bar** (see Figure 1-9 on page PP 1.12) displays the name of the current PowerPoint document. Until you save your presentation, PowerPoint assigns the default name Presentation.

MENU BAR   The **menu bar** (see Figure 1-9) displays the PowerPoint menu names. Each menu name represents a list of commands that allows you to retrieve, store, print, and change objects in your presentation. To display a menu, such as the File menu, click the name File on the menu bar.

STATUS BAR   Located at the bottom of the PowerPoint window, the **status bar** consists of a message area, a presentation Design Template identifier, and two buttons: the New Slide button and the Slide Layout button (see Figure 1-9). Most of the time, the current slide number and the total number of slides in the presentation display in the message area. For example, in Figure 1-9, the message area displays Slide 1 of 1. Slide 1 is the current slide, and of 1 indicates there is only one slide in the presentation. When you point to a command or a button, however, the status bar provides a short message about that command or button.

NEW SLIDE BUTTON   Clicking the **New Slide button** (see Figure 1-9) inserts a new slide into a presentation after the current slide.

SLIDE LAYOUT BUTTON   Clicking the **Slide Layout button** (see Figure 1-9) displays the Slide Layout dialog box. Selecting a slide layout from the options in a dialog box allows you to change the existing layout.

SCROLL BARS   The **vertical scroll bar** (see Figure 1-9), located on the right side of the PowerPoint window, allows you to move forward or backward through your presentation. Clicking the **Next Slide button** (see Figure 1-9), located on the vertical scroll bar, advances to the next slide in the presentation. Clicking the **Previous Slide button** (see Figure 1-9), located on the vertical scroll bar, backs up to the slide preceding the current slide.

The **horizontal scroll bar** (see Figure 1-9), located on the bottom of the PowerPoint window, allows you to display a portion of the window when the entire window does not fit on the screen.

It should be noted that in Slide view, both the vertical and horizontal scroll bar actions are dependent upon **Zoom Control**. You control how large or small a document appears on the PowerPoint window with Zoom Control. If you are in Slide view and Zoom Control is set such that the entire slide is not visible in the Slide window, clicking the up arrow on the vertical scroll bar displays the next portion of your slide, not the previous slide. Recall that to go to the previous slide, click the Previous Slide button. To go to the next slide, click the Next Slide button.

AUTOLAYOUT OBJECT AREA   The **AutoLayout object area** (see Figure 1-9) is a collection of placeholders for the title, text, clip art, graphs, tables, and media clips (video and sound). These placeholders display when you create a new slide. You can change the AutoLayout any time during the creation of your presentation by clicking the Slide Layout button on the status bar and then selecting a different slide layout.

PLACEHOLDERS   Surrounded by a dashed line, **placeholders** are the empty objects on a new slide. Depending on the AutoLayout selected, placeholders will display for the title, text, graphs, tables, organization charts, media clips, and clip art. Once you place contents in a placeholder, the placeholder becomes an object. For example, text typed in a placeholder becomes a text object.

TITLE PLACEHOLDER Surrounded by a dashed line, the **title placeholder** is the empty title object on a new slide (see Figure 1-9 on page PP 1.12). Text typed in the title placeholder becomes the **title object**.

SUB-TITLE PLACEHOLDER Surrounded by a dashed line, the **sub-title placeholder** is the empty sub-title object that displays below the title placeholder on a title slide (see Figure 1-9).

MOUSE POINTER The **mouse pointer** can become one of several different shapes depending on the task you are performing in PowerPoint and the pointer's location on the screen. The different shapes are discussed when they display in subsequent projects. The mouse pointer in Figure 1-9 has the shape of a left-pointing block arrow.

TOOLBARS PowerPoint **toolbars** consist of buttons that allow you to perform tasks more quickly than when using the menu bar. For example, to save, click the Save button on the Standard toolbar. Each button face has a graphical representation that helps you remember its function. Figure 1-10 below, and Figures 1-11 and 1-12 on the next page illustrate the buttons on each of the three toolbars that display when you start PowerPoint and display a slide in Slide view. They are the Standard toolbar, the Formatting toolbar, and the Drawing toolbar. Each button is explained in detail when it is used.

PowerPoint has several additional toolbars you can display by clicking View on the menu bar. You also can display a toolbar by pointing to a toolbar and right-clicking to display a shortcut menu, which lists the available toolbars. A **shortcut menu** contains a list of commands or items that relate to the item to which you are pointing when you right-click.

PowerPoint allows you to customize all toolbars and to add the toolbar buttons you use most often. In the same manner, you can remove those toolbar buttons you do not use. To customize a toolbar, click Tools on the menu bar, and then click Customize to modify the toolbar to meet your requirements.

STANDARD TOOLBAR The **Standard toolbar** (Figure 1-10) contains the tools to execute the most common commands found on the menu bar, such as Open, Print, Save, Copy, Cut, Paste, and many more. The Standard toolbar contains a button for setting Zoom Control. Recall that you control how large or small a document appears in the PowerPoint window with Zoom Control.

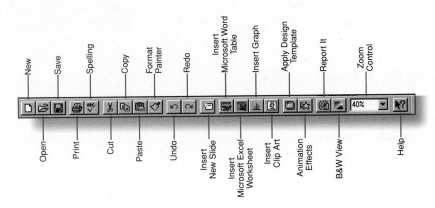

FIGURE 1-10

FORMATTING TOOLBAR The **Formatting toolbar** (Figure 1-11) contains the tools for changing text attributes. The Formatting toolbar allows you to quickly change font, font size, and alignment. It also contains tools to bold, italicize, underline, shadow, color, and bullet text. The five **attribute buttons**, **Bold**, **Italic**, **Underline**, **Text Shadow**, and **Bullet On/Off**, are on/off switches, or toggles. Click the button once to turn the attribute on; then click it again to turn the attribute off.

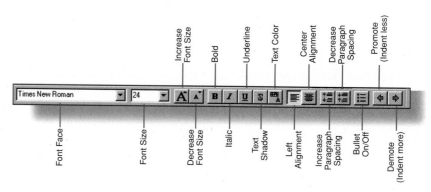

FIGURE 1-11

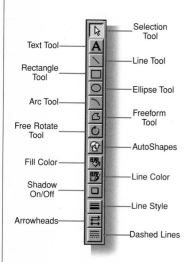

FIGURE 1-12

DRAWING TOOLBAR The **Drawing toolbar** (Figure 1-12) is a collection of tools for drawing objects such as lines, circles, and boxes. The Drawing toolbar also contains tools to edit the objects once you have drawn them. For example, you can add text to an object by clicking the **Text Tool button**, change the color of an object with the **Fill Color button**, or rotate an object by clicking the **Free Rotate Tool** button.

Creating a Title Slide

The purpose of a title slide is to introduce the presentation to the audience. PowerPoint assumes the first slide in a new presentation is the title slide. With the exception of a blank slide, PowerPoint also assumes every new slide has a title. To make creating your presentation easier, any text you type after a new slide displays becomes the title object. In other words, you do not have to first select the title placeholder before typing the title text. The AutoLayout for the title slide has a title placeholder near the middle of the window and a sub-title placeholder directly below the title placeholder (see Figure 1-13).

Entering the Presentation Title

The presentation title for Project 1 is College Survival. Type the presentation title in the title placeholder on the title slide. Perform the following step to create the title slide for this project.

Steps To Enter the Presentation Title

1 **Type** College Survival **in the title placeholder. Do not press the ENTER key.**

*College Survival displays in the title text box (Figure 1-13). When you type the first character, a slashed outline, called the **selection box**, displays around the title place-holder. A blinking vertical line (|), called the **insertion point**, indicates where the next character will dis-play. The highlighted (colored) box is the **text box**, and it indicates you are in text mode.*

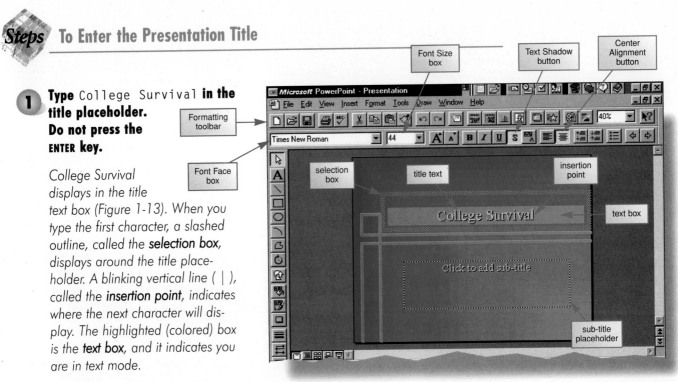

FIGURE 1-13

Notice that you do not press the ENTER key after the word Survival. If you press the ENTER key after typing the title, PowerPoint creates a new paragraph. A **paragraph** is a segment of text with the same format that begins when you press the ENTER key and ends when you press the ENTER key again. Pressing the ENTER key creates a new line in a new paragraph. Therefore, do not press the ENTER key unless you want to create a two-paragraph title. Additionally, PowerPoint **line wraps** text that exceeds the width of the placeholder. For example, if the title were College Survival, the Freshman Experience, it would exceed the width of the title placeholder and display on two lines.

The title is centered in the window because the Embossed Design Template alignment attribute is centered. The Center Alignment button is recessed on the Formatting toolbar in Figure 1-13.

Correcting a Mistake When Typing

If you type the wrong letter and notice the error before pressing the ENTER key, press the BACKSPACE key to erase all the characters back to and including the one that is incorrect. If you mistakenly press the ENTER key after entering the title and the cursor is on the new line, simply press the BACKSPACE key to return the insertion point to the right of the letter l in the word Survival.

When you first install PowerPoint, the default setting allows you to reverse up to the last twenty changes by clicking the Undo button on the Standard toolbar, or by clicking the Undo Typing command on the Edit menu. The number of times you can click the Undo button to reverse changes can be modified. To increase or decrease the number of undos, click Tools on the menu bar, click Options, and then click the Advanced tab. Use the up and down arrows in the Maximum Number of Undos box to change the number of undos. The maximum number of undos is 150; the minimum number is 3.

More *About* **Presentation Design**

Uppercase letters are less distinct, therefore, more difficult to read than lowercase letters. For emphasis, it is acceptable to use all uppercase letters in short titles. Capitalize only the first letter in all words in long titles, except for short articles, unless the article is the first word in the title.

You can reapply a change that you reversed with the Undo button by clicking the Redo button on the Standard toolbar. Clicking the **Redo button** reverses the last undo action.

Entering the Presentation Subtitle

The next step in creating the title slide is to enter the subtitle text into the sub-title placeholder. Complete the steps below to enter the presentation subtitle.

 Steps **To Enter the Presentation Subtitle**

1 **Click the label, Click to add sub-title, located inside the sub-title placeholder.**

The insertion point is in the sub-title text box (Figure 1-14). The mouse pointer changes to an I-beam. The I-beam mouse pointer indicates the mouse is within a text placeholder. The selection box indicates the sub-title placeholder is selected.

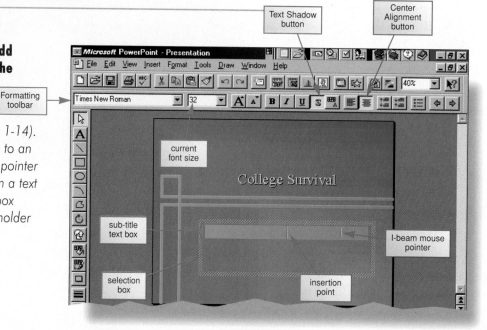

FIGURE 1-14

2 **Type** A Guide to Success **and press the ENTER key two times. Type** Presented by: **and press the ENTER key. Type** J. D. Michaels **but do not press the ENTER key.**

The text displays in the sub-title object as shown in Figure 1-15. The insertion point displays after the letter s in Michaels.

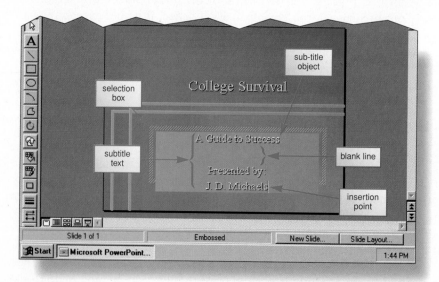

FIGURE 1-15

The previous section created a title slide using an AutoLayout for the title slide. PowerPoint displayed the title slide layout because you created a new presentation. You entered text in the title placeholder without selecting the title placeholder because PowerPoint assumes every slide has a title. You could, however, click the title placeholder to select it and then type your title. In general, to type text in any text placeholder, click the text placeholder and begin typing. You also added a subtitle that identifies the presenter. While this is not required, it is often useful information for the audience.

Text Attributes

This presentation is using the Embossed Design Template that you selected from the Presentation Designs sheet. Each Design Template has its own text attributes. A **text attribute** is a characteristic of the text, such as font face, font size, font style, or text color. You can adjust text attributes any time before, during, or after you type the text. Recall that a Design Template determines the color scheme, font face and size, and layout of your presentation. Most of the time, you use the Design Template's text attributes and color scheme. There are times when you wish to change the way your presentation looks, however, and still keep a particular Design Template. PowerPoint gives you that flexibility. You can use the Design Template you wish and change the text color, text size, text font face, and text style. Table 1-2 explains the different text attributes available in PowerPoint.

<table>
<tr><td colspan="2">**Table 1-2**</td></tr>
<tr><td>*ATTRIBUTE*</td><td>*DESCRIPTION*</td></tr>
<tr><td>Font face</td><td>Defines the appearance and shape of letters, numbers, and special characters.</td></tr>
<tr><td>Text color</td><td>Defines the color of the text. Displaying text in color requires a color monitor. Printing text in color requires a color printer or plotter.</td></tr>
<tr><td>Font size</td><td>Specifies the size of the characters on the screen. Character size is gauged by a measurement system called points. A single *point* is about 1/72 of an inch in height. Thus, a character with a point size of eighteen is about 18/72 (or 1/4) of an inch in height.</td></tr>
<tr><td>Text style</td><td>Defines text characteristics. Text styles include plain, italic, bold, shadowed, and underlined. Text may have one or more styles at a time.</td></tr>
<tr><td>Subscript</td><td>Defines the placement of a character in relationship to another. A subscript character displays or prints slightly below and immediately to one side of another character.</td></tr>
<tr><td>Superscript</td><td>Defines the placement of a character in relationship to another. A superscript character displays or prints above and immediately to one side of another character.</td></tr>
</table>

The next two sections explain how to change the font size and text style attributes.

Changing the Font Size

The Embossed Design Template default font size is 32 points for body text and 44 points for title text. A point is 1/72 of an inch in height. Thus, a character with a point size of 44 is about 44/72 (or 11/18) of an inch in height. Slide 1 requires you to decrease the font size for the paragraph, Presented by:. Perform the steps on the next pages to change font size.

Steps To Decrease Font Size

1 **Triple-click the paragraph, Presented by:, in the sub-title object.**

The paragraph, Presented by:, is highlighted (Figure 1-16).

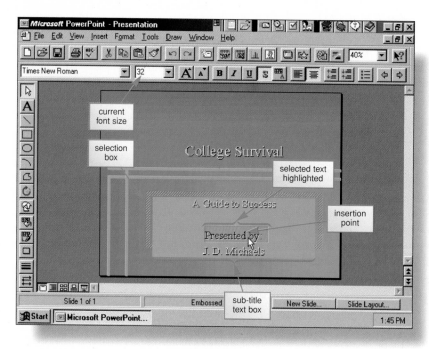

FIGURE 1-16

2 **With Presented by: highlighted, point to the Decrease Font Size button on the Formatting toolbar.**

*When you point to a button on a toolbar, PowerPoint displays a ToolTip. A **ToolTip** contains the name of the tool to which you are pointing. When pointing to the **Decrease Font Size button**, the ToolTip displays the words, Decrease Font Size (Figure 1-17).*

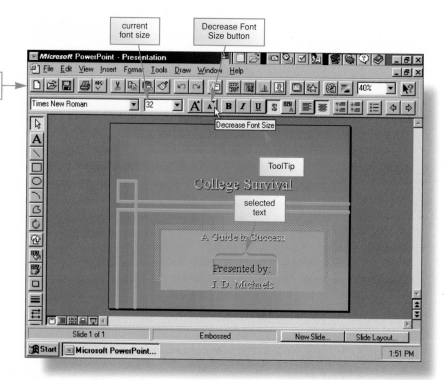

FIGURE 1-17

3 Click the Decrease Font Size button twice so that 24 displays in the Font Size box on the Formatting toolbar.

The paragraph, Presented by:, reduces to 24 points (Figure 1-18). The Font Size box displays the new font size as 24.

FIGURE 1-18

If you need to increase the font size, click the **Increase Font size button**, located immediately to the left of the Decrease Font Size button on the Formatting toolbar.

Changing the Style of Text to Italic

Text styles include plain, italic, bold, shadowed, and underlined. PowerPoint allows you to use one or more text styles in your presentation. Perform the following steps to add emphasis to the title slide by changing plain text to italic text.

 Steps To Change the Text Style to Italic

1 With the paragraph, Presented by:, highlighted, click the Italic button on the Formatting toolbar.

The text is italicized and the Italic button is recessed (Figure 1-19).

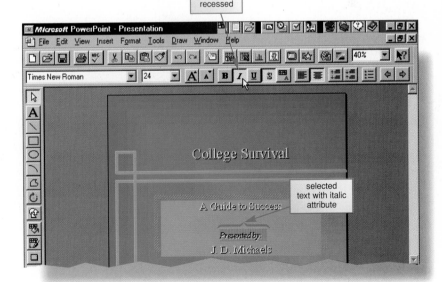

FIGURE 1-19

OtherWays

1. Right-click selected text, click Font on shortcut menu, click new font size in Size list box

2. Click Font Size arrow on Formatting toolbar, click one of listed font sizes, or click Font Size box on Formatting toolbar, type font size between 1 and 4000

3. On Format menu click Font, click new font size in Size list box

OtherWays

1. Right-click selected text, click Font on shortcut menu, click Italic in Font Style list box

2. On Format menu click Font, click Italic in Font Style list box

3. Press CTRL+I

More *About*
Saving

Before you make extreme changes to your presentation, save a copy of it with a different filename using the Save As command on the File menu. This way, if you decide you do not like the new version, you will still have a copy of the original presentation.

To remove italics from text, select the italicized text and then click the Italic button. As a result, the Italic button is not recessed and the text does not have the italic font style.

Saving a Presentation to a Floppy Disk

While you are building your presentation, the computer stores it in main memory. It is important to save your presentation frequently because, if the computer is turned off or you lose electrical power, the presentation is lost. Another reason to save your work is that if you run out of lab time before completing your project, you may finish the project later without having to start over. Therefore, you must save any presentation you will use later. Before you continue with Project 1, save the work completed thus far. Perform the following steps to save a presentation to a floppy disk in drive A using the Save button on the Standard toolbar.

Steps **To Save a Presentation to a Floppy Disk**

1 **Insert a formatted floppy disk in drive A. Then click the Save button on the Standard toolbar.**

The File Save dialog displays (Figure 1-20). The insertion point displays in the File name drop-down list box. The default folder, My Documents, displays in the Save in drop-down list box. Presentations displays in the Save as type drop-down list box. The Save button is dimmed (not available) because you have not yet entered a name in the File name drop-down list box. The Cancel button is available, as indicated by the black text on the button. Clicking the Cancel button closes the File Save dialog box and returns to the PowerPoint window.

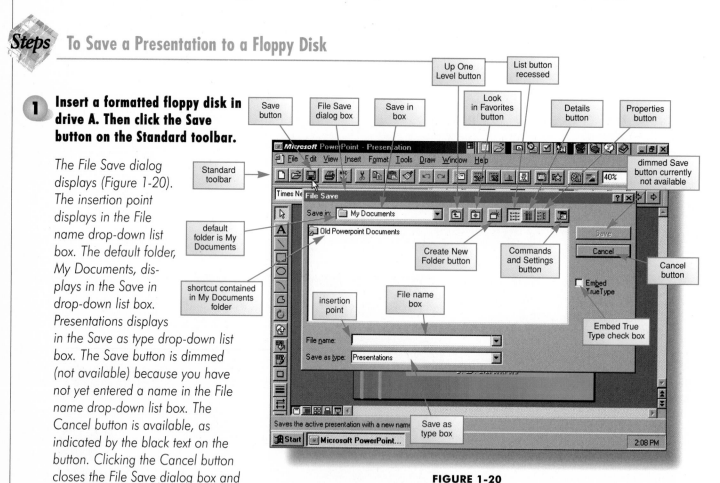

FIGURE 1-20

2 Type College Survival **in the File name box. Do not press the ENTER key after typing the filename. Click the Save in box arrow.**

The name, College Survival, displays in the File name drop-down list box. The Save in drop-down list box displays a list of locations to which you can save your presentation (Figure 1-21). Your list may look different depending on the configuration of your system. The black text on the Save button indicates it is available.

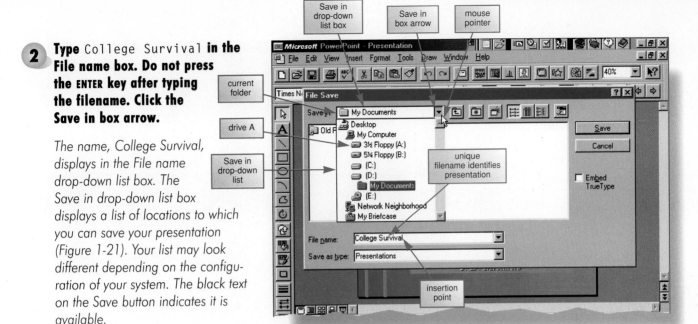

FIGURE 1-21

3 Point to 3½ Floppy [A:] in the Save in drop-down list.

3½ Floppy [A:] is highlighted (Figure 1-22).

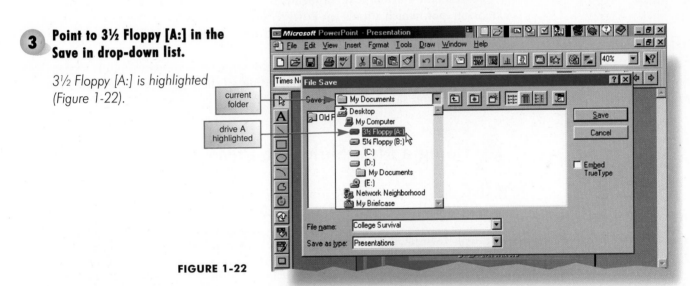

FIGURE 1-22

4 Click 3½ Floppy [A:]. Then point to the Save button.

Drive A becomes the current drive (Figure 1-23).

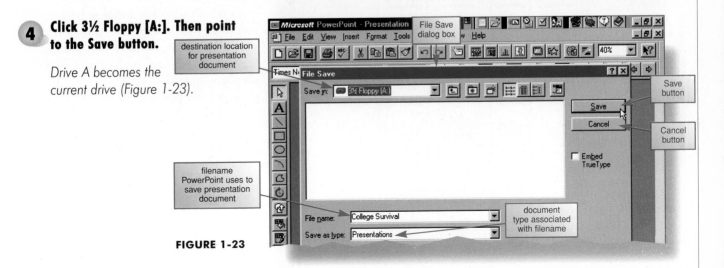

FIGURE 1-23

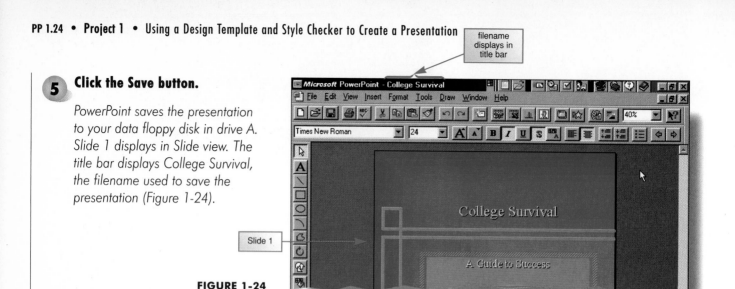

filename displays in title bar

5 **Click the Save button.**

PowerPoint saves the presentation to your data floppy disk in drive A. Slide 1 displays in Slide view. The title bar displays College Survival, the filename used to save the presentation (Figure 1-24).

Slide 1

FIGURE 1-24

PowerPoint automatically appends to the filename, College Survival, the extension **.ppt**, which stands for **P**ower**P**oint. Although the presentation, College Survival, is saved on a floppy disk, it also remains in main memory and displays on the screen.

It is a good practice to save periodically while you are working on a project. By doing so, you protect yourself from losing all the work you have done since the last time you saved.

Adding a New Slide to a Presentation

The title slide for your presentation is created. The next step is to add the first bulleted list slide in Project 1. Clicking the New Slide button on the status bar adds a slide into the presentation immediately after the current slide. Usually when you create your presentation, you are adding slides with text, graphics, or charts. When you add a new slide, PowerPoint displays a dialog box for you to choose one of the AutoLayouts. These AutoLayouts have placeholders for various objects, such as a title, text, graphics, graphs, and charts. Some placeholders provide access to other PowerPoint objects by allowing you to double-click the placeholder. Figure 1-25 displays the twenty-four different AutoLayouts available in PowerPoint. More information about using Auto-Layout placeholders to add graphics follows in subsequent projects. Perform the following steps to add a new slide using the Bulleted List AutoLayout.

Bulleted List AutoLayout

twenty-four different AutoLayouts

Title Slide	Bulleted List	2 Column Text	Table
Text & Graph	Graph & Text	Organization Chart	Graph
Text & Clip Art	Clip Art & Text	Title Only	Blank
Text & Object	Object & Text	Large Object	Object
Text & Media Clip	Media Clip & Text	Object over Text	Text over Object
Text & 2 Objects	2 Objects & Text	2 Objects over Text	4 Objects

FIGURE 1-25

Steps To Add a New Slide Using the Bulleted List AutoLayout

1 **Point to the New Slide button on the status bar (Figure 1-26).**

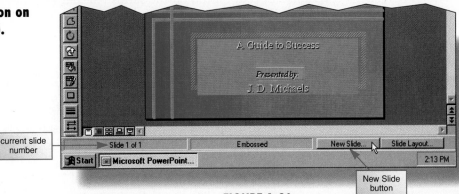

FIGURE 1-26

2 **Click the New Slide button. When the New Slide dialog box displays, point to the OK button.**

The New Slide dialog box displays (Figure 1-27). The Bulleted List AutoLayout is selected and the AutoLayout title, Bulleted List, displays at the bottom right corner of the New Slide dialog box.

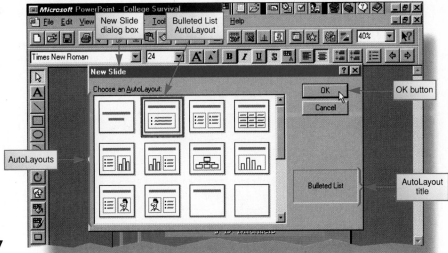

FIGURE 1-27

3 **Click the OK button.**

Slide 2 displays, keeping the attributes of the Embossed Design Template (Figure 1-28). Slide 2 of 2 displays on the status bar.

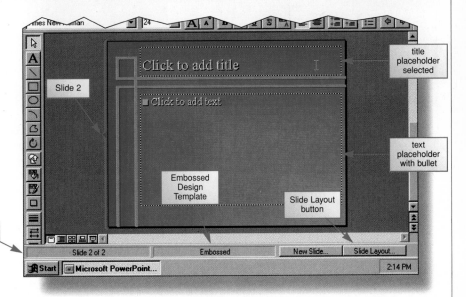

Other Ways

1. Click Insert New Slide button on Standard toolbar
2. On Insert menu click New Slide
3. Press CTRL+ENTER or press CTRL+M

FIGURE 1-28

Because you selected the Bulleted List AutoLayout, PowerPoint displays Slide 2 with a title placeholder and a text placeholder with a bullet. You can change the layout for a slide at any time during the creation of your presentation by clicking the Layout button on the status bar and then double-clicking the AutoLayout of your choice.

Creating a Bulleted List Slide

The bulleted list slides in Figure 1-2 on page PP 1.9, contain more than one level of bulleted text. A slide with more than one level of bulleted text is called a **multi-level bulleted list slide**. A **level** is a position within a structure, such as an outline, that indicates a magnitude of importance. PowerPoint allows for five paragraph levels. Each paragraph level has an associated bullet. The bullet font is dependent on the Design Template. Figure 1-29 identifies the five paragraph levels and the bullet fonts for the Embossed Design Template. Beginning with the Second Level, each paragraph indents .5 inch to the right of the preceding level. For example, the Level Two paragraph indents .5 inch to the right of the Level One paragraph. The Level Three paragraph indents .5 inch to the right of the Level Two paragraph or 1 inch to the right of the Level One paragraph.

An indented paragraph is said to be **demoted**, or pushed down to a lower level. For example, if you demote a First Level paragraph, it becomes a Second Level paragraph. This lower level paragraph is a subset of the higher level paragraph. It usually contains information that supports the topic in the paragraph immediately above it. You demote a paragraph by clicking the **Demote (Indent more) button** on the Formatting toolbar.

When you want to raise a paragraph from a lower level to a higher level, you **promote** the paragraph by clicking the **Promote (Indent less) button** on the Formatting toolbar.

Creating a multi-level bulleted list slide requires several steps. Initially, you enter a slide title. Next, you select a text placeholder. Then you type the text for the multi-level bulleted list, demoting and promoting paragraphs as needed. The next several sections explain how to add a multi-level bulleted list slide.

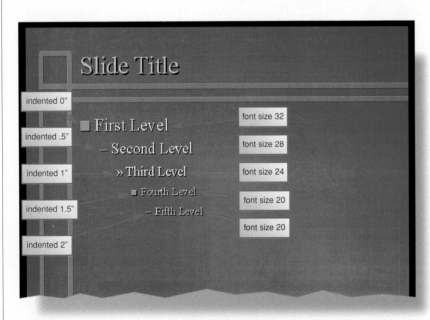

FIGURE 1-29

Entering a Slide Title

PowerPoint assumes every new slide has a title. Therefore, any text you type after a new slide displays becomes the title object. The title for Slide 2 is Dormitory Survival. Perform the following step to enter this title.

Steps To Enter a Slide Title

1 **Type** Dormitory Survival **in the title placeholder. Do not press the ENTER key.**

The title, Dormitory Survival, displays in the title object (Figure 1-30). The insertion point displays after the l in Survival.

FIGURE 1-30

Selecting a Text Placeholder

Before you can type text into the text placeholder, you must first select it. Perform the following step to select the text placeholder on Slide 2.

Steps To Select A Text Placeholder

1 **Click the bulleted paragraph labeled, Click to add text.**

The insertion point displays immediately after the bullet on Slide 2 (Figure 1-31). The Bullet On/Off button is recessed.

FIGURE 1-31

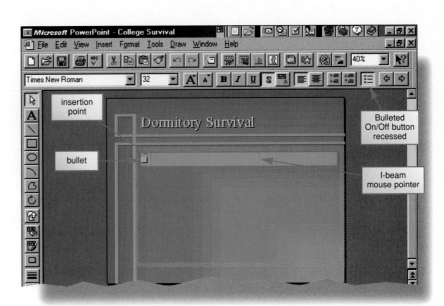

OtherWays

1. Press CTRL+ENTER

Typing a Multi-level Bulleted List

Recall that a bulleted list is a list of paragraphs, each of which is preceded by a bullet. Also recall that a paragraph is a segment of text ended by pressing the ENTER key. The next step is to type the multi-level bulleted list, which consists of the six entries shown in Figure 1-2 on page PP 1.9. Perform the following steps to type a multi-level bulleted list.

 Steps To Type a Multi-level Bulleted List

1 **Type** Be considerate of roommate **and press the ENTER key.**

The paragraph, Be considerate of roommate, displays. The font size is 32. The insertion point displays after the second bullet (Figure 1-32). When you press the ENTER key, the word processing feature of PowerPoint marks the end of one paragraph and begins a new paragraph. Because you are using the Bulleted List AutoLayout, PowerPoint places a bullet in front of the new paragraph.

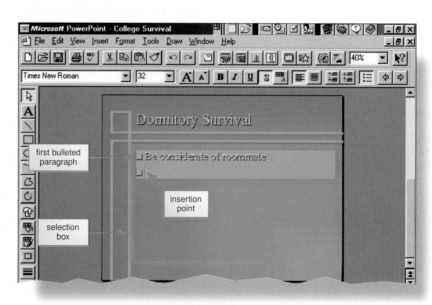

FIGURE 1-32

2 **Point to the Demote (Indent more) button on the Formatting toolbar (Figure 1-33).**

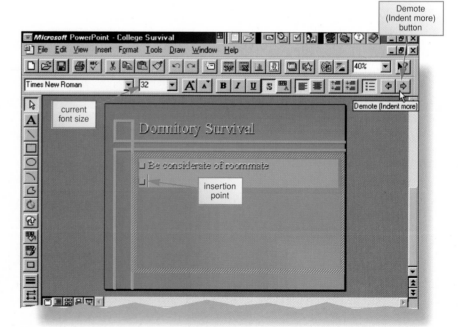

FIGURE 1-33

3 **Click the Demote (Indent more) button.**

The second paragraph indents under the first and becomes a Second Level paragraph (Figure 1-34). Notice the bullet in front of the second paragraph changes from a block to a dash and the font size for the demoted paragraph is now 28. The insertion point displays after the dash.

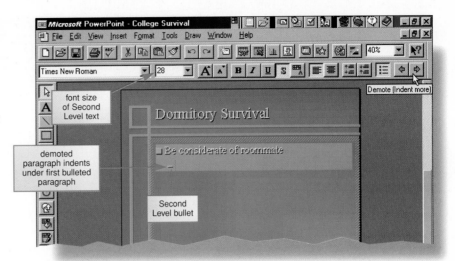

FIGURE 1-34

4 **Type** Organize room together **and press the ENTER key.**

A new Second Level paragraph displays with a dash bullet (Figure 1-35). When you press the ENTER key, PowerPoint adds a new paragraph at the same level as the previous paragraph.

FIGURE 1-35

5 **Point to the Promote (Indent less) button on the Formatting toolbar (Figure 1-36).**

FIGURE 1-36

6 **Click the Promote (Indent less) button.**

The Second Level paragraph becomes a First Level paragraph (Figure 1-37). Notice the bullet in front of the new paragraph changes from a dash to a block and the font size for the promoted paragraph is 32. The insertion point displays after the block bullet.

FIGURE 1-37

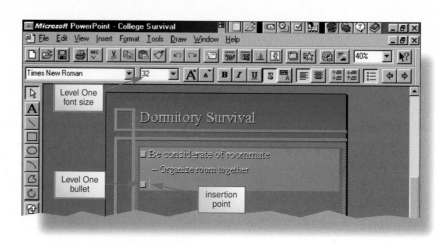

Perform the following steps to complete the text for Slide 2.

TO TYPE THE REMAINING TEXT FOR SLIDE 2

Step 1: Type `Obey rules` and press the ENTER key.
Step 2: Type `Schedule meals` and press the ENTER key.
Step 3: Click the Demote (Indent more) button.
Step 4: Type `Avoid high calorie snacks` and press the ENTER key.
Step 5: Click the Promote (Indent less) button.
Step 6: Type `Get enough sleep` but do not press the ENTER key.

The insertion point displays after the p in sleep (Figure 1-38).

Notice that you did not press the ENTER key after typing the last paragraph in Step 6. If you press the ENTER key, a new bullet displays after the last entry on this slide. To remove an extra bullet, press the BACKSPACE key.

Adding a New Slide with the Same AutoLayout

When you add a new slide to a presentation and want to keep the same AutoLayout used on the previous slide, PowerPoint gives you a shortcut. Instead of clicking the New Slide button and clicking an Auto-Layout in the New Slide dialog box, you can press and hold down the SHIFT key and click the New Slide button. Perform the following step to add a new slide (Slide 3) and keep the Bulleted List AutoLayout used on the previous slide.

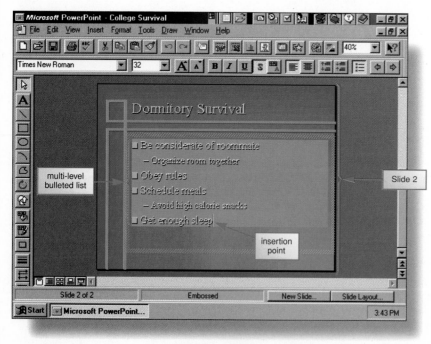

FIGURE 1-38

Steps **To Add a New Slide with the Same AutoLayout**

1 **Press and hold down the SHIFT key. Click the New Slide button on the status bar. Then release the SHIFT key.**

Slide 3 displays with the Bulleted List AutoLayout (Figure 1-39). Slide 3 of 3 displays on the status bar.

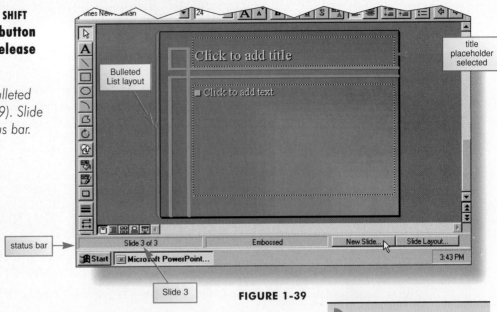

FIGURE 1-39

Other Ways

1. Press SHIFT+CTRL+M

Slide 3 is added to the presentation. Perform the following steps to add text to Slide 3 and create a multi-level bulleted list.

TO CREATE SLIDE 3

Step 1: Type Classroom Survival in the title placeholder.
Step 2: Click the text placeholder.
Step 3: Type Learn your way around campus and press the ENTER key.
Step 4: Type Buy books and supplies and press the ENTER key.
Step 5: Type Attend class and press the ENTER key.
Step 6: Click the Demote (Indent more) button. Then type Be punctual and press the ENTER key.
Step 7: Type Participate and press the ENTER key.
Step 8: Click the Promote (Indent less) button. Then type Develop good study skills and press the ENTER key.
Step 9: Click the Demote (Indent more) button. Then type Budget homework time but do not press the ENTER key.

Slide 3 displays as shown in Figure 1-40.

Slide 4 is the last slide in this presentation. It, too, is a multi-level bulleted list. Perform the steps on the next page to create Slide 4.

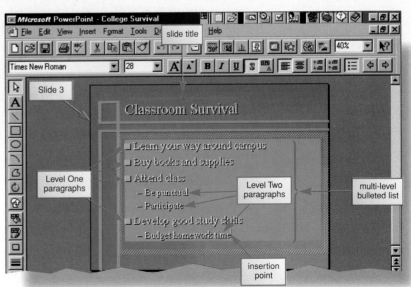

FIGURE 1-40

TO CREATE SLIDE 4

Step 1: Press and hold down the SHIFT key and click the New Slide button on the status bar. Release the SHIFT key.

Step 2: Type Social Survival in the title placeholder.

Step 3: Click the text placeholder.

Step 4: Type Budget time for fun and relaxation and press the ENTER key.

Step 5: Click the Demote (Indent more) button. Then type Join extracurricular clubs and press the ENTER key.

Step 6: Click the Promote (Indent less) button. Then type Preserve your values and press the ENTER key.

Step 7: Click the Demote (Indent more) button. Then type Choose friends with care and press the ENTER key.

Step 8: Click the Promote (Indent less) button. Then type Stay physically fit and press the ENTER key.

Step 9: Type Stay in touch with family but do not press the ENTER key.

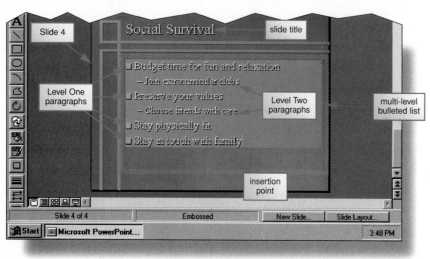

FIGURE 1-41

The slide title and text object display as shown in Figure 1-41.

All slides for the College Survival presentation are created. This presentation consists of a title slide and three multi-level bulleted list slides.

Saving a Presentation with the Same Filename

Saving frequently never can be overemphasized. When you first saved the presentation, you clicked the Save button on the Standard toolbar and the File Save dialog box displayed. When you want to save the changes made to the presentation after your last save, you again click the Save button. This time, however, the File Save dialog box does not display because PowerPoint updates the document called College Survival.ppt on your data floppy disk. Perform the following steps to save the presentation again.

TO SAVE A PRESENTATION WITH THE SAME FILENAME

Step 1: Be sure your data floppy disk is in drive A.

Step 2: Click the Save button on the Standard toolbar.

PowerPoint overwrites the old College Survival.ppt document on the data floppy disk in drive A with the revised presentation document, College Survival.ppt. Slide 4 displays in the PowerPoint window.

Moving to Another Slide in Slide View

When creating or editing a presentation in Slide view, you often want to display a slide other than the current one. Dragging the vertical scroll bar box up or down moves you through your presentation. The box on the vertical scroll bar is called the **elevator** and is shown in Figure 1-42. When you drag the elevator, the **slide indicator** displays the number and the title of the slide you are about to display. Releasing the mouse button displays the slide.

Using the Vertical Scroll Bar to Move to Another Slide

Before continuing with Project 1, you want to display the title slide. Perform the following steps to move from Slide 4 to the Slide 1 using the vertical scroll bar.

Other Ways

1. Click Next Slide button on vertical scroll bar to move forward one slide, or click Previous Slide button on the vertical scroll bar to move back one slide

2. Press PAGE DOWN to move forward one slide, or press PAGE UP to move back one slide

Steps: To Use the Vertical Scroll Bar to Move to Another Slide

1 Position the mouse pointer on the elevator. Press and hold down the left mouse button.

Slide: 4, Social Survival, displays in the slide indicator (Figure 1-42).

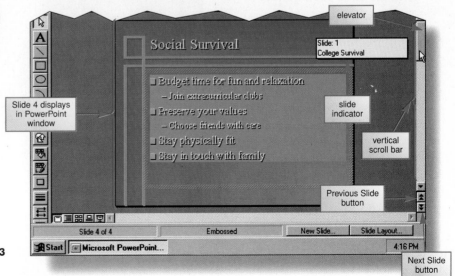

FIGURE 1-42

2 Drag the elevator up the vertical scroll bar until Slide: 1 College Survival displays in the slide indicator.

Slide: 1, College Survival, displays in the slide indicator. Slide 4 still displays in the PowerPoint window (Figure 1-43).

3 Release the left mouse button.

Slide 1, titled College Survival, displays in the PowerPoint window.

FIGURE 1-43

Viewing the Presentation Using Slide Show

The **Slide Show button**, located at the bottom left of the PowerPoint window, allows you to display your presentation electronically using a computer. The computer acts like a slide projector, displaying each slide on a full screen. The full screen slide hides the toolbars, menus, and other PowerPoint window elements.

Starting Slide Show View

Slide Show view begins when you click the Slide Show button. PowerPoint then displays the current slide on the full screen without any of the PowerPoint window objects, such as the menu bar or toolbars. Perform the following steps to start Slide Show view.

 Steps To Start Slide Show View

1 **Point to the Slide Show button on the View Button bar.**

The Slide View button is recessed because you are still in Slide view (Figure 1-44).

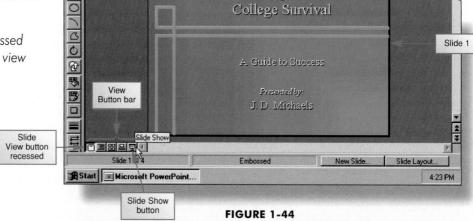

FIGURE 1-44

2 **Click the Slide Show button.**

The title slide fills the screen (Figure 1-45). The PowerPoint window is hidden.

FIGURE 1-45

OtherWays

1. On View menu click Slide Show

Advancing through a Slide Show Manually

After you begin Slide Show view, you can move forward or backward through your slides. PowerPoint allows you to advance through your slides manually or automatically. Automatic advancing is discussed in a later project. Perform the step below to manually move through your slides.

 Steps To Manually Move Through Slides in a Slide Show

Slide 4 in Slide Show view

1 **Click each slide until the last slide of the presentation, Slide 4, Social Survival, displays.**

Each slide in your presentation displays on the screen, one slide at a time. Each time you click the mouse button, the next slide displays (Figure 1-46).

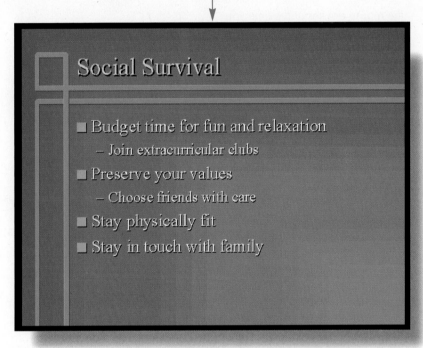

FIGURE 1-46

Other Ways

1. Press PAGE DOWN to advance one slide at a time, or press PAGE UP to go backward one slide at a time

Displaying the Popup Menu in Slide Show View

Slide Show view has a shortcut menu, called **Popup Menu**, that displays when you right-click a slide in Slide Show view. The Popup Menu contains commands to assist you during a slide show. For example, clicking the **Next command** moves you to the next slide. Clicking the **Previous command** moves you to the previous slide. You can jump to any slide in your presentation by clicking the **Go To command**, which displays the Slide Navigator dialog box. The Slide Navigator dialog box contains a list of the slides in your presentation. Jump to the requested slide by double-clicking the name of that slide.

Additional Popup Menu commands allow you to create a list of action items during a slide show, change the mouse pointer from an arrow to a pen, blacken the screen, and end the slide show. Popup Menu commands are discussed in subsequent projects. Perform the step on the next page to display the Slide Show View Popup Menu.

More *About*
Slide Show View

The Pen command on the Popup Menu turns the mouse pointer into a pen that you can use to mark on the slides. The effect is similar to the electronic white board used by television sports announcers as they explain a play. The markings are not saved with the presentation.

To Display the Slide Show View Popup Menu

1 With Slide 4 displaying in Slide Show view, right-click the slide.

The Popup menu displays on Slide 4 (Figure 1-47). Your screen may look different because the Popup menu displays near the location of the mouse pointer at the time you right-click.

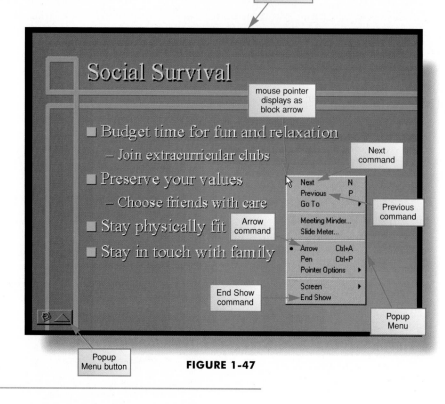

FIGURE 1-47

Other Ways

1. Move mouse pointer during slide show to display the Popup Menu button, then click Popup Menu button

Some presenters prefer to right-click to move backward through a slide show. Because you can display the Slide Show view Popup menu by clicking the Slide Show view Popup Menu button, you can turn off an option setting that displays the Slide Navigator when you right-click. To turn off the Popup Menu on the Right Mouse Click, on the Tools menu, click Options, click the View tab to display the View sheet, click Popup Menu on Right Mouse Click, and then click the OK button. After turning off the Popup Menu on the Right Mouse Click option setting, you can right-click to move backward, one slide at a time, in Slide Show view.

Using the Popup Menu to End a Slide Show

The **End Show command** on the Popup Menu exits Slide Show view and returns to the view you were in when you clicked the Slide Show button. Perform the following step to end Slide Show view.

Steps To Use the Popup Menu to End a Slide Show

1 **Click End Show on the Popup Menu.**

PowerPoint exits Slide Show view and displays the slide last displayed in Slide Show view, which in this instance, is Slide 4 (Figure 1-48).

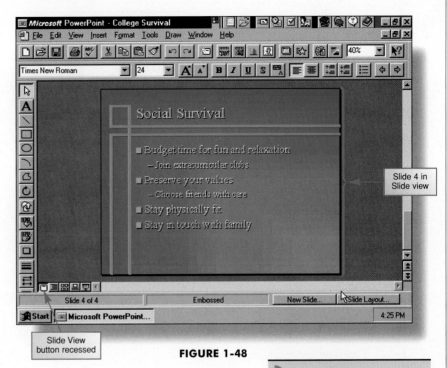

FIGURE 1-48

Slide Show view is excellent for rehearsing a presentation. You can start Slide Show view from any view: Slide view, Outline view, Slide Sorter view, or Notes Pages view.

Closing PowerPoint

The College Survival presentation now is complete. When you close PowerPoint, PowerPoint prompts you to save any changes made to the presentation since the last save, closes all PowerPoint windows, and then quits PowerPoint. Closing PowerPoint returns control to the desktop. Perform the steps on the next page to close PowerPoint.

*Other*Ways

1. Click the last slide in presentation to return to the slide at which you began Slide Show view

2. Press ESC to display slide last viewed in Slide Show view

Steps **To Close PowerPoint**

1 Point to the Close button on the title bar (Figure 1-49).

2 Click the Close button.

If you made changes to the presentation since your last save, the Microsoft PowerPoint dialog box displays asking the question, Save changes to "College Survival"? Click the Yes button to save the changes to the College Survival presentation before closing PowerPoint. Click the No button to close PowerPoint without saving the changes to the College Survival presentation. Click the Cancel button to terminate the Close command and return to the presentation. If you did not make changes to your presentation since your last save, this dialog box does not display.

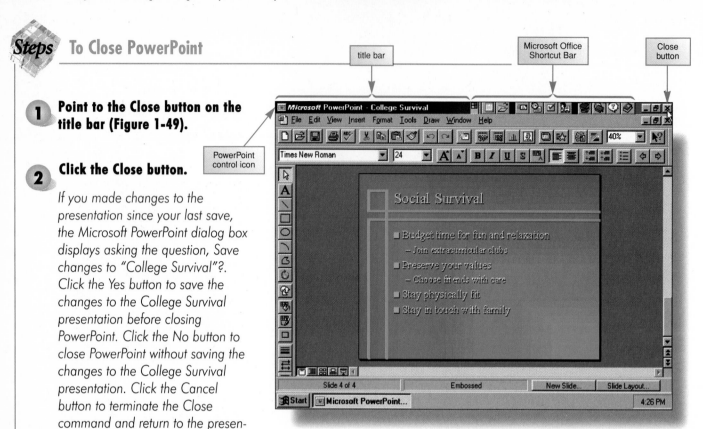

FIGURE 1-49

OtherWays

1. On title bar double-click PowerPoint control icon; or on title bar, click PowerPoint control icon click Close
2. On File menu click Exit
3. Press CTRL+Q, or press ALT+F4

Opening a Presentation

Earlier, you saved the presentation on a floppy disk using the filename, College Survival.ppt. Once you create and save a presentation, you may need to retrieve it from the floppy disk to make changes. For example, you may want to replace the Design Template or modify some text. Recall that a presentation is a PowerPoint document. Use the **Open Office Document command** to open an existing presentation.

Opening an Existing Presentation

Ensure that the data floppy disk used to save College Survival.ppt is in drive A. Then perform the following steps to open the College Survival presentation using the Open Office Document command on the Start menu.

Steps **To Open an Existing Presentation**

1 Click the Start button on the taskbar and point to Open Office Document.

The Windows 95 Start menu displays (Figure 1-50). Open Office Document is highlighted.

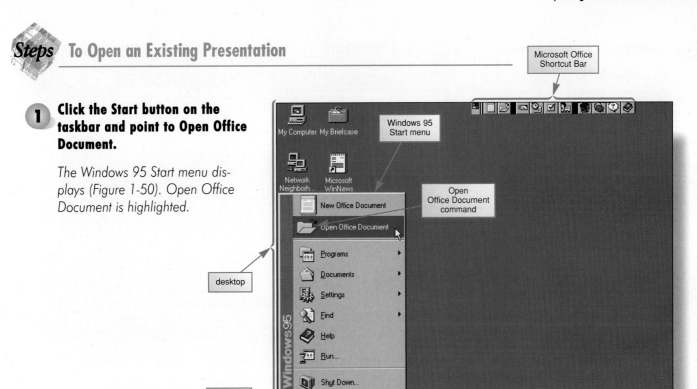

FIGURE 1-50

2 Click Open Office Document. When the Open dialog box displays, click the Look in box arrow and then click 3½ Floppy [A:] (see Figures 1-21 and 1-22 on page PP 1.23 to review this process).

The Open dialog box displays (Figure 1-51). A list of existing files on drive A displays because your data floppy disk is in drive A. Notice that Office Files displays in the Files of type drop-down list box. The file, College Survival, is highlighted. Your list of existing files may be different depending on the files saved on your data floppy disk.

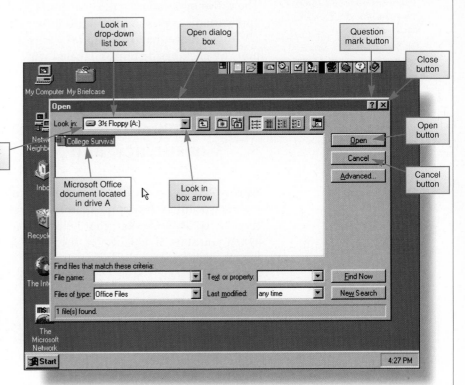

FIGURE 1-51

3 Double-click College Survival.

PowerPoint starts and opens College Survival.ppt from drive A into main memory and displays the first slide on the screen (Figure 1-52). The presentation displays in Slide view because PowerPoint opens presentations in the same view in which they were saved.

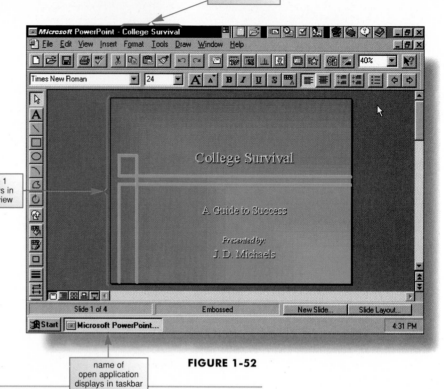

presentation name displays in title bar

Slide 1 displays in Slide view

name of open application displays in taskbar

FIGURE 1-52

OtherWays

1. Click Open a Document button on Microsoft Office Shortcut Bar, click folder or drive name in Look in drop-down list box, double-click document name
2. On Start menu click Documents, click document name

When an application is open, its name displays on a button on the taskbar. The **active application** is the one displaying in the foreground of the desktop. That application's corresponding button on the taskbar appears recessed.

When more than one application is open, you can switch between applications by clicking the button labeled with the name of the application to which you want to switch.

Checking a Presentation for Visual Clarity, Consistency, and Style

After you create a presentation, you should proofread it for errors. Typical errors include spelling errors, punctuation errors, and design errors. PowerPoint has a tool, called **Style Checker**, that helps you identify errors in your presentation. When you start Style Checker, the Style Checker dialog box displays three check boxes: Spelling, Visual Clarity, and Case and End Punctuation. A check mark in a check box instructs Style Checker to look for that particular type of inconsistency. For example, a check mark in the Spelling check box causes Style Checker to check the presentation for spelling errors. Table 1-3 identifies the purpose of each check box in the Style Checker dialog box.

Table 1-3

CHECK BOX	PURPOSE
Spelling	Checks the presentation for spelling errors.
Visual Clarity	Checks the presentation for design and style errors, such as fonts too small for the audience to read, too many bullets on a slide, or too many words per paragraph.
Case and End Punctuation	Checks the presentation for consistent usage of capitalization and end punctuation.

PowerPoint checks your presentation for spelling errors using a standard dictionary contained in the Microsoft Office group. This dictionary is shared with the other Microsoft Office applications such as Word and Excel. A **custom dictionary** is available if you want to add special words such as proper names, cities, and acronyms. When checking a presentation for spelling errors, PowerPoint opens the standard dictionary and the custom dictionary file, if one exists. If a word is not found in either dictionary, PowerPoint displays a dialog box. When a word appears in the Spelling dialog box, you have several options which are explained in Table 1-4.

Table 1-4

OPTION	DESCRIPTION
Manually correct the word	Retype the word with the proper spelling and click Change. PowerPoint continues checking the rest of the presentation.
Ignore the word	Click Ignore when the word is spelled correctly but not found in the dictionaries. PowerPoint continues checking the rest of the presentation.
Ignore all occurrences of the word	Click Ignore All when the word is spelled correctly but not found in the dictionaries. PowerPoint ignores all occurrences of the word and continues checking the rest of the presentation.
Select a different spelling	Click the proper spelling of the word from the list in the Suggestions box. Click Change. PowerPoint corrects the word and continues checking the rest of the presentation.
Change all occurrences of the misspelling to a different spelling	Click the proper spelling of the word on the list in the Suggestions box. Click Change All. PowerPoint changes all occurrences of the misspelled word and continues checking the rest of the presentation.
Add a word to the custom dictionary	Click Add. PowerPoint opens the custom dictionary, adds the word, and continues checking the rest of the presentation.
Suggest alternative spellings	Click Suggest. PowerPoint lists suggested spellings. Click the correct word from the Suggestions box or type the proper spelling. Then Click Change. PowerPoint continues checking the rest of the presentation.

The standard dictionary contains commonly used English words. It does not, however, contain proper names, abbreviations, technical terms, poetic contractions, or antiquated terms. PowerPoint treats words not found in the dictionaries as misspellings.

Starting Style Checker

Start Style Checker by clicking the Style Checker command on the Tools menu. Perform the steps on the next pages to start Style Checker.

More *About* **Presentation Design**

Keep to one concept per slide. Highlight the subject rather than presenting a page of text. Limit your slide to five to seven words per line and five to seven lines per slide. Do not clutter; use empty space effectively.

Steps To Start Style Checker

1 **Click Tools on the menu bar. Then point to Style Checker (Figure 1-53).**

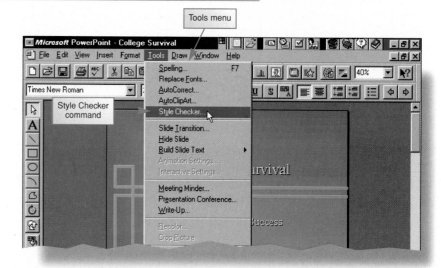

FIGURE 1-53

2 **Click Style Checker. When the Style Checker dialog box displays, point to the Start button.**

The Style Checker dialog box displays (Figure 1-54). A check mark displays in each of the three check boxes in the Check For box. The mouse pointer points to the Start button.

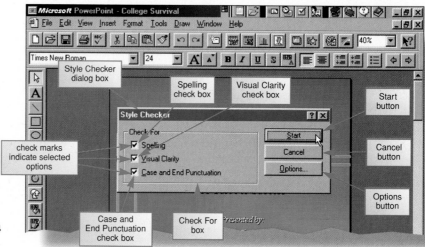

FIGURE 1-54

3 **Click the Start button.**

PowerPoint launches the spelling feature and displays the Spelling dialog box (Figure 1-55). Michaels displays in the Not in Dictionary box. Because it is a common proper name, two suggested spellings display in the Suggestions box. PowerPoint suggests that Michaels should be the possessive form, Michael's, and displays the suggested spelling in the Change To box.

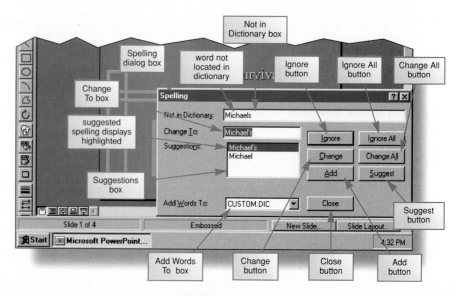

FIGURE 1-55

4 **Click the Ignore button.**

PowerPoint ignores the word Michaels and continues searching for additional misspelled words. PowerPoint may stop on additional words depending on your typing accuracy. When PowerPoint has checked all slides for misspellings, it begins checking for style errors and displays the Style Checker dialog box (Figure 1-56). The Style Checker dialog box displays a message indicating the slide number currently being checked and displays punctuation errors. If you have punctuation errors, you can click one of the buttons to ignore or change them. If you want to stop Style Checker and return to the current slide, click the Cancel button.

FIGURE 1-56

5 **If the Style Checker lists visual clarity inconsistencies in the Style Checker Summary dialog box, write the slide number and the message on a sheet of paper (Figure 1-57).**

6 **Click the OK button.**

PowerPoint closes Style Checker and returns to the current slide, Slide 1, or to the slide where a misspelled word occurred.

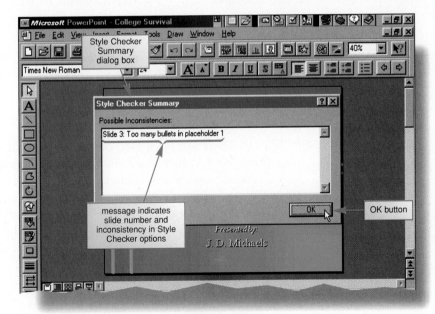

FIGURE 1-57

The Style Checker dialog box contains an **Options button** (see Figure 1-54), which when clicked, displays the Style Checker Options dialog box. The Style Checker Options dialog box has two tabbed sheets: Case and End Punctuation, and Visual Clarity. Each tabbed sheet has several options that can be changed to suit your design specifications. Table 1-5 on the next page identifies each option available in Style Checker and each default setting.

OPTION	SETTING
Table 1-5	
CASE	
Slide Title Style	Title Case
Body Text Style	Sentence Case
END PUNCTUATION	
Slide Title Periods	Remove
Body Text Periods	Remove
VISUAL CLARITY	
Number of Fonts Should Not Exceed	3
Title	36 points
Body Text Size Should Be at Least	24 points
Number of Bullets Should Be at Least	6
Number of Lines per Title Should Be at Least	2
Number of Lines per Bullet Should Be at Least	2
Check for Title and Placeholder Text Off Slide	On

Correcting Errors

After creating a presentation and running Style Checker, you may find that you must make changes. Changes may be required because a slide contains an error, the scope of the presentation shifts, or Style Checker found a style inconsistency. This section explains the types of errors that commonly occur when creating a presentation.

Types of Corrections Made to Presentations

There usually are three types of corrections to text in a presentation: additions, deletions, and replacements.

▶ **Additions** — Additions are necessary when you omit text from a slide and need to add it later. You may need to insert text in the form of a sentence, word, or single character. For example, you may want to add the rest of the presenter's first name on your title slide.

▶ **Deletions** — Deletions are required when text on a slide is incorrect or is no longer relevant to the presentation. For example, Style Checker identified too many bullets on Slide 3. Therefore, you may want to remove one of the bulleted paragraphs.

▶ **Replacements** — Replacements are needed when you want to revise the text in your presentation. For example, you may want to substitute the word their for the word there.

Editing text in PowerPoint is basically the same as editing text in a word processing package. The following sections illustrate the most common changes made to text in a presentation.

Deleting Text

There are three methods for deleting text. One is to use the BACKSPACE key to remove text just typed. The second is to position the insertion point to the left of the text you wish to delete and then press the DELETE key. The third method is to drag through the text you wish to delete and press the DELETE key. (Use the third method when deleting large sections of text.)

Previously, Style Checker identified that Slide 3 has too many bullets. Perform the following steps to delete one of the bulleted paragraphs.

TO DELETE A PARAGRAPH

Step 1: Drag the elevator to display Slide 3.
Step 2: Click the bullet in front of the first paragraph, Learn your way around campus.
Step 3: Press the DELETE key.

The selected paragraph is deleted from Slide 3. The remaining 6 bulleted paragraphs move up one paragraph in the text object to take the place of the deleted paragraph. Slide 3 now satisfies the Style Checker design rule, not to exceed 6 bullets per slide.

Recall from the beginning of this project that if you make a mistake (such as deleting text), you can click the Undo button on the Standard toolbar to reverse your mistake.

▶ **OtherWays**
1. On Edit menu click Clear

Replacing Text into an Existing Slide

When you need to correct a word or phrase, you can replace the text by selecting the text to be replaced and then typing the new text. As soon as you press any key on the keyboard, the highlighted text is deleted and the new text displays.

PowerPoint inserts text to the left of the insertion point. The text to the right of the insertion point moves to the right (and shifts downward if necessary) to accommodate the added text. Perform the following steps to replace the period after the letter J with the rest of J. D. Michaels' first name, Jerry.

TO REPLACE TEXT

Step 1: Drag the elevator to display Slide 1. Select the period between the J and the D in J. D. Michaels by dragging the I-beam mouse pointer.

Step 2: Type erry to replace the period and insert the rest of the first name, Jerry.

The title slide now displays Jerry D. Michaels first name, as shown in Figure 1-2 on page PP 1.9, instead of his initials.

Changing Line Spacing

The bulleted lists on Slides 2, 3, and 4 look crowded; yet, there is ample blank space that could be used to separate the paragraphs. You can adjust the spacing on each slide, but when several slides need to be changed, you should change the Slide Master. Each PowerPoint component (slides, audience handouts, and notes pages) has a **master**, which controls its appearance. Slides have two masters, Title Master and Slide Master. The **Title Master** controls the appearance of the title slide. The **Slide Master** controls the appearance of the other slides in your presentation.

Each Design Template has a specially designed Slide Master; so if you select a Design Template, but want to change one of its components, you can override that component by changing the Slide Master. Any change to the Slide Master results in changing every slide in the presentation, except the title slide. For example, if you change the line spacing to .5 inches before each paragraph on the Slide Master, each slide (except the title slide) changes line spacing after each paragraph to .5 inches. The Slide Master components most frequently changed are listed in Table 1-6.

Table 1-6	
COMPONENT	**DESCRIPTION**
Font face	Defines the appearance and shape of letters, numbers, and special characters.
Font size	Specifies the size of the characters on the screen. Character size is gauged by a measurement system called points. A single point is about 1/72 of an inch in height. Thus, a character with a point size of eighteen is about 18/72 (or 1/4) of an inch in height.
Text style	Text styles include plain, italic, bold, shadowed, and underlined. Text may have more than one style at a time.
Text position	Positions of text in a paragraph left aligned, right aligned, centered, or justified. Justified text is proportionally spaced across the object.
Color scheme	A coordinated set of eight colors designed to complement each other. Color schemes consist of background color, line and text color, shadow color, title text color, object fill color, and three different accent colors.
Background items	Any object other than the title object or text object. Typical items include borders, graphics—such as a company logo, page number, date, and time.
Slide number	Inserts the special symbol used to print the slide number.
Date	Inserts the special symbol used to print the date the presentation was printed.
Time	Inserts the special symbol used to print the time the presentation was printed.

Additionally, each view has its own master. You can access the master by holding down the SHIFT key while clicking the appropriate view button. For example, holding down the SHIFT key and clicking the Slide view button displays the Slide Master. To exit a master, click the view button to which you wish to return. To return to Slide view, for example, click the Slide View button.

Displaying the Slide Master

Before you can change line spacing on the Slide Master, you first must display it. Perform the following steps to display the Slide Master.

Steps To Display the Slide Master

1 **Drag the elevator to display Slide 2. Press and hold down the SHIFT key and then point to the Slide View button.**

When you hold down the SHIFT key, the ToolTip box displays Slide Master (Figure 1-58).

FIGURE 1-58

2 **While holding down the SHIFT key, click the Slide View button. Then release the SHIFT key.**

The Slide Master displays (Figure 1-59).

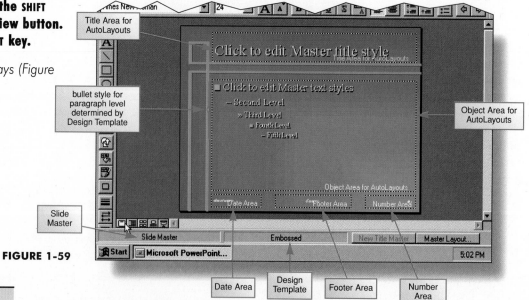

FIGURE 1-59

Other Ways

1. On View menu click Master, click Slide Master

Changing Line Spacing on the Slide Master

Change line spacing by clicking the Line Spacing command on the Format menu. When you click the **Line Spacing command**, the Line Spacing dialog box displays. The Line Spacing dialog box contains three boxes, Line Spacing, Before Paragraph, and After Paragraph, which allow you to adjust line spacing within a paragraph, before a paragraph, and after a paragraph, respectively.

In this project, you change the number in the amount of space box to increase the amount of space that displays before every paragraph, except the first paragraph, on every slide. For example, increasing the amount of space box to 0.5 lines increases the amount of space that displays before each paragraph. The first paragraph on every slide, however, does not change. Perform the following steps to change the line spacing.

 Steps **To Change Line Spacing on the Slide Master**

1 **Click the bulleted paragraph labeled, Click to edit Master text styles.**

The insertion point displays at the point you clicked (Figure 1-60). The text object area is selected.

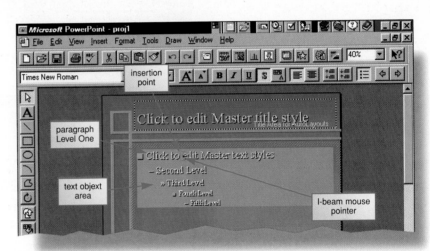

FIGURE 1-60

2 **Click Format on the menu bar and then point to Line Spacing (Figure 1-61).**

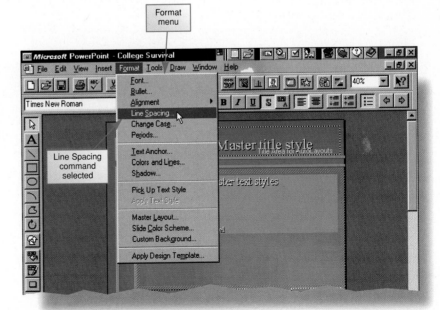

FIGURE 1-61

3 **Click Line Spacing. Point to the up arrow in the amount of space box in the Before Paragraph box.**

PowerPoint displays the Line Spacing dialog box (Figure 1-62).

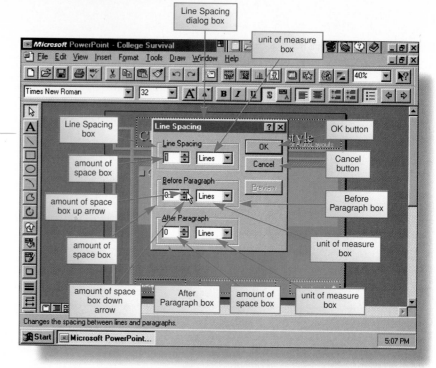

FIGURE 1-62

4 **Click the amount of space box up arrow six times so that 0.5 displays.**

The amount of space box displays 0.5 (Figure 1-63). The Preview button is available after a change is made in the Line Spacing dialog box.

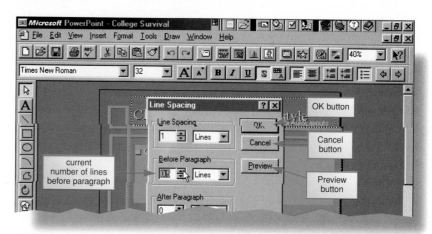

FIGURE 1-63

5 **Click the OK button.**

The Slide Master text placeholder displays the new Before Paragraph line spacing (Figure 1-64). Depending on the video drivers installed, the spacing on your screen may appear slightly different than this figure.

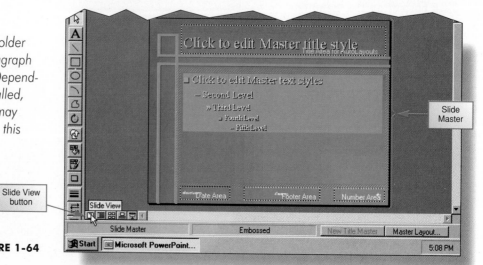

FIGURE 1-64

6 **Click the Slide View button to return to Slide view.**

Slide 2 displays with the Before Paragraph line spacing set to 0.5 lines (Figure 1-65).

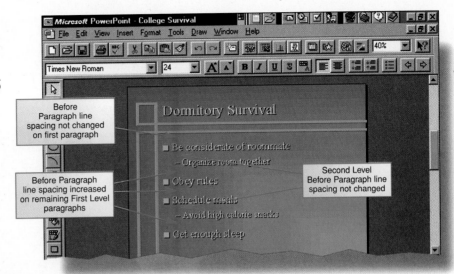

FIGURE 1-65

To display your line spacing changes without making them permanent, click the Preview button. If you want to close the Line Spacing dialog box without applying the changes, click the Cancel button.

Before Paragraph line spacing is controlled by setting the number of units before a paragraph. Units are either lines or points; lines are the default unit. Points may be selected by clicking the down arrow next to the Before Paragraph drop-down list box (see Figure 1-62). Recall from page PP 1.19 that a single point is about 1/72 of an inch in height.

The Line Spacing box and the After Paragraph box each contain an amount of space box and a unit of measure box. To change the amount of space displaying between paragraphs, click the amount of space box up arrow or down arrow in the Line Spacing box. To change the amount of space displaying after a paragraph, click the amount of space box up arrow or down arrow in the After Paragraph box. To change the unit of measure from Lines to Points in either the Line Spacing box or the After Paragraph box, click the down arrow next to the unit of measure drop-down list box and then click Points.

The placeholder at the top of the Slide Master (Figure 1-64) is used to edit the Master title style. The large placeholder under the Master title placeholder is used to edit the Master text styles. Here you make changes to the various bullet levels. Changes can be made to line spacing, bullet font, text and line color, alignment, and text shadow. It is also the object area for AutoLayouts.

Displaying a Presentation in Black and White

This project explains how to print a presentation for the purpose of making transparencies. PowerPoint's **B&W View button** allows you to display the presentation in black and white before you print it. Table 1-7 identifies how PowerPoint objects display in black and white.

More *About*
Line Spacing

Resist the temptation to regard blank space on a slide as wasted space. Blank space added for the purpose of directing the attention of the audience to specific text or graphics is called **white space**. White space is a powerful design tool. Used effectively, white space improves audience attention.

Table 1-7	
OBJECT	**APPEARANCE IN BLACK AND WHITE VIEW**
Text	Black
Text shadows	Hidden
Embossing	Hidden
Fills	Grayscale
Frame	1 point frame
Pattern fills	Grayscale
Lines	Black
Object shadows	Gray
Bitmaps/Pictures	Grayscale
Slide backgrounds	White

Perform the following steps to display the presentation in black and white.

Steps **To Display a Presentation in Black and White**

1 **Point to the B&W View button on the Standard toolbar (Figure 1-66).**

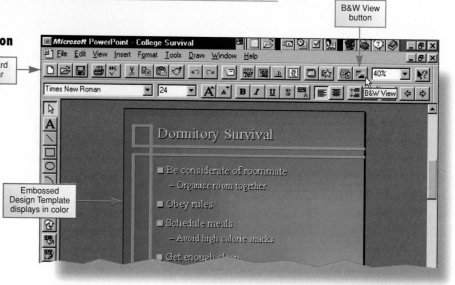

FIGURE 1-66

2 **Click the B&W View button.**

The presentation displays in black and white (Figure 1-67). The B&W View button is recessed. The Color View box displays a miniature of the current slide in color.

FIGURE 1-67

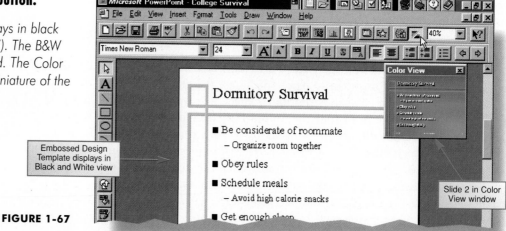

OtherWays

1. On View menu click Black and White

To return to the color view of the presentation, click the B&W View button again.

Printing a Presentation

After you create a presentation, you often want to print it. A printed version of the presentation is called a **hard copy**, or **printout**. The first printing of the presentation is called a **rough draft**. The rough draft allows you to proofread the presentation to check for errors and readability. After correcting errors, you print the final copy of your presentation.

Saving Before Printing

Prior to printing your presentation, you should save your work in the event you experience difficulties with the printer. You occasionally may encounter system problems that can be resolved only by restarting the computer. In such an instance, you will need to reopen your presentation. As a precaution, always save your presentation before you print. Perform the following steps to save the presentation before printing.

TO SAVE A PRESENTATION BEFORE PRINTING

Step 1: Verify that your data floppy disk is in drive A.
Step 2: Click the Save button on the Standard toolbar.

All changes made after your last save are now saved on a floppy disk.

Printing the Presentation

After saving the presentation, you are ready to print. Because you are in Slide view, clicking the **Print button** on the Standard toolbar causes PowerPoint to print all slides in the presentation. Additionally, because you are currently viewing the presentation in black and white, the slides print in black and white, even if you have a color printer. Perform the following steps to print the presentation slides.

 To Print a Presentation

1 **Ready the printer according to the printer instructions. Then, click the Print button on the Standard toolbar.**

The mouse pointer momentarily changes to an hourglass. PowerPoint then displays a message on the status bar indicating it is preparing to print the presentation in the background. An animated printer icon displays on the status bar identifying which slide is being prepared. After several moments, the presentation begins printing on the printer. The printer icon, next to the clock on the taskbar, indicates there is a print job processing (Figure 1-68). When the presentation is finished printing, the printer icon on the taskbar disappears.

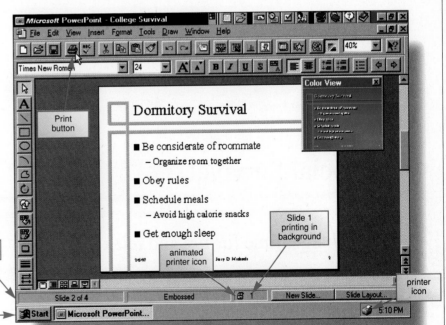

FIGURE 1-68

2 **When the printer stops, retrieve the printouts of the slides.**

The presentation, College Survival, prints on four pages (Figure 1-69).

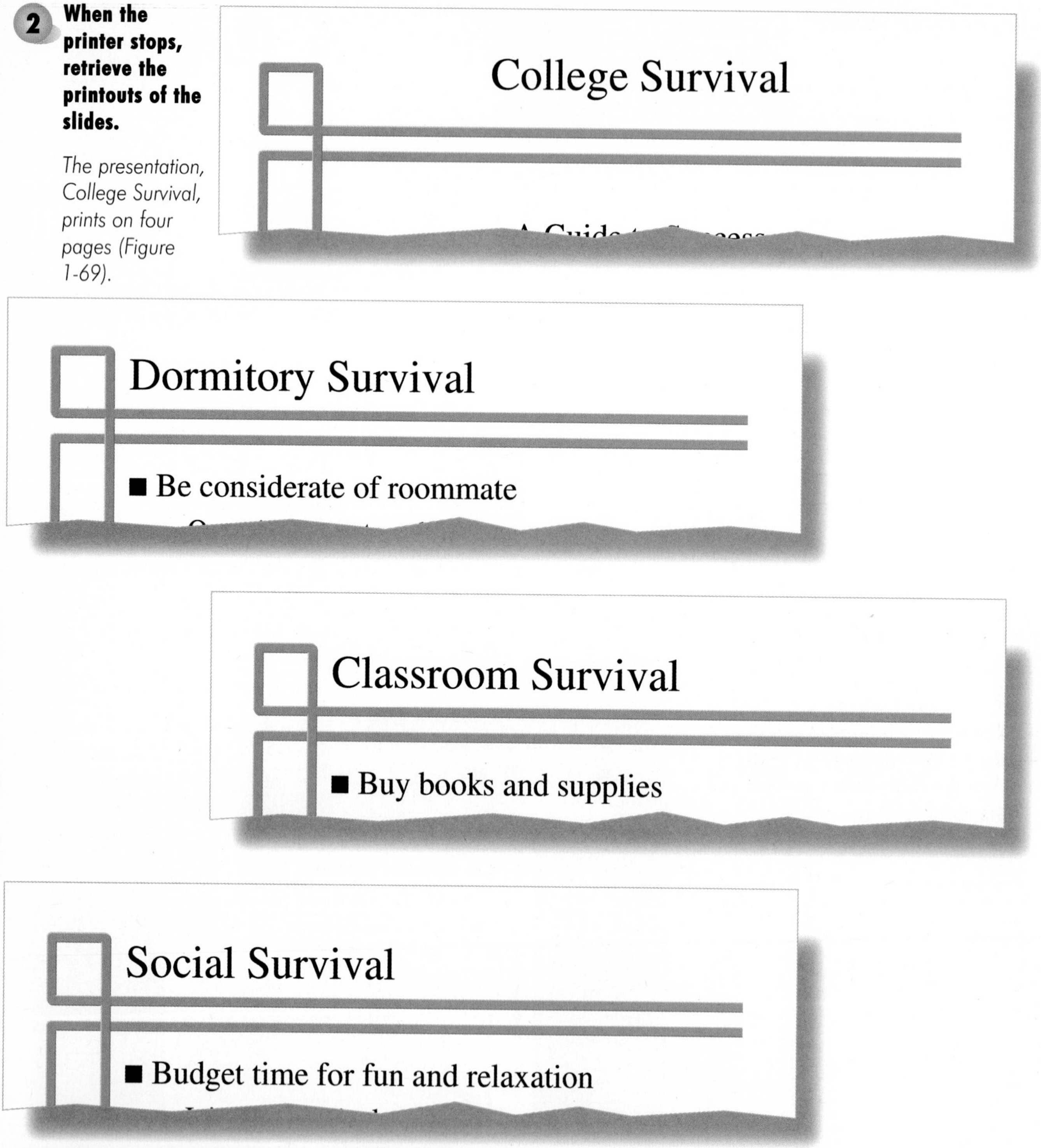

College Survival

A Guide to Success

Dormitory Survival

■ Be considerate of roommate

Classroom Survival

■ Buy books and supplies

Social Survival

■ Budget time for fun and relaxation

FIGURE 1-69

OtherWays

1. On File menu click Print
2. Press CTRL+P, or press CTRL+SHIFT+F12

Double-clicking the animated printer icon on the status bar cancels the printing process.

Making a Transparency

This project requires you to make overhead transparencies. You make transparencies using one of several devices. One device is a printer attached to your computer, such as an ink jet printer or a laser printer. Transparencies produced on a printer may be in black and white or color, depending on the printer. Another device is a photocopier. A third device is a thermal copier. A thermal copier transfers a carbonaceous substance, like toner from a photocopier, from a paper master to an acetate film. Because each of the three devices requires a special transparency film, check the user's manual for the film requirement of your specific device, or ask your instructor.

PowerPoint Help

You can get assistance anytime while you are working in PowerPoint using **online help**. When used effectively, online help can increase your productivity and reduce the amount of time you spend learning how to use PowerPoint. Table 1-8 summarizes the six categories of online help.

The following sections show examples of each category of online help described in Table 1-8.

Using the Contents Sheet to Obtain Help

The **Contents sheet** in the Help Topics dialog box assists you in finding help about a specific subject. Use the Contents sheet in the same manner you use the table of contents in a book. Perform the steps on the next page to use the Contents sheet to obtain help on using the Slide Master to change the appearance of your presentation.

Table 1-8

HELP CATEGORY	SUMMARY	HOW TO START
Answer Wizard sheet	Allows you to enter, in your own words, an English-type question. For example, How do I change bullet fonts?	Double-click the Help button on the Standard toolbar; or on the Help menu, click Microsoft PowerPoint Help Topics, and then click the Answer Wizard tab.
Contents sheet	Groups help topics by general categories. Use when you know, in general, what you want.	Double-click the Help button on the Standard toolbar; or on the Help menu, click Microsoft PowerPoint Help Topics, and then click the Contents tab.
Find sheet	Searches the index for all phrases that include the term you specify. For example, bullets.	Double-click the Help button on the Standard toolbar; or on the Help menu, click Microsoft PowerPoint Help Topics, and then click the Find tab.
Help button	Provides an explanation of objects on the screen.	Click the Help button on the Standard toolbar and then click an object on the screen.
Index sheet	Lists help topics alphabetically. Similar to an index in a book. Use when you know exactly what you want. For example, adding footers.	Double-click the Help button on the Standard toolbar; or on the Help menu, click Microsoft PowerPoint Help Topics, and then click the Index tab.
Question mark button	Provides an explanation of objects on the screen.	In a dialog box, click the Question mark button and then click a dialog box object.

Steps To Obtain Help Using the Contents Sheet

1 **Double-click the Help button on the Standard toolbar.**

The Help Topics: Microsoft PowerPoint dialog box displays.

2 **If necessary, click the Contents tab to activate the Contents sheet. In the list box, double-click the book icon labeled Changing the Appearance of Your Presentation.**

*An icon precedes each entry in the list box. A **Book icon** indicates there are subtopics. A **Question mark icon** indicates information will display when the title is double-clicked (Figure 1-70).*

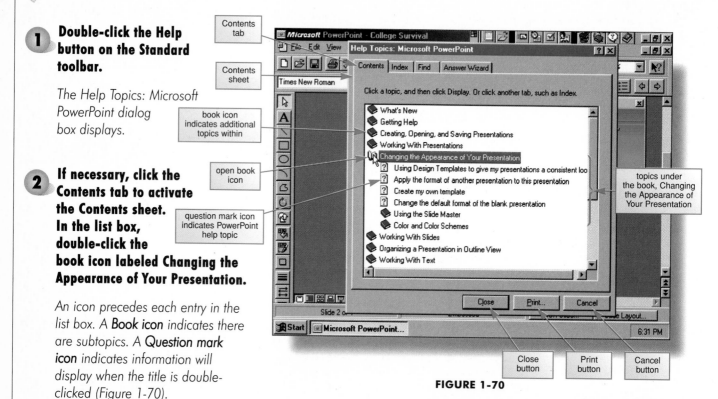

FIGURE 1-70

3 **Double-click the topic labeled Using Design Templates to give my presentations a consistent look.**

A Microsoft PowerPoint window displays information about using Design Templates to give a presentation a consistent look (Figure 1-71).

4 **After reading the information, click the Close button in the Microsoft PowerPoint window.**

The Microsoft PowerPoint window closes.

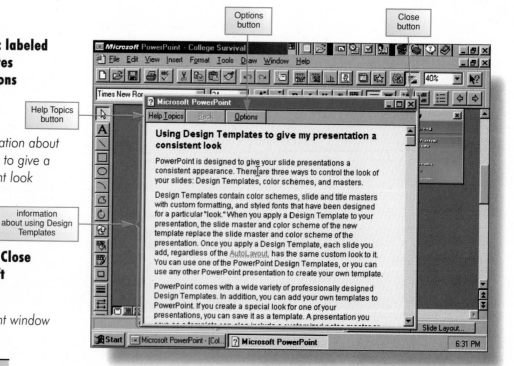

FIGURE 1-71

OtherWays

1. On Help menu click Microsoft PowerPoint Help Topics, click Contents tab
2. Press F1

As an alternative to double-clicking the topic name in the list box, you can click it and then use the buttons at the bottom of the Microsoft PowerPoint window to display information on a topic or print information on a topic (Figure 1-70). Additionally, you can print information on a topic by pointing to the help window, right-clicking, and then clicking Print Topic; or by clicking the Options button at the top of the Microsoft PowerPoint window, and then clicking Print Topic (Figure 1-71). To close or cancel the Microsoft PowerPoint window, click the Close button to return to PowerPoint, or click the **Help Topics button** to return to the Contents sheet.

Using the Index Sheet to Obtain Help

Use the **Index sheet** in the Help Topics: Microsoft PowerPoint dialog box when you know the term about which you are seeking help. You can locate the term you are looking for by typing part or all of the word, or you can scroll through the alphabetical list and click the term. You use the Index sheet in the same manner you use an index at the back of a book.

Many of the online help topics provide you with a demonstration of how to accomplish a task. For example, if you want to find out how to add footers to the Slide Master, PowerPoint shows you by pointing to the View menu and then pointing to the Header and Footer command. Perform the following steps to obtain information about adding footers to the Slide Master by typing foo, the first three letters of the word footer.

Steps **To Obtain Help Using the Index Sheet**

1 **Double-click the Help button on the Standard toolbar.**

The Help Topics: Microsoft PowerPoint dialog box displays.

2 **If necessary, click the Index tab to display the Index sheet. Type** foo **in the box labeled 1.**

The term footers is highlighted in the box labeled 2 (Figure 1-72).

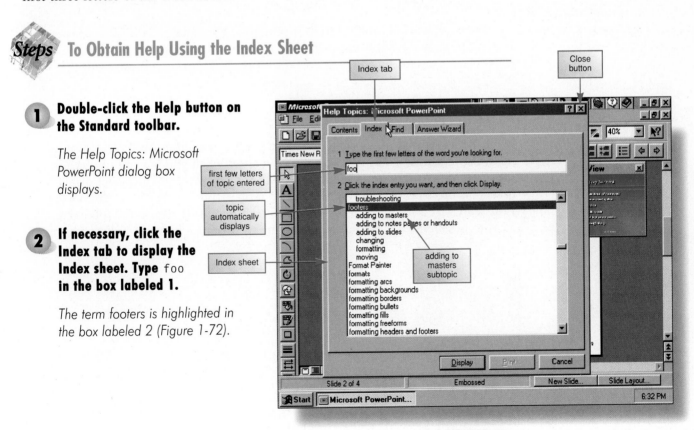

FIGURE 1-72

3 Double-click the subtopic labeled adding to masters (see Figure 1-72 on the previous page).

PowerPoint demonstrates how to add footers to the Slide Master. After which, PowerPoint displays a ScreenTip about the Slide Master (Figure 1-73).

4 After reading the information, click anywhere outside the ScreenTip to close it.

The ScreenTip closes.

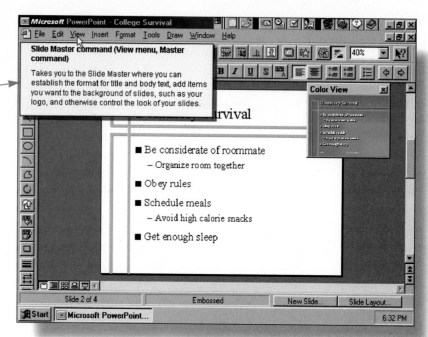

FIGURE 1-73

Other Ways

1. On Help menu click Microsoft PowerPoint Help Topics, click Index tab
2. Press F1

More *About* **Presentation Design**

Two acronyms pertain directly to presentation design:
— K.I.S. (Keep It Simple)
— C.C.C. (Clutter Creates Confusion)

Not all online help information is printable. For example, the Slide Master ScreenTip (Figure 1-73) is not printable. Generally speaking, if the window contains an Options button (Figure 1-71 on page PP 1.54), you can print the information.

Using the Find Sheet to Obtain Help

The **Find sheet** in the Help Topics: Microsoft PowerPoint dialog box locates the word or phrase you want. Use the Find sheet when you wish to find information about a term or a word contained within a phrase. The Find sheet displays a list of all topics pertaining to the specified term or phrase. You then can narrow your search by selecting words or phrases from the list. Perform the following steps to obtain information about changing the distance between bullets and text.

Steps To Obtain Help Using the Find Sheet

1 **Double-click the Help button on the Standard toolbar.**

The Help Topics: Microsoft PowerPoint dialog box displays.

2 **If necessary, click the Find tab. Type** bulleted **in the box labeled 1. Then point to the topic in the box labeled 3, change the distance between bullets and text.**

Three topics display in the box labeled 3 that contain the word bulleted. The topic, Add, change, or remove a bullet, is highlighted (Figure 1-74).

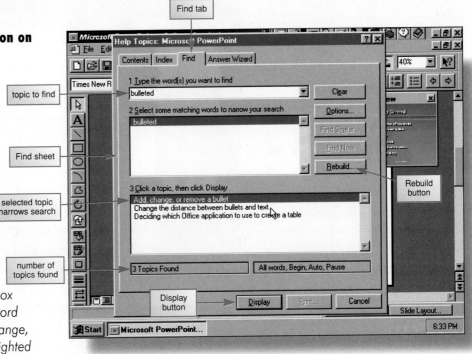

FIGURE 1-74

3 **Double-click the topic, Change the distance between bullets and text, in the box labeled 3 on the Find sheet. When the Microsoft PowerPoint window displays the information about changing the distance between bullets and text, point to the green underlined words, slide master, located in the Note at the bottom of the Microsoft PowerPoint window.**

A Microsoft PowerPoint window displays information about changing the distance between bullets and text. The green underlined text at the bottom of the Microsoft PowerPoint window identifies a jump to additional information (Figure 1-75a).

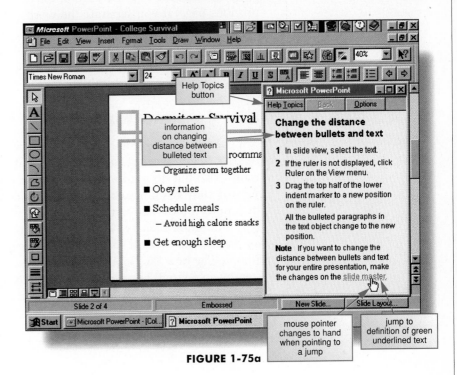

FIGURE 1-75a

4 **Click slide master.**

Clicking the green underlined text displays a ScreenTip (Figure 1-75b). The ScreenTip provides additional information about the word (often a definition).

5 **Read the ScreenTip, and then click the Close button on the Microsoft PowerPoint window two times.**

Clicking the Close button once closes the ScreenTip. Clicking the Close button a second time closes the Microsoft PowerPoint window and returns to PowerPoint.

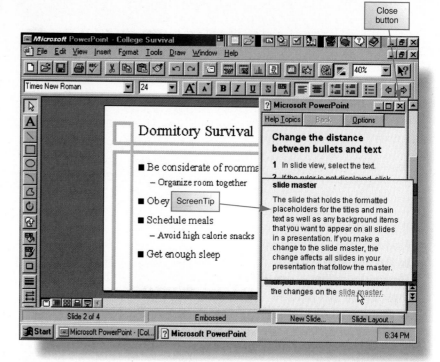

FIGURE 1-75b

OtherWays

1. On Help menu click Microsoft PowerPoint Help Topics, click Find tab
2. Press F1

You may specify more than one word in the box labeled 1 (Figure 1-74 on the previous page) if you separate the words with a space. If you specify words in uppercase letters, then only uppercase occurrences of the words (within the Help Topics) are found. If you specify words in lowercase letters, however, both uppercase and lowercase occurrences of the words are found. Search options can be changed by clicking the Options button on the Find sheet.

Using the Answer Wizard Sheet to Obtain Help

The last sheet in the Help Topics: Microsoft PowerPoint dialog box is the Answer Wizard sheet. Use the **Answer Wizard sheet** when you know what you want to do but do not know what the task is called. Recall that the Answer Wizard allows you to ask a question in your own words. The Answer Wizard then finds topics that contain the words in your question. For example, when you type a question such as, What is new? (to find the new features in PowerPoint 95) on the Answer Wizard sheet, it displays two sections: How Do I and Tell Me About. The **How Do I topics** provide you with easy-to-follow instructions. Some step-by-step visual answers take you to the command or option you need to complete the task. The **Tell Me About topics** give you background information about the selected topic.

Perform the following steps to obtain information on the new features in PowerPoint 95 by typing the question, What is new?

Steps **To Obtain Help Using the Answer Wizard**

1 **Double-click the Help button on the Standard toolbar.**

The Help Topics: Microsoft PowerPoint dialog box displays.

2 **If necessary, click the Answer Wizard tab. Type** What is new? **in the box labeled 1. Click the Search button. Then, in the box labeled 2, in the Tell Me About section, point to the topic, What's new in Microsoft PowerPoint 95.**

The Answer Wizard displays two sections in the box labeled 2: How Do I and Tell Me About (Figure 1-76).

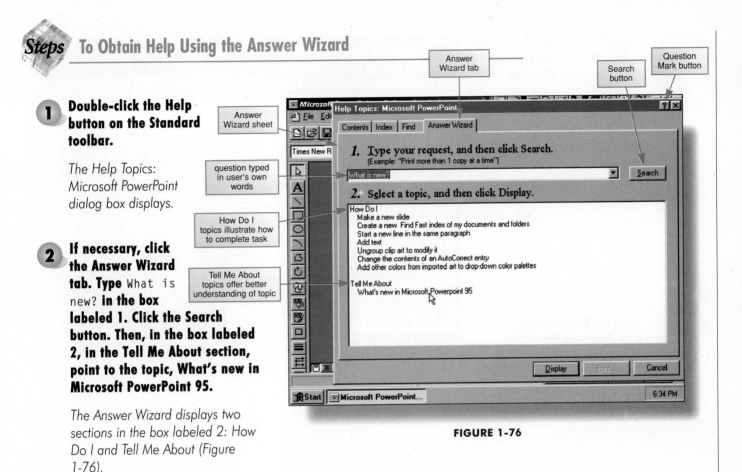

FIGURE 1-76

3 **Double-click What's new in Microsoft PowerPoint 95. Then point to the button in front of AutoCorrect in the Microsoft PowerPoint for Windows 95 window.**

The Microsoft PowerPoint for Windows 95 window displays a list of features new to PowerPoint 95. A button displays in front of each topic. When you point to a topic, the mouse pointer changes to a hand (Figure 1-77).

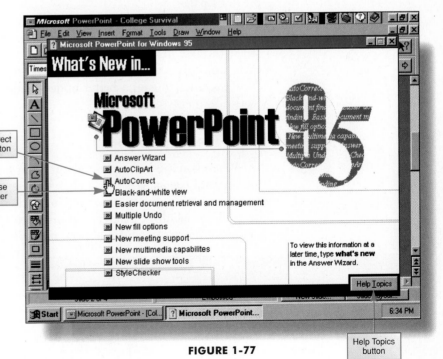

FIGURE 1-77

4 Click the button in front of AutoCorrect. Click the box labeled Easier to be effective.

PowerPoint displays a Microsoft PowerPoint for Windows 95 window containing jump boxes that point to specific items on a slide. When you click the jump box labeled Easier to be effective, a ScreenTip displays containing information about AutoCorrect (Figure 1-78).

5 Read the ScreenTip. Then click the Close button in the Microsoft PowerPoint for Windows 95 window to return to PowerPoint.

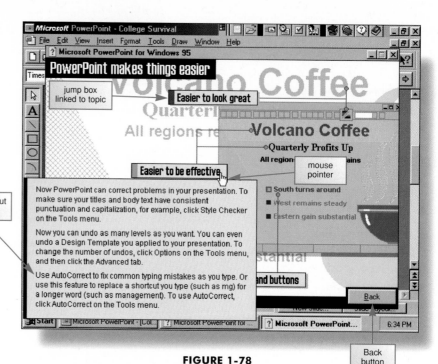

FIGURE 1-78

Other Ways

1. From Help menu click Microsoft PowerPoint Help Topics or Answer Wizard
2. Press F1

As an alternative to clicking the Close button in Step 5, you can click the **Back button** to return to the previous dialog box shown in Figure 1-77 on the previous page.

The four online help features of PowerPoint (Contents, Index, Find, and Answer Wizard) are easy to use, yet powerful. The best way to familiarize yourself with these help tools is to use them. In the Student Assignments at the end of each project is a section titled Use Help. It is recommended that you step through these exercises to gain a better understanding of how PowerPoint online help works.

Using the Help button

When you are not certain about what an object is in the PowerPoint window, use the **Help button**. When you click the Help button, the mouse pointer changes to an arrow with a question mark. Then, when you click an object in the PowerPoint window, a ScreenTip displays. Once you click the Help button, you can move the arrow and question mark pointer to any menu name, button, or object, and click to display a ScreenTip. For example, clicking the Help button, and then clicking the Spelling button on the Standard toolbar results in the ScreenTip shown in Figure 1-79. Click anywhere on the PowerPoint window to close the ScreenTip.

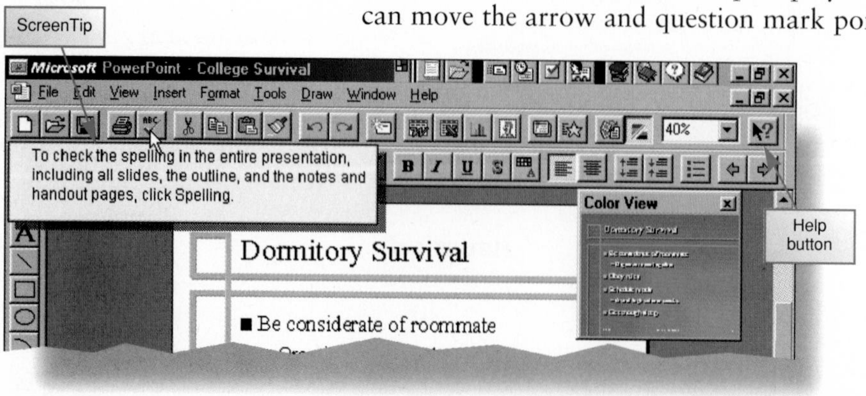

FIGURE 1-79

Using the Question Mark button

The **Question mark button** (see Figure 1-76 on page PP 1.59) is similar to the Help button. Use the Question mark button when you are not certain about the purpose of an object in a dialog box. When you click the Question mark button, the mouse pointer changes to an arrow with a question mark. Then, when you click an object in a dialog box, a ScreenTip displays.

Closing PowerPoint

Project 1 is complete. The final task is to close the presentation and PowerPoint. Perform the following steps to close PowerPoint.

TO CLOSE POWERPOINT

Step 1: Click the Close button on the title bar.
Step 2: Click the Yes button in the Microsoft PowerPoint dialog box.

The Microsoft PowerPoint dialog box displays when you close PowerPoint without first saving any changes (Figure 1-80).

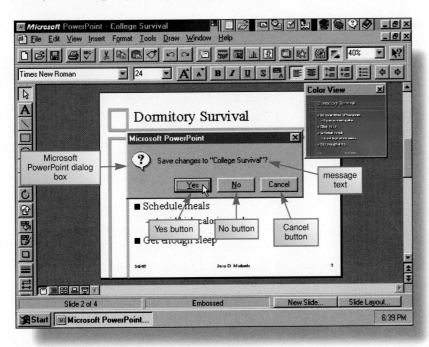

FIGURE 1-80

Clicking the No button in the Microsoft PowerPoint dialog box closes the presentation and PowerPoint without saving the changes made after your last save. Clicking the Cancel button, returns to PowerPoint and the current presentation.

Project Summary

Project 1 introduced you to starting PowerPoint and creating a multi-level bulleted list presentation. You learned about PowerPoint Design Templates, objects, and attributes. Project 1 illustrated how to change the text style to italic and decrease font size on the title slide. Completing these tasks, you saved your presentation. Then, you created three multi-level bulleted list slides. Next, you learned how to view the presentation in Slide Show view. After which, you learned how to close PowerPoint and how to open an existing presentation. Using Style Checker, you learned how to look for spelling errors and identify inconsistencies in design specifications. After running Style Checker, you edited the presentation to correct the design errors and insert text. Using the Slide Master, you adjusted the Before Paragraph line spacing to make better use of white space. You learned how to display the presentation in black and white before printing it; and then, you learned how to print hard copies of your slides. Finally, you learned how to use PowerPoint online help.

What You Should Know

Having completed this project, you now should be able to perform the following tasks:

- Add a New Slide with the Bulleted List Auto-Layout *(PP 1.25)*
- Add a New Slide with the Same AutoLayout *(PP 1.30)*
- Change Line Spacing on the Slide Master *(PP 1.47)*
- Change the Style Text to Italic *(PP 1.21)*
- Close PowerPoint *(PP 1.38, PP 1.61)*
- Decrease Font Size *(PP 1.20)*
- Delete a Paragraph *(PP 1.44)*
- Display a Presentation in Black and White *(PP 1.50)*
- Display the Slide Master *(PP 1.46)*
- Display the Slide Show View Popup Menu *(PP 1.36)*
- Enter the Presentation Subtitle *(PP 1.18)*
- Enter the Presentation Title *(PP 1.17)*
- Enter a Slide Title *(PP 1.27)*
- Manually Move through Slides in a Slide Show *(PP 1.35)*

- Obtain Help Using the Answer Wizard *(PP 1.59)*
- Obtain Help Using the Contents Sheet *(PP 1.54)*
- Obtain Help Using the Find Sheet *(PP 1.57)*
- Obtain Help Using the Index Sheet *(PP 1.55)*
- Open an Existing Presentation *(PP 1.38)*
- Print a Presentation *(PP 1.51)*
- Replace Text *(PP 1.45)*
- Save a Presentation to a Floppy Disk *(PP 1.22)*
- Save a Presentation with the Same Filename *(PP 1.32, PP 1.51)*
- Select a Text Placeholder *(PP 1.27)*
- Start a New Presentation *(PP 1.10)*
- Start Slide Show View *(PP 1.34)*
- Start Style Checker *(PP 1.42)*
- Type a Multi-level Bulleted List *(PP 1.28)*
- Use the Popup Menu to End a Slide Show *(PP 1.37)*
- Use the Vertical Scroll Bar to Move to Another Slide *(PP 1.33)*

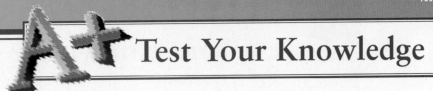 Test Your Knowledge

1 True/False

Instructions: Circle T if the statement is true or F if the statement is false.

T F 1. A PowerPoint document is called a presentation.
T F 2. The basic unit of a PowerPoint presentation is a slide.
T F 3. The menu bar displays the name of the current PowerPoint file.
T F 4. Toolbars consist of buttons that access commonly used PowerPoint tools.
T F 5. Objects are the building blocks for a PowerPoint slide.
T F 6. In PowerPoint, the Formatting toolbar contains tools for changing text attributes.
T F 7. Every time you add a slide to an open presentation, PowerPoint prompts you to choose an AutoLayout.
T F 8. PowerPoint assumes the first slide in a presentation is the Slide Master.
T F 9. The function of the Undo button is limited to reversing the last action.
T F 10. The slide indicator shows the slide number and slide title.

2 Multiple Choice

Instructions: Circle the correct response.

1. When the mouse pointer is pointing to a menu, it has the shape of a(n) _____.
   a. hand
   b. hourglass
   c. I-beam
   d. left-pointing block arrow
2. To close a presentation and PowerPoint, click the _____ button.
   a. Save
   b. Save As
   c. Close
   d. Exit
3. _____ displays a single slide in the PowerPoint window as it appears in your presentation.
   a. Slide view
   b. Outline view
   c. Notes Pages view
   d. Slide Sorter view
4. To display online help information by asking a question in your own words, use the _____.
   a. Content sheet
   b. Index sheet
   c. Find sheet
   d. Answer Wizard sheet

(continued)

A+ Test Your Knowledge

Multiple Choice *(continued)*

5. The Design Template controls the layout and attributes of the _____.
   a. title object
   b. title text
   c. body object
   d. all of the above

6. Before you italicize a paragraph, you must first _____.
   a. highlight the first word in the paragraph to be formatted
   b. highlight the paragraph to be formatted
   c. position the mouse pointer beside the first character in the paragraph to be formatted
   d. underscore the paragraph to be formatted

7. If you add objects to the Slide Master, they display on _____.
   a. the Slide Master
   b. every slide
   c. every slide except the title slide
   d. both a and c

8. To erase a character to the left of the insertion point, press the _____ key.
   a. DELETE
   b. INSERT
   c. BACKSPACE
   d. both a and c

9. When you close PowerPoint, _____.
   a. control is returned to the desktop
   b. the presentation is erased from a floppy disk
   c. the presentation is removed from the screen
   d. both a and c

10. PowerPoint automatically appends the extension _____ to a filename when you save a presentation.
    a. .DOC
    b. .PPT
    c. .TXT
    d. .XLS

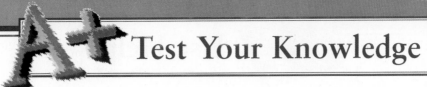

Test Your Knowledge

3 Understanding the PowerPoint Window

Instructions: In Figure 1-81, arrows point to the major components of the PowerPoint window. Identify the various parts of the window in the space provided.

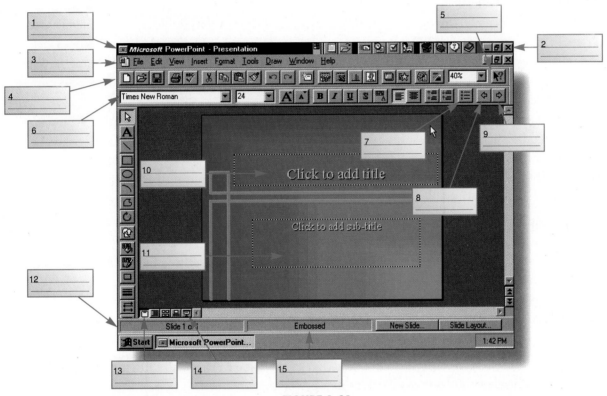

FIGURE 1-81

4 Understanding the PowerPoint Toolbars

Instructions: In Figure 1-82, arrows point to several buttons on the Standard and Formatting toolbars. Identify the buttons in the space provided.

FIGURE 1-82

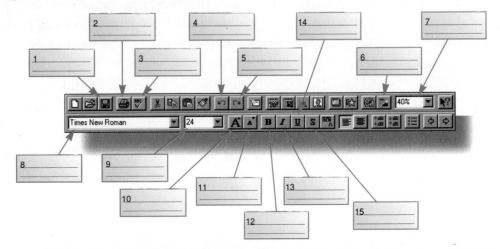

Use Help

1 Reviewing Project Activities

Instructions: Perform the following tasks using a computer.

1. Start PowerPoint. Double-click the Help button on the Standard toolbar to display the Help Topics: Microsoft PowerPoint dialog box.
2. Click the Contents tab. Double-click the Working With Presentations book icon. Double-click What PowerPoint creates. Click the Overhead transparencies link and read the help information. Click the remaining four links and read their help information. Click the Help Topics button in the lower right corner of the Microsoft PowerPoint for Windows 95 dialog box to return to the Help Topics: Microsoft PowerPoint dialog box.
3. Click the Find tab. Type print in box 1. Click printed in box 2. Double-click Printing a presentation in box 3. When the Microsoft PowerPoint window displays, read the information, right-click the window, and click Print Topic. When the Print dialog box displays, click the OK button. Click the Close button to return to PowerPoint. Submit the printout to your instructor.

2 Expanding on the Basics

Instructions: Use PowerPoint online help to better understand the topics listed below. Begin each of the following by double-clicking the Help button on the Standard toolbar. If you cannot print the help information, answer the question on a separate piece of paper.

1. Using the Changing the Appearance of Your Presentation book icon on the Contents sheet in the Help Topics: Microsoft PowerPoint dialog box, answer the following questions. (a) How do you display the Slide Master? (b) What is the function of the Slide Master and the Title Master? and (c) How do you display an object on all slides in a presentation?
2. Using the key term, line spacing, and the Index sheet in the Help Topics: Microsoft PowerPoint dialog box, display and print the answers for the following questions. (a) How do you change the After Paragraph line spacing? (b) How do you change the amount of space within a paragraph? and (c) How do you change the alignment of all text in a text placeholder?
3. Use the Find sheet in the Help Topics: Microsoft PowerPoint dialog box to display and then print information about the function keys. Then answer the following questions: (a) Which key, or combination of keys, do you press to create a new slide? (b) Which key, or combination of keys, do you press to create a new slide without a New Slide dialog box? (c) Which key, or combination of keys, do you press to move up one paragraph? (d) Which key, or combination of keys, do you press to open a new presentation? and (e) Which key, or combination of keys, do you press to save a presentation with a different name?
4. Use the Answer Wizard sheet on the Help Topics: Microsoft PowerPoint dialog box to display and then print the information about masters. (a) How do you create a slide that is different from the Slide Master? (b) What happens to a slide when its master changes? and (c) What is master text and how do you apply it to a slide?

Apply Your Knowledge

CAUTION: It is recommended that you create a backup copy of the Student Floppy Disk that accompanies this book and then remove unneeded folders on the backup floppy disk to free up space. Do the following: (1) insert the Student Floppy Disk in drive A; (2) start Explorer; (3) right-click the 3½ Floppy [A:] folder in the All Folders side of the window; (4) click Copy Disk; (5) click Start and OK as required; (6) insert the backup floppy disk when requested; (7) delete folders on the backup floppy disk except the PowerPoint folder.

1 Formatting a Slide

Instructions: Read the CAUTION box. Start PowerPoint. Open the presentation, Insurance Plan, from the PowerPoint folder on the Student Floppy Disk that accompanies this book. This slide lists the features of a new student insurance plan. Perform the following tasks to change the slide so it looks like the one in Figure 1-83.

1. Press and hold down the SHIFT key, and then click the Slide View button to display the Slide Master. Click the paragraph, Click to edit Master text styles. Click Format on the menu bar and then click Line Spacing. Increase the Before Paragraph line spacing to 0.75 lines. Click the OK button. Then click the Slide View button to return to Slide view.
2. Select the title text. Click the Bold button on the Formatting toolbar.
3. Select the No deductible paragraph. Click the Underline button on the Formatting toolbar.

Student Health Benefits

- No deductible
  - No out-of-pocket expense
- Choose your physician
- Health maintenance
  - Preventative care
  - Annual check-up

FIGURE 1-83

4. Click the paragraph, No out-of-pocket expense, and then click the Demote (Indent more) button on the Formatting toolbar. Then, demote the paragraphs, Preventative care and Annual check-up.
5. Click File on the menu bar and then click Save As. Type Student Insurance in the File name box. If drive A is not already displaying in the Save in box, click the Save in down arrow and click drive A. Then, click the Save button.
6. Click the B&W View button on the Standard toolbar to display the presentation in black and white.
7. Click the Print button on the Standard toolbar.
8. Close PowerPoint.
9. Submit the printout to your instructor.

In the Lab

1 Designing and Creating a Presentation

Problem: You are the Assistant Director for the Career Development and Placement Center at San Baarbo University. An emergency arises and you have been asked to substitute for an instructor this afternoon. The instructor suggests you discuss strategies for interviewing. To prepare for the class, you quickly create the presentation shown in Figure 1-84.

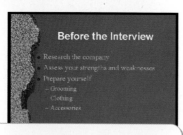

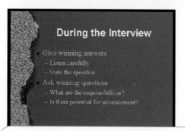

FIGURE 1-84

Instructions: Perform the following tasks.

1. Create a new presentation using the Bedrock Design Template.
2. Using the typewritten notes illustrated in Figure 1-85, create the title slide shown in Figure 1-84 using your name in place of Dana Fox. Decrease the font size of the paragraphs, Presented by:, Assistant Director, and Career Development Center, to 24. Increase the font size of your name to 36.
3. Using the typewritten notes in Figure 1-85, create the three multi-level bulleted list slides shown in Figure 1-84.

1)   The Successful First Interview
         Presented by: Dana Fox
         Assistant Director
         Career Development Center

2)   Before the Interview
  ·   Research the company
  ·   Assess your strengths and weaknesses
  ·   Prepare yourself
     *   Grooming
     *   Clothing
     *   Accessories

3)   During the Interview
  ·   Give winning answers
     *   Listen carefully
     *   State the specifics
  ·   Ask winning questions
     *   What are the responsibilities?
     *   Is there potential for advancement?

4)   After the Interview
  ·   Document interview details
  ·   Send thank you letter
  ·   Make follow-up telephone call

FIGURE 1-85

In the Lab

4. Run Style Checker to check spelling, visual clarity, and case and end punctuation. Correct your errors.
5. Save the presentation on your data floppy disk using the filename First Interview.
6. Display the presentation in black and white.
7. Print the black and white presentation.
8. Close PowerPoint.

2 Using Masters to Modify a Design Template

Problem: You are the Health & Safety Director for your company. This week's health and safety topic is Repetitive Strain Injuries. You select a Design Template but want to modify it. *Hint:* Use Help to solve this problem.

Instructions: Perform the following tasks.

1. Create a new presentation using the Blue Weave Design Template.
2. Using the notes in Figure 1-86, create the title slide shown in Figure 1-87 on the next page using your name in place of John Albrey. Decrease the font size of the paragraphs, Presented by:, and Health & Safety Director, to 24. Increase the font size of your name to 36.
3. Using the notes in Figure 1-86, create the multi-level bulleted list slides shown in Figure 1-87.
4. Display the Slide Master. Click the paragraph, Click to edit Master title style, and then click the Text Shadow button on the Formatting toolbar. Click the paragraph, Click to edit Master text styles. On the Format menu, click Line Spacing, and then increase the Before Paragraph line spacing to 0.75 lines. Drag the mouse pointer to select the paragraphs, Second level and Third level. On the Format menu, click Line Spacing, and then increase the After Paragraph spacing to 0.2 lines.

1)   Repetitive Strain Injuries
             Presented by:
          John Albrey
          Health & Safety Director

2)   What Is Repetitive Strain Injury (RSI)?
    ·   Injury to the hands and/or wrists
        *   Tendons or muscles are strained or torn
        *   Blood circulation is impaired
        *   Tissues deprived of nutrients
        *   Toxins allowed to build

3)   Who Gets RSI?
    ·   People with jobs that require repetitive hand or wrist motion
    ·   Examples:
        *   Computer users
        *   Typists
        *   Assembly-line workers
        *   Meat cutters

4)   How Do You Prevent RSI?
    ·   Before Work
        *   Perform wrist and hand warm-up exercises
    ·   During Work
        *   Relax and keep hands warm
        *   Maintain good posture
        *   Keep wrists and forearms parallel to floor

FIGURE 1-86

(continued)

In the Lab

Using Masters to Modify a Design Template *(continued)*

5. Drag the elevator to display the Title Master. Click the paragraph, Click to edit Master title style, and then click the Text Shadow button on the Formatting toolbar. On the View menu, click Header and Footer. Then add the current date, slide number, and your name to the footer. Display the footer on all slides. Return to Slide view.

6. Run Style Checker to check spelling, visual larity, and case and end punctuation. Correct your errors.

7. Drag the elevator to display Slide 1. Click the Slide Show button to start Slide Show view. Then click to display each slide.

8. Save the presentation on your data floppy disk using the filename, Repetitive Strain Injuries.

9. Display and print the presentation in black and white.

10. Close PowerPoint.

FIGURE 1-87

3 Creating a Training Presentation

Problem: You are a financial planner conducting a personal finance seminar. Over the years, you have accumulated many proven methods for saving money and spending less.

Instructions: Using the list in Figure 1-88, design and create a presentation. The presentation is to include a title slide and five bulleted list slides. Modify the list to conform to Style Checker defaults. Perform the following tasks:

1. Create a new presentation using the Blue Green Design Template.

2. Create a title slide titled Money. Include Are You Saving or Slaving? as the subtitle.

3. Using Figure 1-88, create five multi-level bulleted list slides. Modify the list illustrated in Figure 1-88 to conform to Style Checker defaults (see Table 1-5 on PP 1.44).

In the Lab

4. Adjust Before Paragraph and After Paragraph line spacing to utilize the available white space.
5. Save the presentation to your data floppy disk with the filename Money.
6. View the presentation in Slide Show view to look for errors. Correct any errors.
7. Print the presentation in black and white.
8. Close PowerPoint.

Money
Are You Saving or Slaving?

I.   Saving Savvy
    A.   Save consistently
        1.   Deposit a little money every week
            a)   Saving $10 a week easier than $40 a month
        2.   Use payroll deductions
            a)   Savings bonds
            b)   401K plan
            c)   Thrift plan
        3.   Make savings part of your budget
            a)   Deposit cash saved from discounts
    B.   Open specialty savings accounts
        1.   Vacation club
        2.   College fund
        3.   Christmas club

II.   Reduce Finance Charges
    A.   Pay cash
        1.   Don't create additional debt
        2.   Save until you can pay cash for an item
    B.   Eliminate high interest debt
        1.   Make larger payments
            a)   Pay more then minimum amount due
            b)   Make more frequent payments
                (1)   Make bimonthly payments
                (2)   Make weekly payments
        2.   Consolidate bills
            a)   Eliminate several bills into one
            b)   Refinance at lower interest rate

III.   Food Savings
    A.   Brown-bag your lunch
        1.   Plan meals for entire week
        2.   Use restaurant "doggie-bag" leftovers for next day's lunch
    B.   Grocery shop from a list
        1.   Resist impulse buying
            a)   Don't shop when hungry
        2.   Read cost-per-unit labels
        3.   Use coupons for what you normally buy
            a)   Don't buy an item because you have a coupon
        4.   Buy in bulk
            a)   Only if you'll use before it spoils

IV.   Car Savings
    A.   Insurance
        1.   Insure all cars with same company
            a)   Look for 15 to 20 percent discount
        2.   Reduce coverage on old cars
            a)   Consider eliminating collision coverage
    B.   Maintenance
        1.   Read warranty carefully
            a)   Dealer might be required to fix
        2.   Buy supplies at discount stores
        3.   Do minor repairs yourself
    C.   Driving
        1.   Get ready before you start engine
            a)   Adjust mirrors and seat
            b)   Fasten seatbelt
        2.   Gradually increase and decrease speed

V.   Bill Paying Strategy
    A.   Organize bills
    B.   Write check when bill arrives
        1.   Mail just before due date
    C.   Don't skip payments
        1.   Send small amounts to every creditor
        2.   Call creditor if you must pay late

FIGURE 1-88

Cases and Places

200 MHz

The difficulty of these case studies varies:

▶ Case studies preceded by a single half moon are the least difficult. You are asked to create the required presentation based on information that has already been placed in an organized form.

▶▶ Case studies preceded by two half moons are more difficult. You must organize the information given before using it to create the required presentation.

▶▶▶ Case studies preceded by three half moons are the most difficult. You must decide on a specific topic, and then obtain and organize the necessary information before using it to create the required presentation.

1 ▶ Pauline Gauguin, an art instructor from the Synthétiste School, is giving a presentation at the next parent-teachers meeting. She has written out a recipe for finger paint (Figure 1-89).

With this recipe, Ms. Gauguin has asked you to prepare four slides that can be used on an overhead projector. Use the concepts and techniques introduced in this project to create the presentation.

Homemade Finger Paint

Ingredients
✔ *1/3 cup cornstarch*
✔ *3 cups sugar*
✔ *2 cups cold water*
✔ *food color*

Preparation
✔ *Mix cornstarch, sugar, and water*
   Use 1-quart saucepan
✔ *Cover and stir over medium heat*
   About 5 minutes or until thickened
✔ *Remove from heat*

Adding Color
✔ *Divide mixture into separate cups*
✔ *Tint each cup with a different food color*
   Stir several times until cool
✔ *Store in airtight container*
   Paint works best if used the same day

FIGURE 1-89

Cases and Places

2 ▶ Bill Henry, managing director for the Skoon County Fair, has prepared some notes for a presentation that will be given to the local chamber of commerce (Figure 1-90).

With these notes, the fair director has asked you to prepare four slides that can be used on an overhead projector. Use the concepts and techniques introduced in this project to create the presentation.

25th Annual Skoon County Fair

P.B. Pillbottom's Midway
- *Over 50 rides and attractions*
  World's largest carousel ·
- *Games of skill and chance ·*
- *The Kiddie Corral*
  Activities for children under 8

Popular Exhibits ·
- *Arts and crafts*
  Prizes in 32 separate categories ·
- *Domesticated animals*
  Prizes in 26 classes ·
- *Commercial demonstrations*

Family Entertainment ·
- *The Neighborhood Bigtop*
  Bring a camera to film the kids ·
- *Western Rodeo Jamboree ·*
- *Music and shows*
  The Bronco Brothers
  "Thank God I'm a Country Boy"

FIGURE 1-90

3 ▶▶ As part of a symposium on the history of American education, you are giving a presentation on the Curriculum of General Schools, as proposed in a letter by Thomas Jefferson to Peter Carr. Jefferson divides the general school curriculum into three departments—language, mathematics, and philosophy. The language department is composed of languages and history (both may be attained by the same course of reading), grammar, belles lettres (poetry, composition, and criticism), and rhetoric and oratory. The department of mathematics includes: mathematics pure, physico-mathematics (physical subjects aided by mathematical calculation), natural history (mineralogy, botany, zoology, and anatomy), and the theory of medicine. The philosophical department encompasses ideology, ethics, law of nature and nations, and government (political economy). In addition to a title slide, you plan to develop three other slides that can be used with an overhead projector. Use the concepts and techniques introduced in this project to create the presentation.

Cases and Places

4 ▶▶ You are a consultant in the field of ergonomics (an applied science devoted to making the equipment people use and the surrounding work area safer and more efficient). You have been hired by a large company to give a presentation on Computer User Health Guidelines, and you have been asked to cover three topics—a well-designed work area, equipment in the workplace, and ways to reduce physical and mental fatigue. A well-designed work area contains a desk approximately 30 inches high; a chair with adjustable backrest, seat, and height and 5 legs for stability; and adequate lighting using nonglare bulbs. Equipment in the workplace should consist of a keyboard at a height apropos to the height of the operator; a monitor at a viewing distance between 18 and 28 inches (a viewing angle of 20° to center of screen); a monitor designed to minimize electromagnetic radiation (EMR); and a document holder placed at the same height and distance as screen. Ways to reduce physical and mental fatigue are to alternate work activities (change the order of work to provide variety); minimize surrounding noise; take frequent breaks (look away from the screen every 15 minutes, get out of the chair at least once each hour, and take a 15 minute break every two hours); and incorporate stretching exercises into breaks. In addition to a title slide, you plan to develop three other slides that can be used with an overhead projector. Use the concepts and techniques introduced in this project to create the presentation.

5 ▶▶▶ Appreciation of local landmarks—historical sites, museums, or natural wonders—often can be increased by a preliminary presentation. Go to an area landmark and gather information on its significance, history, popularity, etc. Using this information, together with the concepts and techniques introduced in this project, prepare a presentation to familiarize visitors with the landmark. Create a title slide and at least three other slides that can be used with an overhead projector to enhance the presentation.

6 ▶▶▶ Some instructors use the first class meeting to provide a broad orientation for their students. At this time, students may learn about course requirements, grading policies, academic deadlines, necessary supplies, or the instructor's office hours. Choose a class you are currently taking and outline the information you feel should be offered to students on the first day of class. Using this information, together with the concepts and techniques introduced in this project, prepare a presentation to orient students on opening day. Create a title slide and at least three other slides that can be used with an overhead projector to enhance the presentation.

7 ▶▶▶ Schools often purchase computer equipment on the basis of a sales representative's presentation. Visit a computer vendor and select the system you feel is most appropriate for an elementary school. Determine the features that would make this system attractive to a grade school, such as ease of use, suitability of software, processing power, and available peripheral devices. Using this information, together with the concepts and techniques introduced in this project, prepare a presentation to sell the system to an elementary school's staff. Create a title slide and at least three other slides that can be used with an overhead projector to enhance the presentation.

Microsoft PowerPoint 7 **Project 2**

Using Outline View and Clip Art to Create an Electronic Slide Show

Objectives:

You will have mastered the material in this project when you can:

▶ Create a presentation in Outline view
▶ Describe the PowerPoint window in Outline view
▶ Insert a blank line in a bulleted list
▶ Change the slide layout
▶ Move text between objects
▶ Insert clip art from the ClipArt Gallery
▶ Change the clip art size
▶ Add a header and a footer to outline pages
▶ Add slide transition effects
▶ Add text build effects
▶ Print a presentation outline
▶ Change printing options
▶ Change the slide order
▶ Copy a slide

Making a Point

The Mad Hatter was right, of course. If Alice meant to say one thing and said something else, no matter how much she meant it, she failed to make her point . . . or at least, made the wrong point.

Every day, in countless diverse situations, speakers are faced with the daunting task of making a point with words. Fortunately, over the years of human history, people have learned an important principle: words go down better with a spoonful of graphics!

Speakers today have an advantage over their predecessors who seldom had the benefit of sparkling visuals to help them make a point. With the double-barreled impact of words teamed up with pictures, a point is made — then made again.

Another subtle benefit also is

"Then you should say what you mean," the March Hare went on.

"I do," Alice hastily replied, "at least — at least I mean what I say — that's the same thing, you know."

"Not the same thing a bit!" said the Mad Hatter.

Alice in Wonderland
by Lewis Carroll

present: good graphics can help a speaker stay on track and on target. Practically everyone, from political candidate to college student to general to salesperson, has the means to create dynamic, attractive slide presentations to reinforce verbal remarks.

Armed with presentation graphics software, a user can generate a complete slide presentation often in less time than it takes to write a speech. Visuals may become the thematic focal points of a paper or oral presentation, around which one or more ideas can be built with written text or speech. By clearly establishing the expectations of the reader or listener, a picture can be the "point guard" for the ideas that follow.

General Norman Schwarzkopf, Marcia Clark, Ross Perot, and every U.S. president from Lyndon Johnson to Bill Clinton are just a few of the famous people who have used computer-generated graphics to emphasize or clarify their remarks.

College students not only are able to make a point, but are able to make *grade* points, as well, using computer-generated graphics in virtually any kind of course, whether for inclusion in a paper or an oral presentation. Every day, sales people deliver countless stand-up presentations using graphic slides to underscore each of their points, known as features and benefits. Aircraft engineers use graphics to point out the characteristics of supersonic aircraft.

In a competitive world, Microsoft PowerPoint and every other available tool should be used to make an argument more persuasive. Then, upon yielding the floor, to hear someone say, "A point well-taken... ," that is the ultimate reward.

Microsoft
PowerPoint 7
Windows 95

Using Outline View and Clip Art to Create an Electronic Slide Show

Case Perspective

Web Island Resort is promoting Web Island to college students as *the* place for spring break vacations. While developing a presentation to promote two new spring break vacation packages to Web Island, your boss, Mr. Hayes, receives a telephone call. During the call, Western University invites Web Island Resort to make a presentation at their Spring Break Vacation Fair. For some unspecified reason, another resort is canceling, thereby giving Web Island Resort an opportunity to present. The Vacation Fair is tomorrow. In order for Mr. Hayes to finalize his travel arrangements, he asks you to put together a short six slide presentation. The purpose of the presentation is to entice students to buy one of the spring break vacation packages.

Web Island Resort's Marketing Department supplies you with an outline to use to create the presentation. The outline contains promotional information about the new spring break vacation packages.

To persuade students to buy a Web Island Resort spring break vacation package, you choose a design template with a tropical theme. You also include pictures to intensify the text.

Creating a Presentation from an Outline

At some time during either your academic or business life, you probably will make a presentation. Most academic presentations are informative—providing detailed information about some topic. Business presentations, however, are usually sales presentations, such as selling a proposal or a product to a client, convincing management to approve a new project, or persuading the board of directors to accept the fiscal budget. As an alternative to creating your presentation in Slide view, as you did in Project 1, PowerPoint provides an outlining feature to help you organize your thoughts. When the outline is complete, it becomes the foundation for your presentation.

You create a presentation outline in Outline view. When you create an outline, you type all of your text at one time, as if you were typing an outline on a sheet of paper. This is different than Slide view where you type text as you create each individual slide.

The first step in creating a presentation in Outline view is to type a title for the outline. The outline title is the subject of the presentation and later becomes the presentation title slide. Then you type the remainder of the outline, indenting appropriately to establish a structure or hierarchy. Once the outline is complete, you make your presentation more persuasive by adding graphics. This project uses outlining to create the presentation and clip art graphics to visually support the text.

Project Two – Spring Break Specials

Project 2 uses PowerPoint to create the six slide Web Island Resort Spring Break Specials presentation shown in Figure 2-1. You create the presentation from the outline in Figure 2-2 on the next page.

FIGURES 2-1a

FIGURES 2-1b

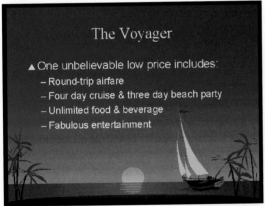

FIGURES 2-1c

FIGURES 2-1f

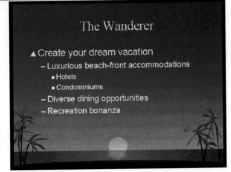

FIGURES 2-1d

FIGURES 2-1e

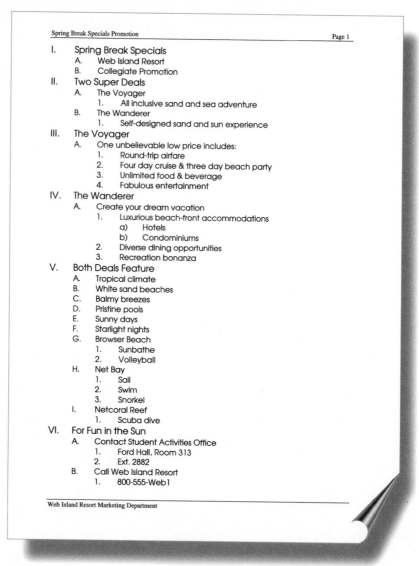

FIGURE 2-2

Presentation Preparation Steps

The preparation steps summarize how the slide presentation shown in Figure 2-1 on page PP 2.5 will be developed in Project 2. The following tasks will be completed in this project.

1. Start a new document and apply a Design Template.
2. Create a presentation in Outline view.
3. Save the presentation.
4. Insert a blank line on Slide 2.
5. Change the Slide 5 layout to 2 Column Text and move text from the left column to the right column.
6. Change the Slide 6 layout to Clip Art and Text and insert a clip art picture into a clip art placeholder.
7. Insert clip art in Slide 3. Move and reduce the size of the clip art picture.
8. Add header and footer text to the outline pages.
9. Add slide transition effects and text build effects.

10. Save the presentation.
11. Print the presentation outline and slides.
12. Edit the presentation in Outline view and in Slide Sorter view.
13. Close PowerPoint.

The following pages contain a detailed explanation of these tasks.

Starting a New Presentation

Project 1 introduced you to starting a presentation document and applying a Design Template. The following steps summarize how to start a new presentation, apply a Design Template, and choose an AutoLayout. For a more detailed explanation, see pages PP 1.9 through PP 1.12. Perform the following steps to start a new presentation.

TO START A NEW PRESENTATION

Step 1: Click the Start button on the taskbar.
Step 2: Click New Office Document.
Step 3: Click the Presentation Designs tab. When the Presentation Designs sheet displays, scroll down the list of Design Templates until Tropical displays.
Step 4: Double-click Tropical.
Step 5: When the New Slide dialog box displays, click the OK button.

PowerPoint displays the Title Slide AutoLayout and the Tropical Design Template on Slide 1 in Slide View (Figure 2-3).

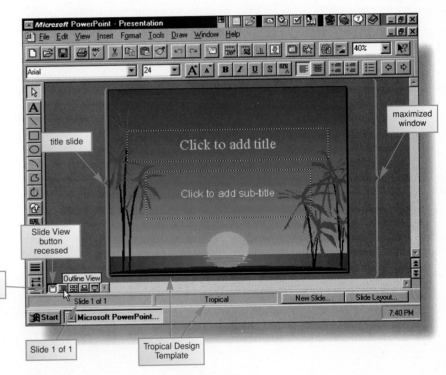

FIGURE 2-3

Using Outline View

Outline view provides a quick, easy way to create a presentation. Outlining allows you to organize your thoughts in a structured format. An outline uses indentation to establish a hierarchy, which denotes levels of importance to the main topic. An **outline** is a summary of thoughts, presented as headings and subheadings, often used as a preliminary draft when you create a presentation.

More *About*
Design Templates

You can build a presentation with the default Design Template and later select a different one. When you change Design Templates, PowerPoint automatically updates color scheme, font attributes, and location of slide objects on every slide in the presentation.

More *About*
Presentation Design

The key to a successful presentation is organization. Begin by jotting down your ideas. Next, look over your list and decide on three or four major topics. Then group the remaining ideas around the major topics, selecting ideas that support the major topics and leaving out those that do not.

In Outline view, title text displays at the left side of the window along with a slide icon and a slide number. Body text is indented under the title text. Graphic objects, such as pictures, graphs, or tables, do not display in Outline view. When a slide contains a graphic object, the slide icon next to the slide title displays with a small graphic on it. The slide icon is blank when a slide does not contain graphics. The attributes for text in Outline view are the same as in Slide view except for color and paragraph style.

PowerPoint limits the number of outline levels to six. The first outline level is the slide title. The remaining five outline levels are the same as the five indent levels in Slide view. Recall from Project 1 that PowerPoint allows for five indent levels and that each indent level has an associated bullet.

The outline begins with a title on **outline level one**. The title is the main topic of the slide. Text supporting the main topic begins on **outline level two** and indents under outline level one. **Outline level three** indents under outline level two and contains text to support outline level two. **Outline level four**, **outline level five**, and **outline level six** indent under outline level three, outline level four, and outline level five, respectively. Use outline levels four, five, and six as required. They are generally used for scientific and engineering presentations requiring vast amounts of detail. Business and sales presentations usually focus on summary information and use outline level one, outline level two, and outline level three.

PowerPoint initially displays in Slide view when you start a new presentation. Change from Slide view to Outline view by clicking the Outline View button on the View Button bar. Perform the following steps to change the view from Slide view to Outline view.

Steps To Change the View to Outline View

1 Point to the Outline View button located on the View Button bar at the lower-left of the PowerPoint window (Figure 2-4).

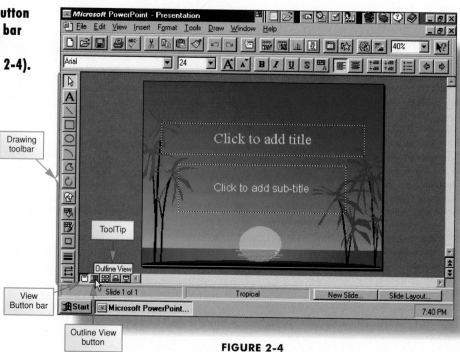

FIGURE 2-4

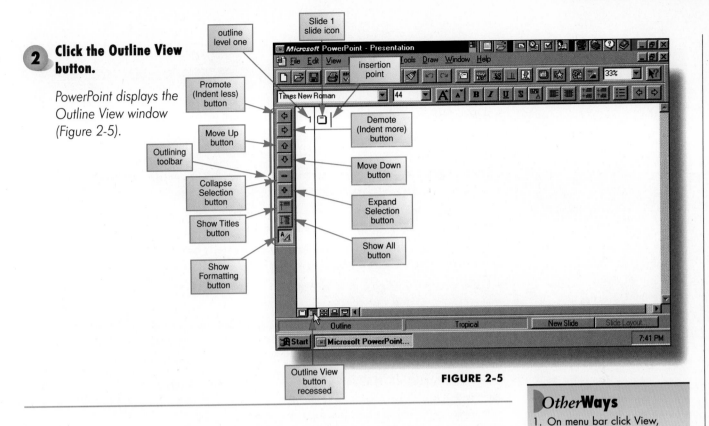

2 **Click the Outline View button.**

PowerPoint displays the Outline View window (Figure 2-5).

FIGURE 2-5

OtherWays

1. On menu bar click View, click Outline

2. Press ALT+V, press O

You can create and edit your presentation in Outline view. Outline view also makes it easy to sequence slides and to relocate title text and body text from one slide to another. In addition to typing text to create a new presentation in Outline view, PowerPoint can produce slides from an outline created in Microsoft Word or another word processor, if you save the outline as an RTF file or as a plain text file. The file extension **RTF** stands for **R**ich **T**ext **F**ormat.

The PowerPoint Window in Outline View

The PowerPoint window in Outline view differs from the window in Slide view because the Outlining toolbar displays and the Drawing toolbar does not display (see Figures 2-4 and 2-5). Table 2-1 on the next page describes the buttons on the Outlining toolbar.

More *About* **Outline Levels**

A topic needing more than six outline levels has too much detail and may overwhelm the audience. Decompose large topics into two or more subtopics. Then, create a new slide for each group of subtopics.

Table 2-1

BUTTON	BUTTON NAME	DESCRIPTION
⇦	Promote button	The Promote (Indent less) button moves the selected paragraph up one level in the outline hierarchy each time you click the button. Promoting a paragraph moves it to the left until you reach outline level one.
⇨	Demote button	The Demote (Indent more) button moves the selected paragraph down, or to the right, one level in the outline hierarchy each time you click the button. You can only demote to the sixth outline level.
⇧	Move Up button	The Move Up button moves selected text up one paragraph at a time while maintaining its hierarchical outline level and text style. The selected text exchanges position with the paragraph located above it.
⇩	Move Down button	The Move Down button moves selected text down one paragraph at time while maintaining its hierarchical outline level and text style. The selected text exchanges position with the paragraph located below it.
▬	Collapse Selection button	The Collapse Selection button hides all outline levels except the slide title of the selected slide. This button is useful when you want to collapse one slide in your outline.
⊕	Expand Selection button	The Expand Selection button displays all outline levels for the selected slide. This button is useful when you want to expand one slide in your outline.
▤	Show Titles button	The Show Titles button collapses all outline levels to show only the slide titles. This button is useful when you are looking at the organization of your presentation and do not care to see all the details.
▤	Show All button	The Show All button expands all outline levels to display the title and text for all slides.
▨	Show Formatting button	The Show Formatting button is a toggle that displays or hides the text attributes in Outline view. This is useful when you want to work with plain text as opposed to working with bolded, italicized, or underlined text. When printing your outline, plain text often speeds up the printing process.

Creating a Presentation in Outline View

Outline view enables you to view title and body text, add and delete slides, **drag and drop** slide text, drag and drop slides to change slide order, promote and demote text, save a presentation, print an outline, print slides, copy and paste slides or text to and from other presentations, apply a Design Template, and import an outline.

Developing a presentation in Outline view is quick because you type the text for all slides on one screen. Once you type the outline, the presentation is fundamentally complete. If you choose, you can then go to Slide view to enhance your presentation with graphics.

Creating a Title Slide in Outline View

Recall from Project 1 that the title slide introduces the presentation to the audience. Additionally, Project 2 uses the title slide to capture the attention of the audience by using a Design Template with a tropical theme. The Tropical Design Template enhances the presentation title with tropical plants and a setting sun. Remember, Web Island Resort is trying to sell vacation packages. They want students to focus on a warm, tropical climate. Perform the following steps to create a title slide in Outline view.

Steps **To Create a Title Slide in Outline View**

1 **Type** Spring Break Specials **and press the ENTER key.**

Spring Break Specials displays as the title for Slide 1 and is called outline level one. A slide icon displays to the left of each slide title. The font for outline level one is Times New Roman and the font size is 44 points. In Outline view, the Zoom Control default setting is 33% of the actual slide size. Pressing the ENTER key moves the insertion point to the next line and maintains the same outline level. The insertion point, therefore, is in position for typing the title for Slide 2 (Figure 2-6).

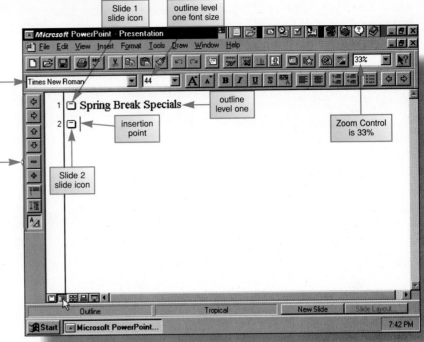

FIGURE 2-6

2 **Point to the Demote (Indent more) button on the Outlining toolbar.**

The Demote (Indent more) ToolTip displays (Figure 2-7).

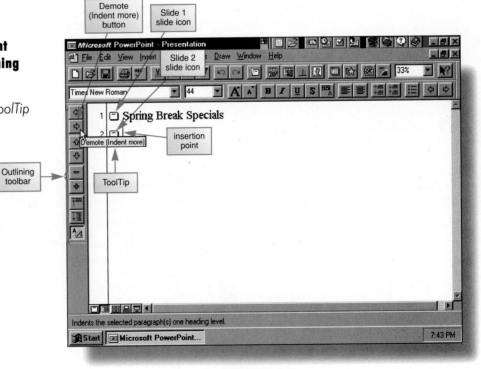

FIGURE 2-7

3 **Click the Demote (Indent more) button.** Type Web Island Resort **and press the ENTER key.** Type Collegiate Promotion **and press the ENTER key.**

The Slide 2 slide icon does not display (Figure 2-8). The lines, Web Island Resort and Collegiate Promotion, are subtitles on the title slide (Slide 1) and demote to outline level two. Outline level two is indented to the right under outline level one. The outline level two font is Arial and the outline level two font size is 32 points.

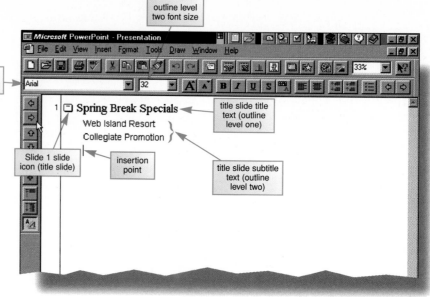

FIGURE 2-8

The title slide for the Spring Break Specials presentation is complete. The next section explains how to add a slide in Outline view.

Adding a Slide in Outline View

Recall from Project 1 that when you add a new slide, PowerPoint defaults to the Bulleted List slide layout. This is true in Outline view as well. One way to add a new slide in Outline view is to promote a paragraph to outline level one. You do this by clicking the Promote (Indent less) button until the insertion point is at outline level one. A slide icon displays when you reach outline level one. Perform the following steps to add a slide in Outline view.

 Steps To Add a Slide in Outline View

1 **Point to the Promote (Indent less) button on the Outlining toolbar.**

The insertion point is still positioned at outline level two (Figure 2-9).

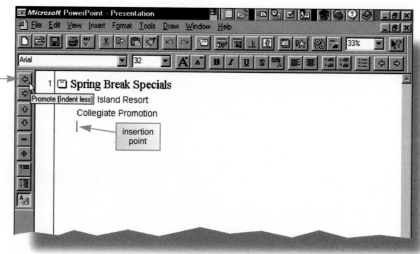

FIGURE 2-9

2 **Click the Promote (Indent less) button.**

The Slide 2 slide icon displays indicating a new slide is added to the presentation (Figure 2-10). The insertion point is in position to type the title for Slide 2 at outline level one.

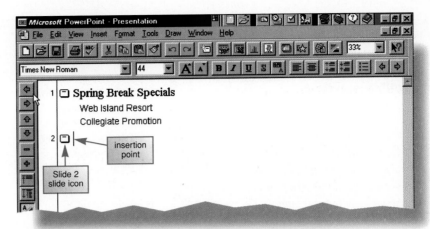

FIGURE 2-10

Other Ways

1. On Standard toolbar click Insert New Slide button
2. On status bar click New Slide button
3. Press CTRL+M

After you add a slide, you are ready to type the slide text. The next section explains how to create a multi-level bulleted list slide in Outline view.

Creating Multi-level Bulleted List Slides in Outline View

To create a multi-level bulleted list slide, you demote or promote the insertion point to the appropriate outline level and then type the paragraph text. Recall from Project 1, when you demote a paragraph, PowerPoint adds a bullet to the left of each outline level. Each outline level has a different bullet font. Also recall that the Design Template determines font attributes, including the bullet font.

Slide 2 is the first informational slide for Project 2. Slide 2 introduces the main topic — two new spring break vacation packages offered by Web Island Resort. Each vacation package displays as outline level two, and each supportive paragraph displays as outline level three. The following steps explain how to create a multi-level bulleted list slide in Outline view.

Steps **To Create a Multi-level Slide in Outline View**

1 **Type** Two Super Deals **and press the ENTER key. Then click the Demote (Indent more) button to demote to outline level two.**

The title for Slide 2, Two Super Deals, displays and the insertion point is in position to type the first bulleted paragraph (Figure 2-11). A triangle shaped bullet displays to the left of the insertion point.

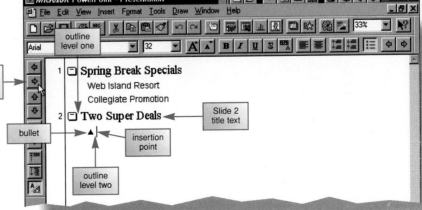

FIGURE 2-11

2 **Type** The Voyager **and press the ENTER key. Then click the Demote (Indent more) button to demote to outline level three.**

Slide 2 displays three outline levels: the title, Two Super Deals, on outline level one, the bulleted paragraph, The Voyager, on outline level two, and the insertion point on outline level three (Figure 2-12). The bullet for outline level two is a triangle. The bullet for outline level three is a dash.

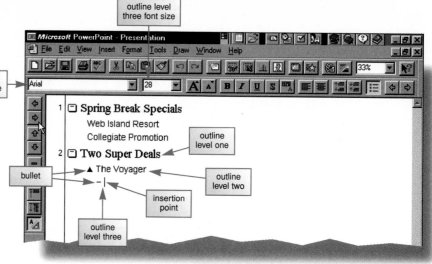

FIGURE 2-12

3 **Type** All inclusive sand and sea adventure **and press the ENTER key. Then click the Promote (Indent less) button.**

Pressing the ENTER key begins a new paragraph at the same outline level as the previous paragraph. Clicking the Promote (Indent less) button moves the insertion point left and elevates the paragraph from outline level three to outline level two (Figure 2-13).

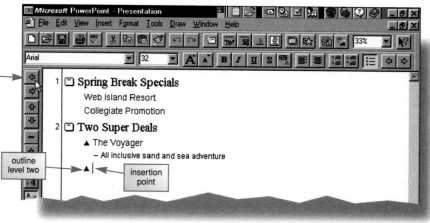

FIGURE 2-13

4 **Type** The Wanderer **and press the ENTER key. Click the Demote (Indent more) button. Type** Self-designed sand and sun experience **and press the ENTER key (Figure 2-14).**

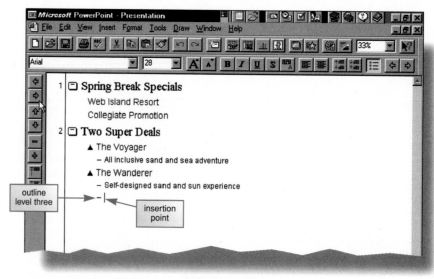

FIGURE 2-14

Other Ways
1. Press TAB to Demote
2. Press ALT+SHIFT+RIGHT ARROW to Demote

Other Ways
1. Press SHIFT+TAB to Promote
2. Press ALT+SHIFT+LEFT ARROW to Promote

Creating a Subordinate Slide

When developing your presentation, begin with a main topic and follow with subsequent slides to support the main topic. Placing all your information on one slide may overwhelm your audience. Decompose your presentation, therefore, into several slides with three to six bullets per slide or per object. The following steps explain how to create a subordinate slide that further explains the spring break package, The Voyager, introduced on Slide 2. This new slide, Slide 3, provides additional information that supports the first outline level two on Slide 2. Later in this project, you will create another subordinate slide to support the second outline level two on Slide 2, The Wanderer.

TO CREATE A SUBORDINATE SLIDE

Step 1: Click the Promote (Indent less) button two times so that Slide 3 is added to the end of the presentation.

Step 2: Type The Voyager and press the ENTER key.

Step 3: Click the Demote (Indent more) button to demote to outline level two.

Step 4: Type One unbelievable low price includes: and press the ENTER key.

Step 5: Click the Demote (Indent more) button to demote to outline level three.

Step 6: Type Round-trip airfare and press the ENTER key.

Step 7: Type Four day cruise & three day beach party and press the ENTER key.

Step 8: Type Unlimited food & beverage and press the ENTER key.

Step 9: Type Fabulous entertainment and press the ENTER key.

The screen displays as shown in Figure 2-15.

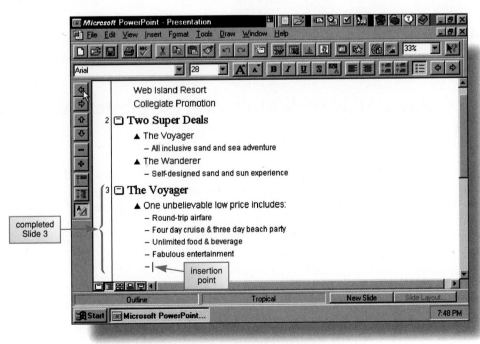

FIGURE 2-15

Creating a Second Subordinate Slide

The next step is to create the slide that supports The Wanderer, which is the second outline level two on Slide 2. Perform the following steps to create this subordinate slide.

TO CREATE A SECOND SUBORDINATE SLIDE

Step 1: Click the Promote (Indent less) button two times so that Slide 4 is added to the end of the presentation. Type The Wanderer and press the ENTER key.

Step 2: Click the Demote (Indent more) button to demote to outline level two. Type Create your dream vacation and press the ENTER key.

Step 3: Click the Demote (Indent more) button to demote to outline level three. Type Luxurious beach-front accommodations and press the ENTER key.

Step 4: Click the Demote (Indent more) button to demote to outline level four. Type Hotels and press the ENTER key. Type Condominiums and press the ENTER key.

Step 5: Click the Promote (Indent less) button to promote to outline level three. Type Diverse dining opportunities and press the ENTER key. Type Recreation bonanza and press the ENTER key.

The screen displays as shown in Figure 2-16.

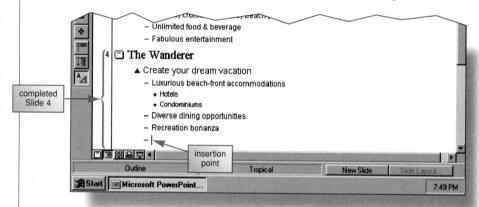

FIGURE 2-16

Creating a Slide with Multiple Text Objects in Outline View

All of the slides you have created to this point consist of a title object and one text object. Occasionally, you need to provide the audience with a long list of items. If you use the Bulleted List slide layout, Style Checker will identify the slide as having too many bullets. Recall from Project 1 that Style Checker checks a presentation for spelling, visual clarity, and end punctuation. One of the design standards Style Checker looks for is too many bullets in an object.

In order to create a slide with more than six bulleted paragraphs and still comply with design standards, break the list into two or more objects. When you divide the text into multiple objects, each object complies with PowerPoint's default settings for visual clarity in Style Checker, as long as the number of bullets per object is less than or equal to six. Six is the default setting for the number of bullets per object.

Because you are creating the presentation in Outline view, type the text for this slide as a bulleted list. Later in this project, you convert the bulleted list slide into a multiple object slide by changing views, changing slide layout, and moving some of the text from the bulleted list to another object. Perform the steps below to create a slide with multiple text objects in Outline view.

TO CREATE A SLIDE WITH MULTIPLE TEXT OBJECTS IN OUTLINE VIEW

Step 1: Click the Promote (Indent less) button two times so that Slide 5 is added to the end of the presentation. Type Both Deals Feature as the slide title and press the ENTER key.

Step 2: Click the Demote (Indent more) button to demote to outline level two. Type Tropical climate and press the ENTER key. Type White sand beaches and press the ENTER key. Type Balmy breezes and press the ENTER key. Type Pristine pools and press the ENTER key. Type Sunny days and press the ENTER key. Type Starlight nights and press the ENTER key. Type Browser Beach and press the ENTER key.

Step 3: Click the Demote (Indent more) button to demote to outline level three. Type Sunbathe, volleyball and press the ENTER key.

Step 4: Click the Promote (Indent less) button to promote to outline level two. Type Net Bay and press the ENTER key.

Step 5: Click the Demote (Indent more) button to demote to outline level three. Type Sail, swim, snorkel and press the ENTER key

Step 6: Click the Promote (Indent less) button to promote to outline level two. Type Net Coral Reef and press the ENTER key.

Step 7: Click the Demote (Indent more) button to demote to outline level three. Type Scuba dive and press the ENTER key.

The screen displays as shown in Figure 2-17.

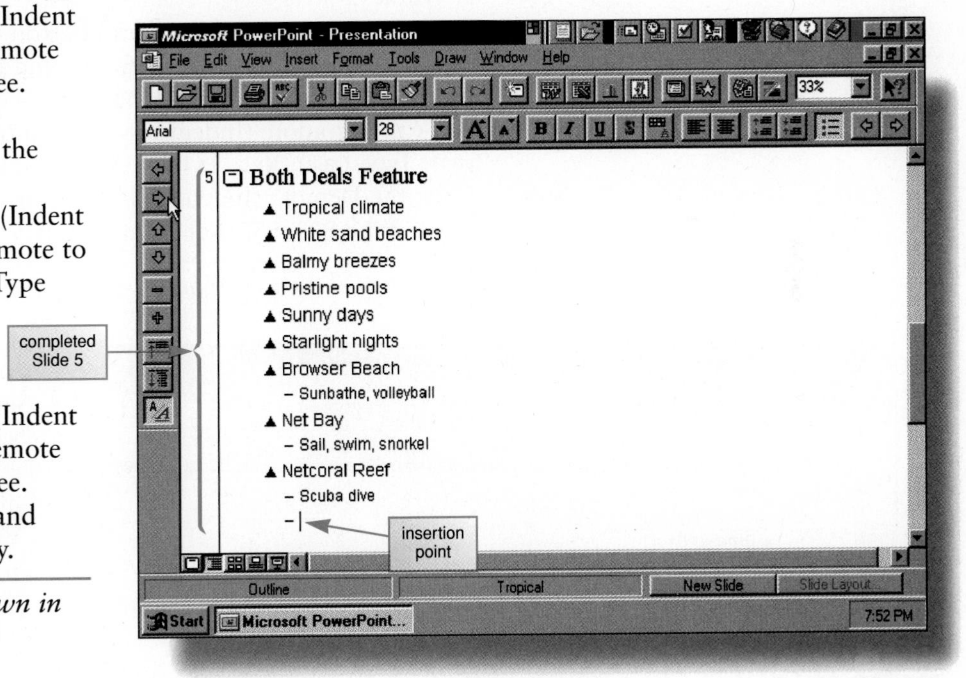

FIGURE 2-17

Creating a Closing Slide in Outline View

The last slide in your presentation is the **closing slide**. A closing slide gracefully ends a presentation. Often used during a question and answer session, the closing slide usually remains on the screen to reinforce the message delivered during the presentation. Professional speakers design the closing slide with one or more of the methods on the next page.

More *About*
Outline View

When working in Outline view, many people prefer to use keyboard keys instead of toolbar buttons. This way their hands never leave the keyboard and their typing is finished more quickly. For example, instead of clicking the Demote button to demote text, press the TAB key.

1. List important information. Tell the audience what to do next.
2. Provide a memorable illustration or example to make a point.
3. Appeal to emotions. Remind the audience to take action or accept responsibility.
4. Summarize the main points of the presentation.
5. Cite a quotation that directly relates to the main points of the presentation. This is most effective if the presentation started with a quotation.

The closing slide in this project combines listing important information and providing an illustration. Because Web Island Resort wants students to buy one of the tropical island vacations, they combine telling students what to do next with providing a list of telephone numbers on the Tropical Design Template. In this presentation, the design template serves as a recurrent illustration. Perform the following steps to create this closing slide.

TO CREATE A CLOSING SLIDE IN OUTLINE VIEW

Step 1: Click the Promote (Indent less) button two times so that Slide 6 is added to the end of the presentation. Type For Fun in the Sun as the slide title and press the ENTER key.

Step 2: Click the Demote (Indent more) button to demote to outline level two. Type Contact Student Activities Office and press the ENTER key.

Step 3: Click the Demote (Indent more) button to demote to outline level three. Type Ford Hall, Room 313 and press the ENTER key. Type Ext. 2882 and press the ENTER key.

Step 4: Click the Promote (Indent less) button to promote to outline level two. Type Call Web Island Resort and press the ENTER key.

Step 5: Click the Demote (Indent more) button to demote to outline level three. Type 800-555-Web1 but do not press the ENTER key.

Slide 6 displays as shown in Figure 2-18.

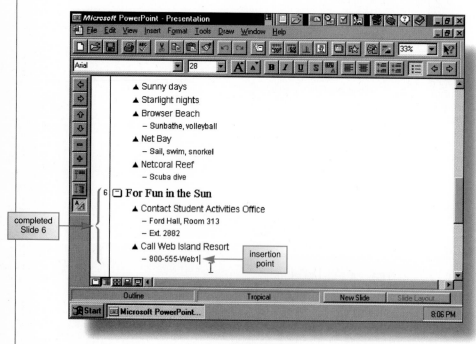

The outline is now complete and the presentation should be saved. The next section explains how to save the presentation.

Saving the Presentation

Recall from Project 1 that it is wise to frequently save your presentation on disk. Because you have created all the text for your presentation, you should save your presentation now. For a detailed explanation of the steps summarized on the next page, refer to pages PP 1.22 through PP 1.24 in Project 1.

FIGURE 2-18

Microsoft **PowerPoint 7** Windows 95

Reviewing a Presentation in Slide Sorter View • PP 2.19

TO SAVE A PRESENTATION

Step 1: Insert a formatted floppy disk in drive A. Then click the Save button on the Standard toolbar.

Step 2: Type Spring Break Specials in the File Name box. Do not press the ENTER key.

Step 3: Click the Save in down arrow. Click 3½ Floppy [A:] in the Save in drop-down list.

Step 4: Click the Save button.

The presentation is saved to drive A under the name Spring Break Specials.

Reviewing a Presentation in Slide Sorter View

When you create a presentation in Outline view, only the text is visible. You cannot see how the text looks on the slide nor how the design template affects the text objects. You must, therefore, see how the text looks on the slides to evaluate necessary changes. Changing to Slide Sorter view allows you to display your presentation slides in miniature so that you can quickly review the slides for content, organization, and overall appearance.

In Project 1, you displayed slides in Slide Show view to look at individual slides. Slide Show view limits you to looking at one slide at a time. Slide Sorter view, however, allows you to look at several slides at one time, which is helpful when you review your presentation for slide order. You will learn how to change slide order in Slide Sorter view later in this project. Perform the following steps to change from Outline view to Slide Sorter view.

 Steps To Change the View to Slide Sorter View

1 **Point to the Slide Sorter View button on the View Button bar at the bottom of the PowerPoint window (Figure 2-19).**

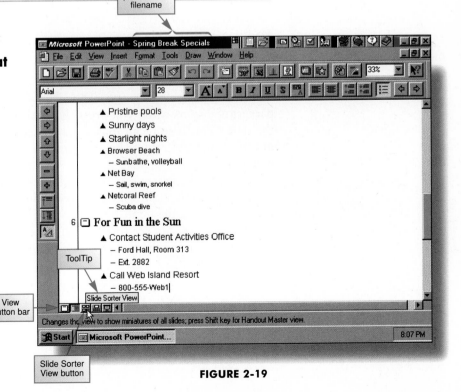

FIGURE 2-19

2 **Click the Slide Sorter View button.**

PowerPoint displays the presentation in Slide Sorter view (Figure 2-20). Slide 6 is selected because it was the current slide in Outline view.

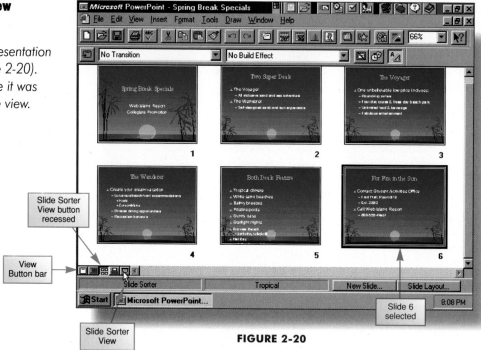

FIGURE 2-20

OtherWays

1. On menu bar click View, click Slide Sorter
2. Press ALT+V, press D

Because there are only six slides in this presentation and Zoom Control is 66%, you can review all slides at this time. Notice that Slide 2, Slide 3, and Slide 6 appear to need changes in line spacing. Slide 5 has text running off the bottom of the slide. Additionally, the presentation lacks pizzazz. To make the presentation more exciting, you may wish to add clip art. The next several sections explain how to improve the presentation by adding a blank line, changing slide layouts, and adding clip art.

Adding a Blank Line

The first improvement to this presentation is adding a blank line to Slide 2. In order to increase white space between paragraphs, add a blank line after the outline level three paragraph, All inclusive sand and sea adventure. Recall that a paragraph begins when you press the ENTER key and ends when you again press the ENTER key. Also recall that in a bulleted list, PowerPoint adds a bullet in front of each new paragraph. Thus, to create a blank line, you must also remove the bullet.

You can change text in both Slide view and Outline view. Recall that if you return to Outline view to add the blank line, you cannot see how the Design Template affects the text object. It is best, therefore, to change the view to Slide view so that you can see the result of editing the text object. Perform the following steps to change the view to Slide view.

Steps To Change the View to Slide View

1 **Point to the slide miniature of Slide 2 (Figure 2-21)**

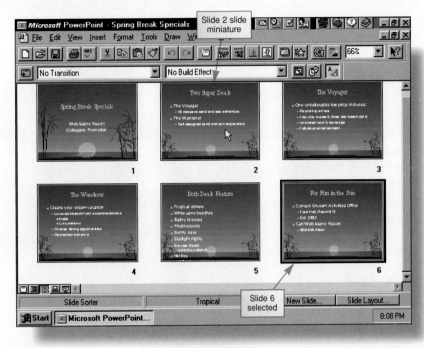

FIGURE 2-21

2 **Double-click the Slide 2 slide miniature.**

Slide 2 displays in Slide view (Figure 2-22). The Slide View button is recessed on the View Button bar.

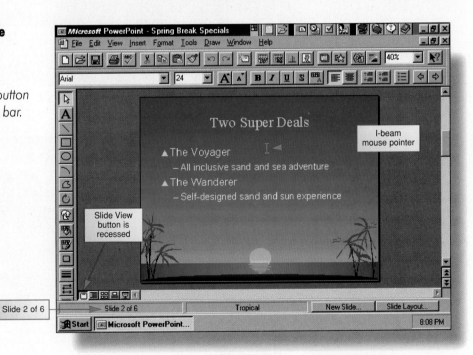

FIGURE 2-22

The next section explains how to add a blank line to Slide 2.

Other Ways

1. On View Button bar click Slide View button
2. On menu bar click View, click Slides
3. Press ALT+V, press S

Adding a Blank Line to Slide 2

Now that Slide 2 displays in Slide view, you are ready to add a blank line after the paragraph, All inclusive sand and sea adventure. Perform the following steps to add a blank line.

Steps To Add a Blank Line

1 **Position the I-beam mouse pointer to the right of the second letter e in the word adventure in the paragraph All inclusive sand and sea adventure. Then click the left mouse button.**

PowerPoint selects the text object and positions the insertion point after the second e in the word, adventure (Figure 2-23). The mouse pointer displays as an I-beam when located in a text object.

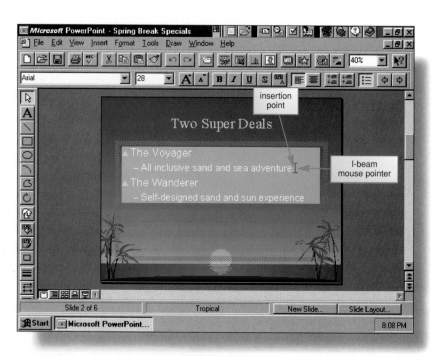

FIGURE 2-23

2 **Press the ENTER key.**

PowerPoint inserts a new paragraph (Figure 2-24). The new paragraph has the same attributes as the previous paragraph. The Bullet On/Off button is recessed on the Formatting toolbar.

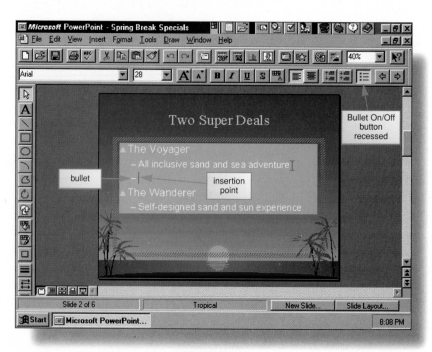

FIGURE 2-24

3 **Click the Bullet On/Off button to remove the bullet.**

The line displays blank because the bullet does not display (Figure 2-25). The Bullet On/Off button is not recessed.

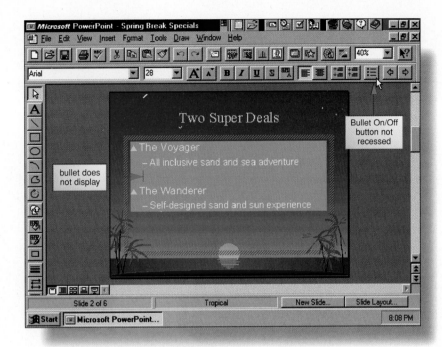

FIGURE 2-25

Other Ways

1. Press and hold down SHIFT, then press ENTER

To display a bullet on a selected paragraph, click the Bullet On/Off button on the Formatting toolbar.

Changing Slide Layout

Recall from Project 1 that when you add a new slide, PowerPoint displays the New Slide dialog box from which you choose one of the slide AutoLayouts. After creating a slide, you can change its layout by clicking the **Slide Layout button** on the status bar. The Slide Layout dialog box then displays. Like the AutoLayout dialog box, the Slide Layout dialog box allows you to choose one of the twenty-four different slide layouts.

When you change the layout of a slide, PowerPoint retains the text and graphics and repositions them into the appropriate placeholders. Using slide layouts eliminates the need to resize objects because PowerPoint automatically sizes the object to fit the placeholder.

To keep your presentation interesting, PowerPoint includes several slide layouts to combine text with nontext objects, such as clip art. The placement of the text, in relationship to the nontext object, depends on the slide layout. The nontext object placeholder may be to the right or left of the text, above the text, or below the text. Additionally, some slide layouts are constructed with two non-text object placeholders. Refer to Project 1 for a list of the available slide layouts (Figure 1-25 on PP 1.24). The instructions on the next page explain how to change the slide layout from a bulleted list to two columns of text.

More *About* **Slide Layout**

Vary your slide layouts to keep a presentation from becoming monotonous. Choose layouts designed for one text object, multiple text objects, graphs, tables, and clip art. While varying slide layouts increases audience attention, be careful to maintain a common theme throughout the presentation by using a Design Template or color scheme.

Steps **To Change Slide Layout**

① **Drag the elevator to display Slide 5 (Figure 2-26).**

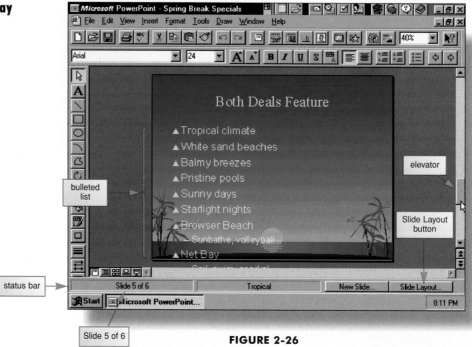

FIGURE 2-26

② **Click the Slide Layout button on the status bar. When the Slide Layout dialog box displays, click the 2 Column Text slide layout located in the row one, column three.**

The Slide Layout dialog box displays (Figure 2-27). The 2 Column Text slide layout is selected. When you click a slide layout, its name displays in the box at the lower right of the Slide Layout dialog box.

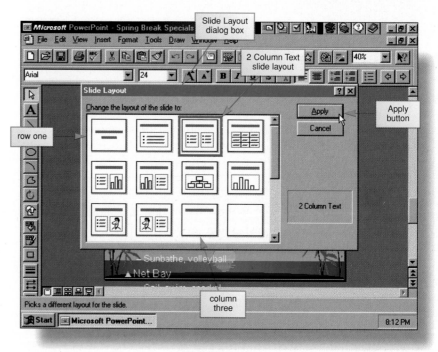

FIGURE 2-27

3 **Click the Apply button.**

Slide 5 displays the bulleted list in the left column text object (Figure 2-28). The right column text placeholder displays the message, Click to add text.

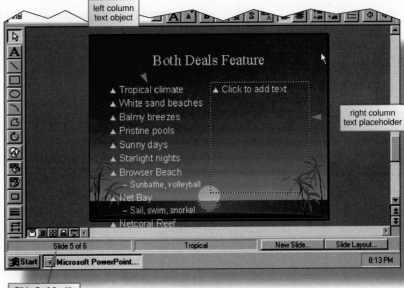

FIGURE 2-28

The text in the left column of Slide 5 is too lengthy to fit into the text object. The next section explains how to move the text at the bottom of the left column to the top of the right column text placeholder.

Moving Text

Because the bulleted list on Slide 5 contains more paragraphs than will fit in the left column text object, select a portion of the list and move it to the right column text placeholder. Perform the following steps to select a portion of the text in the left column and then move it to the right column.

 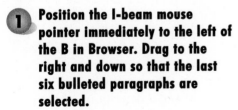 **To Move Text**

1 **Position the I-beam mouse pointer immediately to the left of the B in Browser. Drag to the right and down so that the last six bulleted paragraphs are selected.**

The six bulleted paragraphs, Browser Beach, Sunbathe, volleyball; Net Bay, Sail, swim, snorkel; Netcoral Reef, and Scuba dive, are selected (Figure 2-29).

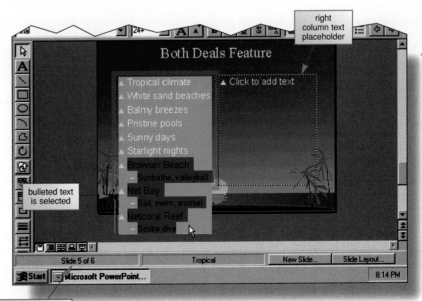

FIGURE 2-29

② Point to the selected text. If the mouse pointer displays as a four-headed arrow, move the mouse pointer to the right of the bullets so that it is positioned over the text. Then drag the selected text to the right column text placeholder.

As you drag the text, the mouse pointer displays as a block arrow with a small dotted box around the arrow shaft. The six selected paragraphs are moved to the right column text placeholder (Figure 2-30). When you insert text into a text placeholder, it becomes a text object.

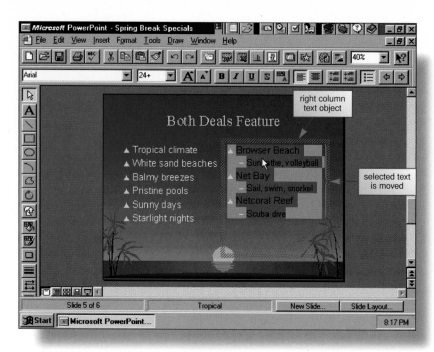

FIGURE 2-30

Recall from Project 1 that you must select an object before you can modify it.

Adding Clip Art to a Slide

Clip art offers a quick way to add professional-looking graphic images to your presentation without creating the images yourself. **Microsoft ClipArt Gallery 2.0** contains a wide variety of graphic images and is shared with other Microsoft Office applications. Microsoft ClipArt Gallery 2.0 combines topic-related clip art images into categories. Insert clip art to your presentation by selecting a clip art image from Microsoft ClipArt Gallery 2.0.

Table 2-2 gives you an idea of the organization of Microsoft ClipArt Gallery 2.0 that accompanies PowerPoint. The table contains four of the categories from Microsoft ClipArt Gallery 2.0 and a description of the clip art contained therein. Clip art image descriptions are nouns and verbs that associate an image with various entities, activities, labels, and emotions. In most instances, the description does not contain the name of the physical object. For example, an image of a magnifying glass in the Academic category

Table 2-2

CATEGORY	DESCRIPTION
Academic	Seven images: Professor Leadership Information text Communication, Meeting Communication Information, Figures Discord, Information, Focus Identify Small, Focus Investigate Identify Small, and Reward Accomplishment.
Cartoons	Ninety-three cartoon and stick people images; e.g., Reward, Worried, Problem Priority, Happy Joy Laugh, Target, Surprise, Idea Brainstorm, Planning Busy Human, Travel Human, and Fast Human.
Household	Eight images: Security Unlock, Security Unlock Solution, Cutback Scissors, Solution Band-Aid, Timeline Schedule Clock, Patience Timeline, Security Unlock Lock and Keys, and Direction.
Transportation	Seven images: Performance Fast Sports Car, Performance Ship, War Battle Powerful Battleship, Performance Fast Plane, Performance Fast War Battle Plane, Performance Fast Plane, and Priority Traffic Light.

has a description of Focus Investigate Identify Small. As a result, you may find it necessary to scroll through several categories to find an appropriate picture.

In this project you use clip art images from the Popular.pcs clip art file. Contact your instructor if you are missing clip art when you perform the following steps. A full installation of PowerPoint is required before all clip art images are available.

Using AutoLayouts to Add Clip Art

PowerPoint simplifies adding clip art to a slide by providing numerous AutoLayouts designed specifically for clip art. Recall from Project 1 that an Auto-Layout is a collection of placeholders for the title, text, clip art, graphs, tables, and media clips. When you use an AutoLayout placeholder, PowerPoint automatically sizes clip art to fit the placeholder. If the clip art is in landscape orientation, PowerPoint sizes it to the width of the placeholder. If the clip art is in portrait orientation, PowerPoint sizes it to the height of the placeholder.

Adding clip art to Slide 6 requires two steps. First, you change the slide layout to Clip Art & Text. Then you insert clip art into the clip art placeholder. The next two sections explain how to add clip art into an AutoLayout placeholder.

Changing Slide Layout to Clip Art & Text

Before you insert clip art into an AutoLayout placeholder, you must first select one of the slide layouts that includes a clip art placeholder. The clip art placeholder on the left side of Slide 6 will hold clip art. Perform the following steps to change the slide layout to Clip Art & Text.

Steps To Change the Slide Layout to Clip Art & Text

1 **Drag the elevator to display Slide 6 (Figure 2-31).**

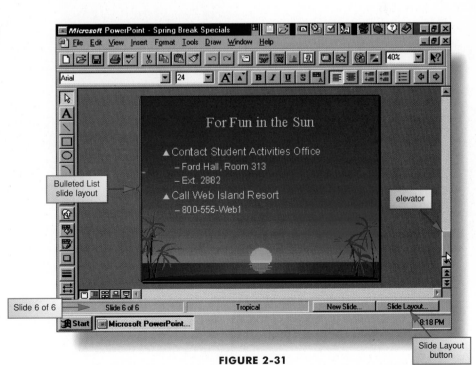

FIGURE 2-31

More *About*
Clip Art

Humor and interest are just two of several reasons to add clip art to your presentation. People have limited attention spans. A carefully placed humorous clip art image can spark attention and interest. When interest is high, it greatly increases the chance that your concept or idea will be remembered.

2 Click the Slide Layout button. When the Slide Layout dialog box displays, click the Clip Art & Text slide layout located in row three, column two. Then point to the Apply button.

The Clip Art & Text slide layout is selected in the Slide Layout dialog box (Figure 2-32).

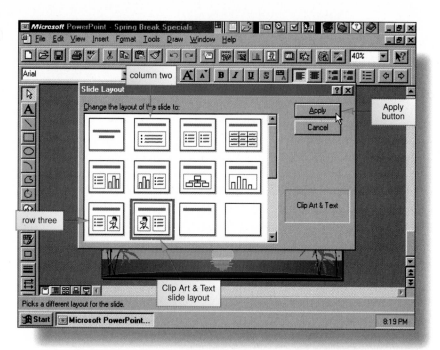

FIGURE 2-32

3 Click the Apply button.

Slide 6 displays the Clip Art & Text slide layout (Figure 2-33). PowerPoint moves the text object and automatically resizes the text to fit the object.

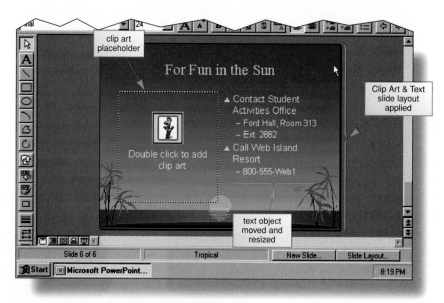

FIGURE 2-33

*Other*Ways

1. Right-click anywhere on slide except placeholders, click Slide Layout

2. On menu bar click Format, click Slide Layout

3. Press ALT+O, press L

You can use an AutoLayout placeholder to insert clip art even if the Auto-Layout doesn't have a clip art placeholder. For example, to insert clip art into the object placeholder of the Object AutoLayout, click the placeholder to select it, click the Insert Clip Art button, and then select a clip art picture.

Inserting Clip Art into a Clip Art Placeholder

Now that the Clip Art & Text placeholder is applied to Slide 6, you must insert clip art into the clip art placeholder. Perform the following steps to insert clip art to the clip art placeholder on Slide 6.

Steps **To Insert Clip Art into a Clip Art Placeholder**

1 **Position the mouse pointer anywhere within the clip art placeholder.**

The mouse pointer is positioned inside the clip art placeholder (Figure 2-34). It is not necessary to point to the picture inside the placeholder.

FIGURE 2-34

2 **Double-click the clip art placeholder on the left side of Slide 6.**

PowerPoint displays the Microsoft ClipArt Gallery 2.0 dialog box (Figure 2-35). When you open Microsoft ClipArt Gallery 2.0, All Categories is the selected category in the Categories box. The Pictures box displays clip art images by category. The selected image is a bear. Your selected image may be different depending on the clip art installed on your computer. If this is the first time you access clip art after an installation, the Microsoft ClipArt Gallery dialog box displays a message asking if you want to add clip art from PowerPoint now. Click the Yes or Add button. PowerPoint then displays the Microsoft ClipArt Gallery 2.0 dialog box.

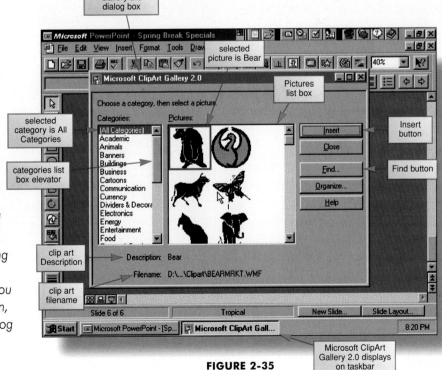

FIGURE 2-35

3 Click the Find button.

The Find ClipArt dialog box displays three boxes in which you enter clip art search criteria (Figure 2-36). The Description box is selected and contains the description, All Descriptions. Use the Description box to find clip art when you know a word from the image's description. Use the Filename containing box when you know the name of the file containing the desired clip art image. Use the Picture type box when you want to find clip art saved in a specific format.

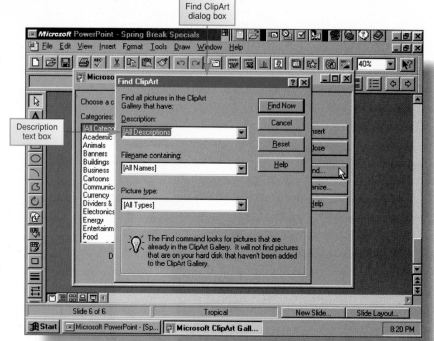

FIGURE 2-36

4 Type disappoint in the Description box and point to the Find Now button.

The Description box contains disappoint, which is a portion of the description, disappointment (Figure 2-37). You do not need to type the full description because the Find feature of Microsoft ClipArt Gallery 2.0 searches for all pictures containing the consecutive letters typed in the Description box. The Find Now button initiates the clip art search. The Reset button resets the Description, Filename containing, and Picture type boxes. Click the Reset button when you wish to begin a new search.

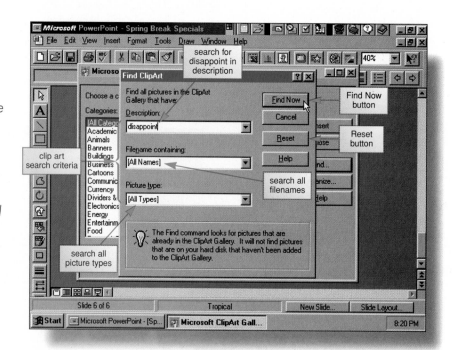

FIGURE 2-37

More *About* Clip Art

Clip art serves a purpose in a presentation – it conveys a message. Clip art should contribute to the understandability of the slide. It should not be used decoratively. Before adding clip art to a presentation, ask yourself: "Does the clip art convey or support the slide topic?" If the answer is yes, put the clip art on the slide.

5 Click the Find Now button.

The Microsoft ClipArt Gallery searches for all pictures that contain disappoint in the description. All pictures that match the description display in the Pictures box (Figure 2-38). The picture of a person sitting at a desk holding a telephone receiver is selected. The selected category changes to Results of Last F(ind). Disappointment displays as the description of the selected picture at the bottom of the Microsoft ClipArt Gallery 2.0 dialog box. Your selected picture may be different depending on the clip art installed on your computer.

FIGURE 2-38

6 Click the Insert button.

The selected picture is inserted into the clip art placeholder on Slide 6 (2-39). PowerPoint automatically sizes the picture to a size that best fits the placeholder. In this instance, the picture is wider it is than tall (landscape orientation), so PowerPoint sizes the picture to fit the width of the placeholder. When a picture is in portrait orientation, PowerPoint sizes the picture to fit the height of the placeholder.

FIGURE 2-39

*Other*Ways

1. Right-click clip art placeholder, click Edit Placeholder Object
2. Click clip art placeholder, on Standard toolbar click Insert Clip Art button
3. Click clip art placeholder, on menu bar click Insert, click Clip Art
4. Click clip art placeholder, press ALT+I, press C

Occasionally, you find a clip art image that enhances your presentation but has a description that does not match your topic. The description is not the factor by which you select your clip art. The effectiveness of the picture determines if you add it to your presentation, not its description.

In addition to the graphic images in Microsoft ClipArt Gallery 2.0, there are other sources for clip art such as retailers specializing in computer software, the Internet, bulletin board systems, and online information systems. Some popular online information systems are Microsoft Network, America Online, CompuServe, and Prodigy. A **bulletin board system** is a computer system that allows users to communicate with each other and share files.

Table 2-3

FORMAT	FILE EXTENSION
AutoCAD Format 2-D	*.dxf
CompuServe GIF	*.gif
Computer Graphics Metafile	*.cgm
CorelDRAW!	*.cdr
DrawPerfect Graphics	*.wpg
Encapsulated PostScript	*.eps
HP Graphics Language	*.hgl
JPEG Filter	*.jpg
Kodak Photo CD	*.pcd
Lotus 1-2-3 Graphics	*.pic
Macintosh PICT	*.pct
Micrografx Designer/Draw	*.drw
PC Paintbrush	*.pcx
Tagged Image File Format	*.tif
Targa	*.tga
Windows Bitmaps	*.dib, *.bmp
Windows Metafile	*.wmf
WordPerfect Graphics	*.wpg

Additionally, you can include pictures into your presentation. These may include scanned photographs, line art, and artwork from compact discs. To insert a picture into a presentation, the picture must be saved in a format that PowerPoint can recognize. Table 2-3 identifies the formats PowerPoint recognizes.

PowerPoint converts pictures saved in the formats listed in Table 2-3 by using filters. These filters are shipped with the PowerPoint installation software and must be installed before PowerPoint can properly convert files.

Inserting Clip Art on a Slide without a Clip Art Placeholder

PowerPoint does not require you to use an AutoLayout containing a clip art placeholder to add clip art to a slide. You can insert clip art on any slide regardless of its slide layout. On Slide 3, you are adding a picture of a sailboat to illustrate the type of sailing vessel used in the Voyager vacation package. Recall that the slide layout on Slide 3 is a Bulleted List. Because the Bulleted List AutoLayout does not contain a clip art placeholder, you click the Insert Clip Art button on the Standard toolbar to start Microsoft ClipArt Gallery 2.0. The picture for which you are searching is a sailing ship. Its description is Performance Ship. Perform the following steps to insert the picture of a ship on a slide that does not have a clip art placeholder.

OtherWays
1. On menu bar click Insert, click Clip Art
2. Press ALT+I, press C

TO INSERT CLIP ART ON A SLIDE WITHOUT A CLIP ART PLACEHOLDER

Step 1: Drag the elevator to display Slide 3, titled The Voyager.
Step 2: Click the Insert ClipArt button on the Standard toolbar (see Figure 2-39 on page PP 2.31).
Step 3: Click the Find button. When the Find ClipArt dialog box displays, type ship in the Description box. Click the Find Now button.
Step 4: When the Pictures box in the Microsoft ClipArt Gallery 2.0 dialog box displays the results, click the down arrow on the Pictures box scroll bar until the sailboat displays. If the sailboat is not installed on your computer, see your instructor for an appropriate replacement picture.
Step 5: Click the picture of the sailboat.
Step 6: Click the Insert button.

The sailboat displays on Slide 3 (Figure 2-40). A selection box indicates the clip art is selected.

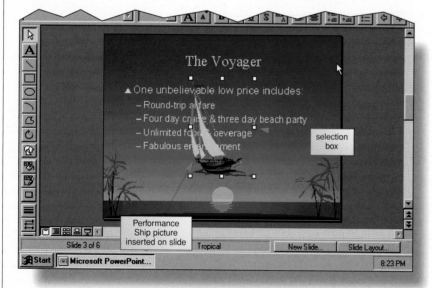

FIGURE 2-40

Moving Clip Art

After you insert clip art on a slide, you may want to reposition it. The picture of the sailboat overlays the bulleted list on Slide 3. Moving the picture to the lower right corner of the slide places the sailboat onto the water and away from the text. Perform the steps below to move the sailboat to the lower-right portion of the slide.

 Steps **To Move Clip Art**

1 **If the picture of the sailboat is not already selected, use the mouse pointer to point to the sailboat and click.**

2 **Press and hold down the left mouse button. Drag the picture of the sailboat down to the bottom of the slide and then to the right until the left edge of the dotted box aligns below the b in beach. Release the left mouse button.**

When you drag an object, a dotted box displays. The dotted box indicates the new position of the object. When you release the left mouse button, the picture of the sailboat displays in the new location (Figure 2-41). Resize handles appear at the corners and along the edges of the selection box.

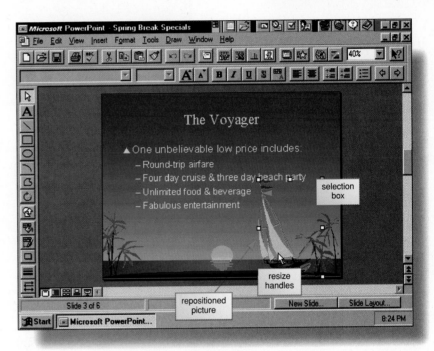

FIGURE 2-41

More *About* **Clip Art**

When used appropriately, clip art reduces misconceptions. If a presentation consists of words alone, the audience creates its own mental picture. The mental picture created may be different than the concept you are trying to convey. The audience better understands the concept when clip art is included.

Changing the Size of Clip Art Using the Scale Command

You may sometimes find it necessary to change the size of clip art. For example, on Slide 3, the mast on the sailboat slightly overlaps the bulleted text. To improve legibility, reduce the size of the picture. To change the size of a clip art picture by an exact percentage, use the Scale command. The advantage of using the Scale command is the ability to maintain the aspect ratio when you resize the picture. The **aspect ratio** is the relationship between the height and width of an object. Additionally, because the Scale dialog box contains a Preview button, you can make changes and see how the picture looks on the slide without permanently changing its size. When you are satisfied with the size of the picture, click the OK button to apply the settings in the Scale dialog box. Perform the steps on the next pages to reduce the size of the sailboat.

*Other***Ways**

1. On status bar click Slide Layout button, click slide layout containing clip art or media clip placeholder

2. Select clip art object, press arrow keys

Steps To Change the Size of Clip Art Using the Scale Command

1 With the picture of the sailboat selected, click Draw on the menu bar. Then point to Scale (Figure 2-42).

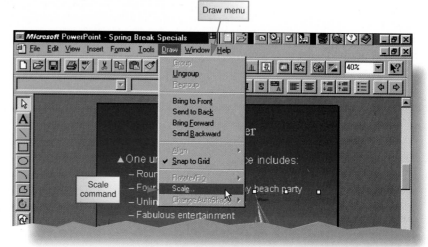

FIGURE 2-42

2 Click Scale.

The Scale dialog box displays (Figure 2-43). The Scale To box displays the current percentage of the sailboat picture, 99.6. A check mark in the Relative to Original Picture Size box instructs PowerPoint to maintain the aspect ratio of the picture.

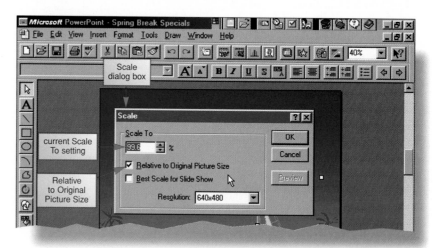

FIGURE 2-43

3 Point to the Scale dialog box title bar and drag it to the upper left corner of the slide window.

The sailboat is fully visible (Figure 2-44).

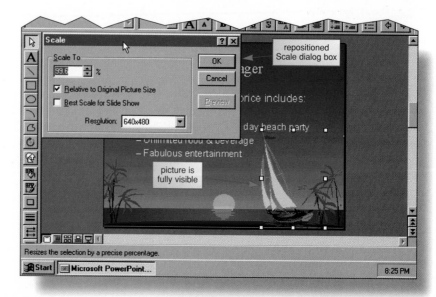

FIGURE 2-44

4 **Type** 85 **and click the Preview button.**

PowerPoint temporarily resizes the sailboat to 85 percent of its original size and displays it on Slide 3 (Figure 2-45). The Preview button is dimmed, or not available at this time. If the sailboat picture were still covering part of the text, you would want to try another scaling percentage to make it smaller. When you type a number in the Scale To box, the Preview button becomes available again. The OK button is used when you are satisfied with the scaling results.

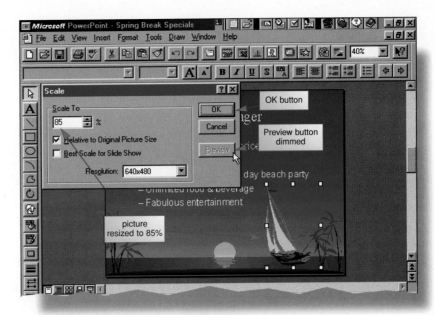

FIGURE 2-45

5 **Click the OK button.**

PowerPoint displays the reduced sailboat picture and closes the Scale dialog box (Figure 2-46).

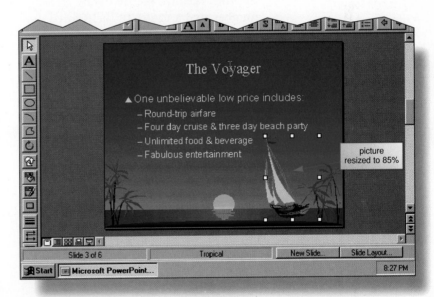

FIGURE 2-46

Other Ways

1. Select clip art object, drag a resize handle
2. Select clip art object, press ALT+D, press E

The Scale command is available only when a selected object displays in Slide view or Notes Pages view.

When you use the Scale command to change the size of a clip art image, the image increases or decreases proportionally to the percentage specified in the Scale To box. For example, if you wish to decrease the size of a picture to one-half its original size, type 50 in the Scale To box. If you wish to double the size of a picture (two times its original size), type 200 in the Scale To box.

Saving the Presentation

To preserve the work completed this far, save the presentation again by clicking the Save button on the Standard toolbar.

Adding a Header and a Footer to Outline Pages

A printout of the presentation outline often is used as an audience handout. Distributing a copy of the outline provides the audience with paper upon which to write notes or comments. Another benefit of distributing a copy of the outline is to help the audience see the text on the slides when lighting is poor or the room is too large. To help identify the source of the printed outline, add a descriptive header and footer.

Using the Notes and Handouts Sheet to Add Headers and Footers

Add headers and footers to outline pages by clicking the Notes and Handouts sheet in the Header and Footer dialog box and entering the information you wish to print. Perform the following steps to add the current date, a header, the page number, and a footer to the printed outline.

Steps To Use the Notes and Handouts Sheet to Add Headers and Footers

1 Click View on the menu bar. Point to Header and Footer (Figure 2-47).

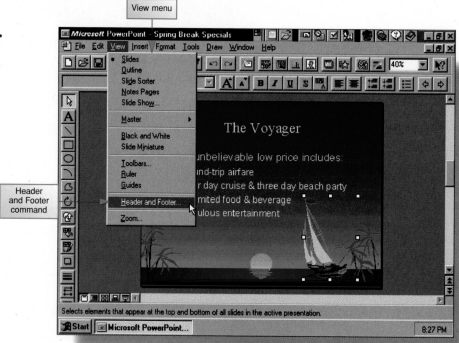

FIGURE 2-47

---

2 Click Header and Footer.

The Header and Footer dialog box displays (Figure 2-48). The Slide sheet displays.

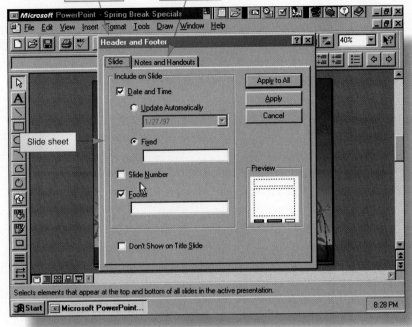

FIGURE 2-48

3 Click the Notes and Handouts tab.

The Notes and Handouts sheet displays (Figure 2-49). Check marks display in the Date and Time, Header, Page Number, and Footer check boxes. The Fixed option button is selected.

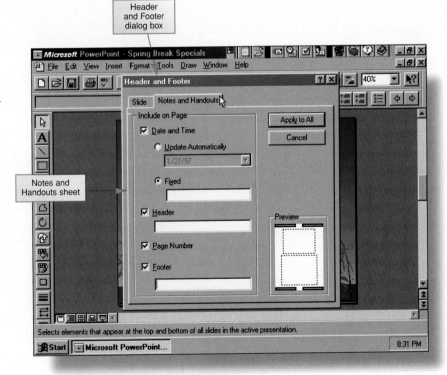

FIGURE 2-49

4 **Click the Update Automatically option button. Type** Spring Break Specials **in the Header text box. Type** Web Island Resort **in the Footer text box. Then point to the Apply to All button (Figure 2-50).**

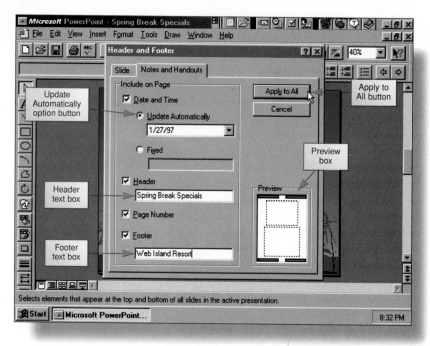

FIGURE 2-50

5 **Click the Apply to All button.**

PowerPoint applies the header and footer text to the outline, closes the Header and Footer dialog box, and displays Slide 3 (Figure 2-51). You cannot see header and footer text until you print the outline.

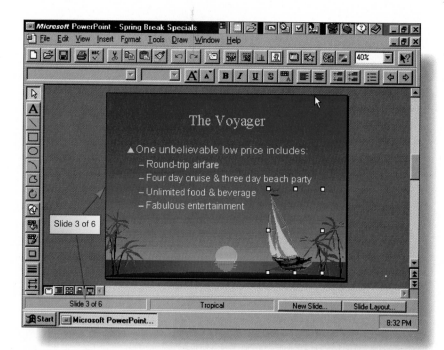

FIGURE 2-51

Checking the Presentation for Spelling and Style Errors

Now that the individual slide changes have been made, you should run Style Checker to identify errors in your presentation. Recall from Project 1 that Style Checker identifies possible errors in spelling, visual clarity, case, and end punctuation. Perform the following steps to run Style Checker.

TO RUN STYLE CHECKER

Step 1: Click Tools on the menu bar.

Step 2: Click Style Checker.

Step 3: When the Style Checker dialog box displays, click the Start button.

Step 4: Correct spelling errors and ignore correct spellings of words not located in the standard dictionary.

Step 5: If Style Checker lists visual clarity inconsistencies in the Style Checker Summary dialog box, write the slide number and the message on a sheet of paper.

Step 6: When the Style Checker Status dialog box displays, press the OK button.

PowerPoint closes Style Checker and displays the slide containing the last word not in the dictionaries, Slide 6 (Figure 2-52). This presentation contains no visual clarity inconsistencies. If Style Checker identifies any visual clarity inconsistencies, review the steps for creating the identified slide and make the appropriate corrections.

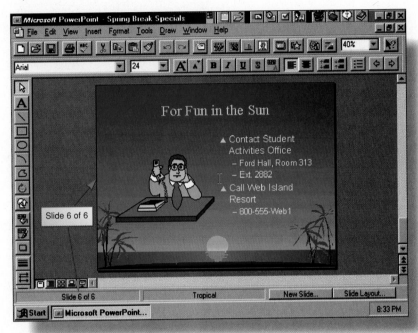

FIGURE 2-52

For more information about Style Checker, see page PP 1.40 in Project 1.

Adding Animation Effects

PowerPoint provides many animation effects to make your slide show presentation look professional. Two of these animation effects are slide transition and text build. **Slide transition effects** control how a slide displays on and exits the screen. **Text build effects** control how the objects on a slide display. The following pages discuss each of these animation effects in detail.

Adding Slide Transitions to a Slide Show

PowerPoint allows you to control the way you advance from one slide to the next by adding slide transitions to an on-screen slide show. Slide transitions are visual effects that display when you move one slide off the screen and bring the next one on. PowerPoint has forty-six different slide transitions. The name of the slide transition characterizes the visual effect that displays. For example, the slide transition effect, Split Vertical In, displays the next slide by covering the previous slide with two vertical boxes moving toward the center of the screen until the two boxes meet. The effect is similar to closing draw drapes over a window.

PowerPoint requires you to select a slide before applying slide transition effects. In this presentation, you apply slide transition effects to all slides except the title slide. Because Slide 6 is already selected, you must select Slides 2 through 5. The technique used to select more than one slide is the **SHIFT+click technique.** To perform the SHIFT+click technique, hold down the SHIFT key as you click each slide. After you click the slides to which you want to add text build effects, release the SHIFT key.

In the Spring Break Specials presentation, you wish to display the Box Out slide transition effect between slides. That is, all slides begin stacked on top of one another, like a deck of cards. As you click the mouse to view the next slide, the new slide enters the screen by starting at the center of the slide and exploding out toward the edges of the slide while maintaining a box shape. Perform the following steps to apply the Box Out slide transition effect to the Spring Break Specials presentation.

 Steps **To Add Slide Transitions to a Slide Show**

1 **Click the Slide Sorter View button at the bottom of the PowerPoint screen.**

PowerPoint displays the presentation in Slide Sorter view (Figure 2-53). Slide 6 is selected. Slide 6 currently does not have a slide transition effect as noted in the Slide Transition Effects box on the Slide Sorter toolbar.

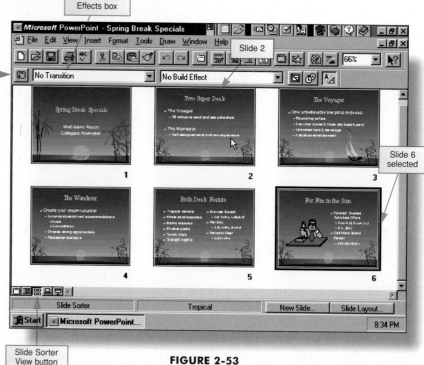

FIGURE 2-53

2 Press and hold down the SHIFT key and click Slide 2, Slide 3, Slide 4, and Slide 5. Release the SHIFT key.

Slides 2 through 6 are selected, as indicated by the heavy border around each slide (Figure 2-54).

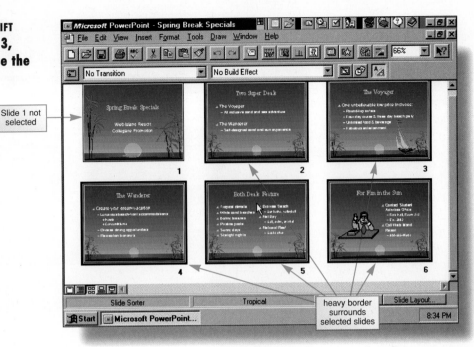

FIGURE 2-54

3 Point to Slide 5 and right-click. When a shortcut menu displays, point to Slide Transition (Figure 2-55).

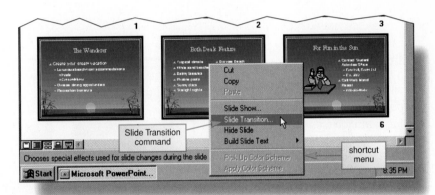

FIGURE 2-55

4 Click Slide Transition. When the Slide Transition dialog box displays, click the Effect box arrow and point to Box Out.

The Slide Transition dialog box displays (Figure 2-56). The Effect drop-down list displays available slide transition effects.

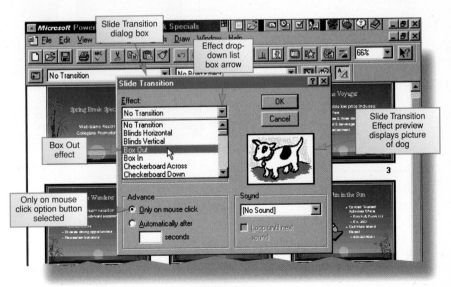

FIGURE 2-56

5 **Click Box Out.**

The Slide Transition Effect preview demonstrates the Box Out effect (Figure 2-57). To see the demonstration again, click the picture in the Slide Transition Effect preview.

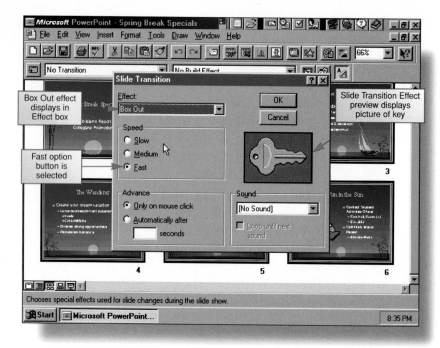

FIGURE 2-57

6 **Click the OK button.**

PowerPoint displays the presentation in Slide Sorter view (Figure 2-58). A slide transition icon displays under each selected slide, which indicates that slide transition effects have been added to those slides. The current slide transition effect, Box Out, displays in the Slide Transition Effects box.

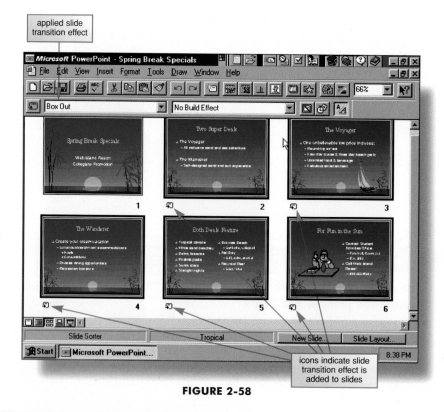

FIGURE 2-58

*Other*Ways

1. On Slide Sorter toolbar click Slide Transition button
2. On menu bar click Tools, click Slide Transition
3. Press ALT+T, press T

Slide Sorter Toolbar

PowerPoint provides you with multiple methods for accomplishing most tasks. Generally, the fastest method is to right-click to display a shortcut menu. Another frequently used method is to click a toolbar button. For example, you can apply slide transition effects by clicking the Slide Transition Effects box on the Slide Sorter toolbar.

The Slide Sorter toolbar displays only when you are in Slide Sorter view. It displays beneath the Standard toolbar, in place of the Formatting toolbar. The Slide Sorter toolbar contains tools to help you quickly add animation effects to your slide show. Table 2-4 explains the function of the buttons and boxes on the Slide Sorter toolbar.

TABLE 2-4

ICON	NAME	FUNCTION
	Slide Transition button	Displays the Slide Transition dialog box, which lists special effects used for slide changes during a slide show.
Box Out ▾	Slide Transition Effects box	Displays a list of slide transition effects. Selecting a slide transition effect from the list applies it to the selected slide(s) and demonstrates it in the preview box.
Fly From Bottom-Left ▾	Text Build Effects box	Displays a list of text build effects.
	Hide Slide button	Excludes a slide from the presentation without deleting it.
	Rehearse Timings button	Records the amount of time spent on each slide during a presentation rehearsal.
	Show Formatting button	Displays or hides character formatting attributes.

A slide transition effect has been applied to the presentation. The next step in creating this slide show is to add animation effects to individual slides.

Applying Text Build Effects to Bulleted Slides

Text build effects are animation effects that are applied to bulleted paragraphs. This special effect instructs PowerPoint to progressively disclose each bulleted paragraph, one at a time, during the running of a slide show. PowerPoint has thirty-eight text build effects and the capability to dim the bulleted paragraphs already on the slide when a new paragraph is displayed.

The next step is to apply the Fly From Bottom-Left build text effect to Slides 2, 3, 4, 5, and 6 in the Spring Break Specials presentation. Perform the steps on the next pages to apply text build effects to the bulleted slides in this presentation.

◆ **More** *About*
Text Build Effects

Clicking the Dim Previous Points check box in the Build dialog box changes the color of the current bulleted paragraph as the next one displays. The default dim color displays in the Dim Previous Points color drop-down list box. To choose a different dim color, click the Dim Previous Points down arrow.

Steps To Apply Text Build Effects to Bulleted Slides

1 If Slides 2 through 6 are not selected, use the SHIFT+click method to select them.

2 Right-click Slide 2. When a shortcut menu displays, point to Build Slide Text.

When Build Slide Text is highlighted, a submenu displays (Figure 2-59). A right-pointing arrow after a menu command indicates a submenu exists. The bullet in front of the Off command in the submenu identifies the current setting.

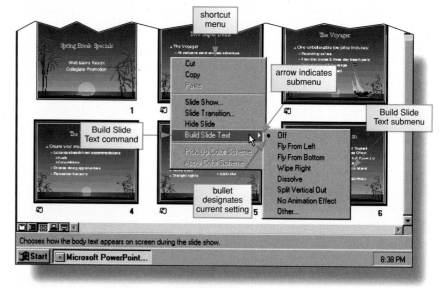

FIGURE 2-59

3 Point to Other in the Build Slide Text submenu (Figure 2-60).

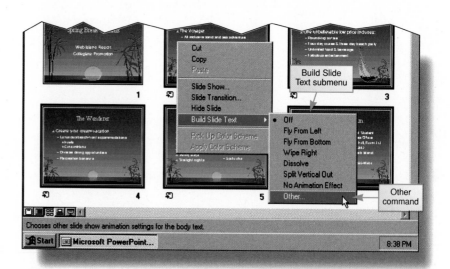

FIGURE 2-60

4 Click Other. When the Animation Settings dialog box displays, click the Build Options box down arrow. Then point to By 3rd Level Paragraphs.

The Build Options drop-down list displays various build options for slide text (Figure 2-61). The current build option is Don't Build as indicated in the Build Options box.

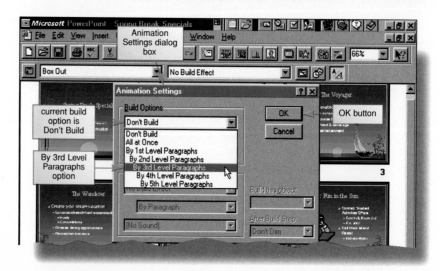

FIGURE 2-61

5 Click **By 3rd Level Paragraphs.**
Click the **Effects box arrow.** Then
point to **Fly From Bottom-Left**
(Figure 2-62).

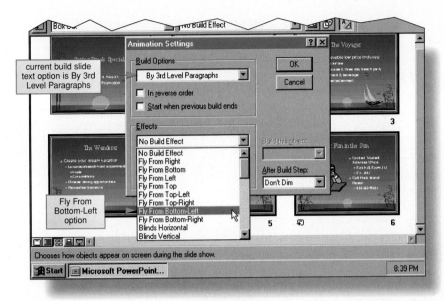

FIGURE 2-62

6 Click **Fly From Bottom-Left.** Then
click the **OK button.**

*PowerPoint applies the Fly From
Bottom-Left text build effect to the
selected slides (Figure 2-63). Fly
From Bottom-Left displays in the Text
Build Effects box. Icons below each
selected slide indicate text build
effects are applied to the slides.*

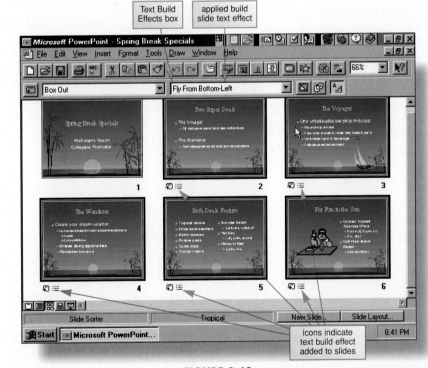

FIGURE 2-63

*Other***Ways**

1. On Slide Sorter toolbar click
   Text Build Effects box

2. In Slide view, click Tools on
   menu bar, click Animation
   Settings

3. In Slide view, press ALT+T,
   press B, press letter of text
   build effect

Slide transition and text build effects complete this presentation. You are now
ready to run the presentation in Slide Show view.

Saving the Presentation Again

Because several changes have been made since your last save, you should save
the presentation again by clicking the Save button on the Standard toolbar.

Running a Slide Show with Animation Effects

Project 1 introduced you to using Slide Show view to look at your presentation one slide at a time. This project introduces you to running a slide show with slide transition effects and text build effects. When you run a slide show with slide transition effects, PowerPoint displays the slide transition effect when you click the mouse to advance to the next slide. When a slide has text build effects, each paragraph level displays as determined by the animation settings. Perform the following steps to run the Spring Break Specials slide show with animation effects.

Steps To Run a Slide Show with Animation Effects

1 **Click Slide 1. Click the Slide Show button on the View Button bar. When Slide 1 displays in Slide Show view, click the slide anywhere except on the Popup Menu button.**

PowerPoint first displays the Box Out slide transition effect and then displays Slide 2 with only the slide title (Figure 2-64). Recall the Popup Menu button displays when you move the mouse pointer during a slide show.

FIGURE 2-64

2 **Click the slide anywhere except on the Popup Menu button.**

PowerPoint displays the first Level One bulleted paragraph using the Fly From Bottom-Left text build effect (Figure 2-65).

FIGURE 2-65

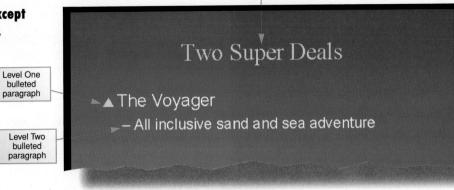

FIGURE 2-66

3 **Click the slide anywhere except on the Popup Menu button.**

PowerPoint displays the first Level Two bulleted paragraph beneath the Level One bulleted paragraph. PowerPoint again uses the Fly From Bottom-Left text build effect (Figure 2-66).

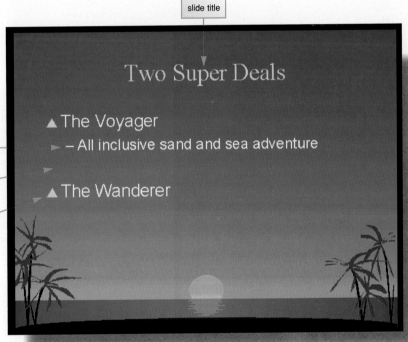

FIGURE 2-67

4 **Click the slide two times anywhere except on the Popup Menu button.**

PowerPoint displays the blank line and the second Level One bulleted list (Figure 2-67). The first click displays the blank line. The second click displays the second Level One bulleted paragraph.

5 **Continue clicking to finish running the slide show and return to Slide Sorter View.**

PowerPoint builds each slide based on the animation settings. When you click the slide after the last paragraph displays, PowerPoint exits Slide Show and returns to Slide Sorter View.

Printing in Outline View

PowerPoint allows you to print a hard copy of the current view using the Print button on the Standard toolbar. Recall from Project 1 that, while in Slide view, you click the Print button to print hard copies of the presentation slides. PowerPoint also allows you print a hard copy of views other than the current view using the Print command in the File menu. The next two sections explain how to use the Print button to print the presentation outline and how to use the Print command to print the presentation slides.

Printing an Outline

During the development of a lengthy presentation, it is often easier to review your outline in print rather than on-screen. Printing your outline also is useful for audience handouts or when your supervisor or instructor wants to review your subject matter before you fully develop your presentation.

When you display a presentation in Slide view, clicking the Print button causes PowerPoint to print all slides in the presentation. Similarly, when you display a presentation in Outline view, clicking the Print button causes PowerPoint to print the outline. The outline, however, prints as last viewed in Outline view. This means that you must select the Zoom Control setting to display the outline text as you wish to print it. If you are uncertain of the Zoom Control setting, you should review it prior to printing. Perform the following steps to print an outline in Outline view.

Steps To Print an Outline

1 **Click the Outline View button on the View Button bar.**

2 **Ready the printer according to the printer instructions. Then click the Print button on the Standard toolbar.**

The mouse pointer momentarily changes to an hourglass shape, and then PowerPoint briefly displays a message on the status bar indicating it is preparing to print the outline in the background. An animated printer icon displays on the status bar, identifying which page is being prepared to print. After several moments, the outline begins printing on the printer. The printer icon next to the clock on the taskbar indicates a print job is processing (Figure 2-68). When the outline is finished printing, the printer icon on the taskbar disappears.

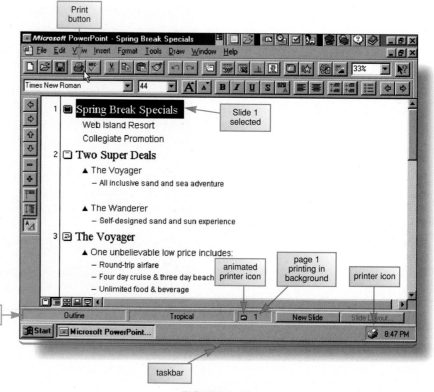

FIGURE 2-68

3 When the printer stops, retrieve the printout of the outline (Figure 2-69).

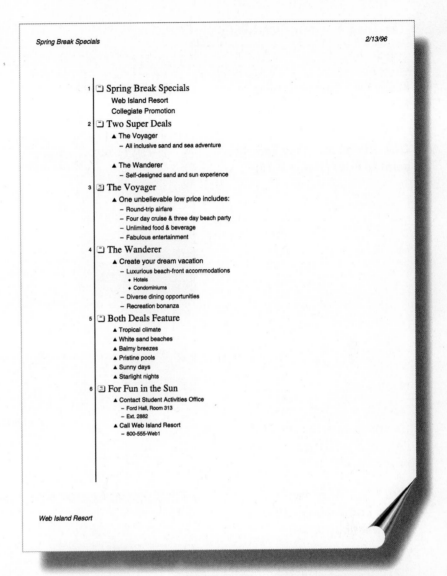

FIGURE 2-69

Printing Presentation Slides in Outline View

After correcting errors, you will want to print a final copy of your presentation. If you made any changes to your presentation since your last save, be sure to save your presentation before you print.

Perform the steps on the next pages to print the presentation slides while in Outline view.

Steps **To Print Presentation Slides**

1 **Ready the printer according to the printer instructions.**

2 **Click File on the menu bar. Then point to Print (Figure 2-70).**

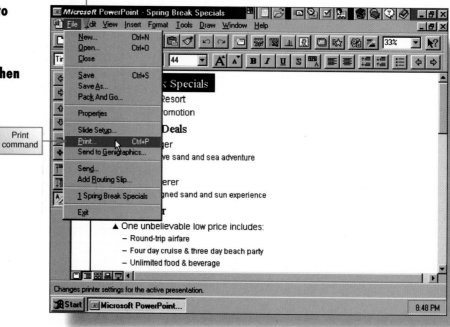

FIGURE 2-70

3 **Click Print. When the Print dialog box displays, click the Print what box arrow.**

The Print dialog box displays (Figure 2-71). The Print what drop-down list box displays hard copy options. Outline View is selected because it is the current view.

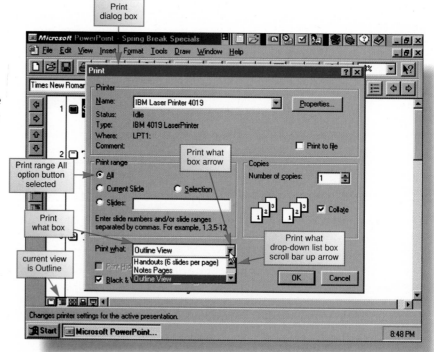

FIGURE 2-71

4 Click the Print what drop-down list scroll bar up arrow until Slides (without Builds) displays. Then point to Slides (without Builds) (Figure 2-72).

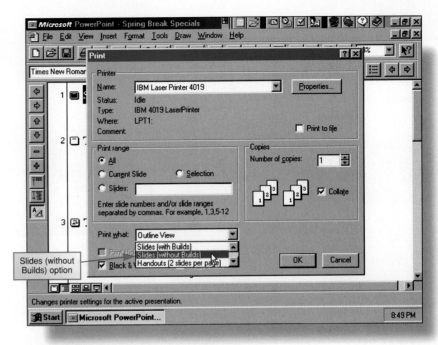

FIGURE 2-72

5 Click Slides (without Builds) (Figure 2-73).

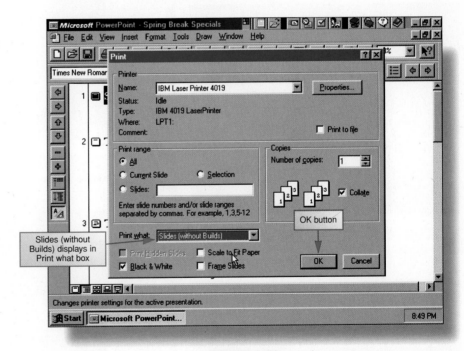

FIGURE 2-73

6 **Click the OK button in the Print dialog box. When the printer stops, retrieve the printouts.**

The printouts should look like the slides in Figure 2-74.

FIGURE 2-74a

FIGURE 2-74b

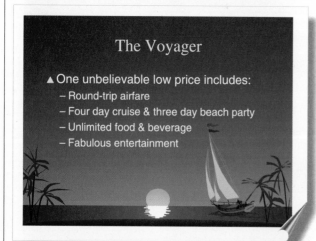

FIGURE 2-74c

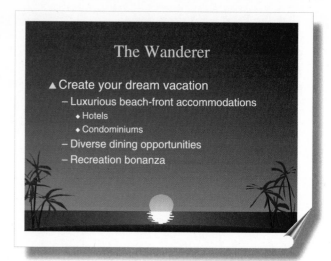

FIGURE 2-74d

FIGURE 2-74e

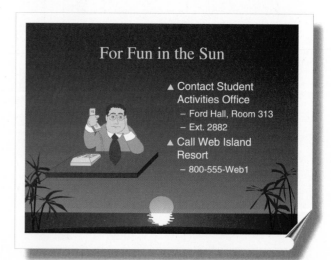

FIGURE 2-74f

> **Other Ways**
>
> 1. On View Button bar click Slide View button, click Print button
> 2. Press CTRL+P, click Slides in Print what box

The Print what drop-down list in the Print dialog box contains options for printing two, three, or six slide images per page. These options are labeled as Handouts [2 slides per page], Handouts [3 slides per page], and Handouts [6 slides per page]. Printing handouts is useful for reviewing a presentation because you print several slides on one page. Additionally, many businesses distribute handouts of the slide show before a presentation so the attendees have a hard copy to which to refer.

Editing a Presentation

Now that the Spring Break Specials presentation is complete, you want to review it for content and presentation flow. If you find that your slides need to be in a different sequence, you can easily change the slide order by dragging the slide to its new position. You can change slide order in either Outline view or Slide Sorter view. The following sections explain several editing features of PowerPoint. First, you will change slide order in Outline view and then in Slide Sorter view. You will also copy a slide and paste it into the presentation. Finally, you will use the Undo button to reverse the last edit action.

Displaying Slide Titles in Outline View

When moving slides in Outline view, it is easier to display only the slide titles. Displaying just the slide titles makes a large presentation more manageable by allowing you to work with one line of text per slide. The nontitle text displays as a gray line under the slide title. Showing only slide titles also prevents you from combining slides by moving one slide into the bulleted text of another. Perform the following steps to display only the slide titles in Outline view.

 Steps To Display Slide Titles in Outline View

1 **Point to the Show Titles button on the Outlining toolbar (Figure 2-75).**

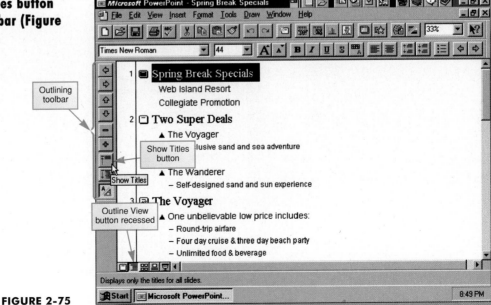

FIGURE 2-75

2 **Click the Show Titles button.**

PowerPoint compresses the slides so that only the six slide titles display in the Outline view window (Figure 2-76). Slide 1 is highlighted because it is the current slide. Nontitle text is indicated by a gray line under the title. Slides containing graphics display with graphic symbols in the slide icon.

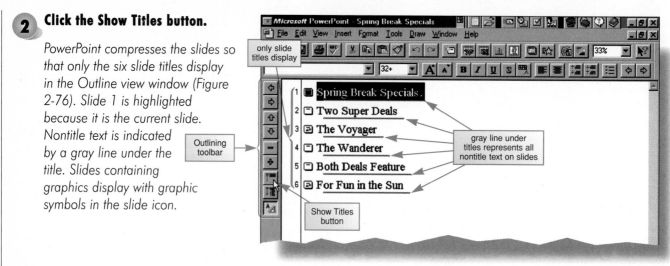

FIGURE 2-76

Changing Slide Order in Outline View

You move a slide to a new location, in Outline view, by dragging the slide icon until the horizontal placement indicator displays at the location where you want to position the slide. Perform the following steps to change slide order in Outline view.

 To Change Slide Order in Outline View

1 **Position the mouse pointer over the slide icon for Slide 5. Click the Slide 5 slide icon.**

Slide 5 is selected (Figure 2-77). The mouse pointer becomes a four-headed arrow when positioned over the slide icon.

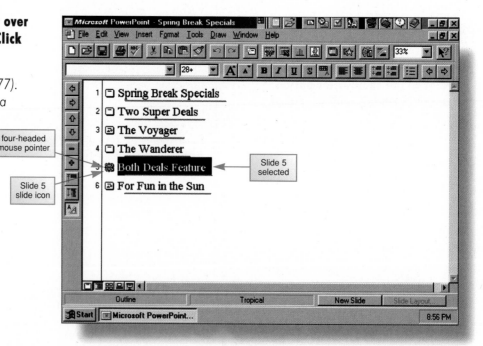

FIGURE 2-77

2 Press and hold down the left mouse button. Drag the Slide 5 slide icon up until the horizontal placement indicator displays below Slide 2, Two Super Deals, and above Slide 3, The Voyager.

The horizontal placement indicator displays below Slide 2 and above Slide 3 (Figure 2-78). The mouse pointer displays as a two-headed arrow.

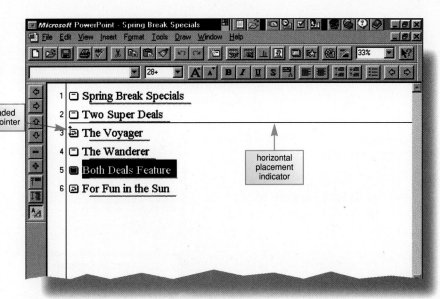

FIGURE 2-78

3 Release the left mouse button.

The slide titled Both Deals Feature becomes Slide 3 (Figure 2-79). PowerPoint automatically renumbers the slides. The mouse pointer displays as a four-headed arrow.

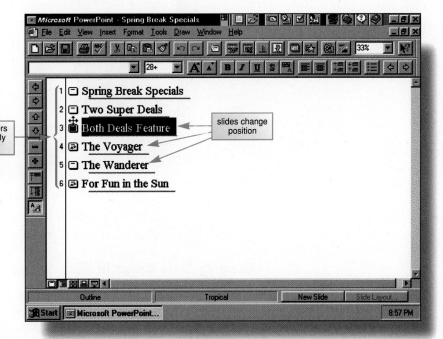

FIGURE 2-79

As you drag the slide icon, a horizontal placement indicator displays as soon as you move off the slide. The horizontal placement indicator is useful for identifying the exact location to drop the slide when changing slide order in Outline view.

Displaying All Text in Outline View

After moving slides, it is advisable to review the presentation again. Before you review the presentation, display the entire outline. Perform the following step to display all outline text.

Steps | To Display All Text in Outline View

1 **Click the Show All button on the Outlining toolbar (see Figure 2-5 on page PP 2.9).**

PowerPoint expands the outline text (Figure 2-80). Slide 3 is the current slide.

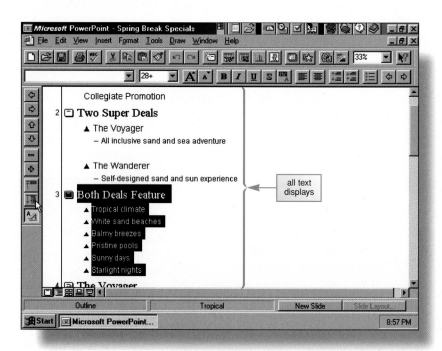

FIGURE 2-80

Changing Slide Order in Slide Sorter View

As previously stated, changing slide order in Slide Sorter view is as simple as dragging and dropping the slide into its new position. When you drag a slide to a new location in Slide Sorter view, a placement indicator displays to identify the slide's new position. The placement indicator is a dotted line. As you drag a slide, the mouse pointer displays as an arrow with a box around the arrow shaft. You move the slide to its new location by dragging the mouse pointer until the placement indicator displays at the location where you want to insert the slide. Because you cannot drop one slide on top of another slide in Slide Sorter view, the placement indicator appears to jump in front of a slide or after a slide as the mouse pointer moves around the window. Perform the following steps to change slide order in Slide Sorter view.

Steps To Change Slide Order in Slide Sorter View

1 **Click the Slide Sorter View button on the View Button bar.**

The presentation displays in Slide Sorter view (Figure 2-81). Slide 3 is selected because it was the current slide in Outline view. PowerPoint assigns a number to each slide.

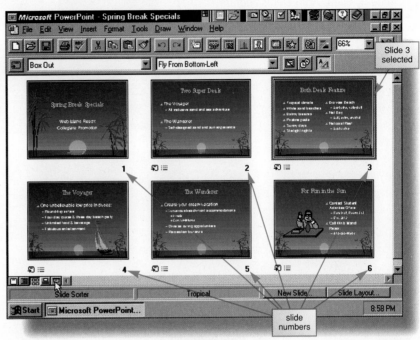

FIGURE 2-81

2 **Point to Slide 3, and then press and hold down the left mouse button. Drag Slide 3 down and to the left until the placement indicator displays after Slide 5 (Figure 2-82).**

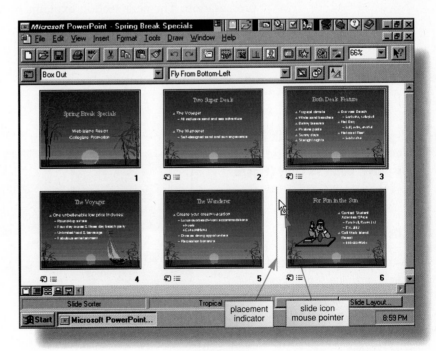

FIGURE 2-82

3 **Release the left mouse button to drop Slide 3 after Slide 5.**

Slide 3, titled, Both Deals Feature, becomes Slide 5 (Figure 2-83). PowerPoint automatically renumbers the slides.

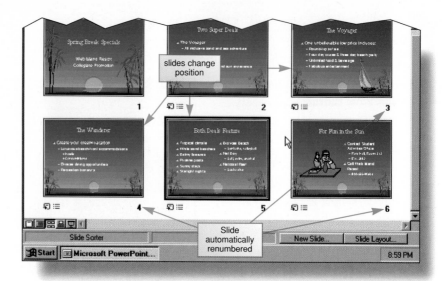

FIGURE 2-83

Copying a Slide

Occasionally you will want to copy a slide and then make changes to it. PowerPoint has a copy command that allows you to quickly duplicate a slide or any object on a slide. After you make a copy, you paste it elsewhere in your presentation. The next section explains how to copy and paste a slide in Slide Sorter view.

Steps To Copy a Slide in Slide Sorter View

1 **Right-click Slide 5, Both Deals Feature. When a shortcut menu displays, point to Copy (Figure 2-84).**

2 **Click Copy.**

A copy of Slide 5 is placed on the Clipboard. The shortcut menu no longer displays.

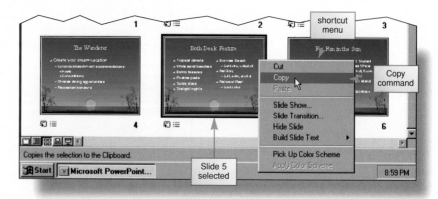

FIGURE 2-84

The Clipboard stores one copy at a time. If you copy another slide to the Clipboard, it replaces the first. To prevent the accidental loss of the contents of the Clipboard, immediately follow the Copy command with the Paste command. The next section explains how to paste the contents of the Clipboard into a presentation.

Pasting a Slide into a Presentation

Because a copy of Slide 5 is on the Clipboard, paste that copy into the presentation between Slide 2 and Slide 3. Perform the following steps to paste the contents of the Clipboard to the presentation.

 Steps To Paste a Slide into a Presentation

1 **Position the mouse pointer between Slide 2 and Slide 3 and right-click. When a shortcut menu displays, point to Paste.**

The insertion point displays after Slide 2 and in front of Slide 3 (Figure 2-85). A shortcut menu displays. To reduce the possibility that you may accidentally replace the contents of the Clipboard, only the Paste and Slide Show commands are available.

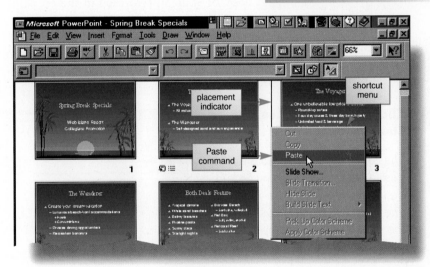

FIGURE 2-85

2 **Click Paste on the shortcut menu.**

A copy of Slide 5, titled Both Deals Feature, is inserted after Slide 2 (Figure 2-86). PowerPoint renumbers the slides. Both Slide 3 and Slide 6 are titled Both Deals Feature. The presence of the elevator in the scroll bar indicates more slides are in the presentation than can display in the Slide Sorter view window. The presentation now has seven slides because you added another slide to the presentation when you pasted a copy of the slide titled Both Deals Feature.

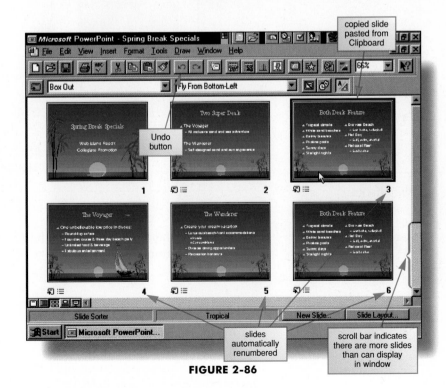

FIGURE 2-86

*Other***Ways**

1. On Standard toolbar click Paste button
2. On menu bar click Edit, click Paste
3. Press CTRL+V

Using the Undo Button to Reverse the Last Edit

PowerPoint has an Undo button to reverse the last edit task. For example, if you delete an object, but realize you still want it to display, click the Undo button and the object again displays. By default, PowerPoint stores twenty edits in a buffer. A **buffer** is an area used temporarily to store data. As soon as you perform another edit task, the new task is stored in the Undo buffer. You can change the number of edits stored by PowerPoint by clicking Tools on the menu bar, clicking Options, clicking the Advanced tab in the Options dialog box, and changing the number in the Maximum Number of Undos box.

Follow the step below to use the Undo button to reverse the pasting of the copy of Slide 5 performed in the previous step.

Steps To Use the Undo Button to Reverse the Last Edit

1 **Click the Undo button on the Standard toolbar.**

The copy of Slide 5, previously pasted between Slide 2 and Slide 3, no longer displays (Figure 2-87). The insertion point displays where the slide previously displayed. PowerPoint renumbers the slides.

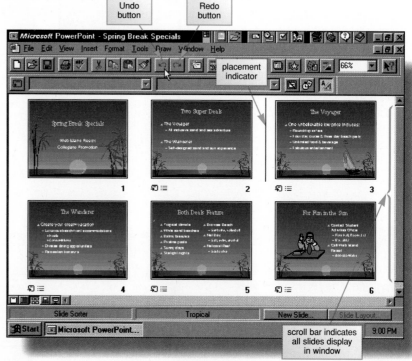

FIGURE 2-87

Located to the right of the Undo button is the Redo button. Clicking the Redo button returns the presentation to the state it was in prior to clicking the Undo button.

Saving and Closing PowerPoint

If you made any changes to your presentation since your last save, you should save it again by clicking the Save button. Close the presentation and PowerPoint by clicking the Close button on the title bar. For more details on closing PowerPoint, refer to page PP 1.37.

Project Summary

Project 2 introduced you to Outline view and clip art. You created a slide presentation in Outline view where you entered all the text in the form of an outline. You arranged the text using the Promote (Indent less) and Demote (Indent more) buttons. Once your outline was complete, you changed slide layouts and added clip art. You added slide transition effects and text build effects. Then you ran the slide show to demonstrate the animation effects, slide transition and text build. You learned how to print the presentation outline and slides in Outline view. Finally, you edited a presentation by rearranging slide order, copying and pasting, and reversing the last edit using the Undo button.

What You Should Know

Having completed this project, you now should be able to perform the following tasks:

- Add a Blank Line *(PP 2.20)*
- Add a Slide in Outline View *(PP 2.12)*
- Add Slide Transitions to a Slide Show *(PP 2.39)*
- Apply Text Build Effects to Bulleted Slides *(PP 2.43)*
- Change Slide Layout *(PP 2.23)*
- Change Slide Layout to Clip Art & Text *(PP 2.27)*
- Change Slide Order in Outline View *(PP 2.54)*
- Change Slide Order in Slide Sorter View *(PP 2.56)*
- Change the Size of Clip Art Using the Scale Command *(PP 2.33)*
- Change View to Outline View *(PP 2.8)*
- Change View to Slide Sorter View *(PP 2.19)*
- Copy a Slide in Slide Sorter View *(PP 2.58)*
- Create a Multi-level Slide in Outline View *(PP 2.13)*

- Create a Title Slide in Outline View *(PP 2.10)*
- Display All Text in Outline View *(PP 2.56)*
- Display Slide Titles in Outline View *(PP 2.53)*
- Insert Clip Art into a Clip Art Placeholder *(PP 2.28)*
- Insert Clip Art on a Slide without a Clip Art Placeholder *(PP 2.32)*
- Move Clip Art *(PP 2.33)*
- Paste a Slide into a Presentation *(PP 2.59)*
- Print an Outline *(PP 2.48)*
- Print Presentation Slides *(PP 2.50)*
- Run a Slide Show with Animation Effects *(PP 2.46)*
- Use the Notes and Handouts Sheet to Add Headers and Footers *(PP 2.36)*
- Use the Undo Button to Reverse the Last Edit *(PP 2.60)*

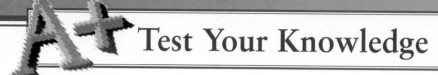

Test Your Knowledge

1 True/False

Instructions: Circle T if the statement is true or F if the statement is false.

T F 1. An outline is a summary of thoughts presented as headings and subheadings.

T F 2. Graphic objects, such as pictures, graphs, and tables, display in Outline view.

T F 3. In Outline view, the subtitle on the title slide displays on outline level one.

T F 4. The Demote (Indent more) button moves the selected paragraph up one level in the outline hierarchy each time you click the button.

T F 5. Clip art provides a quick way to add professional-looking graphic images to your presentation without creating the images yourself.

T F 6. The Scale command resizes clip art while maintaining its aspect ratio.

T F 7. PowerPoint automatically sizes clip art to fit a clip art placeholder.

T F 8. Slide view Zoom Control affects the size of text when printing an outline.

T F 9. Double-clicking a slide miniature in Slide Sorter view displays that slide in Outline view.

T F 10. Print slides from Outline view by clicking the Print button on the Standard toolbar.

2 Multiple Choice

Instructions: Circle the correct response.

1. Outline view provides a quick, easy way to _____.
   a. insert clip art
   b. change slide layout
   c. display slide miniatures
   d. create a presentation

2. To add a new slide to a presentation in Outline view, _____.
   a. click the New Slide button on the status bar
   b. click the Promote (Indent less) button until the insertion point displays at outline level one
   c. press CTRL+M
   d. all of the above

3. A presentation outline begins with a title on _____.
   a. outline level zero
   b. outline level two
   c. outline level one
   d. none of the above

4. Move a slide in Outline view by dragging the _____ to its new position.
   a. paragraph
   b. slide icon
   c. bullet
   d. none of the above

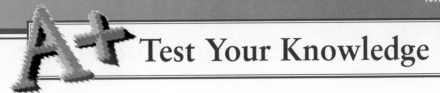

5. PowerPoint provides a(n) _____ button to reverse the latest edit task.
   a. Paste
   b. Undo
   c. Edit
   d. Copy

6. The presentation outline may be printed by selecting the Print command from the File menu when in _____.
   a. Notes Pages view
   b. Slide view
   c. Slide Sorter view
   d. all of the above

7. The animation effect that instructs PowerPoint to progressively disclose each bulleted paragraph during the running of a slide show is called _____.
   a. Slide Show
   b. Slide Transition
   c. Build Slide Transition
   d. Build Slide Text

8. The Scale command _____.
   a. is available in Outline view
   b. changes the size of a clip art image by a specific percentage
   c. changes the aspect ratio of the clip art image
   d. all of the above

9. Insert clip art on a slide that has a(n) _____.
   a. object placeholder
   b. clip art placeholder
   c. text placeholder
   d. all of the above

10. The horizontal placement indicator is useful for identifying the exact location to drop a slide when changing slide order in _____.
    a. Outline view
    b. Slide view
    c. Slide Sorter view
    d. all of the above

3 Understanding the Outlining View Window

Instructions: Arrows in Figure 2-88 point to the major components of a PowerPoint window in Outline view. Identify the various parts of the window in the space provided.

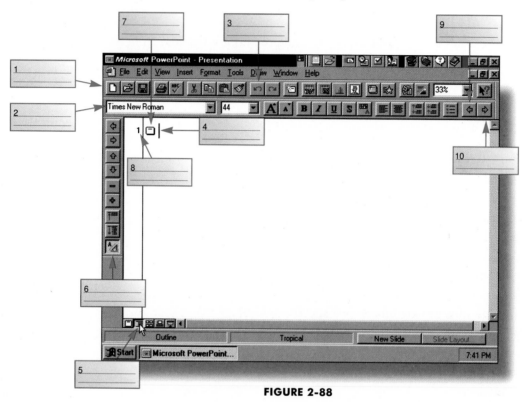

FIGURE 2-88

4 Understanding the Outlining Toolbar

Instructions: In Figure 2-89 below, arrows point to several of the buttons on the Outlining toolbar. In the space provided, briefly explain the purpose of each button.

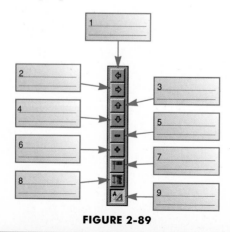

FIGURE 2-89

? Use Help

1 Learning More about PowerPoint

Instructions: Perform the following tasks using a computer.

1. If PowerPoint is not already started, start a new PowerPoint presentation and select any AutoLayout.
2. Double-click the Help button on the Standard toolbar to display the Help Topics: Microsoft PowerPoint dialog box.
3. Click the Index tab. Type templates in box 1 and then double-click templates in box 2. When the Topics Found dialog box displays, double-click Using Design Templates to give my presentation a consistent look. When the Microsoft PowerPoint window displays, read the information, right-click within the dialog box, and click Print Topic. When the Print dialog box displays, click the OK button. Click the Help Topics button to return to the Help Topics: Microsoft PowerPoint dialog box.
4. Type bullets in box 1 and then press the ENTER key. When the Topics Found dialog box displays, double-click Add, change, or remove a bullet. When the Microsoft PowerPoint window displays, read and print the information. Click Change the distance between the bullet and the text. When the Microsoft PowerPoint window displays, read and print the information. Click the Help Topics button to return to the Help Topics: Microsoft PowerPoint dialog box.
5. Type trouble in box 1 and then double-click troubleshooting bullets in box 2. When the Microsoft PowerPoint window displays, read and print the I can't select a bullet information. Click the Close button to exit Help. Submit the printouts to your instructor.

2 Expanding on the Basics

Instructions: Use PowerPoint online help to better understand the topics listed below. Begin each of the following by double-clicking the Help button on the Standard toolbar. If you can't print the help information, answer the question on a separate piece of paper.

1. When in Outline view, how do you change the color of a bullet for all slides in a presentation?
2. How do you prevent a bullet from displaying?
3. How do you change the bullet character from a dot to an open file folder?
4. How do you change the size of a bullet?
5. How do you add a period to the end of every paragraph in a list?
6. How do you replace one clip art picture in a slide with another picture?
7. How do you build a slide with a clip art image that appears to fly onto the slide?

Apply Your Knowledge

1 Intensifying a Presentation by Applying a Design Template, Changing Slide Layout, and Adding Clip Art.

Instructions: Start PowerPoint. Open the presentation Triathlon from the PowerPoint folder on the Student Floppy Disk that accompanies this book. Perform the following tasks to change the presentation to look like Figure 2-90. *Hint:* Use Help to solve this problem.

1. Apply the Soaring Design Template. Add the current date, slide number, and your name to the footer. Display the footer on all slides.

2. Change the Slide Master line spacing for the First Level bullet to 0.5-lines before each paragraph.

3. On Slide 1, insert one blank paragraph after the August 16, 1997 paragraph. Insert the runner clip art image shown in Figure 2-90 that has the description, Victory Performance. Drag the runner clip art image to align the left side of the dotted box under the letter l in the word Triathlon and to display the image of the runner in the middle of the light blue pathway as shown in Figure 2-90. Decrease font size of Sponsored by: to 24 points.

4. Go to Slide 3. Change the slide layout to 2 Column Text. Move the six female categories to the right column placeholder.

5. Go to Slide 4. Change the slide layout to Text & Clip Art. Insert the trophy clip art image shown in Figure 2-90 that has the description, Goal Success. Scale the trophy clip art image to 90%.

6. Go to Slide 5. Change the slide layout to Clip Art & Text. Insert the hourglass clip art image shown in Figure 2-90 that has the description, Patience Timeline. Scale the hourglass clip art image to 95%. Change the line spacing for the First Level bullets to 1 line before each paragraph.

7. Check the presentation for spelling errors.

8. Add the Strips Down-Right slide transition effect to all slides except the title slide.

9. Save the presentation on your data floppy disk using the filename, Two-State Triathlon.

10. Print the presentation in black and white.

11. Close PowerPoint.

Apply Your Knowledge

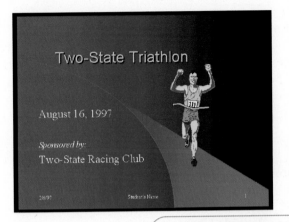

FIGURE 2-90

In the Lab

1 Adding Clip Art and Animation Effects to a Presentation Created in Outline View

Problem: You are a student in Psych 101. Your psychology professor assigns a research paper and requires you to present your findings during a five minute presentation. Your topic is having a positive attitude. To prepare for the presentation, you create the outline shown in Figure 2-91. You then use the outline to create the slide show shown in Figure 2-92. Because of your research findings, you create a unique closing slide. *Hint:* Use Help to solve this problem.

Instructions: Perform the following tasks:

1. Create a new presentation using the Cheers Design Template.

2. Using the outline shown in Figure 2-91, create the title slide shown in Figure 2-92. Use your name instead of the name Adam East. Increase the font size of your name to 36 points.

3. Using the outline in Figure 2-91, create the three bulleted list slides shown in Figure 2-92.

4. Change the slide layout on Slide 2 to Clip Art & Text. Using the clip art placeholder, insert the clip art shown in Figure 2-92 that has the description, Happy Joy Laugh. Increase the bulleted list font size to 36 points.

I.	Improving Your Attitude
	Adam East
	Psychology 101
II.	Positive Attitude Characteristics
A.	Cheerful
B.	Friendly
C.	Neat
D.	Courteous
E.	Thoughtful
F.	Considerate
III.	How to Improve Your Attitude
A.	Associate with positive people
B.	Speak well of others
C.	Isolate negative thoughts
D.	Treat others with respect
E.	Forgive and forge on
IV.	Anything is Possible with a Positive Attitude

FIGURE 2-91

5. Change the slide layout on Slide 3 to Text & Clip Art. Using the clip art placeholder, insert the clip art shown in Figure 2-92 that has the description, Consensus. Increase the bulleted list line spacing to 0.3-lines before each paragraph.

6. Drag the slide title on Slide 4 to the text placeholder. Change the case of Possible, Positive, and Attitude to lowercase letters. Increase the text font size to 66 points.

7. Add the slide number and your name to the slide footer. Display the footer on all slides except the title slide. Add your name to the outline header and your school's name to the outline footer.

8. Apply the Dissolve slide transition effect to all slides. Apply the Wipe Right text build effect to all First Level paragraphs on Slide 2 and Slide 3.

In the Lab

9. Run Style Checker to check spelling, visual clarity, case, and end punctuation. Ignore the Visual Clarity Error on Slide 4 in order to create this special effect. Correct any other errors identified by Style Checker.
10. Save the presentation on your data floppy disk using the filename, Improving Your Attitude.
11. Print the presentation outline.
12. Print the black and white presentation.
13. Close PowerPoint.

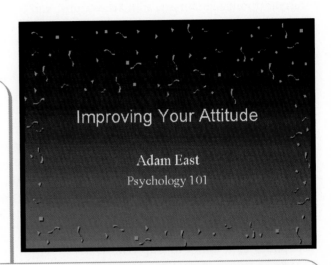

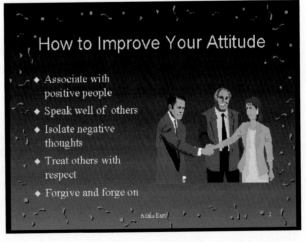

FIGURE 2-92

In the Lab

2 Using Clip Art, Slide Transition Effects, and Text Build Effects to Refine a Presentation

Problem: You are the Director of Career Development and Placement at Green Valley University. A local middle school principal has asked you to speak to his eighth grade students about career opportunities. You create the presentation using the outline shown in Figure 2-93. You then refine the presentation using clip art, slide transitions, and text build effects to create the slide show shown in Figure 2-94.

Instructions: Perform the following tasks.

1. Create a new presentation using the Splatter Design Template and the outline in Figure 2-93.

2. On the title slide, use your name instead of the name Ms. Janet Jakoby. Decrease the font size of the paragraphs, Presented by: and Green Valley University, to 24 points.

3. Change the slide layout on Slides 2, 3, and 4 to Clip Art & Text.

4. Use Figure 2-94 as a reference. On Slide 2, insert the clip art that has the description, Future Forecast. On Slide 3, insert the clip art that has the description, Surprise. On Slide 4, insert the clip art that has the description, Confusion Dilemma.

5. Add the slide number and your name to the slide footer. Display the footer on all slides except the title slide. Add your name to the outline header, and the name of the school, Green Valley University, to the outline footer.

I.	**The Future Is Yours** **What to Consider** **Presented by:** **Ms. Janet Jakoby** **Green Valley University**

II. What Is In Your Future?
    A. Education
        1. College
        2. Technical School
        3. Apprenticeship
    B. Work
        1. On the job training

III. Possible Career Choices
    A. Chef
    B. Engineer
    C. Entertainer
    D. Flight attendant
    E. Machinist
    F. Nurse
    G. Teacher
    H. Veterinarian

IV. How Do You Choose?
    A. Consider likes and dislikes
        1. Working with your hands
        2. Reading and writing
        3. Working with people
        4. Working with computers
        5. Working with animals

FIGURE 2-93

6. Check the presentation for spelling errors.
7. Apply the Uncover Right-Down slide transition effect to all slides. Apply the Split Vertical Out text build effect by 2nd level paragraphs to Slides 2 through 4.
8. Save the presentation on your data floppy disk using the filename, The Future is Yours.
9. Run the electronic slide show.
10. Print the presentation outline. Print the presentation slides without builds in black and white.
11. Close PowerPoint.

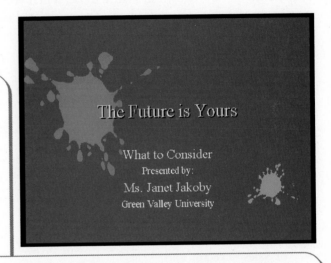

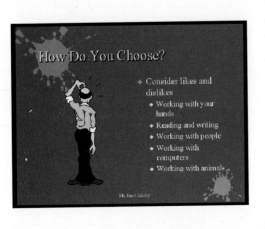

FIGURE 2-94

In the Lab

3 Animating a Slide Show

Problem: You are the sales director for Olympic Pharmaceuticals, a manufacturer of vitamins and other nutritional supplements. Experience tells you that sales are directly related to the quality of the sales presentation. Sales quotas are higher than last year and you want to make sure your sales staff understands the importance of practicing the delivery of a presentation. After much research, you prepare the outline shown in Figure 2-95. When you practice your presentation, you decide to add animation effects to the slide show. The completed slide show is shown in Figure 2-96 on pages PP 2.73 and PP 2.74.

Instructions: Perform the following tasks.

1. Create a new presentation using the Blue Green Design Template and the outline shown in Figure 2-95.

2. On the title slide, use your name instead of the name Les Deal. Decrease the font size of Presented by: to 20 points. Decrease the font size of Sales Director and Olympic Pharmaceuticals to 24 points.

3. On Slide 2, increase the font size of the Level One bullets to 36 points and Level Two bullets to 32 points. Increase the line spacing for Level Two bullets to 0.75-lines before each paragraph. Using Figure 2-96 as a reference, insert the clip art that has the description, Target. Scale the clip art to 120% and drag it to the lower-right corner of the slide.

4. On Slide 3, insert the clip art shown in Figure 2-96 that has the description, Happy Joy Laugh. Drag the clip art to the right side of the slide.

I. Polishing Your Presentation
    Presented by:
    Les Deal
    Sales Director
    Olympic Pharmaceuticals
II. Practice Makes Perfect
    A. Three key factors for a successful presentation
        1. Practice
        2. Practice
        3. Practice
III. Why Practice?
    A. Increase confidence
    B. Develop rhythm
        1. Pause for emphasis
    C. Improve articulation
        1. Vary pitch and inflection
    D. Establish timings
    E. Identify problems
IV. How To Practice
    A. Speak out loud
        1. Make a recording
            a) Video
            b) Audio
        2. Look into a mirror
        3. Find a live audience
            a) Friend or co-worker
            b) Group or team
    B. Go to delivery site
        1. Inspect equipment
            a) Audio-visual
            b) Lectern
        2. Check environment
            a) Noise
            b) Lighting
            c) Room temperature
V. Practice Makes Perfect

FIGURE 2-95

In the Lab

5. On Slide 4, change the slide layout to 2 Column Text. Drag the text into the right column placeholder so that your slide looks like Slide 4 in Figure 2-96. Increase the line spacing to 0.4-lines before each paragraph.

6. On Slide 5, change the slide layout to Object. Insert the clip art that has the description, Target.

7. Add the current date, slide number, and your name to the slide footer. Display the footer on all slides except the title slide. Include the current date and your name on the outline header. Include Olympic Pharmaceuticals and the page number on the outline footer.

8. Apply the Strips Up-Right slide transition effect to all slides. Apply the Fly From Bottom text build effect to Slides 2 through 4.

9. Animate the clip art on Slide 2 using the Fly From Left text build effect so it displays immediately after the slide title when you run the slide show.

10. Save the presentation on your data floppy disk using the filename, Polishing Your Presentation.

11. Print the presentation outline. Print the presentation slides without builds in black and white.

12. Close PowerPoint.

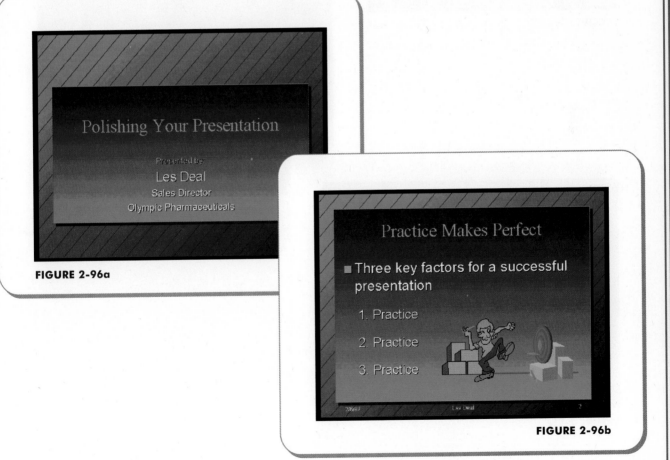

FIGURE 2-96a

FIGURE 2-96b

(continued)

In the Lab

Animating a Slide Show *(continued)*

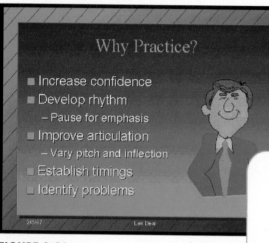

FIGURE 2-96c

FIGURE 2-96e

FIGURE 2-96d

Cases and Places

The difficulty of these case studies varies:

▶ Case studies preceded by a single half moon are the least difficult. You are asked to create the required document based on information that has already been placed in an organized form.

▶▶ Case studies preceded by two half moons are more difficult. You must organize the information presented before using it to create the required document.

▶▶▶ Case studies preceded by three half moons are the most difficult. You must decide on a specific topic, then obtain and organize the necessary information before using it to create the required document.

1 ▶ Easy Rider Limousine Service plans to show programs in local high schools to promote their prom night packages. The owner of the limousine service has outlined the presentation.

With this outline, the owner has asked you to develop slides for the presentation, using clip art and special effects to add interest. The owner also would like a printed outline that can be distributed to students at the presentation's conclusion. Use the concepts and techniques introduced in this project to create the presentation.

I. Easy Rider Limousine Service
   A. A special ride on your special night
   B. Safe transportation to and from the prom
II. Three Great Packages
   A. The Dance
      1. Secure transport at reasonable rates
   B. The Promenade
      1. Conveyance with an extra flair
   C. The Cotillion
      1. A once-in-a-lifetime adventure
III. The Dance
   A. Our basic package provides:
      1. Terra Nova minivan
      2. Courteous, licensed driver
IV. The Promenade
   A. Our most popular package offers:
      1. Jackson World Town Car
      2. Courteous, licensed driver in chauffer's cap
      3. Refreshments
         a. Soft drinks and hors d'oeuvres
      4. Eight-speaker CD sound system
V. The Cotillion
   A. Our aristocratic package presents:
      1. La'Hambra Classic Limousine
      2. Courteous, licensed driver in top hat and tails
      3. Refreshments
         a. Soft drinks and hors d'oeuvres
         b. Lobster salad or prime rib sandwiches
      4. Live music
         a. Concert violinist performs a selection of songs
VI. To experience a prom trip remembered forever
   A. Call Easy Rider Limousine
      1. 555-EASY
   B. Talk to Your High School Guidance Office

FIGURE 2-97

Cases and Places

2 ▶ Phrank Ishua, director of the Ishua Institute, has outlined a presentation plugging the institute that will be given at various adult education classes and club meetings.

With this outline, Professor Ishua has asked you to develop slides for the presentation, using clip art and special effects to add interest. The owner also would like a printed outline that can be distributed to attendees at the presentation's conclusion. Use the concepts and techniques introduced in this project to create the presentation.

I. The Ishua Institute
A. Expand physical and intellectual horizons
B. Revelations for people of all ages
II. The Institute's Programs
A. Training the body
    1. Practices that promote health and wellness
B. Educating the mind
    1. Activities that enhance spiritual awareness
III. Training the Body
A. Reach new levels of fitness through:
    1. Aerobic exercise sessions
    2. Interpretive dance
    3. Non-competitve games
    4. Rigorous isometric exercise
IV. Educating the Mind
A. Learn to think in new ways with:
    1. Consciousness-raising workshops
    2. Alternative thought classes
        a. Extraterrestrial metaphysics
        b. Dynamics of contemplation
        c. Animated introspection
    3. Incidental meditation

V. Each Stay at the Ishua Institue Includes:
A. Modest solitary accomodations
B. Three nourishing meals daily
    1. Nutritionally complete fare
    2. Organically grown vegetables
    3. Salubrious confections and desserts
C. Nightly self-examination
D. Evening enrichment
E. Use of extraordinary facilities
    1. Antediluvian mud baths
    2. Primeval hot springs
F. Tours of Reflection Lake
G. Lectures by guest instructors
VI. For a week, month, or year of rejuvenation
A. Call Phrank Ishua
    1. 800-555-0609
B. Write the Ishua Institute
    1. Mountbatten, WY 43721

FIGURE 2-98

Cases and Places

3 ▶▶ This summer you are working at Our Four Footed Friends, the largest pet shop in the community. The shop deals in all aspects of animal care: selling pets, providing supplies, and offering services. In addition to traditional pets, such as dogs and cats, the store peddles more unusual quadrupeds— raccoons, mongooses, wart hogs, etc. The shop stocks food, medicine, collars, grooming aids, and clothing for almost every type of pet. The store also makes pets presentable (clipping both fur and nails), supplies basic veterinary maintenance, and gives obedience classes. The workers are knowledge-able, helpful, and caring. The shop is open from 9:00 a.m. to 9:00 p.m. Monday through Saturday, and customers can call 555-PETS for information or appointments. As a break from cleaning cages, you have offered to develop a presentation marketing Our Four Footed Friends that will be exhibited at the county fair. Use the concepts and techniques introduced in this project to create the presentation. Enhance the presentation with clip art and special effects. Print an outline of the presentation that can be distributed to fair visitors.

4 ▶▶ As a well-known historian, you have been asked to develop a presentation for the International Association of Aliment Preservationists (IAAP) on the origin of canned food. You've decided to focus on two early 19th century innovators—Nicholas Appert, a wine bottler and cook, and Bryan Donkin, a one-time wallpaper manufacturer. Appert invented the canning process by placing foods in champagne bottles, corking the bottles, and then preserving the foods by boiling the bottles for varying lengths of time. The food, found to be in perfect condition after eight months, soon provisioned Napoleon's armies. Appert's methods were published in a book entitled L'art de conserver pendant plusieurs années toutes les substances animales or végétales. When Donkin's wallpaper business failed, he purchased the canning process patent and turned his idle machines to the manufacture of canned goods. Because of England's metal working industry, Donkin used tin cans (about twice the size of today's average can) instead of glass bottles. Although the canned food was lauded by the royal family and utilized on Arctic explorations, it was unpopular with the general public. The cans were expensive, in limited supply, and required a hammer and chisel to open. The trade was further crippled when some cans were found to have spoiled food. In the early 19th century the work of Louis Pasteur led to proper sterilization of food and the rebirth of the canning industry. Using this information, together with the concepts and techniques introduced in this project, create your presentation on the birth of the canned food. Enhance the presentation with clip art and special effects. Print an outline of the pre-sentation that can be distributed to members of the IAAP.

5 ▶▶▶ While at one time most American businesses manufactured a some type of product, today an increasing number of companies instead offer a service. To be successful, service-oriented businesses must be able to clearly and convincingly explain how they can benefit prospective clients. Visit a business that provides a service and learn all you can about the service and the people to whom it is being offered. Using this information, together with the concepts and techniques introduced in this project, prepare a presentation promoting the company's services. Enhance the presentation with clip art and special effects and print an outline of the presentation.

Cases and Places

6 ▶▶▶ Visuals not only add interest to a class, they also make the class more memorable. Studies show that people recall only about ½ of what they hear, but more than ¾ of what they see and hear. Think of a lecture you have heard recently that could be improved with the addition of graphic materials. Outline the lecture's content. Use your outline, together with the concepts and techniques introduced in this project, to prepare a presentation that would augment the lecture. Enhance the presentation with clip art and special effects and print the outline of the presentation. Make an appointment with the instructor who delivered the lecture, show your presentation, and solicit comments or suggestions. Using the instructor's critique, rework the presentation. Give a copy of the presentation to the instructor.

7 ▶▶▶ In addition to Microsoft PowerPoint, other presentation graphics software packages include Aldus Persuasion, Lotus Freelance Graphics, and SPC Harvard Graphics. Visit a software vendor and try one of these, or another presentation graphics package. Use current computer magazines or other resources to learn more about the package you tested. Based on what you have discovered, together with the concepts and techniques introduced in this project, prepare a presentation comparing the package you tested to Microsoft PowerPoint. Contrast the capabilities, strengths, weaknesses, ease of use, and cost of each package. End by noting which package you prefer and why. Enhance the presentation with clip art and special effects and print the outline of the presentation.

Linking an Excel Chart to a PowerPoint Presentation

INTEGRATION FEATURE

Case Perspective

Because of the success of the spring break promotion, Mr. Hayes, your boss at Web Island Resort, decides to run the promotion every year. You suggest that he include the results of the annual guest satisfaction survey to emphasize the quality of the resort. Mr. Hayes agrees and asks you to add a slide with a chart that illustrates the high percentage of guest satisfaction into the Spring Break Specials presentation. You contact the Marketing Department for the previous year's survey results. They e-mail you a file containing an Excel worksheet and a pie chart that summarizes the results of the 1996 guest satisfaction survey. Because you know Mr. Hayes is going to use this presentation every year and the chart will change each time the survey results change, you decide to link the pie chart to the presentation. Linking the chart ensures that you always present the most current survey results.

Introduction

This Integration Feature uses the Object Linking and Embedding (OLE) feature of Microsoft Office to insert an Excel chart into a PowerPoint slide. OLE allows you to incorporate parts of documents or entire documents from one application into another. In this section, you will open the Spring Break Specials presentation created in Project 2, insert a new slide, and link the pie chart shown in Figure 1 on the next page to a new slide shown in Figure 2 on the next page. The pie chart in Excel is called the **source document** and the Spring Break Specials presentation is the **container document.**

The three most common methods of copying objects between applications are copy and paste, copy and embed, and copy and link. This Integration Feature introduces a fourth method called insert object. Use the **insert object** method when you want to insert an entire file. The insert object method allows you to insert the source file without opening the source document. In this section, you use the insert object method to link the guest satisfaction survey file to the presentation.

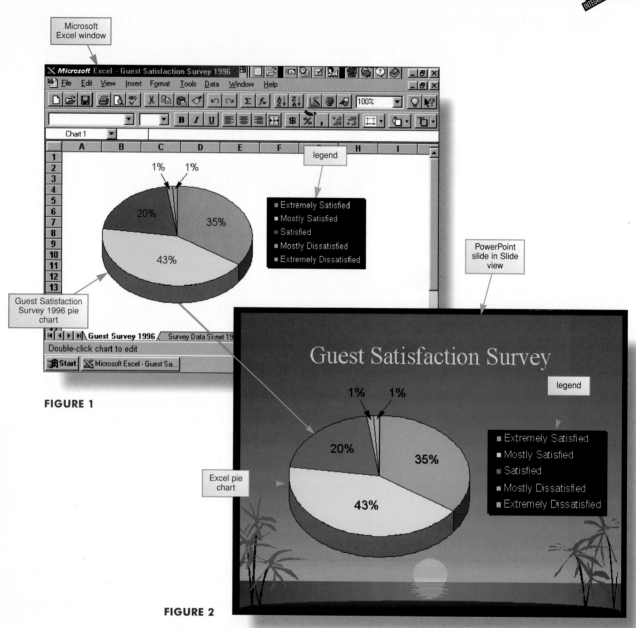

FIGURE 1

FIGURE 2

Opening an Existing Presentation and Saving It with a New Filename

To add a chart to the Spring Break Specials presentation created in Project 2, the first step is to open the presentation. To keep the original Spring Break Specials presentation intact, you save the presentation with a new name, Spring Break Specials Chart. You then add a new slide to the Spring Break Specials Chart presentation and link the chart to the guest satisfaction survey.

Before adding a new slide, first you must open the presentation. Perform the following steps to open the Spring Break Specials presentation.

TO OPEN AN EXISTING PRESENTATION

Step 1: Insert your data floppy disk that contains the Spring Break Specials presentation created in Project 2 into drive A.

Step 2: Click the Start button on the taskbar. Click Open Office Document. Click 3½ Floppy [A:] in the Look in drop-down list box.

Step 3: Double-click the presentation Spring Break Specials.

PowerPoint opens and displays the presentation in the view it was in when last saved. Project 2 last saved the presentation in Slide Sorter view.

To preserve the original Spring Break Specials presentation, you save the open presentation with a new filename. Then, you make the changes to the new presentation. Essentially you are making a duplicate copy of a file. Perform the following steps to save the Spring Break Specials presentation with a new filename using the Save As command.

TO SAVE A PRESENTATION WITH A NEW FILENAME

Step 1: Click File on the menu bar. Click Save As.

Step 2: Type Spring Break Specials Chart in the File name box.

Step 3: Click the Save button.

The Spring Break Specials presentation is saved with the filename Spring Break Specials Chart. The new filename displays in the title bar.

Creating a Chart Slide

Several steps are necessary to create a slide containing a linked Excel chart. You must insert a new slide with the Object AutoLayout between Slides 5 and 6. Next, you type the slide title. Finally, you link the Excel chart. The steps on the following pages explain how to create a slide containing a linked Excel chart.

Inserting a New Slide Between Two Slides

The slide containing the Excel chart displays after Slide 5, Both Deals Feature. Perform the following steps to insert a new slide with the Object AutoLayout.

TO INSERT A NEW SLIDE

Step 1: Click between Slide 5 and Slide 6.

Step 2: Click the New Slide button on the status bar.

Step 3: When the New Slide dialog box displays, scroll down to display the Object AutoLayout. Double-click the Object AutoLayout.

PowerPoint inserts a slide after Slide 5, numbers the new slide as Slide 6 and renumbers the original Slide 6 as Slide 7 (Figure 3 on the next page). Slide 7 is not visible in Figure 3.

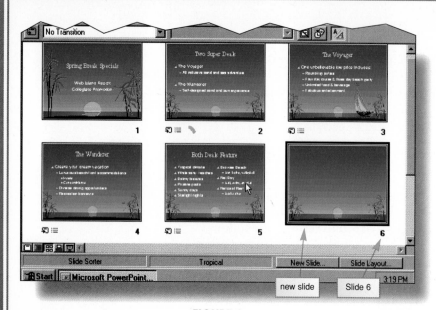

FIGURE 3

Typing a Slide Title

The next step is to type the slide title. The chart represents the results of the guest satisfaction survey. The slide title, therefore, is Guest Satisfaction Survey. Before typing, you must change views. Perform the following steps to type the slide title.

TO TYPE A SLIDE TITLE

Step 1: Double-click Slide 6 to display the slide in Slide view.

Step 2: Type Guest Satisfaction Survey in the title placeholder.

The slide title for Slide 6 displays.

More *About*
Linked Objects

When the name or location of a source document changes, you must reconnect the link. Click the linked object and then click Links on the Edit menu. In the Links box, click the source document, click the Change Source button, and select the renamed or moved source document. Click the Update Now button.

Linking an Excel Chart to a Presentation

The Web Island Resort Marketing Department created the chart from the results of the 1996 Guest Satisfaction Survey. You link the existing chart to Slide 6 so the chart always reflects the current survey results. The Student Floppy Disk contains the chart, Guest Satisfaction Survey 1996, in the PowerPoint folder. Perform the following steps to link the Excel chart to Slide 6 in the Spring Break Specials Chart presentation.

Steps To Link the Excel Chart to Slide 6

1 **Remove your data floppy disk from drive A. Insert the Student Floppy Disk that accompanies this book into drive A. Double-click the Object placeholder on Slide 6.**

The Insert Object dialog box displays (Figure 4). Create New is the default. AutoSketch is selected as the default object type. The default object type on your computer may be different depending on options selected during the installation of Microsoft Office 95.

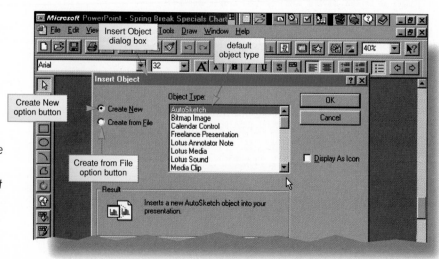

FIGURE 4

2 **Click Create from File. Point to the Browse button (Figure 5).**

3 **Click the Browse button. When the Browse dialog box displays, double-click the PowerPoint folder. Click Guest Satisfaction Survey.**

The Guest Satisfaction Survey file is highlighted in the Name box.

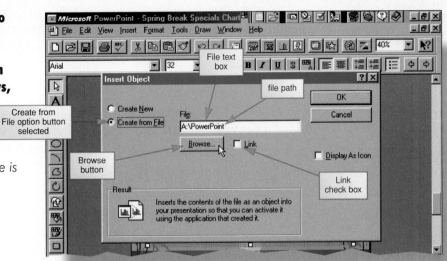

FIGURE 5

4 **Click the OK button. When the Insert Object dialog box displays, click Link.**

The File text box displays the path, or location, of the Excel chart (Figure 6). The check mark in the Link check box indicates the file listed in the File text box will be linked to the presentation.

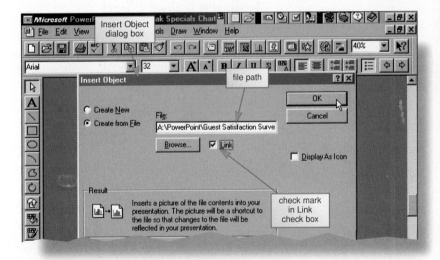

FIGURE 6

5 **Click the OK button.**

PowerPoint automatically sizes and displays the chart to fit the Object placeholder on Slide 6 (Figure 7). PowerPoint links the Customer Satisfaction Survey 1996 file, located on the Student Floppy Disk in drive A, to the presentation.

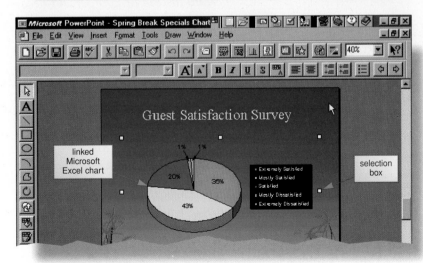

FIGURE 7

More *About* Linking Objects

If you deliver a presentation containing linked objects on a computer other than the one on which it was created, be certain to include a copy of the source files. The source files must be stored in the location as originally specified when you linked them to the presentation.

More *About* Linking Charts

To edit a linked chart, right-click the chart and then click Edit Worksheet Link. With the help of OLE, PowerPoint displays the chart without running Excel. When you finish your edits, select the worksheet to link to PowerPoint and then save the workbook. PowerPoint displays the top worksheet in the linked object.

When you click Create from File in the Insert Object dialog box, the dialog box changes (Figure 5 on page PPI 1.5). The Object Type list box no longer displays and is replaced by the File text box. Another change to the dialog box is the Link check box. The **Link** check box inserts the object as a linked object. A **linked object** maintains a connection to its source. If the original object changes, the linked object on the slide also changes. The linked object itself is stored in the source file where it was created, not in the presentation.

For example, the Excel chart you inserted into the slide is stored in the Guest Satisfaction Survey file on the Student Floppy Disk. Because you linked the Guest Satisfaction Survey file to the presentation, the Guest Satisfaction Survey file changes to display automatically on the chart on Slide 6. The PowerPoint presentation stores a representation of the original Guest Satisfaction Survey file and information about its location. Later, if you move or delete the source file, the link is broken and the object is not available.

Now that the linked pie chart displays on Slide 6, you want to improve the readability of the chart by increasing its size. The next section explains how to increase the size of the chart to best fit the slide.

Scaling a Linked Object

Increasing the size of the pie chart on Slide 6 improves the readability of the chart and improves the overall appearance of the slide. You increase the size of the pie chart using the Scale command on the Draw menu. Recall from Project 2 that the Scale command maintains the aspect ratio of the object. Perform the following steps to increase the size of the pie chart.

TO SCALE A LINKED OBJECT

Step 1: If not already selected, click the pie chart.
Step 2: Click Draw on the menu bar. Click Scale.
Step 3: Type 200 and then press the ENTER key. Click the OK button.

PowerPoint resizes the chart. PowerPoint limits the scaling percentage to the maximum height or width of a slide. The chart, therefore, is limited to 187.1 percent instead of 200 percent because of the width of the slide.

The changes to Slide 6 are complete. The next section explains how to save and print the linked presentation.

Saving and Printing a Linked Presentation

Perform the following steps to save and then print the Spring Break Specials Chart presentation.

TO SAVE AND PRINT A LINKED PRESENTATION

Step 1: Click the Save button on the Standard toolbar.
Step 2: Click the Print button on the Standard toolbar.

Summary

This Integration Feature introduced you to linking an object to a presentation. First, you opened an existing presentation, saved it with a new filename, and inserted a new slide onto which the chart from Excel was linked. Then, you performed the linking process. When you open a linked presentation, the object linking and embedding function of Microsoft Office 95 opens the presentation and updates the link to the chart file, providing the most current version of the chart. Next, you scaled the linked object to improve the readability. Finally, you saved and printed the linked presentation.

What You Should Know

Having completed this Integration Feature, you should be able to perform the following tasks:

▶ Insert a New Slide *(PPI 1.3)*
▶ Link the Excel Chart to Slide 6 *(PPI 1.4)*
▶ Open an Existing Presentation *(PPI 1.3)*
▶ Save a Presentation with a New Filename *(PPI 1.3)*

▶ Save and Print a Linked Presentation *(PPI 1.6)*
▶ Scale a Linked Object *(PPI 1.6)*
▶ Type a Slide Title *(PPI 1.4)*

In the Lab

1 Using Help

Instructions: Perform the following tasks using a computer.

1. Start PowerPoint. Double-click the Help button on the Standard toolbar to display the Help Topics: Microsoft PowerPoint dialog box.
2. Click the Answer Wizard tab. Type ole in box 1 and then click the Search button. In the Tell Me About section in box 2, double-click Exchanging information with other applications. Read the Help information about Sharing information, Linking information, and Embedding objects. Click the Help Topics button.
3. Click the Search button in the Help Topics: Microsoft PowerPoint dialog box. In the Tell Me About section, double-click Updating a link. Read and print the Help information. Click the Help Topics button.
4. Type linked objects in box 1 and then click the Search button. In the How Do I section, double-click Update a link manually. Read and print the Help information. Click the Help Topics button.
5. Click the Search button. In the How Do I section, double-click Reconnect links to renamed or moved documents. Read and print the Help information. Click the Close button.
6. Label each printout with your name. Submit the printouts to your instructor.

In the Lab

2 Linking a 3-D Bar Chart to a Slide

Problem: You are the general manager of Vacation Vistas travel agency applying for a short-term loan to cover operating expenses. The bank requests that you present an analysis of your first-quarter expenses, both budgeted and actual. Wanting to appear professional, you create a PowerPoint slide show. Knowing the bank will request this analysis again, you link the chart to the presentation.

Instructions: Perform the following tasks.
1. Open the document, Vacation Vistas, from the PowerPoint folder on the Student Floppy Disk that accompanies this book.
2. On Slide 2, link the file, Expense Comparison 1st Quarter 1997, located in the PowerPoint folder on the Student Floppy Disk. Scale the chart to 150%. Center the chart on the slide.
3. Add your name in the footer on all slides.
4. Save the presentation as Vacation Vistas Budget on your data floppy disk. Print the presentation in black and white. Close PowerPoint.

3 Linking Two-Column Charts to a Presentation

Problem: Your manager at Mega-Money Management, Mr. Richard Rich, conducts weekly investment seminars at which he displays Excel charts to illustrate his topic. He recently learned that you could create a PowerPoint presentation and link his Excel charts. He asks you to create a PowerPoint presentation and link two Excel charts to illustrate this week's topic, Risky Money.

Instructions: Perform the following tasks.
1. Open the document, Risk, from the PowerPoint folder on the Student Floppy Disk that accompanies this book.
2. Use the Large Object AutoLayout and insert a new slide after Slide 2. Link the file, Secured Fund, located in the PowerPoint folder on the Student Floppy Disk. Scale the chart to 170%. Center the chart on the slide.
3. Use the Large Object AutoLayout and insert a new slide after Slide 3. Link the file, Index 500 Stock, located in the PowerPoint folder on the Student Floppy Disk. Scale the chart to 170%. Center the chart on the slide.
4. Add your name in the footer on all slides.
5. Save the presentation as Risky Money on your data floppy disk. Print the presentation in black and white. Close PowerPoint.

▶ PROJECT THREE

EMBEDDED VISUALS

Objectives   PP 3.3
Creating Exciting Presentations Using
   Embedded Visuals   PP 3.6
Project Three – Microsoft Office 95 Workshop
   PP 3.6
Importing Outlines Created in Another
   Application   PP 3.8
Changing Presentation Design Templates
   PP 3.11
Saving the Presentation   PP 3.14
Creating a Custom Background   PP 3.14
Embedding an Organization Chart   PP 3.20
Creating a PowerPoint Clip Art Object
   PP 3.38
Grouping Objects   PP 3.48
Embedding a Picture into a Slide   PP 3.54
Creating a Blank Closing Slide   PP 3.60
Project Summary   PP 3.63
What You Should Know   PP 3.63
Test Your Knowledge   PP 3.64
Use Help   PP 3.68
Apply Your Knowledge   PP 3.69
In the Lab   PP 3.71
Cases and Places   PP 3.75

▶ PROJECT FOUR

CREATING A PRESENTATION CONTAINING INTERACTIVE OLE DOCUMENTS

Objectives   PP 4.1
Introduction   PP 4.4
Project Four — Customizing an Exisiting
   Presentation   PP 4.6
Selecting a New Color Scheme   PP 4.10
Creating a Logo   PP 4.15
Creating a Graphic Object with Text   PP 4.21
Scaling an Object   PP 4.30
Grouping Objects   PP 4.30
Adding an Object to the Slide
   Master   PP 4.31
Creating an Interactive Document   PP 4.36
Replacing a Picture   PP 4.45
Ending a Presenation with a Black
   Slide   PP 4.52
Hiding Slides   PP 4.54
Animating an Object   PP 4.55
Running a Slide Show with a Hidden Slide
   and Interactive Documents   PP 4.58
Project Summary   PP 4.59
What You Should Know   PP 4.59
Test Your Knowledge   PP 4.60
Use Help   PP 4.62
Apply Your Knowledge   PP 4.63
In the Lab   PP 4.64
Cases and Places   PP 4.71

▶ INTEGRATION FEATURE

EMBEDDING A WORD TABLE INTO A POWERPOINT PRESENTATION

Introduction   PPI 2.1
Adding a Word Table to a PowerPoint
   Presentation   PPI 2.2
Formatting a Word Table in PowerPoint
   PPI 2.6
Saving and Printing an Embedded Presentation
   PPI 2.7
Summary   PPI 2.8
In the Lab   PPI 2.8

Index   PP I.2

Microsoft *PowerPoint* 7

Windows 95

Embedded Visuals

Objectives:

You will have mastered the material in this project when you can:

▶ Import an outline created in Microsoft Word
▶ Create a slide background using a picture
▶ Embed an organization chart
▶ Scale objects
▶ Disassemble clip art
▶ Embed an Excel chart
▶ Group objects
▶ Layer objects
▶ Send objects to the bottom of a stack
▶ Resize objects
▶ Add a border to a picture
▶ Create a closing slide
▶ Print handouts

THE POWER OF PREPARATION

Death. Finacial problems. Heights. Flying. These are the things Americans fear most, right? Wrong! By a wide margin, fear of public speaking leads the list.

Although speakers are sometimes faced with obstacles of their own making, such as the renowned Greek orator, Demosthenes, who taught himself to speak more forcefully by talking with a mouthful of pebbles, the most daunting hurdle to overcome is usually nerves. Sometimes, this can be hilarious, such as the gaffe-prone minister in the movie, *Four Weddings and a Funeral*. For the person struck with an attack of the jitters, however, the situation is far from funny.

Accomplished speakers agree that the key to overcoming nervousness and hesitation when giving a public speech is *preparation*. One of the tools you can use to prepare your speech is a graphic presentation system such as Microsoft PowerPoint. Well-done

Preparat

visuals you create using PowerPoint provide a means of building confidence through practice, which can leave an audience thirsting for more.

And it's a good thing this help is available because leaders in business, government, science, religion, and virtually all vocations agree that the ability to present one's views clearly, while keeping the audience involved, is fundamental to a successful career. Though you probably spend more time in front of the lectern than behind it, your college years are a good time to get a leg up on the competition by learning how to develop power presentations on your PC.

Even with this help, however, it is not enough merely to present dry, static details. A presentation needs zest to grab and hold the attention of today's sophisticated audiences.

Among the many features in PowerPoint are the capabilities to add exciting visual effects and to build on a concept step by step. Including pictures, graphs, and tables in a slide series gives the audience a visual association to help assimilate the speaker's words. Going one step further, a variety of pleasing transitions can be achieved to make one image blend into the next, rather than making abrupt frame changes.

Build effects allow a concept to be presented one point at a time, preventing the visual overload that occurs if all the information is presented at once. In psychology, this is called "chunking," recognizing that the human brain absorbs information more readily in small bites than in one huge mass.

Demosthenes became one of the great orators in history, but with PowerPoint, who knows? He might have been king.

Project 3

Microsoft
PowerPoint 7

Windows 95

Embedded Visuals

Case Perspective

ETT, Executive Training Tours, specializes in software training. They tour the world conducting training workshops in resort locations and focus on corporate executives who need training in word processing, spreadsheet, database, and presentation graphics applications. ETT needs a presentation for their Microsoft Office 95 Workshop in Maui, Hawaii.

The workshop organizing team created an outline using Microsoft Word. They used this outline to develop their advertisements and sales literature. You develop the orientation session presentation from the existing Word outline. You then enhance the presentation by creating a custom background, embedding an organization chart, embedding an Excel chart, and embedding a photograph.

Create Exciting Presentations Using Embedded Visuals

Bulleted lists and simple graphics are the starting point for most presentations; but they can become boring. Advanced PowerPoint users want exciting presentations—something to impress their audience. With PowerPoint, it is easy to develop impressive presentations by creating a custom background, embedding organization charts, creating new graphics by combining objects, and inserting pictures.

One problem you may experience when developing a presentation is finding the proper graphic to convey your message. One way to overcome this obstacle is to create a graphic by combining multiple pictures from the Microsoft ClipArt Gallery. Another solution is to modify clip art or combine clip art and an embedded object, thereby creating the graphic that best conveys your message. Because PowerPoint Design Templates offer a limited number of slide backgrounds, PowerPoint allows you to create your own background using a picture or clip art. This project introduces several techniques to make your presentations more exciting.

Project Three – Microsoft Office 95 Workshop

Project 3 expands on PowerPoint's basic presentation features by importing existing files and embedding objects. This project creates a presentation that is used in the orientation session of the Microsoft Office 95 Workshop. The seminar provides intense training sessions for Microsoft Office 95 Professional application software. The project begins by building the presentation from an outline created in Microsoft Word and saved as a Rich Text Format (RTF) file. Then several objects are inserted to customize the presentation. These objects include pictures, an Excel chart, and an organization chart.

Slide Preparation Steps

The preparation steps summarize how the slide presentation shown in Figure 3-1 will be developed in Project 3. The following tasks will be completed in this project.

1. Start PowerPoint.
2. Import the Office Workshop outline from the Student Floppy Disk that accompanies this book.
3. Apply a Design Template.
4. Save the presentation as Office 95 Workshop.
5. Insert a picture to create a slide background (see Figure 3-1a).
6. Embed an organization chart on Slide 2 (see Figure 3-1b).
7. Embed an Excel chart in a clip art picture on Slide 3 (see Figure 3-1c).
8. Insert a picture in Slide 4.
9. Add a border to the picture in Slide 4 (see Figure 3-1d).
10. Create a closing slide (see Figure 3-1e).
11. Apply Slide Transition and Text Build effects.
12. Save the presentation again.
13. Print handouts.
14. Close PowerPoint.

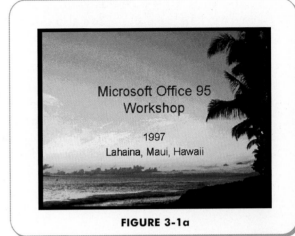

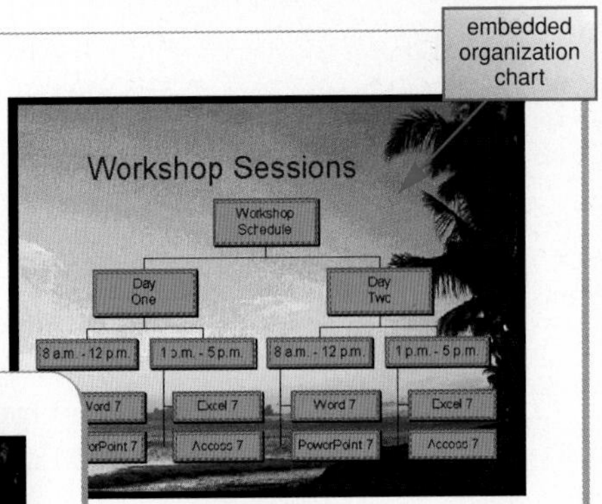

FIGURE 3-1a

FIGURE 3-1b

FIGURE 3-1c

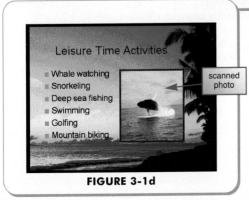

FIGURE 3-1d

FIGURE 3-1e

Importing Outlines Created in Another Application

Someday, you may be asked to present the findings of a research paper. Instead of typing the presentation outline, you can import the outline from the research paper. If you did not create an outline for the research paper, you can create it by first saving the research paper document as an RTF file, removing all text except topic headings, and then saving the RTF file again. Once the research paper outline is saved as an RTF file, you can import the outline into PowerPoint.

You also can create a presentation by opening an outline created in Microsoft Word or another word processor. The advantage of using an outline saved as a Microsoft Word document or as an RTF file is the text attributes and outline heading levels are maintained. Documents saved as plain text files (TXT) can be opened in PowerPoint but do not maintain text attributes and outline heading levels. Consequently, each paragraph becomes a slide title.

To create a presentation using an existing outline, select All Outlines from the Files of type box in the File Open dialog box. When you select All Outlines, PowerPoint displays a list of outlines. Next, you select the file that contains the outline. PowerPoint then creates a presentation using your outline. Each major heading in your outline becomes a slide title and subheadings become a bulleted list.

Opening an Existing Outline Created in Another Application

After starting PowerPoint, the first step in this project is to open an outline created in Microsoft Word. PowerPoint can produce slides from an outline created in Word or another word processor if the outline was saved in a format that PowerPoint can recognize. The outline created by the workshop organizing team was saved as an RTF file.

Opening an outline into PowerPoint requires two steps. First, you must tell PowerPoint you are opening an existing presentation. Then, in order to open the outline, you need to select the proper file type from the Files of type box in the File Open dialog box. The following steps explain how to open an outline created in Microsoft Word.

More *About*
Presentation Design

When designing a presentation create your conclusion, or closing, first. Then, design the rest of the presentation to reach the conclusion. This causes you to focus on the objective of the presentation.

Note: The Student Floppy Disk that accompanies this book contains a PowerPoint folder with two executable files that include compressed versions of the files for Projects 3 and 4 of PowerPoint. Some of these files are required if you plan to step through the PowerPoint projects on a PC. The other files are required for the exercises at the end of the projects. It is recommended that you copy the executable file for a project to a blank floppy disk and then expand it. The file required for the Integration Feature following Project 4 is part of the executable file for Project 4. The paragraph below explains how to expand the files for Project 3. To expand the files for Project 4, replace Project3 with Project4.

To expand the executable file for Project 3, do the following: (1) insert the Student Floppy Disk in drive A; (2) start Explorer and, if necessary, click the Restore button so that part of the desktop displays; (3) click the plus sign to the left of the 3½ Floppy [A:] icon in the All Folders side of the window and then click the PowerPoint icon; (4) right-drag Project3 on to the desktop and click Copy Here on the shortcut menu; (5) insert a blank floppy disk in drive A; (6) right-drag Project3 from the desktop on to the 3½ Floppy [A:] icon in the All Folders side of the window and then click Move Here on the shortcut menu; (7) double-click Project3 in the Contents of '3½ Floppy [A:]' side of the window and then click the Proceed button when the PowerPoint 7 Project 3 Student Files dialog box displays (do not change the folder location unless installing to a hard disk); (8) right-click Project3 and click Delete on the shortcut menu, and then click the Yes button in the Confirm File Delete dialog box; (9) clearly label the newly created floppy disk as PowerPoint 7 Project 3 Student Files.

 **To Open an Outline**

1 **Insert the floppy disk with the Project 3 files that accompanies this book into drive A. Click the Start button. When the Windows 95 Start menu displays, point to the Programs submenu. When the Programs submenu displays, point to Microsoft PowerPoint.**

The Windows 95 Start menu displays the names of several programs. The mouse pointer points to Microsoft PowerPoint (Figure 3-2).

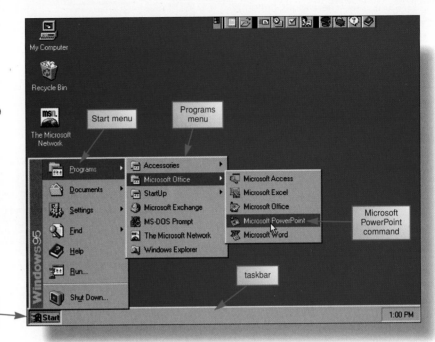

FIGURE 3-2

2 **Click Microsoft PowerPoint. When the PowerPoint startup dialog box displays, click Open an Existing Presentation. Then point to the OK button.**

The PowerPoint startup dialog box displays (Figure 3-3). The Open an Existing Presentation option button is selected.

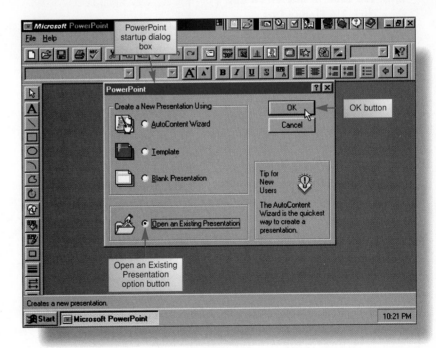

FIGURE 3-3

3 **Click the OK button.**

The File Open dialog box displays (Figure 3-4). The Details button is recessed. If your Details button is not recessed, click it. The current folder is My Documents. The current file type is Presentations as displayed in the Files of type drop-down list box.

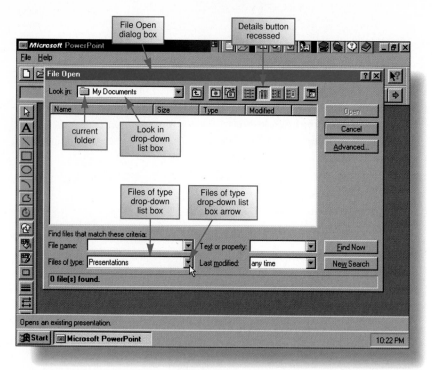

FIGURE 3-4

4 **Click the Look in box arrow and then click 3½ Floppy [A:]. Double-click the PowerPoint folder in the Name list box. Click the Files of type box arrow and then point to All Outlines.**

A drop-down list displays the types of files that PowerPoint can open (Figure 3-5). Your list may be different depending on the software installed on your computer. The Open button is dimmed because no files are selected in the File name box.

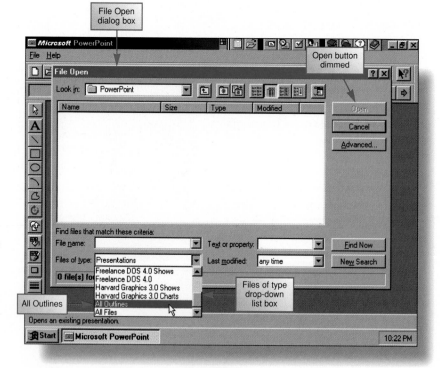

FIGURE 3-5

5 **Click All Outlines. Then double-click Office Workshop in the File name list box.**

PowerPoint opens Office Workshop and displays it in Outline view (Figure 3-6). The title on Slide 1 is highlighted. The outline text displays bulleted, indicating the slide layout is Bulleted List. The position of the elevator in the scroll bar indicates there is more outline text than can display in the Outline view window. The current Design Template is Default Design as identified on the status bar.

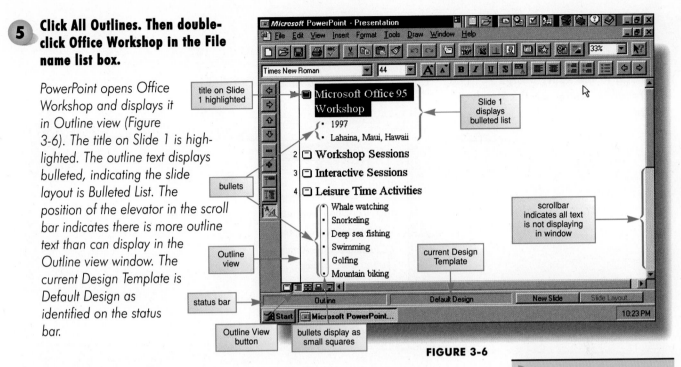

FIGURE 3-6

When opening a file created in another presentation graphics program, such as Harvard Graphics or Aldus Persuasion, PowerPoint picks up the outline structure from the styles used in the file (heading level one becomes a title, heading level two becomes the first level of text, and so on). If the file does not contain heading styles, PowerPoint uses paragraph indents to create the outline. For **plain text files**, which are files saved without formatting, PowerPoint uses the tabs at the beginning of paragraphs to define the outline structure. Imported outlines can have up to nine outline levels, whereas PowerPoint outlines have only six (one for titles and five for text). When you import an outline, all text in outline levels six through nine is treated as outline level six.

Other Ways

1. Click Start button, click Open Office Document, click All Files in Files of type box
2. On Office toolbar click Open a Document button, click All Files in Files of type box
3. On PowerPoint Standard toolbar click Open button, click All Outlines in Files of type box
4. On PowerPoint File menu click Open, click All Outlines in Files of type box

Changing Presentation Design Templates

Recall that Design Templates format the look of your presentation. You can change the Design Template any time you wish to change the appearance of your presentation, not just when you create a new presentation. The current Design Template is Default Design. You wish to apply the Tatami Design Template because it compliments the custom slide background you will create later in this project.

Perform the steps on the next page to change Design Templates.

Steps To Change Design Templates

1 **Point to the Apply Design Template button on the Standard toolbar (Figure 3-7).**

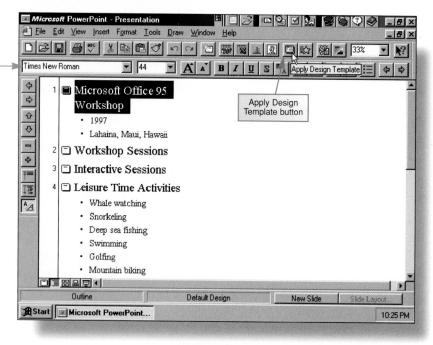

FIGURE 3-7

2 **Click the Apply Design Template button. Click the Preview button if it is not already recessed.**

The Apply Design Template dialog box displays (Figure 3-8). The Preview button is recessed. Azure, the first Design Template in the Name list box, is selected. A sample of the selected Design Template displays in the preview area.

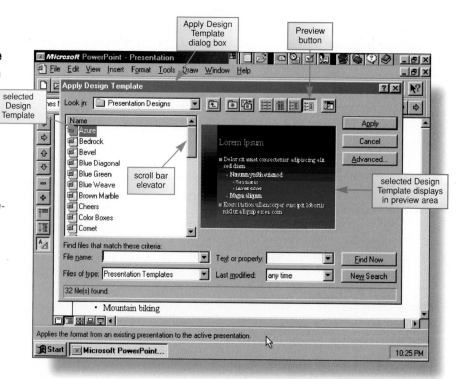

FIGURE 3-8

3 Drag the scroll bar elevator in the Name list box until Tatami displays. Then click Tatami.

Tatami is highlighted in the Name list box and a preview of the Tatami Design Template displays in the preview area (Figure 3-9).

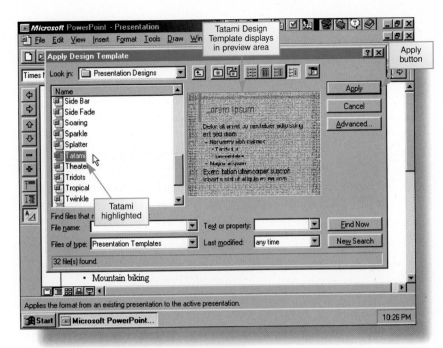

FIGURE 3-9

4 Click the Apply button.

PowerPoint applies the Tatami Design Template as indicated by the change to the font name and bullet (Figure 3-10). The font size remains the same.

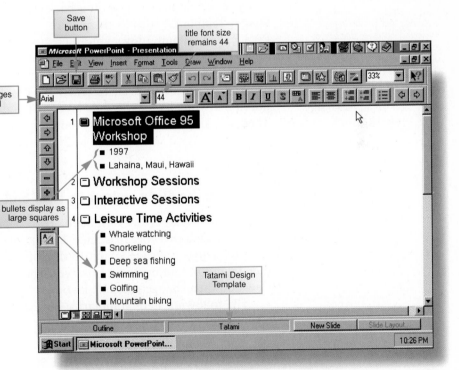

FIGURE 3-10

Recall that slide attributes change when you select a different Design Template. The Tatami Design Template format determines the slide attributes of the Slide Master and the Title Master. For example, when you compare Figure 3-6 on page PP 3.11 to Figure 3-10, you see that the font changed from Times New Roman to Arial and the bullets changed from small squares to large squares.

Other Ways

1. Double-click name of current Design Template on status bar

2. On Format menu click Apply Design Template

3. Press ALT+O, press M

Saving the Presentation

Because you created a presentation from an RTF file and changed Design Templates, you now should save your presentation. The following steps summarize how to save a presentation.

TO SAVE A PRESENTATION

Step 1: Click the Save button on the Standard toolbar.
Step 2: Type Office 95 Workshop in the File name box.
Step 3: Click the Save button.

The presentation is saved with the filename, Office 95 Workshop. The presentation title, Office 95 Workshop, displays in the title bar, instead of the default, Presentation.

Creating a Custom Background

PowerPoint has thirty-two Design Templates in the Presentation Designs folder. However, sometimes you want a background that is not found in one of the Design Templates, such as the picture of the ocean bay in Figure 3-1 on page PP 3.7. PowerPoint allows you to create that background by inserting a picture. PowerPoint also allows you to customize the background color, shading, pattern, and texture.

You perform two tasks to create the customized background for this presentation. First, you change the slide layout of Slide 1 to the Title Slide AutoLayout. Then, you create the slide background by inserting a picture of an ocean bay.

The next two sections explain how to create a slide background using a picture.

Changing the Slide Layout to Title Slide

When you import an outline to create a presentation, PowerPoint assumes the text is bulleted text. Because Slide 1 is the title slide for this presentation, you want to change the slide layout to the Title Slide layout. You cannot change the slide layout in Outline view, however. Therefore, you want to change to Slide view and then change the slide layout.

The following steps summarize how to change to Slide view and change the layout of Slide 1 to the Title Slide layout.

TO CHANGE SLIDE LAYOUT TO TITLE SLIDE

Step 1: Click the Slide View button.
Step 2: Click the Slide Layout button on the status bar.
Step 3: Double-click Title Slide, the first layout in the Slide Layout dialog box.

Slide 1 displays in Slide view with the Tatami Design Template (Figure 3-11).

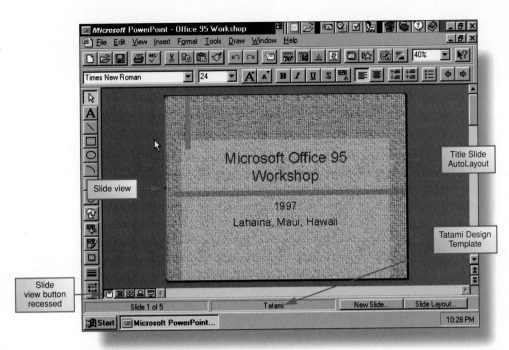

FIGURE 3-11

PowerPoint provides two alternative methods to double-clicking the slide layout in Step 3 above. The first alternative is to type the layout number of one of the twenty-four slide layouts and press the ENTER key. The second alternative is to type the layout number and click the Apply button. PowerPoint interprets the number you type as the corresponding slide layout and applies it when you press the ENTER key (alternative one) or click the Apply button (alternative two). For example, the Title Slide layout is layout number one. When the Slide Layout dialog box displays, type 1 and press the ENTER key instead of double-clicking the Title Slide layout.

Inserting a Picture to Create a Custom Background

The next step in creating the Microsoft Office 95 Workshop presentation is to insert a picture to create a custom background. In PowerPoint, a **picture** is any graphic created in another application. Pictures usually are saved in one of two **graphic formats**: bit-map or vector.

A **bit-mapped graphic** is a piece of art that has been stored as a pattern of dots called pixels. A **pixel,** short for **picture element,** is one dot in a grid. A picture that is produced on the computer screen or on paper by a printer is composed of thousands of these dots. Just as a bit is the smallest unit of information a computer can process, a pixel is the smallest element that displays or print hardware and software can manipulate in creating letters, numbers, or graphics. For example, the letter A shown in Figure 3-12 is actually made up of a pattern of pixels in a grid.

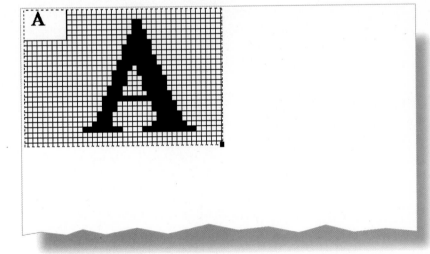

FIGURE 3-12

Bit-mapped graphics are created in paint programs such as Microsoft Windows Paintbrush. Bit-mapped graphics also can be produced from **digitizing** art, pictures, or photographs by passing the artwork through a scanner. A **scanner** is a hardware device that converts lines and shading into combinations of the binary digits, 0 and 1, by sensing different intensities of light and dark. The scanner shines a beam of light on the picture being scanned. The beam passes back and forth across the picture sending a digitized signal to the computer's memory. A **digitized signal** is the conversion of input, such as the lines in a drawing, into a series of discrete units represented by the binary digits, 0 and 1. **Scanned pictures** are bit-mapped pictures and have jagged edges (see Figure 3-12 on the previous page). The jagged edges are caused by the individual pixels that create the picture. Bit-mapped graphics also are known as **raster images**. Additionally, bit-mapped files cannot be disassembled into smaller object groups.

The other graphic format in which pictures are stored is vector graphics. A **vector graphic** is a piece of art that has been created by a drawing program such as CorelDRAW! or AutoCAD. Vector graphic objects are created as a collection of lines instead of patterns of individual dots (pixels), as are bit-mapped graphics. Vector graphic files store data as picture descriptions, or calculations. These files describe a picture mathematically as a set of instructions for creating the objects in the picture. These mathematical descriptions determine the position, length, and direction in which the lines are to be drawn. These calculations allow the drawing program to recreate the picture on-screen as necessary. Because vector graphic objects are described mathematically, they also can be layered, rotated, and magnified relatively easily. Vector graphics also are known as object-oriented pictures. Clip art pictures in the Microsoft ClipArt Gallery that have the file extension of .PCS or .WMF are examples of vector files. Vector files can be disassembled and manipulated by their component objects.

PowerPoint allows you to insert either bit-mapped or vector files because it uses **graphic filters** to convert the various graphic formats into a format PowerPoint can use. These filters are installed with the initial PowerPoint installation or can be added later by running the Setup program.

Because the Microsoft Office 95 Workshop presentation is given at the first organized session of the seminar, you want to stress the relaxed learning atmosphere by emphasizing the beaches surrounding Maui. To create the desired effect, you insert a picture of an ocean bay to cover the Tatami Design Template. Additionally, you omit the background graphics on the Slide Master and Title Master to prevent the graphic attributes from displaying on the picture.

Perform the following steps to create a custom background.

More *About*
Presentation Design

Use pictures and graphics to convey a message. An audience can scan a graphic faster than text, thereby allowing the audience to focus on what the presenter is saying.

Steps To Insert a Picture to Create a Custom Background

1 Right-click anywhere on Slide 1 except the title object or sub-title object. When a shortcut menu displays, point to Custom Background (Figure 3-13).

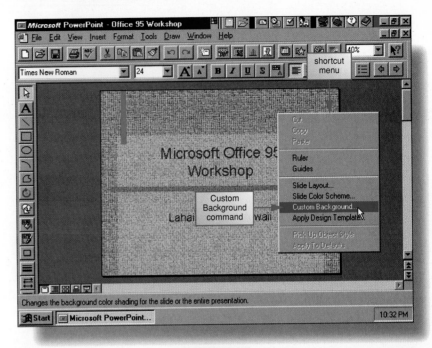

FIGURE 3-13

2 Click Custom Background on the shortcut menu. When the Custom Background dialog box displays, point to the down arrow in the Background Fill area.

The Custom Background dialog box displays (Figure 3-14).

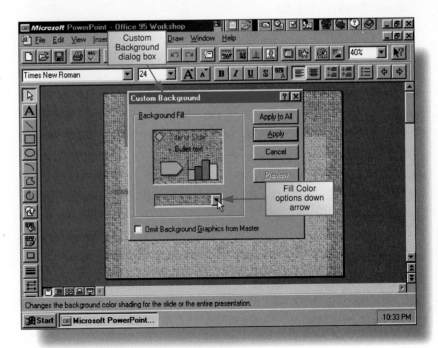

FIGURE 3-14

3 **Click the down arrow. When the Fill Color menu displays, point to Picture.**

The Fill Color menu displays options for filling the slide background (Figure 3-15). The current background fill is Automatic, which is the Tatami Design Template default.

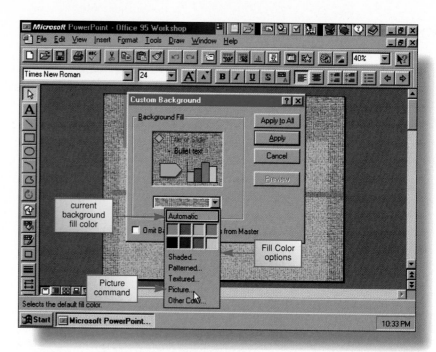

FIGURE 3-15

4 **Click Picture on the Fill Color menu. Double-click the PowerPoint folder in the Name list box. Then, click the Preview button if it is not already recessed.**

The Insert Picture dialog box displays (Figure 3-16). The Preview button is recessed. The selected file is Bay View and it displays in the Preview box.

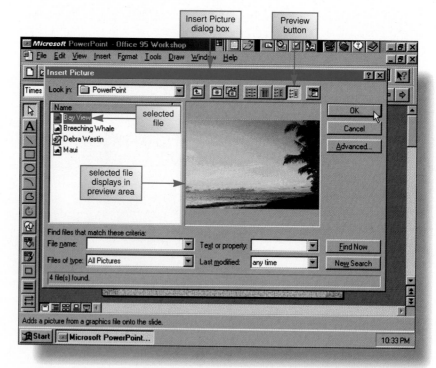

FIGURE 3-16

5 Double-click Bay View in the Name list box. When the Custom Background dialog box displays, click Omit Background Graphics from Master. Then point to the Apply to All button.

The Custom Background dialog box displays the Bay View picture in the Background Fill area (Figure 3-17). A check mark displays in the Omit Background Graphics from Master check box.

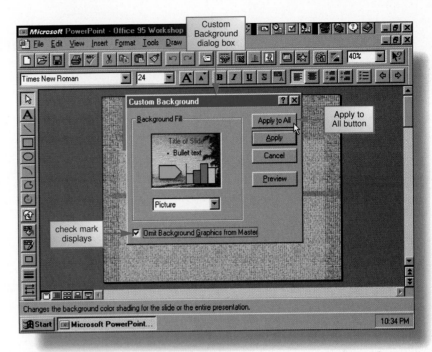

FIGURE 3-17

6 Click the Apply to All button in the dialog box.

Slide 1 displays the Bay View picture as the slide background (Figure 3-18). Although not shown in this figure, the Bay View picture is the background for all slides in the presentation. The Tatami Design Template text attributes display on the slide.

FIGURE 3-18

When you customize the background, the Design Template text attributes remain the same, but the slide background changes. For example, inserting the Bay View picture for the slide background changed the appearance of the slide background but maintained the text attributes of the Tatami Design Template.

*Other***Ways**

1. On Format menu click Custom Background
2. Press ALT+O, press G

Embedding an Organization Chart

Slide 2 contains a chart that elaborates on the daily schedule for the Microsoft Office workshop as shown in Figure 3-19. This type of chart is called an organization chart. An **organization chart** is a hierarchical collection of elements depicting various functions or responsibilities that contribute to an organization or to a collective function. Typically, an organization chart is used to show the structure of people or departments within an organization, hence the name, organization chart.

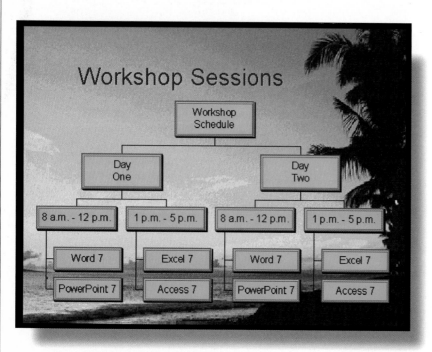

FIGURE 3-19

Figure 3-20 illustrates how a company uses an organization chart to describe the relationships between the company's departments. In the information sciences, organization charts are often used to show the decomposition of a process or program. When used in this manner, the chart is called a **hierarchy chart**.

PowerPoint contains a supplementary application called **Microsoft Organization Chart** that allows you to create an organization chart. When you open Microsoft Organization Chart, its menus, buttons, and tools are available to you directly on the PowerPoint screen. Microsoft Organization Chart is an object linking and embedding (OLE) application. The organization chart you create for Slide 2 (see Figure 3-19) is an embedded object because it is created in an application other than PowerPoint.

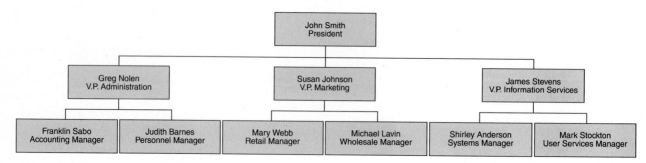

FIGURE 3-20

Creating an organization chart requires several steps. First, you display the slide that will contain the organization chart in Slide view and change the slide layout to the organization chart layout. Then, you open the Microsoft Organization Chart application. Finally, you enter and format the contents of the boxes in the organization chart.

Perform the steps on the following pages to create the organization chart for this project.

Changing Slide Layouts

Because you imported the presentation outline, the current slide layout is a bulleted list. Before you open Microsoft Organization Chart, you need to display Slide 2 and change the slide layout to the Organization Chart layout.

TO DISPLAY THE NEXT SLIDE AND CHANGE THE SLIDE LAYOUT

Step 1: Click the Next Slide button.
Step 2: Click the Slide Layout button.
Step 3: When the Slide Layout dialog box displays, double-click the seventh layout, Organization Chart.

Slide 2 displays the organization chart placeholder and the slide title (Figure 3-21).

FIGURE 3-21

Slide 2 now displays the placeholder for the organization chart. The next section explains how to open the Microsoft Organization Chart application.

Opening the Organization Chart Application

In order to create the organization chart on Slide 2, you must first open the organization chart application, Microsoft Organization Chart, which is included within PowerPoint. Recall that this supplementary application opens and the menus, buttons, and tools in the organization chart application are made available on the PowerPoint screen. Once open, Organization Chart displays a sample four-box organization chart in a work area in the middle of the PowerPoint screen, as explained in the steps on the next pages.

Steps To Open Organization Chart

1 **Double-click the organization chart placeholder in the middle of Slide 2.**

Organization Chart displays the Microsoft Organization Chart - [Object in Office 95 Workshop] window in a work area on the PowerPoint screen (Figure 3-22). Notice the sample organization chart is composed of four boxes connected by lines. When Organization Chart opens, the first line of the top box is automatically selected. Depending on the version of Organization Chart installed on your computer, the display on the screen may vary slightly.

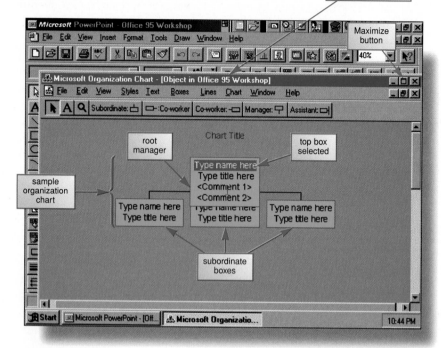

FIGURE 3-22

Organization Chart displays a sample organization chart to help you create your organization chart. The sample is composed of one **manager box**, located at the top of the chart, and three **subordinate boxes**. A manager box is one that has one or more subordinates. The topmost manager is called the **root manager**. A subordinate box is located at a level lower than its manager. A subordinate box has only one manager. When a lower-level subordinate box is added to a higher-level subordinate box, the higher-level subordinate box becomes the manager of the lower-level subordinate box.

Maximizing the Organization Chart Window

When Microsoft Organization Chart opens, the Organization Chart window is not maximized. Maximizing the Organization Chart window makes it easier to create your organization chart because it displays a larger area in which to view the chart.

TO MAXIMIZE THE ORGANIZATION CHART WINDOW

Step 1: Click the Maximize button in the upper right corner of the Organization Chart window.

The Organization Chart window fills the desktop (Figure 3-23). Clicking the Restore button returns the Organization Chart window to its original size.

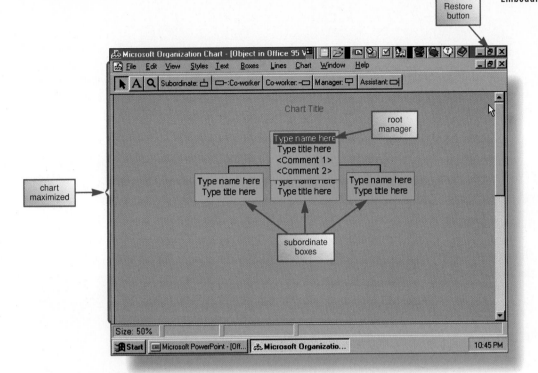

FIGURE 3-23

Creating the Title for the Root Manager Box

In this presentation, the organization chart is used to communicate the daily workshop schedule. The topmost box, the root manager, identifies the purpose of this organization chart: Workshop Schedule. Recall that when Organization Chart opened, the first line in the root manager box was selected. The following step explains how to create the title for the root manager box.

Steps To Create the Title for the Root Manager Box

1 **Type** Workshop **and then press the ENTER key. Type** Schedule **on the second line.**

Workshop Schedule displays in the root manager box (Figure 3-24). Comment 1 and Comment 2 prompts display in brackets under the root manager box title.

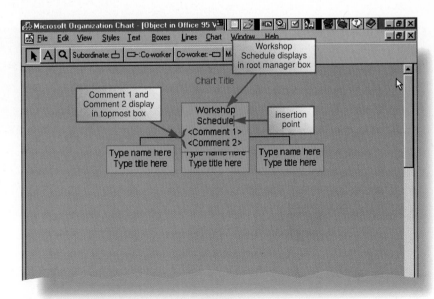

FIGURE 3-24

Deleting Subordinate Boxes

The organization chart in this presentation has two boxes on the level immediately below the root manager. Because the schedule for day one and day two are identical, you create the schedule for day one, copy it, and change day one to day two. Before proceeding with the remaining boxes for day one, you want to delete the unnecessary boxes as shown in the following steps.

Steps **To Delete Subordinate Boxes**

---

1 **Click the middle subordinate box located directly under the root manager box.**

2 **Press and hold down the SHIFT key. Then click the rightmost subordinate box.**

The middle and right subordinate boxes are selected (Figure 3-25). Comment 1 and Comment 2 do not display in the root manager box because text was not entered at their prompts. Name and Title prompts, however, display without entering text at their prompts. The technique of selecting more than one object by holding down the SHIFT key while clicking the objects is called SHIFT+click.

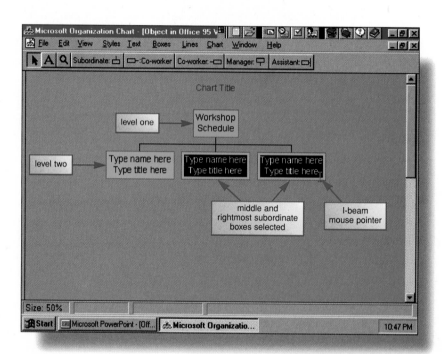

FIGURE 3-25

3 **Press the DELETE key.**

Organization Chart displays two boxes: the root manager and one subordinate (Figure 3-26).

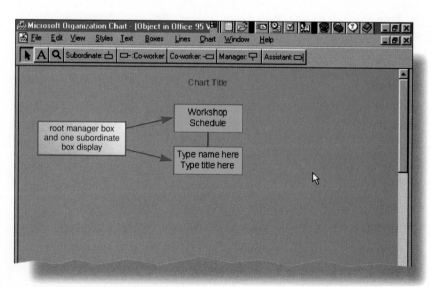

FIGURE 3-26

Titling the Subordinate Box

The process of adding a title to a subordinate box is the same as adding the title to the root manager box except that you first must select the subordinate box. The following step explains how to title a subordinate box.

Steps To Title a Subordinate Box

1 **Click the subordinate box. Type** Day **and then press the ENTER key. Type** One **on the second line.**

Day One displays as the title for the subordinate box (Figure 3-27).

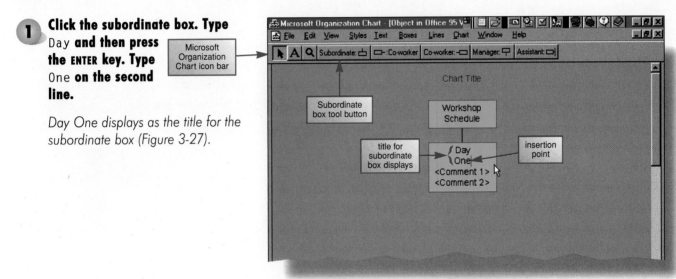

FIGURE 3-27

Adding Subordinate Boxes

Organization Chart has five types of boxes you can add to a chart. Each box type has a corresponding box tool on the Organization Chart icon bar. Because the daily activities for the workshop in this project are divided into morning and afternoon sessions, you need to add two subordinate boxes to day one.

To add a single subordinate box, click the Subordinate box tool button and then click the box on the organization chart to which the subordinate reports. On the occasions you wish to add several subordinate boxes, you can hold down the SHIFT key and click the Subordinate box tool. This keeps the Subordinate box tool active so that you do not have to click it each time before you click the manager box to which you are adding the subordinate. When you hold down the SHIFT key, you can click a box tool once for each box you want to add to the organization chart. For example, if you wish to add two subordinate boxes, hold down the SHIFT key and click the Subordinate box tool button two times. As long as the box tool is active, you can add the boxes repeatedly without selecting the box tool again. Once activated, the Subordinate box tool button stays recessed on the icon bar until you deselect it. You deselect the Subordinate box tool by clicking the Select button on the Organization Chart icon bar or pressing the ESC key.

The steps on the next page explain how to use the SHIFT key and the Subordinate box tool to add two subordinate boxes to the Day One box.

Steps To Add Multiple Subordinate Boxes

1 **Press and hold down the SHIFT key and then click the Subordinate box tool on the Organization Chart icon bar two times. Then point to the Day One box.**

The Subordinate box tool is recessed (Figure 3-28). The status bar displays the number of subordinate boxes Microsoft Organization Chart is creating. The mouse pointer changes shape to a subordinate box.

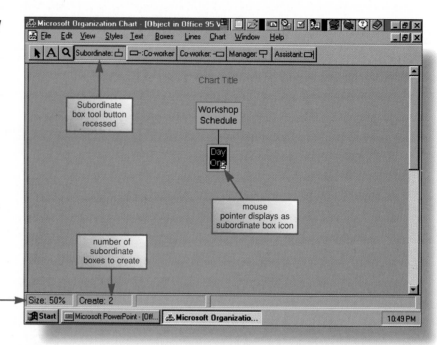

FIGURE 3-28

2 **Click the Day One box.**

Two subordinate boxes display below the Day One box (Figure 3-29). The new subordinate boxes display one level lower than the box to which they are attached. Day One is now the manager to the new subordinate boxes. The left subordinate box on level three is selected. The Subordinate box tool is still recessed indicating that it is active.

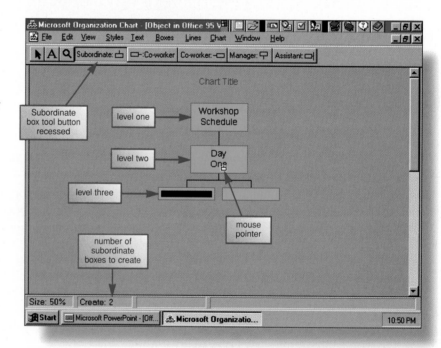

FIGURE 3-29

Adding Another Level of Subordinate Boxes

To further develop the organization chart in this project, you need to add a fourth level of subordinate boxes for the workshop sessions. This workshop presents two classes during the morning session and two classes during the afternoon session. Workshop participants must decide which four-hour class they want to attend. For example, a participant can attend the Word session the morning of day one and then attend the PowerPoint session on day two. The same decision will need to be made for the afternoon sessions.

The following steps summarize adding multiple subordinate boxes to a higher-level box.

TO ADD ANOTHER LEVEL OF SUBORDINATE BOXES

Step 1: With the Subordinate box tool still active, click the left subordinate box on level three.

Step 2: Click the right subordinate box on level three.

Two subordinate boxes display under each level three subordinate box (Figure 3-30).

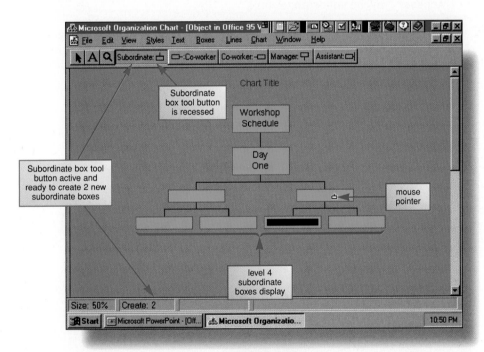

FIGURE 3-30

The structure of the organization chart is complete. The next step is to add titles to the boxes in the chart.

Adding Names to the Subordinate Boxes

To complete the organization chart, you add names to all boxes subordinate to the Day One box. However, before you can add the names, you must deactivate the Subordinate box tool and activate the Select button. When the **Select button** is active, the mouse pointer displays as a left-pointing block arrow. Because the subordinate boxes in this project have names but do not have titles, the Title, Comment 1, and Comment 2 prompts display in brackets under the box name when the box is selected. The brackets indicate the label is optional and it displays only when replaced by text. You use the Select button to select a subordinate box before you type its title. The following steps summarize how to activate the Select button and add a title to each subordinate box.

TO ADD NAMES TO SUBORDINATE BOXES

Step 1: Click the Select button on the Organization Chart icon bar.

Step 2: Click the left subordinate box on level three. Type 8 a.m. - 12 p.m. in the subordinate box.

Step 3: Click the right subordinate box on level three. Type 1 p.m. - 5 p.m. in the subordinate box.

Step 4: Click the left subordinate box under the 8 a.m. - 12 p.m. box. Type Word 7 in the subordinate box.

Step 5: Click the right subordinate box under the 8 a.m. - 12 p.m. box. Type PowerPoint 7 in the subordinate box.

Step 6: Click the left subordinate box under the 1 p.m. - 5 p.m. box. Type Excel 7 in the subordinate box.

Step 7: Click the right subordinate box under the 1 p.m. - 4 p.m. box. Type Access 7 in the subordinate box.

All subordinate boxes under the Day One box display session names (Figure 3-31).

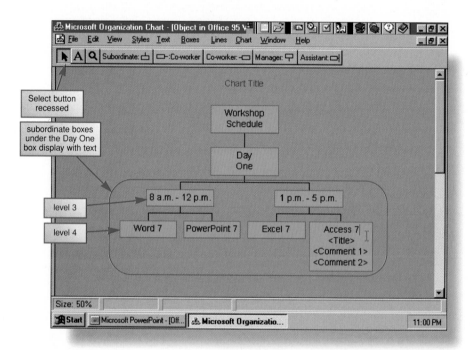

FIGURE 3-31

Changing Organization Chart Styles

Now that the boxes for the Day One branch are labeled, you want to change the way the organization chart looks. With the addition of each new box, the chart expanded horizontally. Before you add the schedule for day two, you will change the style of selected boxes from horizontal to vertical.

Steps To Change the Organization Chart Style

1 **Press and hold down the SHIFT key. Then click the four lowest-level boxes: Word 7, PowerPoint 7, Excel 7, and Access 7.**

The four lowest-level boxes are selected (Figure 3-32).

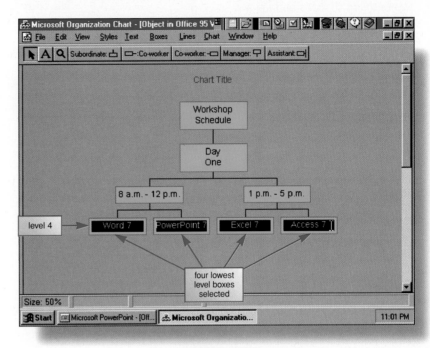

FIGURE 3-32

2 **Click Styles on the menu bar and then point to the vertical style box, which is the second box from the left in the top row of the Groups menu.**

Because it is the default, the horizontal style box is currently recessed (Figure 3-33). The vertical style box is highlighted because the mouse pointer is positioned over it.

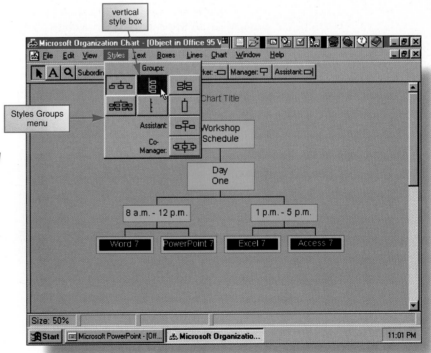

FIGURE 3-33

3 **Click the vertical style box.**

The organization chart displays the two morning sessions and the two afternoon sessions vertically (Figure 3-34). The 8 a.m. - 12 p.m. box and the 1 p.m. - 5 p.m. box still display horizontally under the Day One box because only the selected boxes change styles.

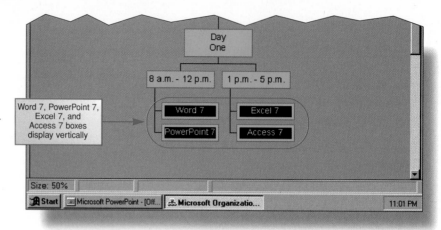

FIGURE 3-34

If you select the wrong style box or wish to return to the previous style, click the Undo Chart Style command from the Edit menu.

Copying a Branch of an Organization Chart

Day one's schedule is complete. Day two follows the same schedule so that participants can attend a workshop session they did not attend on day one. Instead of creating the day two schedule by adding and labeling boxes, you copy the day one schedule and add it under the Daily Schedule box. When you work with a whole section of an organization chart, it is referred to as working with a **branch**, or an appendage, of the chart. The following steps explain how to copy a branch of the chart.

 Steps To Copy a Branch of an Organization Chart

1 **Press and hold down the SHIFT key. Then click the Day One box, the 8 a.m. - 12 p.m. box, the 1 p.m. - 5 p.m. box. If not already selected, click the Word 7 box, the Excel 7 box, the PowerPoint 7 box, and the Access 7 box. Then release the SHIFT key (Figure 3-35).**

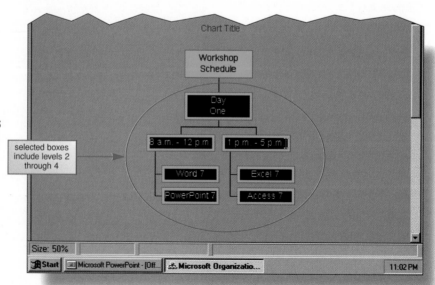

FIGURE 3-35

2 Right-click one of the selected boxes. When a shortcut menu displays, point to Copy (Figure 3-36).

3 Click Copy on the shortcut menu.

Organization Chart copies the Day One branch of the organization chart to the Clipboard. Recall that the Clipboard is a temporary Windows storage area.

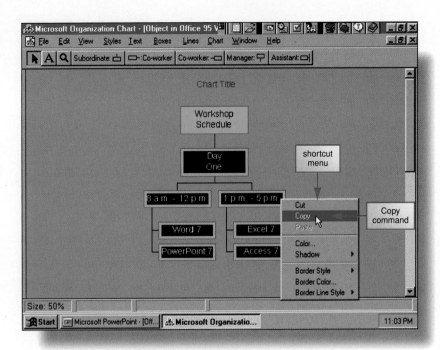

FIGURE 3-36

The next section explains how to paste the Day One branch of the organization chart to another location on the chart.

Pasting a Branch of an Organization Chart

Now that a copy of the Day One branch of the organization chart is on the Clipboard, the next step is to paste it from the Clipboard to the Daily Schedule slide.

 Steps To Paste a Branch of an Organization Chart

1 Right-click the root manager box labeled Workshop Schedule. Then point to Paste Boxes on the shortcut menu.

Paste Boxes is highlighted on the shortcut menu (Figure 3-37). The Workshop Schedule box is selected.

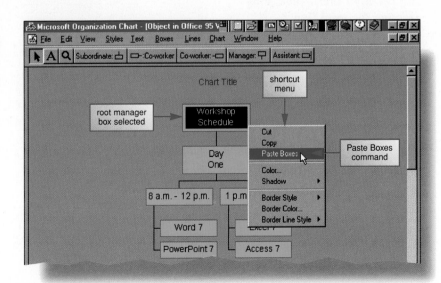

FIGURE 3-37

2 Click Paste Boxes on the shortcut menu.

The organization chart displays two Day One branches (Figure 3-38).

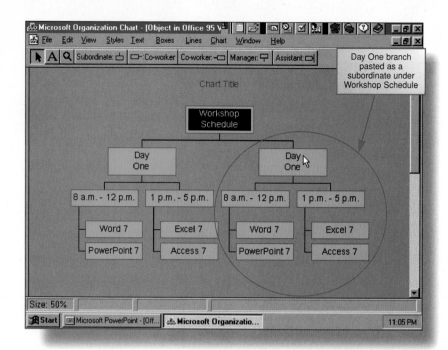

FIGURE 3-38

Editing an Organization Chart

After you have copied and pasted a branch of the organization chart, you need to edit the title of the first subordinate level so that it displays as Day Two. Editing a box requires you to first select the box and then make your edits.

 Steps To Edit Text in an Organization Chart

1 Click the Day One box at the top of the right branch of the organization chart. Then, drag through the word One.

The word One is selected (Figure 3-39).

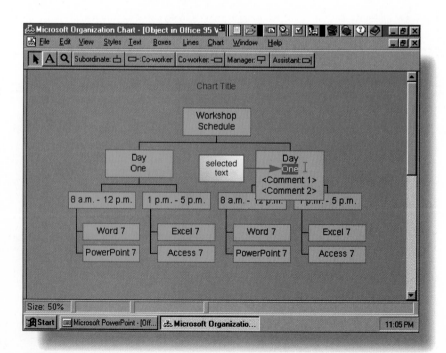

FIGURE 3-39

2 **Type** Two **in the subordinate box.**

The word Two replaces the word One (Figure 3-40).

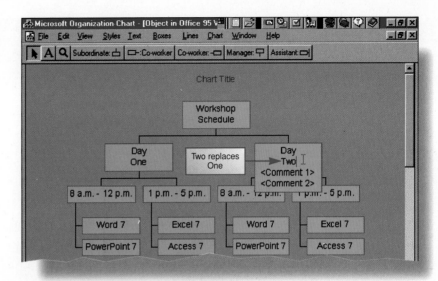

FIGURE 3-40

The text on the organization chart is complete. The next section explains how to format an organization chart.

Formatting an Organization Chart

Organization Chart allows you to format a box simply by selecting it. To make your organization chart look like Figure 3-19 on page PP 3.20, you add shadow effects and a border to every box. The following sections explain how to quickly select all boxes in the chart and change the box attributes to shadow and border.

 Steps **To Select All Boxes in an Organization Chart**

1 **Click Edit on the menu bar, point to Select, and then point to All (Figure 3-41).**

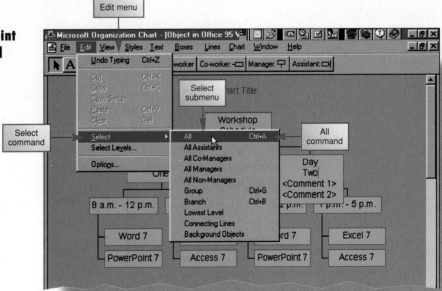

FIGURE 3-41

More *About* **Microsoft Organization Chart**

Microsoft Organization Chart allows you to make changes to text in an organization chart. You can change font, font style, font size, and font color. You also can change text alignment to left-aligned, right-aligned, or center-aligned.

2) Click All on the submenu.

Organization Chart selects all boxes in the chart (Figure 3-42).

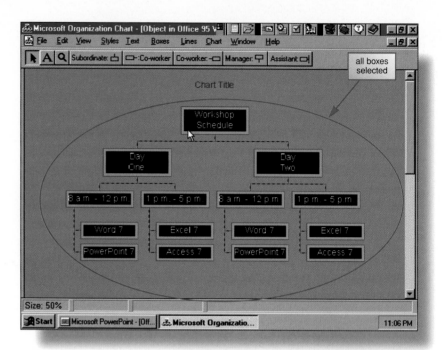

FIGURE 3-42

Adding Shadow Effects to Boxes in an Organization Chart

Now that all the boxes are selected, you add shadow effects. The following steps explain how to add shadow effects to all boxes in an organization chart.

 Steps To Add Shadow Effects to Boxes in an Organization Chart

1) With all the boxes in the organization chart still selected, right-click one of the selected boxes. Point to Shadow on the shortcut menu and then point to the third shadow option in the second column on the Shadow submenu.

Organization Chart displays the Shadow submenu (Figure 3-43). The default shadow setting for Organization Chart is None. The third shadow option in column two is highlighted because you pointed to it.

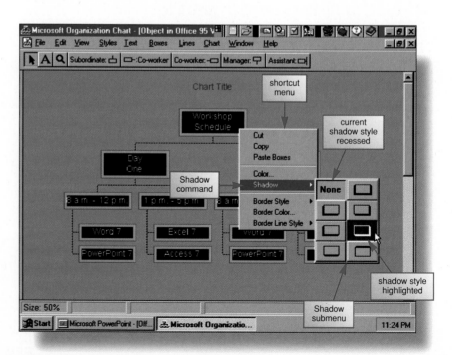

FIGURE 3-43

2 **Click the third shadow option in column two on the submenu.**

Organization Chart adds the shadow effect to all boxes in the organization chart (Figure 3-44).

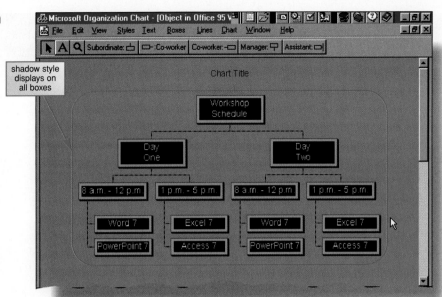

FIGURE 3-44

Changing Border Styles in an Organization Chart

To enhance the boxes in the organization chart, you want to change the border style. Organization Chart has twelve border styles from which to choose. One style is None, or no border. The default border style is a thin line, which is visible in Figure 3-44. The following steps explain how to change border styles.

 Steps To Change Border Style

1 **With all boxes in the organization chart still selected, right-click one of the selected boxes. Point to Border Style on the shortcut menu and then point to the fourth border style in the second column on the Border Style submenu.**

Organization Chart displays the Border Style submenu (Figure 3-45). The default border style for Organization Chart is a thin line, which is the second border style in column one. The fourth border style in column two is highlighted because you pointed to it.

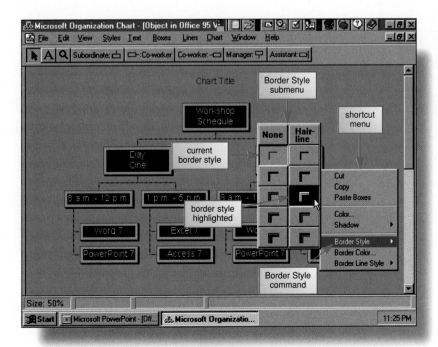

FIGURE 3-45

2 Click the fourth border style in column two on the submenu.

Organization Chart applies the new border style to all boxes in the organization chart (Figure 3-46).

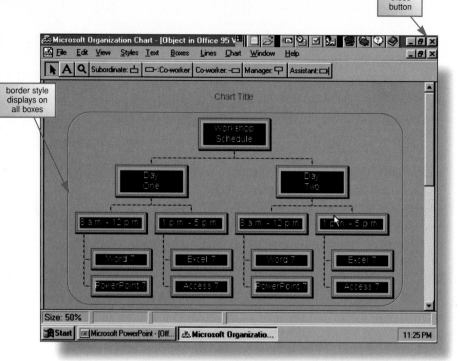

FIGURE 3-46

The organization chart is now complete. The next step is to return to PowerPoint.

Closing Organization Chart and Returning to PowerPoint

After you create and format an organization chart, you close Organization Chart and return to the PowerPoint screen. The following steps explain how to return to PowerPoint.

 To Close Organization Chart and Return to PowerPoint

1 Click the Close button on the Microsoft Organization Chart - [Object in Office 95 Workshop] title bar. When the Microsoft Organization Chart dialog box displays, point to the Yes button.

The Microsoft Organization Chart dialog box warns you that the organization chart object has changed and asks you if you want to update the object in the PowerPoint presentation, Office 95 Workshop, before proceeding (Figure 3-47).

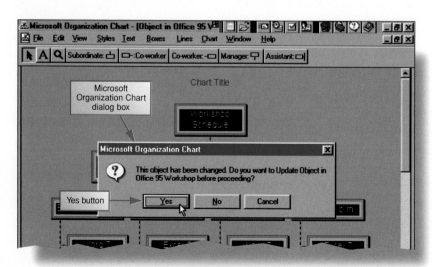

FIGURE 3-47

2 **Click the Yes button.**

Microsoft Organization Chart updates the organization chart object, closes, and then PowerPoint displays the organization chart on Slide 2 (Figure 3-48).

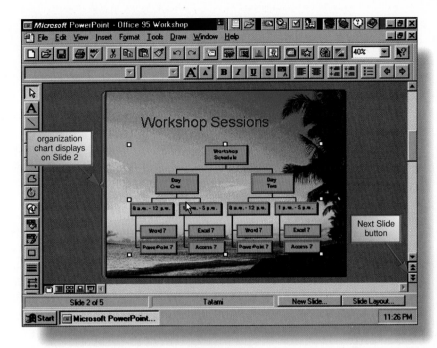

FIGURE 3-48

Scaling an Organization Chart Object

The organization chart on Slide 2 is sized to fit the Organization Chart place-holder. The organization chart would be easier to read if it was enlarged. Recall that the Scale command, on the Draw menu, allows you to enlarge or reduce an object by very precise amounts while retaining the object's original proportions. Perform the following steps to scale an organization chart object.

TO SCALE AN ORGANIZATION CHART OBJECT

Step 1: With the organization chart selected, click Draw on the menu bar. Then click Scale.

Step 2: Type 115 in the Scale To box.

Step 3: Click the OK button.

The organization chart is scaled to 115 percent of its original size (Figure 3-49).

More *About*
Scaling Objects

The Preview button in the Scale dialog box allows you to check the object's new size without applying it. When you want to make an object bigger, enter a number greater than 100 in the Scale To box. To make an object smaller, enter a number less than 100.

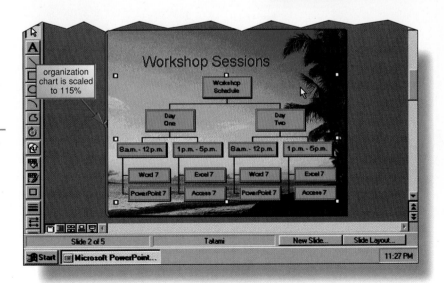

FIGURE 3-49

Creating a PowerPoint Clip Art Object

A clip art picture is composed of many objects grouped together to form one object. PowerPoint allows you to alter clip art by disassembling the objects. **Disassembling** a clip art object, also called **ungrouping**, separates one object into multiple objects. Once disassembled, you manipulate the individual objects as needed to form a new object. When you disassemble a clip art picture in PowerPoint, it becomes a **PowerPoint object** and loses its link to the Microsoft ClipArt Gallery. Therefore, you cannot double-click the new picture to open the Microsoft ClipArt Gallery.

Slide 3 contains the Leadership picture from the Microsoft ClipArt Gallery that has been modified by embedding an Excel chart onto the screen object (Figure 3-50). There are numerous reasons why you may wish to modify clip art. Many times you cannot find clip art that precisely illustrates your topic. For example, you want a picture of a man and woman shaking hands, but the only available clip art picture has two men and a woman shaking hands.

From time to time you may wish to remove or change a portion of a clip art picture. For example, you are making a presentation to a group of people who do not believe in wearing jewelry, so you want to delete all jewelry from the clip art picture.

Sometimes you wish to combine two or more clip art pictures. For example, you choose to use one clip art picture for the background and another picture as the foreground. Still other times, you may wish to combine clip art with another type of object. The types of objects you can combine with clip art depend on the software installed on your computer. The Object Type list box in the Insert Object dialog box identifies the types of objects you can combine with clip art.

Modifying the clip art picture on Slide 3 requires several steps. First, you display Slide 3. Then, you change the slide layout to Object. Next, you insert the Leadership clip art into the object placeholder. Then, you scale the clip art to cover most of the slide, and disassemble the clip art. Then, you embed an Excel chart into the screen. Later in this project, you combine the disassembled objects into one object.

The steps on the following pages explain in detail how to insert, scale, and disassemble clip art, and embed an Excel chart in Slide 3.

FIGURE 3-50

Inserting Clip Art

The first step in modifying a clip art picture is to insert the picture on a slide. You insert the Leadership clip art from the Microsoft ClipArt Gallery. In a later step, you modify the clip art by combining it with an Excel chart.

The following steps explain how to insert the Leadership clip art into Slide 3 of this presentation.

TO INSERT CLIP ART

Step 1: Click the Next Slide button to display Slide 3.
Step 2: Click the Slide Layout button. Scroll to display the Object AutoLayout, layout number 16. Then double-click the Object AutoLayout.
Step 3: Click the object placeholder to select it.
Step 4. Click the Insert Clip Art button on the Standard toolbar. Then click the Find button in the Microsoft ClipArt Gallery 2.0 dialog box.
Step 5: When the Find ClipArt dialog box displays, type Leadership in the Description box.
Step 6: Click the Find Now button. Then click the picture with a description of Leadership which is a picture of a woman conducting a meeting while standing in front of a blue screen (see Figure 3-50).
Step 7: Click the Insert button in the Microsoft ClipArt Gallery dialog box.

Slide 3 displays the Leadership clip art picture (Figure 3-51).

FIGURE 3-51

Scaling Clip Art

Now that the clip art picture is inserted onto Slide 3, you increase its size by scaling. Perform the following steps to scale clip art.

TO SCALE CLIP ART

Step 1: If not selected, click the Leadership clip art picture.
Step 2: Click Draw on the menu bar and then click Scale.
Step 3: Type 175 in the Scale To box and click the OK button.

The Leadership clip art picture is scaled to 175 percent of its original size (Figure 3-52).

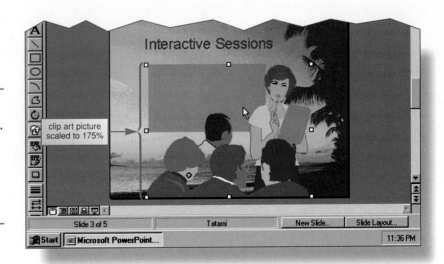

FIGURE 3-52

Using the View Menu to Display the Drawing+ Toolbar

In order to modify the clip art on Slide 3, you use the Disassemble Picture button on the Drawing+ toolbar. The **Drawing+ toolbar** contains buttons that modify objects as explained in Table 3-1.

Table 3-1		
BUTTON	**BUTTON NAME**	**DESCRIPTION**
	Bring Forward	Moves an object one level closer to the top of a stack of objects.
	Send Backward	Moves an object one level closer to the bottom of a stack of objects.
	Group Objects	Creates a set of objects that can be used as a single object. PowerPoint requires you to select two or more objects.
	Disassemble Picture	Separates the selected picture or object into PowerPoint objects.
	Rotate Left	Rotates the selected object or group of objects 90 degrees to the left. Pictures and OLE objects cannot be rotated.
	Rotate Right	Rotates the selected object or group of objects 90 degrees to the right. Pictures and OLE objects cannot be rotated.
	Flip Horizontal	Flips a selected object or group of objects horizontally 180 degrees. Pictures and OLE objects cannot be horizontally flipped.
	Flip Vertical	Flips a selected object or group of objects vertically 180 degrees. Pictures and OLE objects cannot be vertically flipped.

You display the Drawing+ toolbar by right-clicking any toolbar and then clicking Drawing+ on the shortcut menu. The following steps explain how to display the Drawing+ toolbar. If the Drawing+ toolbar already displays in the PowerPoint window, read the next two steps without doing them and then proceed to the next section, Disassembling Clip Art.

Steps To Display the Drawing+ Toolbar

1 Right-click the Drawing toolbar. When a shortcut menu displays, point to Drawing+ (Figure 3-53).

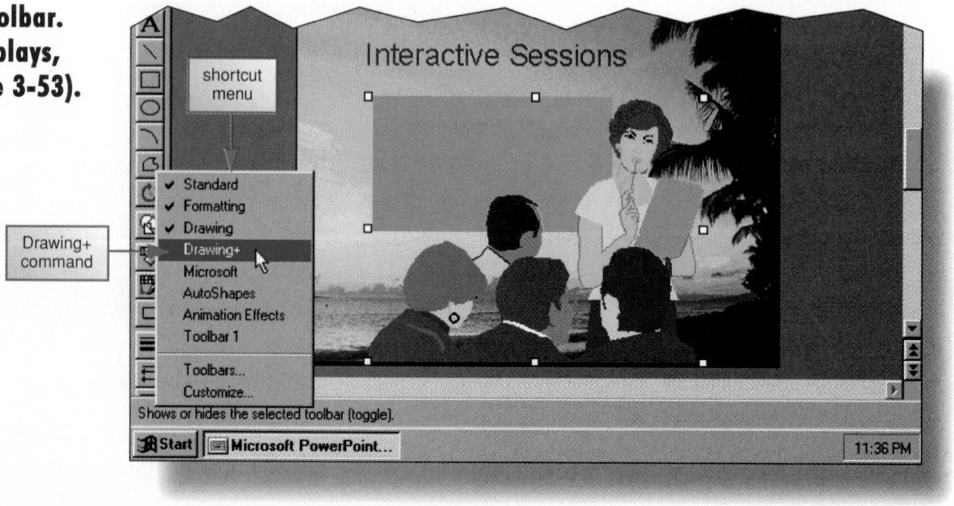

shortcut menu

Drawing+ command

Interactive Sessions

✓ Standard
✓ Formatting
✓ Drawing
  Drawing+
  Microsoft
  AutoShapes
  Animation Effects
  Toolbar 1

  Toolbars...
  Customize...

Shows or hides the selected toolbar (toggle).

Start | Microsoft PowerPoint...   11:36 PM

FIGURE 3-53

2 **Click Drawing+.**

The Drawing+ toolbar displays on the PowerPoint screen (Figure 3-54).

Drawing+ toolbar →

FIGURE 3-54

Disassembling Clip Art

The next step is to disassemble the Leadership clip art picture on Slide 3. When you disassemble a clip art picture, PowerPoint breaks it into its component objects. These new groups can be repeatedly disassembled until they decompose into individual objects. Depending on the clip art picture, it may be composed of a few individual objects or several complex groups of objects.

The following steps explain how to disassemble clip art.

Steps To Disassemble Clip Art

1 **With the Leadership clip art picture selected, point to the Disassemble Picture button on the Drawing+ toolbar (Figure 3-55).**

Disassemble Picture button →

Disassemble Picture

selected object →

Drawing+ toolbar →

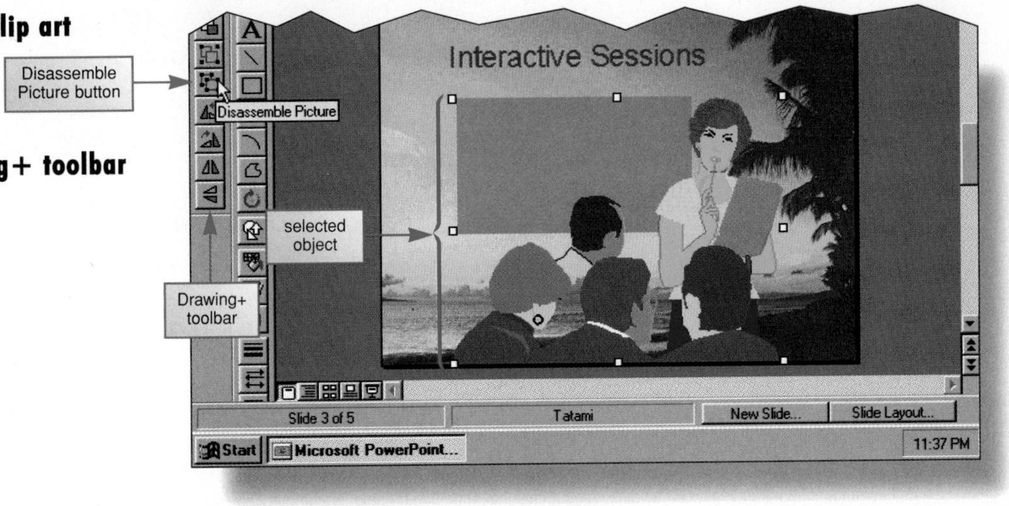

FIGURE 3-55

2 Click the Disassemble Picture button.

A Microsoft PowerPoint dialog box displays explaining that this clip art object is an imported object and that converting it to a PowerPoint drawing permanently discards any embedded data or linking information it contains (Figure 3-56). Finally, you are asked if you want to convert the object to a PowerPoint drawing.

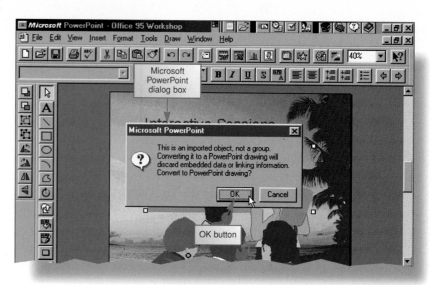

FIGURE 3-56

3 Click the OK button.

The clip art picture now displays as several PowerPoint objects (Figure 3-57). Selection rectangles display around the disassembled objects. Recall that a selection rectangle is the box framed by the resize handles when a graphic is selected.

FIGURE 3-57

When you disassemble a clip art object and click the Yes button in the Microsoft PowerPoint information box (Steps 2 and 3 above), PowerPoint converts the clip art object to a PowerPoint object. Recall that a PowerPoint object is an object *not* associated with a supplementary application. As a result, you lose the ability to double-click the clip art picture to open the Microsoft ClipArt Gallery. To replace a PowerPoint object with a clip art object, click the Insert Clip Art button on the Standard toolbar or click the Insert Clip Art command from the Insert menu. If, for some reason, you decide not to disassemble the clip art picture, click the Cancel button in the Microsoft PowerPoint information box. Clicking the Cancel button terminates the Disassemble Picture command, and the clip art picture displays on the slide as a clip art object.

Because clip art is a collection of complex groups of objects, you may need to disassemble a complex object into less complex objects before being able to modify a specific object. In the PowerPoint object in Figure 3-57, for example, the woman on the left is wearing an earring. To modify or delete the earring, you must further disassemble the object until her earring is a separate object.

If you accidentally disassemble an object, you can immediately **regroup** it by clicking the Group button on the Drawing+ toolbar. If only one composite object is selected or you made changes to the composite objects, however, you can regroup the composite objects using the **Regroup command** from the Draw menu. The Regroup command is also available from a shortcut menu. To display the shortcut menu, point somewhere within the disassembled object and right-click. Then click the Regroup command from the shortcut menu.

Recall that clip art is an object imported from the Microsoft ClipArt Gallery. Disassembling imported, embedded, or linked objects eliminates the embedding data or linking information the object contains that ties it back to its original source.

Use caution when objects are not completely regrouped. Dragging or scaling affects only the selected object, not the entire collection of objects.

Deselecting Clip Art Objects

All of the disassembled objects Figure 3-57 are selected. Before you can manipulate an individual object, you must **deselect** all selected objects to remove the selection rectangles, and then select the object you wish to manipulate. For example, in this project you wish to modify the light blue screen. The following step explains how to deselect objects.

 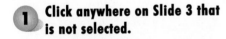 **To Deselect a Clip Art Object**

① **Click anywhere on Slide 3 that is not selected.**

Slide 3 displays without selection rectangles around the objects (Figure 3-58).

FIGURE 3-58

The Leadership clip art picture is now disassembled into many objects. The next section explains how to embed an Excel chart into the presentation and display it on the light blue screen of the disassembled Leadership clip art picture.

Embedding an Existing Excel Chart

PowerPoint allows you to embed many types of objects into a presentation. In this project, you embed an existing Excel chart onto the screen in the disassembled clip art picture. The Excel chart is on the Student Floppy Disk that accompanies this book.

Embedding an existing Excel chart is similar to embedding other objects. Because the Excel chart already exists, you retrieve it from the file in which it was saved rather than opening the supplementary application and creating the object. To make placing and sizing the Excel chart easier, you drag the screen object away from the other PowerPoint objects. Once the screen object is fully visible, you embed and scale the Excel chart.

The next two sections explain how to drag a PowerPoint object and embed an Excel chart.

Moving a PowerPoint Object

To make working with the screen object easier, you move it away from the other objects to the upper-left corner of the PowerPoint window. Perform the following steps to move a PowerPoint object.

Steps To Move a PowerPoint Object

1 **Click the screen object.**

A selection rectangle displays around the screen object (Figure 3-59). If you inadvertently selected a different object, click the center of the screen object.

FIGURE 3-59

2 Drag the screen object to the upper left corner of Slide 3 (Figure 3-60).

FIGURE 3-60

The reason you moved the screen object away from the other objects was to avoid placing the Excel chart on top of the other screen objects. Later in this project, you combine the screen object and an Excel chart. Moving the screen object now makes this process less complicated.

Embedding an Excel Chart

The next step in modifying the PowerPoint object for Slide 3 is to embed an Excel chart. The Excel chart is already created and saved on the Student Diskette. The following steps explain how to embed an existing Excel chart.

Steps **To Embed an Excel Chart**

1 **Click Insert on the menu bar. Then click Object.**

The Insert Object dialog box displays (Figure 3-61). Depending on your installation, the list of object types on your computer may look different from the one in this figure.

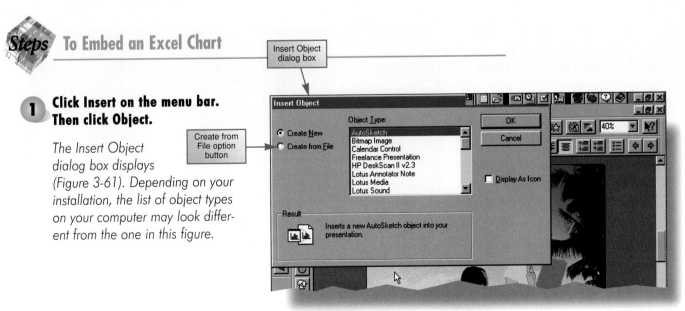

FIGURE 3-61

2 **Click Create from File.**

The Insert Object dialog box now displays the File text box (Figure 3-62). Drive A is the current drive and PowerPoint is the current folder.

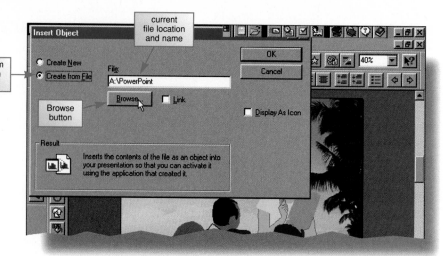

FIGURE 3-62

3 **Click the Browse button. When the Browse dialog box displays, double-click the PowerPoint folder in the Look in list box. Then point to Sales Report.**

The Browse dialog box displays the files in the PowerPoint folder (Figure 3-63).

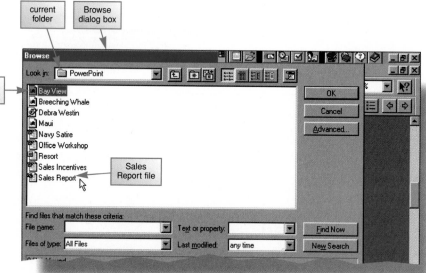

FIGURE 3-63

4 **Double-click Sales Report. When the Insert Object dialog box displays, point to the OK button.**

The Insert Object dialog box now displays A:\PowerPoint\Sales Report.xls in the File text box (Figure 3-64). When you double-clicked Sales Report, you selected the file from which you will embed the Excel chart into Slide 3.

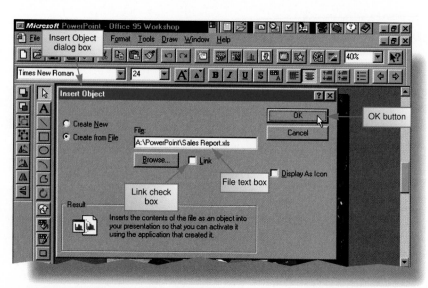

FIGURE 3-64

⑤ Click the OK button.

After a short time, Slide 3 displays the Quarter 1 Sales chart in the middle of the slide (Figure 3-65).

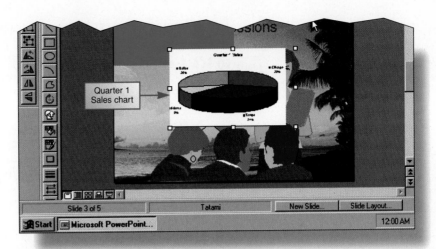

FIGURE 3-65

PowerPoint displays the chart in the middle of Slide 3 because you did not have a placeholder selected. Later in this project, you will scale the chart and position it on the screen object.

When you click the Create from File option button in the Insert Object dialog box, the dialog box changes (Figure 3-62). The Object Type list box is replaced by the File box. Another change to the dialog box is the Link check box. The **Link** check box inserts the object as a linked, instead of an embedded, object. Like an embedded object, a **linked object** also is created in another application but maintains a connection to its source. If the original object is changed, the linked object on the slide also changes. The linked object is stored in the source file where it was created. For example, the Excel chart you inserted onto the screen is stored in the Sales Report file on the Student Floppy Disk. If you were to link the Sales Report file to your presentation, every time the Sales Report file changed in Excel, the changes would display on the chart in Slide 3. Your PowerPoint presentation stores a representation of the original Sales Report file and information about its location. Therefore, if you later move or delete the source file, the link will be broken and the object will not be available. Hence, if you make a presentation on a computer other than the one on which the presentation was created and the presentation contains linked objects, be certain to include a copy of the source files. The source files must be stored in the exact location as originally specified when you linked them to your presentation.

When you select a source file from the Browse dialog box, PowerPoint associates the file with a specific application, which is based on the file extension. For example, if you select a source file with the file extension .DOC, PowerPoint recognizes the file as a Word file. Additionally, if you select a source file with the file extension .XLS, PowerPoint recognizes the file as an Excel file.

Scaling an Embedded Object

The Excel chart is too large to place on the clip art screen in Figure 3-65. Before you position the Excel chart on the screen, you want to scale it. Scaling the chart before you move it helps you to center the chart both vertically and horizontally. You scale the Excel chart using the Scale command from the Draw menu.

The following steps explain how to scale an object using the Scale command.

TO SCALE AN EMBEDDED OBJECT

Step 1: With the Excel chart selected, click Draw on the menu bar and then click Scale.

Step 2: Type 75 in the Scale To text box.

Step 3: Click the OK button.

The Excel chart is scaled to 75% of its original size (Figure 3-66).

Recall if you do not know the number to type in the Scale To text box (Step 2 above), you can type a number and then click the Preview button. You can see if you need to increase the number in the Scale To box to increase the size of the object or decrease the number in the Scale To box to decrease the size of the object. You can continue to change the number in the Scale To box and click the Preview button until the object displays at the proper scale.

FIGURE 3-66

Grouping Objects

The next step in creating Slide 3 requires you to move the Excel chart onto the screen object and then combine the two objects into one. Combining two or more objects into one object is called **grouping**. Grouping multiple objects together allows you to move the combined objects at the same time. If the objects are not grouped, you must move them one object at a time. To make grouping objects more efficient, PowerPoint has a **Group Object button** on the Drawing+ toolbar. After selecting the objects you want to group, click the Group Object button.

Finalizing Slide 3 requires several steps. First, you layer the Excel chart over the screen object and then group the chart and the screen into one object. Then, you move the grouped screen and chart to the screen's original position in the Leadership clip art picture. Because the disassembled Leadership clip art picture is composed of multiple layered objects, you send the grouped screen and chart to the bottom of the stack of objects so that it displays behind the speaker's shoulder. Finally, you group all the objects in the PowerPoint object into one object.

The next sections explain how to create a layered object, group the two layered objects into one modified screen object, return the modified screen object to the PowerPoint object, send the modified screen object to the background of the PowerPoint object, and combine the disassembled objects of the clip art picture into one PowerPoint object.

Overlaying Objects

PowerPoint has four commands to help you manipulate objects that have been layered. **Layered objects** are objects that have been positioned on top of each other like a stack of cards (see Figure 3-67). The object at the bottom of the stack is the **background object**. Only a portion of the background object is visible because it is covered by the objects layered on top. Each layer hides a portion of the object on which it is overlaid. The top layer, the **foreground object,** is the part of slide closest to the viewer and is fully visible.

A layered object is created by overlaying one or more objects. An **overlay** is something that is laid over, or covers, something else. You create the layered screen object by overlaying the Excel chart on the screen object. The following steps summarize how to overlay the Excel chart on the clip art screen to create the layered object.

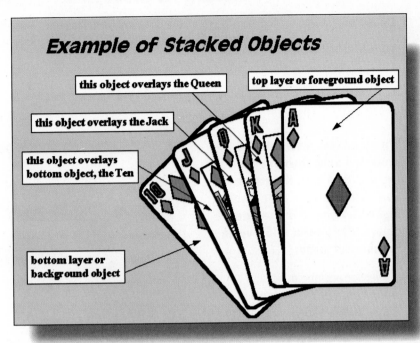

FIGURE 3-67

TO OVERLAY OBJECTS

Step 1: Drag the Excel chart to the center of the screen object in the upper left corner of the slide.

Step 2: Drop the Excel chart onto the center of the screen object by releasing the left mouse button.

The Excel chart displays in the center of the screen object (Figure 3-68). The Excel chart overlays the screen object.

FIGURE 3-68

Grouping the Two Layered Objects into One Modified Screen Object

Now that the chart overlays the screen object, you want to group the two objects into one. The following steps explain how to group two objects into one.

Steps To Group Layered Objects into One Object

1 **With the Excel chart selected, press and hold down the SHIFT key and then click the screen object. Release the SHIFT key. Right-click one of the selected objects. Then point to Group on the shortcut menu.**

A selection rectangle displays around each of the two objects (Figure 3-69). The Group command is highlighted.

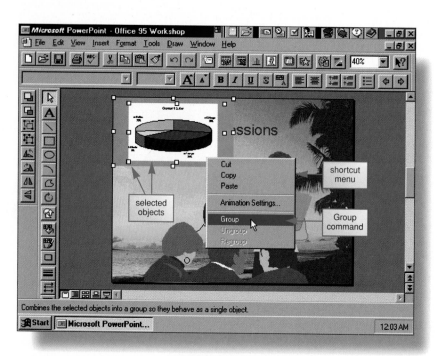

FIGURE 3-69

2 **Click Group on the shortcut menu.**

The two objects become one object (Figure 3-70). One selection rectangle displays around the grouped object.

FIGURE 3-70

If you make an error and do not want the objects grouped, you can click the Undo button on the Standard toolbar or click the Disassemble Picture button on the Drawing+ toolbar.

Dragging a Modified Object

The next step in creating Slide 3 is to return the modified screen object to the PowerPoint object. The following steps summarize moving an object.

TO DRAG A MODIFIED OBJECT

Step 1: Drag the modified screen object down to the right until the upper right resize handle is positioned at the top and center of the speaker's head.

Step 2: Release the left mouse button to drop the modified screen object on top of the PowerPoint object.

The modified screen object overlays the PowerPoint object (Figure 3-71).

Sending an Object to the Background

The modified screen object hides portions of the objects beneath it because it overlays the stack of objects that constitute the PowerPoint object. To make the hidden portions visible, you send the modified screen object to the bottom of the stack of objects. Perform the following step to send an object to the background.

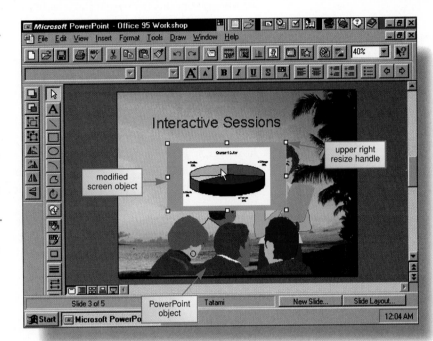

FIGURE 3-71

 Steps To Send an Object to the Background

1 **With the modified screen object selected, click Draw on the menu bar, and then click Send to Back.**

The modified screen object displays behind the speaker's shoulder at the bottom of the stack of PowerPoint objects (Figure 3-72).

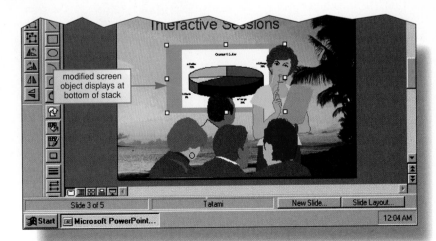

FIGURE 3-72

OtherWays

1. Press ALT+D, press K

In the previous steps, you used the Send to Back command to move the screen object to the bottom of a stack of objects. When you are working with several layered objects and want to move an object back just one layer in the stack, use the **Send Backward command.** You also can move an object to the top of the stack or up just one layer. To send a selected object to the top of the stack, use the **Bring to Front command.** To move a selected object one layer up toward the top of the stack, use the **Bring Forward command.**

Selecting Objects

Before you can group all the clip art objects into a new PowerPoint object, first you must select the objects to be grouped. When you have a few objects to select, you can use the SHIFT+CLICK method. When you have many objects to select, however, it is easier to use the Select All command from the Edit menu. When the Select All command is chosen, every object on the slide is selected. For example, if you select all objects on Slide 3, you select all of the clip art objects and the title object.

If you select objects you do not want included in the object you are grouping, you must deselect those objects. The following steps explain how to select all the objects on Slide 3 and then deselect the title object.

More *About*
Selecting Objects

If the object on which you wish to work is in a stack of layered objects, press the TAB key to cycle through the stack until the object you want is selected. Press SHIFT+TAB to cycle backward. Resize handles display on a selected object.

Steps To Select All Objects on a Slide

1 **Click Edit on the menu bar and then click Select All.**

All objects on Slide 3 are selected (Figure 3-73). A selection rectangle displays around every object.

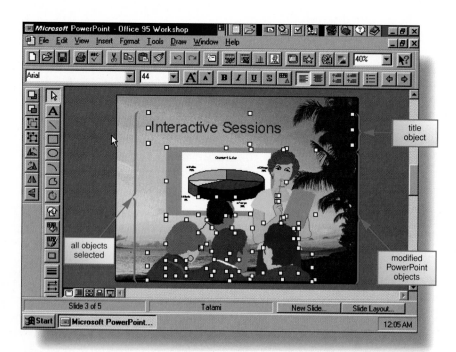

FIGURE 3-73

2 Press and hold down the SHIFT key. Then click one of the words in the title object. Release the SHIFT key.

The title text is not selected (Figure 3-74). All PowerPoint objects on Slide 3 still are selected.

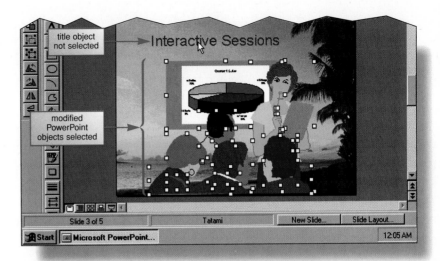

FIGURE 3-74

Grouping Selected Objects

Now that the PowerPoint objects are selected, the final step in creating Slide 3 is to group those objects into one object. Perform the following step to group selected objects into one object.

 To Group Selected Objects

1 Right-click one of the selected PowerPoint objects. Click Group on the shortcut menu.

The selected objects are grouped into one object (Figure 3-75). Notice only one selection rectangle displays.

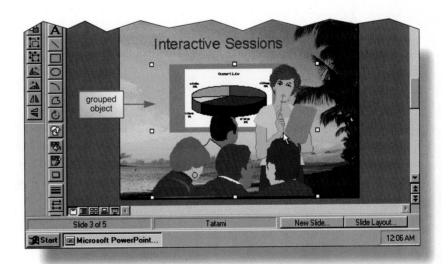

FIGURE 3-75

Slide 3 is now complete. The next section introduces you to embedding a picture into a slide.

> **OtherWays**
> 1. Click Group Objects button on Drawing+ toolbar
> 2. On Draw menu click Group
> 3. Press ALT+D, press G

Embedding a Picture into a Slide

Another graphic object often inserted into a slide is a picture. Slide 4 contains an embedded picture as shown in Figure 3-76. Recall that a picture is any graphic image from another application.

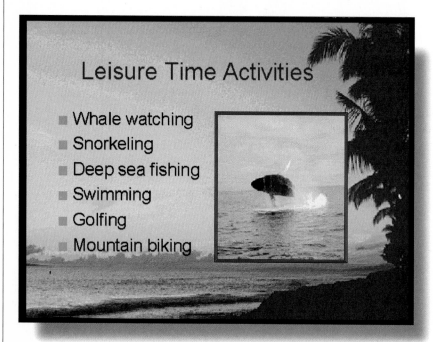

FIGURE 3-76

Inserting a Picture

Slide 4 is included in this presentation to encourage prospective seminar attendees to combine educational activities with recreational activities. You insert a picture to reinforce that message. The picture you insert on Slide 4 is a scanned picture that has been stored as a bit-map graphic and saved as a TIF file. The Breeching Whale file is on the Student Floppy Disk that accompanies this book. Perform the following steps to insert this picture.

  To Insert a Picture

1 Click the Next Slide button.

Slide 4 displays the Bulleted List slide layout (Figure 3-77).

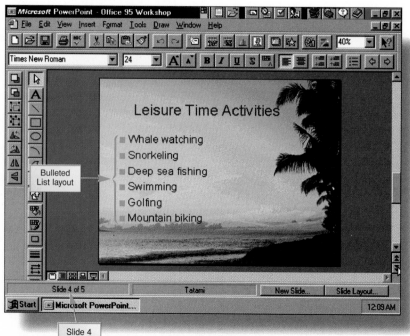

FIGURE 3-77

2 Ensure the Student Floppy Disk is in drive A. Click Insert on the menu bar and then click Picture. When the Insert Picture dialog box displays, click Breeching Whale in the Name list box.

The Insert Picture dialog box displays Breeching Whale in the Name list box (Figure 3-78). A preview of the picture displays in the preview area.

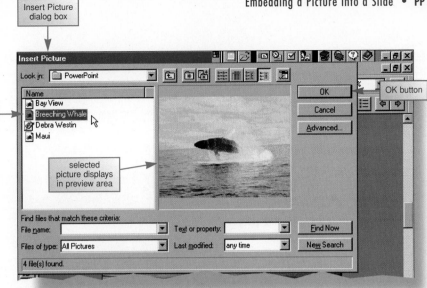

FIGURE 3-78

3 Double-click Breeching Whale.

PowerPoint displays a dialog box with a message that it is importing the Breeching Whale.tif file from the PowerPoint folder on drive A. The dialog box also indicates the percentage completed of the file importation. Once the file is imported, the Breeching Whale.tif file displays (3-79).

FIGURE 3-79

> **Other Ways**
> 1. Press ALT+I, press P, select picture, click OK button

When the Insert Picture dialog box displays, PowerPoint does not require that you specify which format your picture is in. The default includes all the formats installed on your system that PowerPoint recognizes.

Resizing a Picture

PowerPoint automatically placed the picture in the middle of Slide 4 because a placeholder was not selected. To balance the text object and the picture, you drag the picture to the right of the bulleted list. **Balance** means that the slide possesses a harmonious, or satisfying, arrangement of proportions of its objects. The height of the picture is not in balance with the bulleted text. To correct this, you change the proportions of the picture.

PowerPoint allows you to **constrain,** or control, resizing an object from its center by holding the CTRL key while dragging a resize handle. This method of constraining is called **resizing about center.** Perform the step on the next page to resize a picture about its center.

Steps To Resize a Picture

1 **Drag the picture to the right of the bulleted list so the left side of the picture aligns under the A in Activities in the title object, and the top of the picture aligns with the top of the text in the bulleted item Snorkeling (Figure 3-80).**

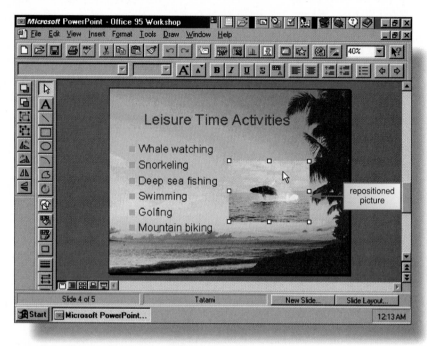

FIGURE 3-80

2 **Point to the bottom center resize handle of the picture.**

The mouse pointer shape changes to a two-headed arrow when it is positioned on a resize handle (Figure 3-81).

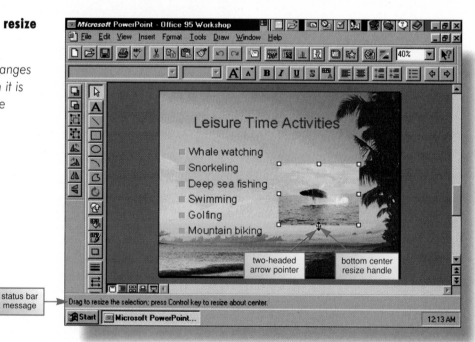

FIGURE 3-81

3 Press and hold down the CTRL key, drag the mouse pointer down until the bottom edge of the picture aligns with the bottom edge of the text in the bulleted item, Mountain biking. Release the left mouse button. Then release the CTRL key.

The picture is resized about its center (Figure 3-82). Resize about center means changing the size of an object proportionally from its center.

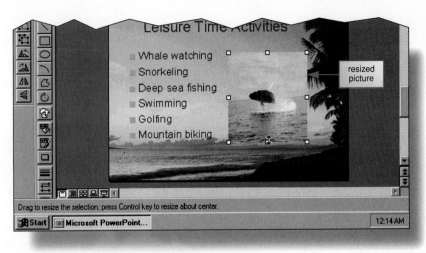

FIGURE 3-82

Caution should be exercised when resizing an object about its center. In Step 3, releasing the CTRL key before releasing the left mouse button does not resize about center; it resizes only the bottom of the picture. To correct this error, click the Undo button and perform Steps 2 and 3 again, making certain to first release the left mouse button and then release the CTRL key.

PowerPoint has other methods of constraining objects when resizing. Table 3-2 explains the various constraining methods.

Restore a resized object to its original proportions by selecting the object, clicking the Scale command from the Draw menu, selecting the Relative to Original Picture Size check box in the Scale dialog box, and then clicking the OK button.

Table 3-2	
METHOD	*CONSTRAINING WHEN RESIZING AN OBJECT*
SHIFT+drag	**Resizes an object vertically, horizontally, or diagonally from one side or corner. Diagonal resizing maintains the height-to-width relationship.**
CTRL+drag	**Resizes an object vertically, horizontally, or diagonally from the center outward.**
CTRL+SHIFT+drag	**Resizes an object vertically, horizontally, or diagonally from the center outward.**

Changing the size of the object can be done simply by dragging a resize handle. This resizes the picture in the direction towards which you drag. Dragging a resize handle, however, changes the proportions of the picture. Recall that evenly resizing the object from a center point in the object is called resizing about center. This method of resizing the clip art picture maintains the object's proportions.

Adding a Border to the Picture

The next step is to add a border to the picture. A **border** is the visible line around the edge of an object. The border draws attention to the object by defining its edges. A border is composed of three attributes: line style, line color, and fill color. The **line style** determines the line thickness and line appearance of the border. For example, you could choose a thick, solid line for your border. **Line color** determines the color of the line that forms the border so you could use black for the line color on a border around a picture. Fill color determines the interior color of the selected object. The picture illustrated in Figure 3-76 on page PP 3.54 has a three-line border. Perform the steps on the next page to add a three-line border.

Steps **To Add a Border to a Picture**

1 **Click the Line Style button on the Drawing toolbar. When the Line Style menu displays, point to the three-line style (narrow, wide, narrow) at the bottom of the list.**

The Line Style menu displays (Figure 3-83).

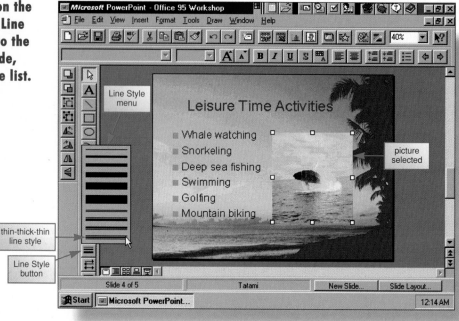

FIGURE 3-83

2 **Click the three-line style (narrow, wide, narrow) on the menu.**

A three-line border displays around the picture (Figure 3-84).

More *About* **Borders**

You delete a border when you remove its color. To delete a border around an object, view the object in Slide view, click the Line Color button on the Drawing toolbar, and then click No Line on the Line Color menu.

FIGURE 3-84

*Other***Ways**

1. On Format menu click Color and Lines, click style box arrow, select last line example, click OK button

2. Press ALT+O, press N, press TAB three times, press DOWN ARROW, press ARROW keys to select line style, press ENTER two times

Changing the Fill Color of the Border

To draw the attention of the audience to the picture, add fill color to the border. Recall that the Design Template establishes the attributes of the Title Master and the Slide Master. When you click the Fill Color button on the Drawing toolbar, a menu displays fill color options. A portion of the menu lists the eight colors used to create the Design Template. One of the colors is identified as the fill color and is listed as the Automatic option on the menu. Recall that the

Design Template used in this project is Tatami. Perform the following steps to add the Tatami Design Template default fill color to the border around the picture on Slide 4.

 Steps To Change Fill Color of the Border

1 **Ensure the picture is selected. Click the Fill Color button on the Drawing toolbar.**

The Fill Color menu displays (Figure 3-85). The current fill color is No Fill.

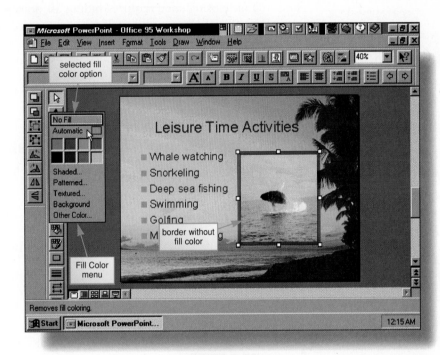

FIGURE 3-85

2 **Click Automatic on the Fill Color menu.**

The Automatic fill color, orange, is the default fill color for the Tatami Design Template (Figure 3-86).

3 **Click the Save button on the Standard toolbar to save the presentation again.**

FIGURE 3-86

Slide 4 is now complete. The next section introduces you to another option for gracefully closing an on-screen slide show.

▶*Other***Ways**

1. On Format menu click Color and Lines, click Fill box arrow, click Automatic, click OK button
2. Press ALT+O, press N, press DOWN ARROW, press ARROW keys to select color, press ENTER two times

More *About*
Fill Color

PowerPoint allows you to create semi-transparent objects. On the Format menu, click Colors and Lines, then click Semi-Transparent in the Fill area of the Colors and Lines dialog box. Change the fill color of the object by clicking the Fill box arrow and then clicking a color.

Creating a Blank Closing Slide

When running a presentation in Slide Show view, PowerPoint returns to the PowerPoint screen when you advance beyond the last slide in your slide show. Using a blank slide to end an on-screen slide show gives the presentation a clean ending and prevents the audience from seeing the PowerPoint screen. Creating a blank closing slide requires hiding all objects that normally display on the Slide Master, which you did earlier in this project when you created the custom slide background.

Because PowerPoint added an extra slide when you opened the Office Workshop outline file, Slide 5, the closing slide, was automatically created. Slide 5 will display the Bay View picture background when you run the presentation in Slide Show view.

Adding Slide Transition and Text Build Effects

The final step in preparing the Office 95 Workshop presentation is to add slide transition effects and text build effects. Perform the following steps to add the slide transition and text build effects.

TO ADD SLIDE TRANSITION AND TEXT BUILD EFFECTS

Step 1: Click the Slide Sorter View button.
Step 2: Press and hold down the SHIFT key, click Slide 2, Slide 3, and Slide 5. Release the SHIFT key.
Step 3: Click the Slide Transition Effects box down arrow. Click Dissolve.
Step 4: Click Slide 1. Press and hold down the SHIFT key and click Slide 4. Release the SHIFT key.
Step 5: Click the Text Build Effects box down arrow. Click Split Horizontal Out.

The presentation displays in Slide Sorter view (Figure 3-87). Slides 1 and 4 are selected. Text build effects are applied to Slide 1 and Slide 4. Slide transition effects are applied to Slides 2, 3, 4, and 5.

More *About*
Presentation Design

Insert a black slide between sections of a large presentation or when you want to pause for discussion. The black slide focuses the audience's attention on the speaker, and away from the screen display. To create a black slide, change the slide background color to black and click Omit Background Graphics from Master.

More *About*
Presentation Delivery

Never pierce the light source with your body or hands. Doing so distorts the information on the slide as it displays on your clothes, making it difficult for the audience to view.

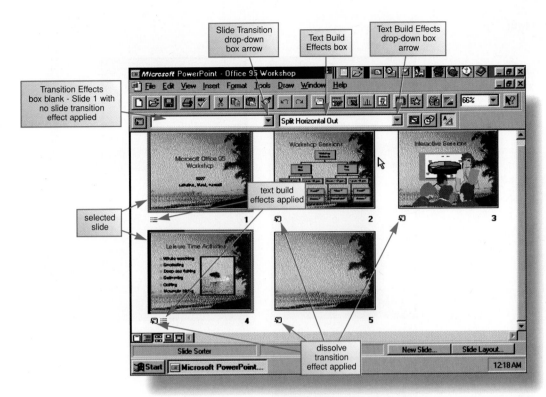

FIGURE 3-87

Printing Slides as Handouts

Perform the following steps to print the presentation slides as handouts, six slides per page.

Steps To Print Slides as Handouts

1 Click File on the menu bar and then click Print. When the Print dialog box displays, click the Print what box arrow, click Handouts [6 slides per page] in the Print what list box. Then click the Scale to Fit Paper check box (Figure 3-88).

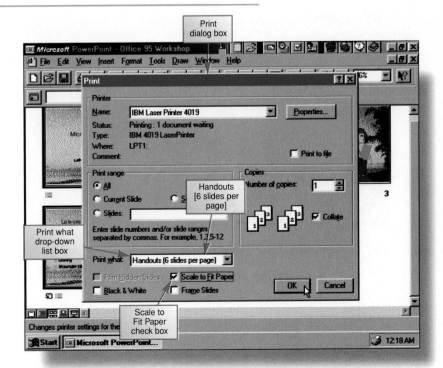

FIGURE 3-88

2 Click the OK button to begin printing.

The handout prints as shown in Figure 3-89.

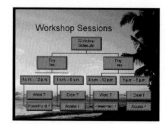

FIGURE 3-89

Project Summary

Project Three introduced you to several methods of enhancing a presentation with embedded visuals. You began the project by creating the presentation from an outline that was created in Word. Then, you learned how to create a special slide background using a picture. Slide 2 introduced you to embedding an organization chart using the supplementary application Microsoft Organization Chart. When you created Slide 3, you learned how to disassemble objects, embed an existing Excel chart, create a layered object, group a layered object, and then group several objects to create a new PowerPoint object. You then learned how to embed a picture, add a border, and change the fill color on Slide 4. Then, you learned how to create a blank closing slide for Slide 5. Finally, you learned how to print your presentation slides as handouts.

What You Should Know

Having completed this project, you now should be able to perform the following tasks:

- Add a Border to a Picture *(PP 3.58)*
- Add Another Level of Subordinate Boxes *(PP 3.27)*
- Add Multiple Subordinate Boxes *(PP 3.26)*
- Add Names to Subordinate Boxes *(PP 3.28)*
- Add Shadow Effects to Boxes in an Organization Chart *(PP 3.34)*
- Add Slide Transition and Text Build Effects *(PP 3.60)*
- Change Border Style *(PP 3.35)*
- Change Design Templates *(PP 3.12)*
- Change Fill Color of the Border *(PP 3.59)*
- Change the Organization Chart Style *(PP 3.29)*
- Change Slide Layout to Title Slide *(PP 3.14)*
- Close Organization Chart and Return to PowerPoint *(PP 3.36)*
- Copy a Branch of an Organization Chart *(PP 3.30)*
- Create the Title for the Root Manager Box *(PP 3.23)*
- Delete Subordinate Boxes *(PP 3.24)*
- Deselect a Clip Art Object *(PP 3.43)*
- Disassemble Clip Art *(PP 3.41)*
- Display the Drawing+ Toolbar *(PP 3.40)*
- Display the Next Slide and Change the Slide Layout *(PP 3.21)*
- Drag a Modified Object *(PP 3.51)*
- Edit Text in an Organization Chart *(PP 3.32)*
- Embed an Excel Chart *(PP 3.45)*
- Group Layered Objects into One Object *(PP 3.50)*
- Group Selected Objects *(PP 3.53)*
- Insert a Picture *(PP 3.54)*
- Insert a Picture to Create a Custom Background *(PP 3.17)*
- Insert Clip Art *(PP 3.39)*
- Maximize the Organization Chart Window *(PP 3.22)*
- Move a PowerPoint Object *(PP 3.44)*
- Open an Outline *(PP 3.9)*
- Open Organization Chart *(PP 3.22)*
- Overlay Objects *(PP 3.49)*
- Paste a Branch of an Organization Chart *(PP 3.31)*
- Print Slides as Handouts *(PP 3.61)*
- Resize a Picture *(PP 3.56)*
- Save a Presentation *(PP 3.14)*
- Scale an Embedded Object *(PP 3.48)*
- Scale an Organization Chart Object *(PP 3.37)*
- Scale Clip Art *(PP 3.39)*
- Select All Boxes in an Organization Chart *(PP 3.33)*
- Select All Objects on a Slide *(PP 3.52)*
- Send an Object to the Background *(PP 3.51)*
- Title a Subordinate Box *(PP 3.25)*

A+ Test Your Knowledge

1 True/False

Instructions: Circle T if the statement is true or F if the statement is false.

T F 1. PowerPoint can create a presentation by opening an outline only if the outline was saved as an RTF file.

T F 2. A scanner is a software device that converts lines and shading into combinations of the binary digits 0 and 1 by sensing different intensities of light and dark.

T F 3. Pictures usually are saved as one of two graphic formats: bit-map or vector.

T F 4. Vector graphic objects are created as collections of pixels and are stored as picture descriptions or calculations.

T F 5. Microsoft Organization Chart is an OLE application that is a supplement of PowerPoint.

T F 6. In Microsoft Organization Chart, the bottom-most manager box is called the root manager.

T F 7. Layered objects are objects that have been positioned on top of each other like a stack of cards.

T F 8. The object at the bottom of a stack of objects is the foreground object.

T F 9. Disassembling clip art converts the objects into individual Organization Chart objects.

T F 10. To resize an object about its center, hold the SHIFT key and drag one of the object's resize handles.

2 Multiple Choice

Instructions: Circle the correct response.

1. An outline saved as a(n) _____ or as a(n) _____ maintains its text attributes and outline heading levels.
   a. Microsoft Word document, RTF file
   b. PowerPoint format file, plain text file
   c. rich text format file, plain text file
   d. Excel format file, plain text file

2. Scanned pictures are _____ pictures and have jagged edges.
   a. bit-mapped
   b. vector
   c. grouped
   d. all of the above

3. A(n) _____ chart is a hierarchical collection of elements depicting various functions or responsibilities that contribute to an organization or to a collective function.
   a. responsibility
   b. organization
   c. Microsoft Excel
   d. Microsoft Word

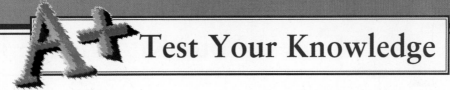 Test Your Knowledge

4. To quickly locate a clip art picture, click the _____ button in the Microsoft ClipArt Gallery dialog box.
   a. Options
   b. Search
   c. Find
   d. Locate

5. PowerPoint allows you to alter clip art by first _____ the objects.
   a. cutting
   b. disassembling
   c. pasting
   d. rearranging

6. Constraining an object from its center point is called _____.
   a. expanding around center
   b. sizing around center
   c. resizing about center
   d. all of the above

7. The object at the bottom of a stack of objects is the _____.
   a. midground object
   b. background object
   c. foreground object
   d. all of the above

8. The _____ button moves an object one level closer to the top of a stack of objects.
   a. Group Objects
   b. Send Backward
   c. Bring to Front
   d. Bring Forward

9. Grouping objects together to create one object is accomplished by _____.
   a. clicking the Group button on the Drawing+ toolbar
   b. clicking the Group command on the Draw menu
   c. clicking the Group command on the shortcut menu
   d. all of the above

10. A(n) _____ object is created in another application and maintains a connection to its source so that if the original object changes so does this object.
    a. embedded
    b. inserted
    c. pasted
    d. linked

 Test Your Knowledge

3 Understanding PowerPoint Menus and Commands

Instructions: Identify the menus and commands that carry out the operation or cause the dialog box to display and allow you to make the indicated changes.

	MENU	COMMAND
1. Disassemble selected object	_____	_____
2. Select all objects on slide	_____	_____
3. Insert a picture	_____	_____
4. Add a border	_____	_____
5. Change the slide background to a picture	_____	_____
6. Resize an object to 130 percent	_____	_____
7. Print audience handouts	_____	_____
8. Insert an organization chart	_____	_____
9. Regroup selected objects	_____	_____
10. Insert clip art	_____	_____

4 Working with an Organization Chart

Instructions: Write the step numbers below to indicate the sequence necessary to create the organization chart shown in Figure 3-90. Assume PowerPoint is open, the Design Template and Organization Chart slide layout are selected, and the border, logo, and title text are already created. Label levels one and two before adding new subordinate boxes. Label new subordinate boxes before changing the chart style. Format the box border style after changing the chart style.

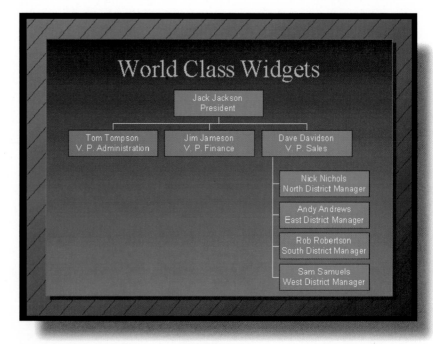

FIGURE 3-90

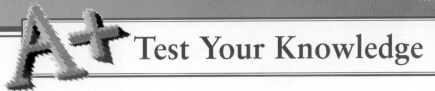 Test Your Knowledge

Step _____: Click the Select button on the Organization Chart icon bar. Click the box to the right of the North District Manager subordinate box. Type Andy Andrews and press the ENTER key. Then type East District Manager in the box.

Step _____: Double-click the organization chart placeholder.

Step _____: On the Organization Chart Edit menu, point to Select and then click Lowest Level on the Select menu.

Step _____: On the Organization Chart Edit menu, point to Select and then click All on the Select menu.

Step _____: Click the Close button. Then click the Yes button in the Microsoft Organization Chart dialog box.

Step _____: On the Organization Chart Styles menu, click the vertical style box in the Groups menu..

Step _____: On the Boxes menu, click Border. Click dark pink (column five, row one in the Color box). Click the OK button.

Step _____: Press and hold down the SHIFT key, click the Subordinate button on the Organization Chart icon bar four times, and then release the SHIFT key. Click the right subordinate box labeled Dave Davidson V. P. Sales. Type Nick Nichols and press the ENTER key. Then type North District Manager in the box.

Step _____: On level two, click the left subordinate box. Type Tom Tompson and press the ENTER key. Type V. P. Administration in the box. Next, click the middle subordinate box. Type Jim Jameson and press the ENTER key. Type V. P. Finance in the box. Then, click the right subordinate box. Type Dave Davidson and press the ENTER key. Type V. P. Sales in the box.

Step _____: Click the box to the right of the East District Manager subordinate box. Type Rob Robertson and press the ENTER key. Then type South District Manager in the box.

Step _____: Click the box to the right of the South District Manager subordinate box. Type Sam Samuels and press the ENTER key. Then type West District Manager in the box.

Step _____: Type Jack Jackson in the root manager box and press the ENTER key. Then type President in the root manager box.

Use Help

1 Learning More about Microsoft Organization Chart

Instructions: Perform the following tasks using a computer:

1. Start PowerPoint. When the PowerPoint startup dialog box displays, double-click Blank Presentation. Then double-click the Organization Chart AutoLayout.
2. Double-click the organization chart placeholder. When the Microsoft Organization Chart window displays, click Help on the menu bar, and then click Index on the Help menu.
3. On the Microsoft Organization Chart Help window, click Menu commands and icons. When the Menu commands and icons Help window displays, click Styles menu. When the Styles menu Help window displays, read the information. Right-click the Styles menu window and click Print Topic on the shortcut menu.
4. Jump to Rearranging boxes by clicking Rearranging boxes at the bottom of the Styles menu Help window. When the Rearranging boxes Help window displays, read the information. Next, click each of the four underlined topics—manager, assistant, subordinates, and group style—and read the information. Then, print the Rearranging boxes information.
5. Click the Back button on the Help toolbar two times to display the Menu commands and icons Help window.
6. Click The icon bar. When The icon bar Help window displays, read and print the information.
7. Jump to General purpose tools. Read and print the information. Click the Back button. Jump to Box tools. Read and print the information. Click the Back button. Jump to Custom drawing tools. Read and print the information.
8. Click the Microsoft Organization Chart Help window Close button. Click the Microsoft Organization Chart - [Object in Presentation] Close button. When the Microsoft Organization Chart dialog box displays, click the No button.
9. When the PowerPoint window displays, close PowerPoint without saving the presentation.
10. Hand in the printouts to your instructor.

2 Expanding on the Basics

Instructions: Use PowerPoint online Help to better understand the topics listed below. Begin each of the following by double-clicking the Help button on the Standard toolbar. If you cannot print the Help information, answer the question on a separate piece of paper.

1. How do you select an object that is hidden behind another?
2. How do you remove a border?
3. In what ways can you modify a picture in your presentation?
4. How do you edit an organization chart?

Apply Your Knowledge

1 Creating a Presentation from an Outline and Changing the Slide Background

Instructions: Start PowerPoint. Perform the following tasks to create the slides shown in Figure 3-91:

1. Open the Sales Incentives outline from the PowerPoint folder on the Student Floppy Disk that accompanies this book. Recall that you need to change the Files of type box to All Outlines.

2. Change slide layout for Slide 1 (Figure 3-91a) to Title Slide. Change slide layout for Slide 2 to 2 Column Text and move the bulleted text to look like Figure 3-91b. Add a blank closing slide at the end of the presentation.

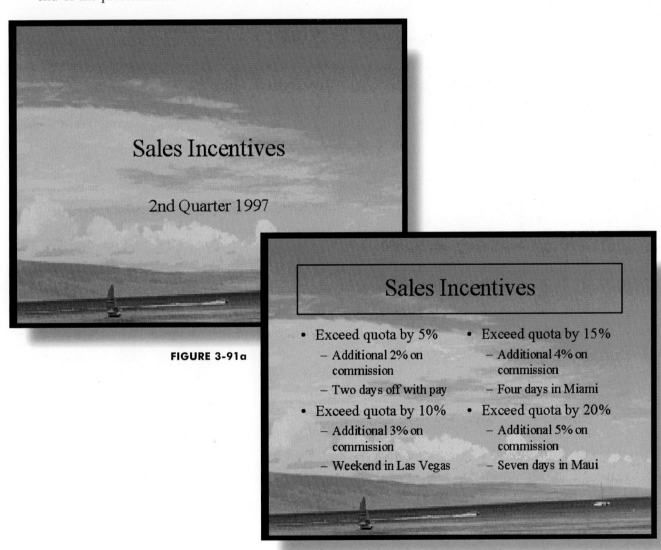

FIGURE 3-91a

FIGURE 3-91b

(continued)

Apply Your Knowledge

Creating a Presentation from an Outline and Changing the Slide Background *(continued)*

3. Create the custom background shown in Figure 3-91c using the Maui picture file from the Student Floppy Disk.
4. Apply a border to the title text on Slide 2 using the second line style on the Line Style menu.
5. Apply the Uncover Right-Down slide transition effect. Then apply the Fly From Top-Left text build effect.
6. Save the presentation with the filename, Sales Incentives.
7. Print the presentation.
8. Close PowerPoint.

FIGURE 3-91c

In the Lab

1 Creating a Custom Background

Problem: You are the marketing manager for a new time-share development. You are creating a sales training presentation and want a title slide with a rendering of the resort as the background. A friend sends you a presentation containing a clip art picture he found in an old version of PowerPoint. You modify that clip art and then border the title text using a picture in the ClipArt Gallery. *Hint:* Use Help to solve this problem.

Instructions: Perform the following tasks to create the slide shown in Figure 3-92:

1. Start PowerPoint, open the Resort presentation on the Student Floppy Disk that accompanies this book. Apply the Comet Design Template. Then change slide layout to Title Only.

2. Change the slide background color to light blue (column four, row two of the Background Fill menu in the Custom Background dialog box). Prevent the comet graphic from displaying.

3. Type Polynesian Princess Resort for the slide title. Change the font to Algerian or a similar font if your computer does not have Algerian. Then change text color to dark blue (column two, row one on the Text Color menu).

4. Insert the clip art picture from the Microsoft ClipArt Gallery with a description of Medieval Frame. Overlay the clip art on the slide title. Resize the clip art about center to frame the slide title as shown in Figure 3-92. Send the clip art back one level in the stack of objects. Then group the title text and the clip art into one object.

5. Resize the Resort clip art picture about center so that the clip art covers the width of the slide.

6. Ungroup the Resort picture two times. Next, select the blue-green water object. Then, drag the middle bottom resize handle down to the edge of the slide so that the water object covers the bottom portion of the slide. Change the fill color of the water object to dark blue (column two, row one on the Fill Color menu).

7. Change the sand object (cream colored object between the water object and the green object) to Sand in the Textured Fill dialog box.

8. Regroup the PowerPoint objects.

9. Save the presentation with the file-name Polynesian Princess.

10. Print the slide using the Black & White option.

11. Close PowerPoint.

FIGURE 3-92

In the Lab

2 Embedding an Organization Chart and Inserting a Picture

Problem: You are the Administrative Assistant for Solar Technology and Radiant Energy Storage Systems. Your boss wants a few slides to familiarize the employees in the four regional sales offices with the senior management team and the newly hired vice president of research. You decide to use PowerPoint to create the organization chart shown in Figure 3-93a and the fact sheet shown in Figure 3-93b. *Hint:* Use Help to solve this problem.

Instructions: Perform the following tasks:

1. Start PowerPoint and click a blank presentation. Apply the Organization Chart slide layout. Then apply the Sparkle Design Template.
2. Type Solar Technology and Radiant Energy Storage Systems for the slide title.
3. Create the organization chart shown in Figure 3-93a. Type your name in the Administrative Assistant box.
4. Change the box color for the president (level one) to yellow (column 1, row 2). Change the box color for the administrative assistant and vice presidents (level two) to cyan (column 3, row 2). Change the box color for the engineers, supervisors, and managers (level three) to lime-green (column 2, row 2).
5. Add borders to all boxes. Use the border style in column 1, row 2 on the Border Style menu. Change the border color for all boxes to white (column 9, row 3).
6. Change the text color for all box text to black (column 7, row 1).
7. Close Microsoft Organization Chart and return to Slide 1. Scale the organization chart to 120 percent. Then drag the organization chart down below the lines under the title object.

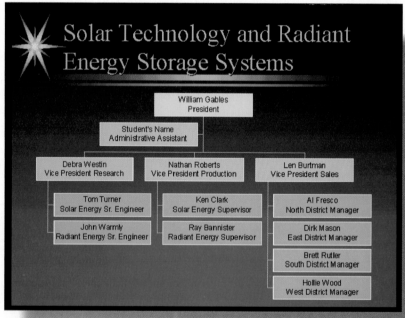

FIGURE 3-93a

8. Insert a new slide with the Text & Object AutoLayout. Type the text shown in Figure 3-93b.
9. Insert the picture shown in Figure 3-93b using the file, Debra Westin, on the Student Floppy Disk. Add a border to the picture using the second to the last line style on the Line Style menu.
10. Save the presentation with the filename, Solar Tech Org Chart.
11. Print handouts [2 slides per page] using the Black & White option. Then close PowerPoint.

In the Lab

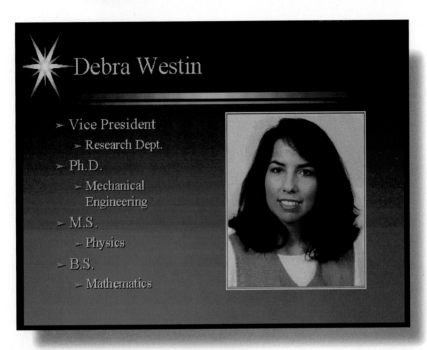

FIGURE 3-93b

3 Opening an Existing Outline and Creating a New Clip Art Picture

Problem: You have written a satire on life in the Navy and have been asked to present your work to the English department at their monthly meeting. You create the presentation from the outline developed for your satire. Because you cannot find a caricature of a person in naval attire, you create the caricature shown in Figure 3-94 on the next page.

Instructions: Perform the following tasks:

1. Start PowerPoint. Open the Navy Satire outline from the Student Floppy Disk that accompanies this book.
2. Apply the Splatter Design Template. Change the slide layout to Clip Art & Text.
3. Select the bulleted list and click the Increase Font Size button four times so that the Font Size box displays 40+. Insert a blank line between the paragraphs, salute it and If it doesn't.
4. Insert the clip art picture with the description of Problem Priority in the Microsoft ClipArt Gallery into the clip art placeholder. Disassemble the clip art picture until the hats display as individual objects.
5. Delete all hats except the sailor's cap. Then, delete the group of curved lines, which indicate motion.
6. Drag the sailor's cap onto the man's head to just above his eyebrows. Next, increase Zoom Control to 100 percent. Then, bring the cap to the foreground.
7. Change the color of the sailor's pants to white.

(continued)

In the Lab

Opening an Existing Outline and Creating a New Clip Art Picture *(continued)*

8. Change the sweater object color to white. Next, change the neckline with the pink tie object color to white. Then, disassemble the neckline with tie object and delete the tie object.
9. Group all the individual PowerPoint objects in the picture into one object.
10. Scale the object to 150 percent.
11. Place your name, the date, and slide number in the slide footer.
12. Save the presentation with the filename, You're in the Navy. Then, print the presentation using the Black & White option. Close PowerPoint.

FIGURE 3-94

Cases and Places

The difficulty of these case studies varies:

▶ Case studies preceded by a single half moon are the least difficult. You are asked to create the required presentation based on information that has already been placed in an organized form.
▶▶ Case studies preceded by two half moons are more difficult. You must organize the information presented before using it to create the required presentation.
▶▶▶ Case studies preceded by three half moons are the most difficult. You must decide on a specific topic, and then obtain and organize the necessary information before using it to create the required presentation.

1 ▶ You are following a prescribed course of study to complete your education. Before you graduate, the department chairperson or another school official is responsible for auditing your transcript. It is important that you carefully organize your classes, semester by semester, so that you finish your prescribed course of study in the least amount of time. Create a presentation to present to your academic advisor that identifies a proposed class list for your junior and senior years. Include a title slide and an organization chart listing your semester courses for your junior year and senior year. Identify the department, your major, and if applicable, your minor area in which you are studying. Identify the department chairperson and insert a picture of that person. If a picture is not available, use one of the pictures in the PowerPoint folder on the Student Floppy Disk that accompanies this book. Design your presentation to flow logically.

2 ▶ If time and money were both unlimited, what would you do? Assume you have unlimited wealth, are healthy, and have many years to live. Design a presentation that explains what you would do and what you would own. Be creative and honest with yourself. Organize your life into three stages: early adulthood, middle adulthood, and late adulthood. In each stage of life, identify what you would accomplish. Create a custom background. Use pictures or clip art where appropriate.

3 ▶▶ Assume you are on the nominating committee for the Humanitarian of the Year Award. One of your responsibilities is to present your nominee to the other committee members. Select a politician, entertainer, sports figure, or other benevolent individual with whom you are familiar. Create a presentation that provides a brief biography and identifies this person's major accomplishments. Insert a bordered picture of this person. Identify why you chose this individual as someone worthy of recognition. Select a suitable Design Template. Close the presentation with a blank closing slide.

Cases and Places

4 ▶▶ Goals are often divided into four categories: spiritual, family, career, and self. A 1973 Yale University economics study concluded that three percent of the 1953 Yale graduating class had written goals and defined a game plan to reach them. Twenty years later, the same three percent had achieved a net worth greater than the rest of the entire class combined. Create a presentation about yourself. Provide a brief biography. Create an organization chart of your goals. Under each of the four goal categories, identify two or more goals. One goal should be a short-term goal, something that will take less than a year to achieve. Another goal should be a long-term goal, something that will take longer than one year to achieve. Format the organization chart as necessary to display the chart on a slide.

5 ▶▶ Every organization has structure. Someone is the leader, and other people are accountable to the leader. Depending on the size of the organization, leadership responsibilities may be separated by function or by department. Create a presentation that explains an organization that you currently work for, one that you previously worked for, or one that you otherwise have knowledge of. The presentation should include the purpose of the organization, a brief history of the organization, a summary of the organization's products or services, and an organization chart. Format the organization chart to highlight the organization's various functions or departments.

6 ▶▶▶ Use the Internet, the library, or a travel agency to research a destination you dream of someday visiting. Include a list of available activities or historical sites. Provide geographical information and a map. Scan a picture of your dream location and use it for the background of the title slide. Include another picture to depict one of the local points of interest (for example, the Eiffel Tower in Paris, France). Close the presentation with a blank slide. Apply slide transition and text build effects where appropriate.

7 ▶▶▶ Just about every day, you read or hear negative news about what we eat. On the other hand, you frequently hear claims of how vitamins prevent disease and improve a person's health. Use the Internet or your local library to research the vitamin industry. For example, how are vitamins made, what is the difference between natural and synthetic vitamins, and can vitamins prevent disease? Use a word processing program to outline your research findings. Create a presentation from your outline. Design a custom background, add pictures with borders, include an organization chart, and close the presentation with a blank slide.

Microsoft PowerPoint 7

Windows 95

Creating a Presentation Containing Interactive OLE Documents

Objectives:

You will have mastered the material in this project when you can:

▶ Open an existing presentation and save it with a new filename

▶ Select a new color scheme

▶ Modify a color scheme

▶ Draw an object

▶ Create a graphic object using Microsoft WordArt

▶ Embed an object on the Slide Master

▶ Use object linking and embedding (OLE) to create a slide containing interactive documents

▶ Use guides to position and size an object

▶ Modify PowerPoint options to end a presentation with a black slide

▶ Hide a slide

▶ Animate an object

▶ Run a slide show to display a hidden slide and activate an interactive document

The Magic of Embedding Visuals

Mr. Twain's humorous aphorism may have been pertinent in his day, but today's audiences are better educated than ever before and know when the facts add up. Baby boomers and Generation X alike have grown increasingly more sophisticated in their expectations for everything from automobiles to zoom lenses. Forty years ago, audiences sat still for the herky-jerky movement of such classics as *King Kong Meets Godzilla*, but nowadays, they are accustomed to the computer-generated seamless motion of the velociraptors in *Jurassic Park*.

Whether the purpose is to dispense entertainment or information, in a universe competing for audiences, higher and more exacting standards have created a high-tech society that demands excitement and stimulation in everything it sees.

Manipulation

> *Get your facts first, and then you can distort them as much as you please.*
>
> Mark Twain

Presentations are no exception. In exchange for their time and attention, people expect presentations to be entertaining, as well as informative.

Fortunately for those who face the daunting task of presenting a visually stimulating, rewarding experience to exacting viewers, Microsoft has provided its own answer to Industrial Light and Magic. Far simpler to use than most software in its class, PowerPoint supplies another kind of magic, called Object Linking and Embedding, otherwise known as OLE (pronounced olay). Somewhat like a Star Fleet transporter, OLE gives users the capability of importing and embedding objects from another source, such as a clip art gallery picture, a cartoon, or a scanned-in photo. With the literally thousands of images in commercially available clip art libraries, it is possible to include the Mona Lisa or even a favorite rock star's portrait in a slide with very little effort.

The freedom to create a picture to the author's specifications is a decided plus over other static preparation tools. After embedding a graphics object, the object can be manipulated in several ways: changing its size, extracting part of the image, rearranging the individual components of the image, or adding objects from other sources to the original. Picture the juxtaposition of Porky Pig kissing Sleeping Beauty. Not exactly the prince charming she had in mind!

The capability of importing from other applications, such as Excel or Word, adds another powerful tool to the presenter's arsenal. Via this route, graphs, charts, tables, worksheets, and special text effects created with WordArt add to the excitement.

Someday, Microsoft may even find a way to provide the capability of dimming the lights and serving refreshments from a replicator. Until then, we can imagine the words of the immortal Captain James Tiberius Kirk, after a visit to the planet Earth: "Don't beam me up, Scotty. There is intelligent life here, after all."

POWERPOINT

Project 4

Microsoft
PowerPoint 7
Windows 95

Creating a Presentation Containing Interactive OLE Documents

Case Perspective

The next Executive Training Tours (E.T.T.) workshop is in Phoenix, Arizona. The organizing team decides to modify the Office 95 Workshop orientation presentation created for the Maui workshop. They want to change Design Templates, but cannot find one that uses the colors associated with the E.T.T. company logo. Therefore, they decide to change Design Templates and select a new color scheme. They use PowerPoint to draw their company logo and then insert text to create a graphic object. They insert the logo onto the Slide Master so that it displays on every slide except the title slide. They then decide to animate the logo to fly across the title slide. They decide to replace the breeching whale picture with a picture of one of the activities in the Phoenix area. Finally, the team decides to add a slide to demonstrate the four Microsoft Office 95 applications featured in the workshop. Then they decide to display that slide only if time permits.

Introduction

Because every presentation is created for a specific audience, subsequent deliveries of the same presentation may require you to make changes. These changes are necessary to accommodate the knowledge base or interest level of the audience. Sometimes, when running a slide show, you want to open another application to show the audience the effect of a change. For example, when presenting next year's projected sales, you may wish to perform a "what if" analysis during the slide show without leaving PowerPoint. PowerPoint allows you to do so using interactive documents. An **interactive document** is a file created in an object linking and embedding (OLE) application, such as Microsoft Excel, and then opened during the running of a slide show. Other times you may wish to refrain from showing one or more slides because they are not applicable to a particular audience. PowerPoint has the capability to hide slides. As the presenter, you decide whether to display them. Occasionally, you need to change the look of your presentation by adding special graphics, such as a company logo, adding borders to objects and text, adding shadow effects to objects, or changing the overall color scheme. Project 4 customizes the Office 95 Workshop presentation created in Project 3 (see Figures 3-1a through 3-1e on page PP 3.7).

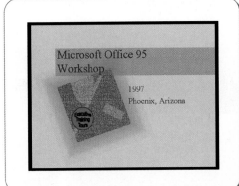

FIGURE 4-1a

Slide Preparation Steps

The preparation steps are an overview of how the slide presentation shown in Figures 4-1a through 4-1k on this and the next page will be developed in Project 4. The following tasks will be completed in this project.

1. Start PowerPoint.
2. Open an existing presentation, save it with a new filename, and apply a new Design Template.
3. Select a new color scheme and then modify it.
4. Create a graphic object using drawing tools and Microsoft WordArt.
5. Embed the graphic object on the Slide Master.
6. Link Word, PowerPoint, and Excel documents, and embed an Access database to create a slide containing interactive documents.
7. Replace the text and picture on the slide titled Leisure Time Activities.
8. Delete the blank closing slide and change the PowerPoint options to end the presentation with a black slide.
9. Hide a slide.
10. Animate the title slide.
11. Save the presentation.
12. Run the slide show to display the hidden slide and activate the interactive documents.
13. Close PowerPoint.

FIGURE 4-1b

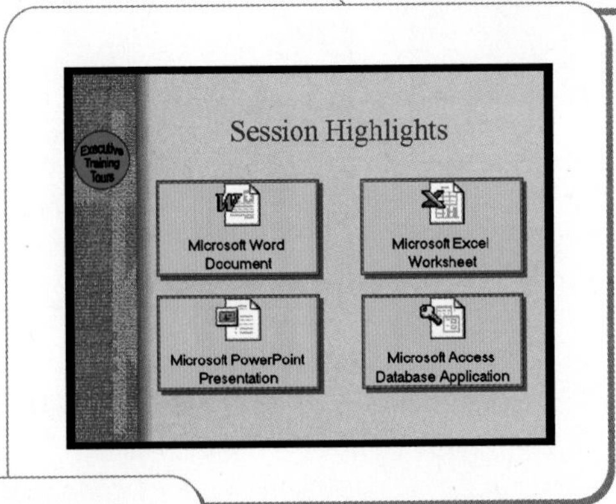

FIGURE 4-1c

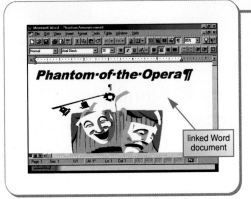

FIGURE 4-1d

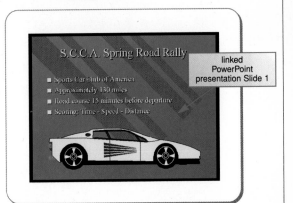

FIGURE 4-1e

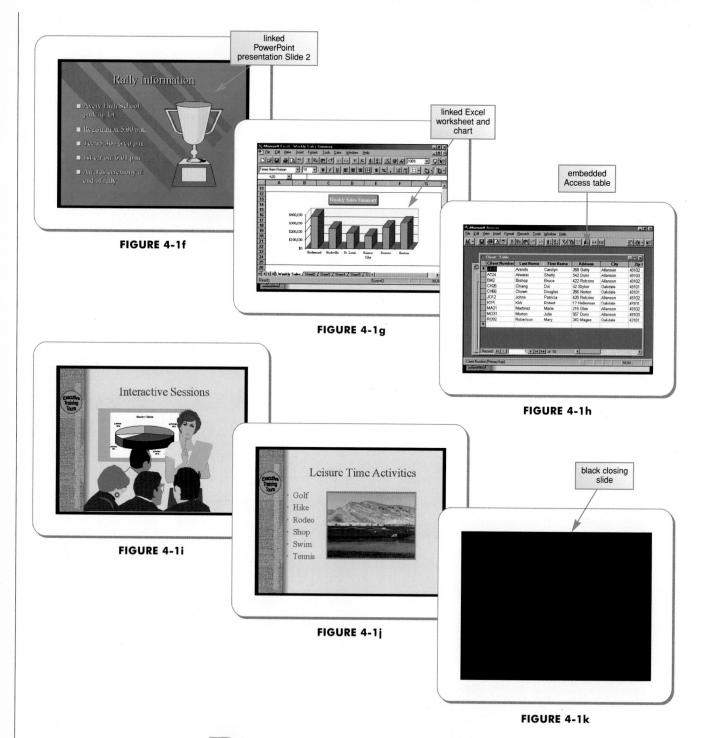

FIGURE 4-1f

FIGURE 4-1g

FIGURE 4-1h

FIGURE 4-1i

FIGURE 4-1j

FIGURE 4-1k

Project Four – Customizing an Existing Presentation

Because you are customizing the Office 95 Workshop presentation created in Project 3, the first step in this project is to open the Office 95 Workshop. So that the original presentation remains intact, you save it with a new filename, Office 95 Workshop Phoenix. Later in this project, you modify the new presentation's slides by changing the Design Template, selecting a new color scheme, replacing a picture and bulleted text, and adding one new slide. The steps on the following pages illustrate these procedures.

Opening a Presentation and Saving It with a New Filename

After starting PowerPoint, the first step in this project is to open the Office 95 Workshop presentation saved in Project 3 and save it with the filename, Office 95 Workshop Phoenix. This procedure should be done immediately to prevent inadvertently saving the presentation with the original filename. Perform the following steps to open an existing presentation and save it with a new filename. If you did not complete Project 3, see your instructor for a copy of the presentation.

TO OPEN A PRESENTATION AND SAVE IT WITH A NEW FILENAME

Step 1: Insert the floppy disk that contains the Project 3 file (created in Project 3), Office 95 Workshop, into drive A.

Step 2: Click the Start button on the taskbar. Click Open Office Document.

Step 3: When the Open dialog box displays, click the Look in down arrow and then click 3½ Floppy [A:]. Double-click Office 95 Workshop.

Step 4: Click File on the menu bar and then click Save As.

Step 5: Type `Office 95 Workshop Phoenix` in the File name box. Do not press the ENTER key.

Step 6: Click the Save button.

The presentation is saved to drive A with the filename, Office 95 Workshop Phoenix (Figure 4-2).

Editing Text

Because the location of the Office 95 Workshop is changing, the subtitle text on the title slide must be changed. Recall that text objects that display on a slide can be edited in Slide view or Outline view. Perform the steps on the next page to display the title slide in Slide view and then revise the subtitle text.

> **More** *About*
> **Using an Existing**
> **Presentation**
>
> When you want to create a new presentation with the same basic design as another presentation, open the existing presentation and save it with a new filename. Then, make changes to the new presentation. The existing presentation acts as a template for the new presentation using Microsoft Paint to change colors.

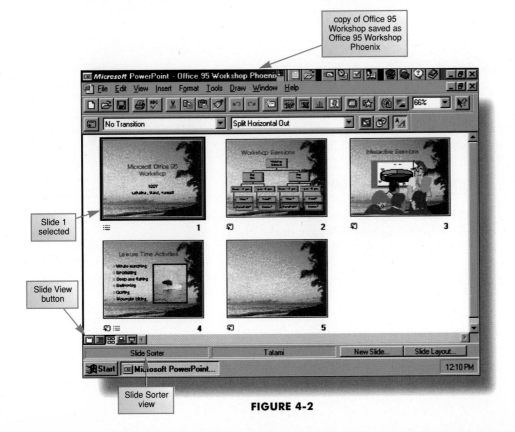

FIGURE 4-2

TO CHANGE TEXT

Step 1: Click the Slide View button on the View button bar if it is not already recessed.
Step 2: Triple-click Lahaina, Maui, Hawaii.
Step 3: Type Phoenix, Arizona in place of the highlighted text.

Slide 1 displays the updated subtitle text (Figure 4-3).

FIGURE 4-3

Changing Design Template

One of the changes requested by the Office 95 Workshop organizing team is the Design Template. The Design Template used in Project 3 was Tatami; the Design Template requested for Project 4 is Blue Weave. Perform the following steps to change the Design Template.

TO CHANGE THE DESIGN TEMPLATE

Step 1: Click the Apply Design Template button on the Standard toolbar.
Step 2: Double-click Blue Weave in the Name box.

PowerPoint displays "Charts are being updated with the new color scheme." After several seconds, Slide 1 displays the new template, Blue Weave, without the Title Master background graphics (Figure 4-4).

Recall from Project 3 that the Omit Background Graphics from Master check box, in the Custom Background dialog box, was clicked to prevent the Design Template graphics from displaying on the picture that composed the slide background. The next step is to display the background graphics for the Blue Weave Design Template.

FIGURE 4-4

Displaying Background Graphics on the Masters

The Blue Weave Design Template in Figure 4-4 looks different from the Blue Weave Design Template in Figure 4-1 on pages PP 4.5 and PP 4.6 because the Omit Background Graphics from Master check box contains a check mark. Recall that the Title Master controls the objects that display on the title slide and the Slide Master controls the objects that display on all the slides except the title slide. To display the Blue Weave Design Template graphics, you remove the check mark from the Omit Background Graphics from Master check box. Perform the following steps to display the background graphics on the Title Master and Slide Master.

TO DISPLAY BACKGROUND GRAPHICS ON THE MASTERS

Step 1: Right-click anywhere on the slide except a text object.

Step 2: Click Custom Background on the shortcut menu.

Step 3: When the Custom Background dialog box displays, click Omit Background Graphics from Master.

Step 4: Click the Apply to All button.

The Blue Weave Design Template background graphics will display on all presentation slides. Slide 1 displays the Title Master background graphics (Figure 4-5). The Title Master background graphics are different from those that display on the Slide Master.

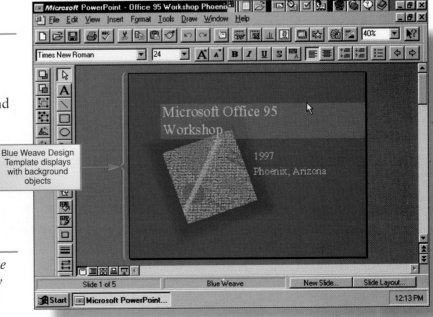

FIGURE 4-5

More *About*
Color Schemes

Color invokes an emotional
response from the audience and
can have a tremendous impact
on the success of a presentation. The attention span for
black and white presentations
(which reflect light) is usually
very short. Color presentations
(which absorb light) are easier
for the audience to look at,
thereby increasing their attention span.

Selecting a New Color Scheme

It is sometimes difficult to find a Design Template that has all the attributes your presentation requires. For example, you may find a Design Template with background objects you like, but you do not like the text and lines color. Fortunately, PowerPoint does not limit you to the default color scheme associated with a Design Template. A **color scheme** is a set of eight colors assigned as the main colors of a slide. It consists of a background color, text and lines color, title text color, shadow color, fill color, and three different accent colors. Table 4-1 explains the components of a color scheme. Changing the color scheme can change the look of your presentation dramatically.

Table 4-1

COMPONENT	DESCRIPTION
Background color	The background color is the fundamental color of a PowerPoint slide. For example, if your background color is white, you can place any other color on top of it, but the fundamental color remains white. The white background shows everywhere you do not add color or other objects. The background color on a slide works the same way.
Text and Lines color	The text and lines color contrasts with the background color of the slide. Together with the background color, the text and lines color sets the tone for a presentation. For example, a gray background with black text and lines color sets a dreary tone. In contrast, a red background with yellow text and lines color sets a vibrant tone.
Title Text color	The title text color contrasts with the background color in a manner similar to text and lines color. Title text displays in the title placeholder on a slide.
Shadow color	The shadow color is applied when you shadow an object. This color is usually a darker shade of the background color.
Fill color	The fill color contrasts with both the background color and the text and lines color. The fill color is used for graphs and charts.
Accent colors	Accent colors are designed as colors for secondary features on a slide. Additionally, accent colors are used as colors on graphs.

Selecting a Color Scheme

PowerPoint provides multiple alternative color schemes for each Design Template. You change color schemes by clicking one of the alternative color schemes as described in the following steps.

 Steps To Select a Color Scheme

1 **Right-click Slide 1 anywhere except the title or subtitle object. Then point to Slide Color Scheme on the shortcut menu (Figure 4-6).**

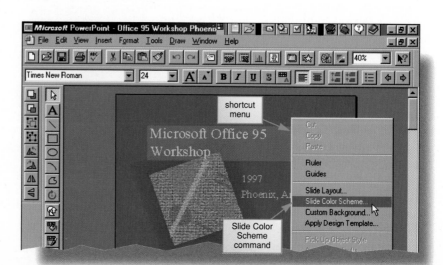

FIGURE 4-6

2 Click Slide Color Scheme on the shortcut menu. When the Color Scheme dialog box displays, click the first color scheme in the second row in the Color Scheme area on the Standard sheet.

The Color Scheme dialog box displays. The Blue Weave Design Template has six color schemes from which to choose. The selected color scheme displays a border (Figure 4-7), a light gray background, a right pointing blue green arrow, and four columns colored blue-green, light purple, light green, and yellow-orange.

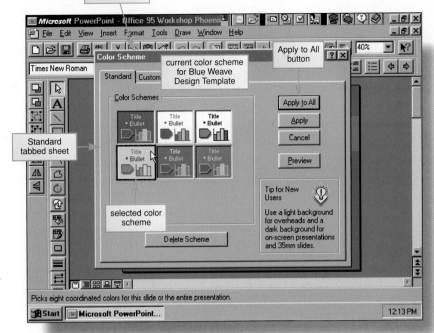

FIGURE 4-7

3 Click the Apply to All button.

PowerPoint displays the message, Charts are being updated with the new color scheme. After a few moments, PowerPoint applies the new color scheme to all slides in the presentation (Figure 4-8).

FIGURE 4-8

Clicking the Apply to All button applies the new color scheme to every slide in the presentation. Clicking the Apply button in the Color Scheme dialog box, however, applies the new color scheme to only the current slide or to any selected slides. If you click the Apply button by mistake, you can correct the error immediately by clicking the Undo button on the Standard toolbar, and then reapplying the color scheme.

Other Ways

1. On Format menu click Slide Color Scheme, click color scheme on Standard sheet, click Apply to All

2. Press ALT+O, press C, press TAB, press ARROW keys to select color scheme, press TAB, press T

More *About*
Color Schemes

To help the audience distinguish between related topics, color code sections of the presentation by applying different color schemes to groups of slides. For example, in a presentation with three distinct sections, such as past history, current trends, and future projections, use three different color schemes in the same color family to uniquely identify each section while maintaining a consistent design.

Modifying a Color Scheme

When you apply a new color scheme, you still may need to adjust one or more of its colors to maintain contrast between objects. For example, the title text in Figure 4-8 on the previous page, displays muted, or faded. Changing the title text color in the new color scheme to a darker color makes the text easier to read. Because this presentation is an on-screen slide show, you also wish to soften the slide background color to light blue.

The Custom sheet in the Color Scheme dialog box displays each of the eight colors that compose the current color scheme. Each of the eight colors in the Scheme Colors area defines a color attribute of an object on the slide. To change a color attribute, first you select the object color and then click the Change Color button. When the specific object's color dialog box displays, you click one of the colors on the Standard sheet and then click the OK button. Perform the following steps to change the slide background and title text colors.

Steps **To Modify a Color Scheme**

1 **Right-click Slide 1 anywhere except the title or subtitle object and then click Slide Color Scheme on the shortcut menu. When the Color Scheme dialog box displays, click the Custom tab. When the Custom sheet displays, click the Background color box and then point to the Change Color button.**

The Color Scheme dialog box displays the Custom sheet. The Background color box is selected (Figure 4-9).

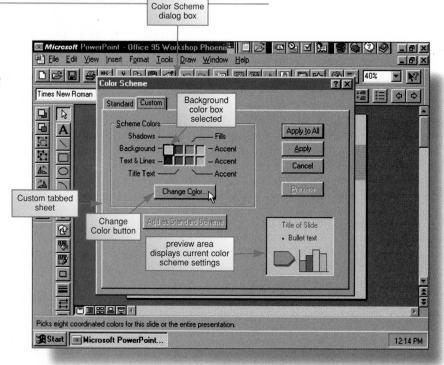

FIGURE 4-9

2 **Click the Change Color button. Then click the seventh color in the sixth row on the Standard sheet.**

The Background Color dialog box displays the Standard sheet (Figure 4-10). The light blue color on the sixth row is selected. Colors on the Standard sheet are arranged in varying shades of the color groups. White, black, and varying shades of gray display at the bottom of the Standard sheet. The box at the lower right of the Standard sheet displays the Current Color and the New Color. The object color on the slide does not change until you click the OK button.

FIGURE 4-10

3 **Click the OK button.**

The Color Scheme dialog box displays (Figure 4-11). The Background color in the Scheme Colors area displays the new background color, light blue. The light blue background color also displays in the preview area.

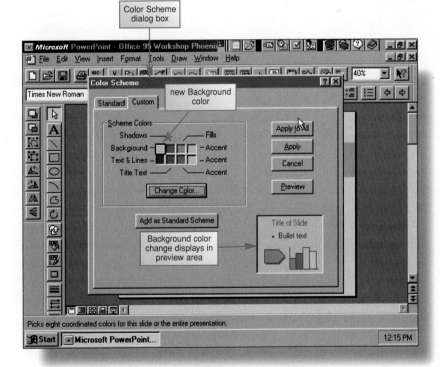

FIGURE 4-11

More *About* **Color Schemes**

Certain color combinations may create problems for some people. Many people have a red/green deficiency with which they cannot distinguish red from green. These people may see purple as blue and green as brown. The difficulty to distinguish colors increases as object size decreases.

4 Click the Title Text color box (Figure 4-12).

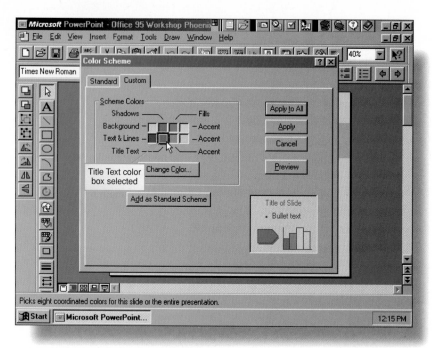

FIGURE 4-12

5 Click the Change Color button. When the Title Text Color dialog box displays, click the eighth color (last color on right) in the second row.

The dark blue color in the second row is selected (Figure 4-13). The dark blue color displays in the New Color box.

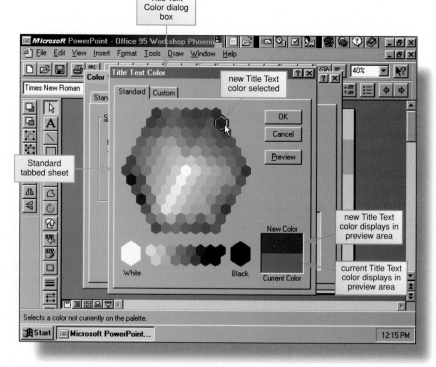

FIGURE 4-13

More *About*
Color Schemes

You can change a color scheme on all slides in the presentation or just selected slides. To change the color scheme of a selected slide, click the Apply button in the Color Scheme dialog box.

6 **Click the OK button.**

The Color Scheme dialog box displays (Figure 4-14). The Title Text color in the Scheme Colors area displays the new title text color, dark blue. The dark blue title text color also displays in the preview area.

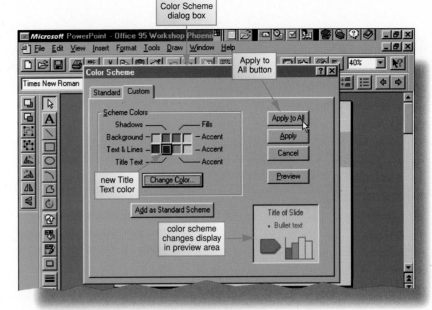

FIGURE 4-14

7 **Click the Apply to All button.**

PowerPoint displays the message, Charts are being updated with the new color scheme. PowerPoint applies the new color scheme to all slides. Slide 1 displays the changes to the title text and background color (Figure 4-15).

8 **Click the Save button on the Standard toolbar to save the presentation again.**

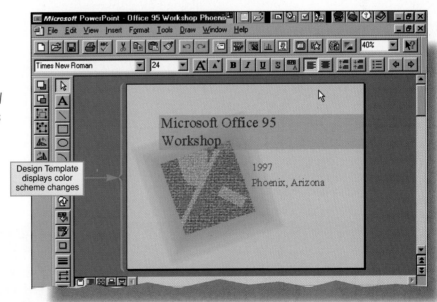

FIGURE 4-15

Creating a Logo

Many companies establish presentation standards to which every presentation must adhere. Very often, a company logo is part of those standards. The Office 95 Workshop Phoenix organizing team is following Executive Training Tours standards by displaying the company logo (Figure 4-16 on the next page) on all slides.

*Other*Ways

1. On Format menu click Slide Color Scheme, click Custom tab, click object color box, click Change Color, click new color, click OK, click Apply to All

2. Press ALT+O, press C, press RIGHT ARROW, press TAB, press ARROW keys to select an object color, press TAB, press O, press TAB, press ARROW keys to select new color, press TAB, press ENTER, press T

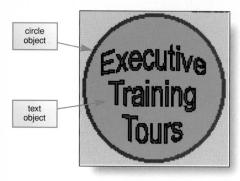

circle
object

text
object

FIGURE 4-16

Displaying the Executive Training Tours logo requires several steps. First, you must open a new presentation and draw the circle object. Next, you apply a border. Then you use the company name to create a graphic text object using Microsoft WordArt. The drawing and graphic text objects are then combined into one logo object. Finally, after copying the logo object onto the Clipboard, you paste it on the Office 95 Workshop Phoenix slide master. The next several sections explain how to create the Executive Training Tours logo.

Opening a New Presentation

Because you may wish to reuse the Executive Training Tours logo in other presentations, you create it in a new presentation. Perform the following steps to open a new presentation.

TO OPEN A NEW PRESENTATION

Step 1: Click the New button on the Standard toolbar.
Step 2: Double-click the Blank Presentation AutoLayout when the New Slide dialog box displays.
Step 3: Click the Maximize button if the PowerPoint window is not already maximized.

Slide 1 displays the Blank AutoLayout in a new presentation titled Presentation (Figure 4-17).

Drawing a Logo

The Executive Training Tours logo is a circle enclosing the company name. The logo is actually two objects, a circle object and a text object. You create the circle object using PowerPoint's drawing tools. Drawing the circle object requires several steps. To help you draw the circle object, display the horizontal and vertical rulers and the horizontal and vertical guides to assist in aligning the objects. Next, you increase the Zoom Control to see the detail of small objects better. Then you draw the outline of the circle object with the Ellipse tool. Finally, you add a border and change its line style. You create the text object later in this project. The next several sections explain how to draw the circle object shown in Figure 4-16.

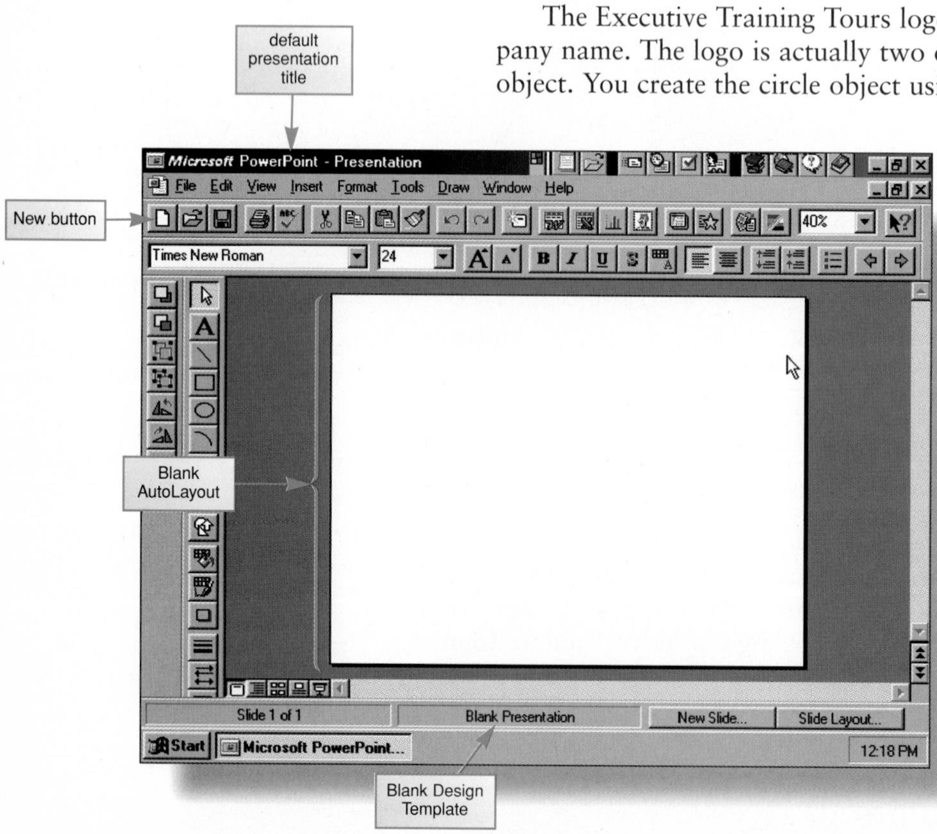

default
presentation
title

New button

Blank
AutoLayout

Blank Design
Template

FIGURE 4-17

Displaying Rulers

To help you align objects, PowerPoint provides two **rulers**: a horizontal ruler and a vertical ruler. The **horizontal ruler** displays at the top of the slide window. The **vertical ruler** displays at the left side of the slide window. Depending on the Zoom Control, **tick marks** on the rulers identify 1/2-inch or 1/8-inch segments. When Zoom Control is 25% or 33%, tick marks displays in 1/2-inch segments. When Zoom Control is 50% or greater, tick marks display in 1/8-inch segments. When you move the mouse pointer, a **pointer indicator** traces the position of the pointer and displays its exact location on both rulers. You use the rulers and pointer indicator later in this project when you draw the circle object. In preparation for creating the logo, you display the rulers now. Perform the following steps to display the horizontal and vertical rulers.

Steps To Display Rulers

1 **Right-click anywhere on the blank slide. Then point to Ruler on the shortcut menu (Figure 4-18).**

2 **Click Ruler on the shortcut menu.**

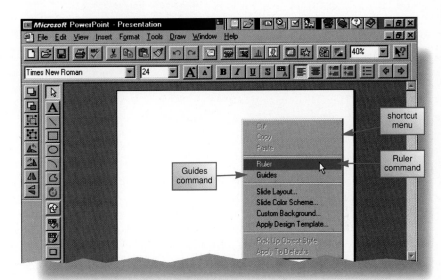

FIGURE 4-18

When the Ruler command is active, a check mark displays in front of the Ruler command on both the shortcut menu and the View menu. When you want to prohibit the rulers from displaying in the PowerPoint window, you hide them. To hide the rulers, right-click anywhere in the PowerPoint window except on an object, and then click Ruler.

Displaying Guides

PowerPoint has **guides,** which are two straight dotted lines, one horizontal and one vertical, used for aligning objects. When an object is close to a guide, its corner or its center (whichever is closer) snaps to, or attaches itself to, the guide. You can move the guides to meet your alignment requirements. Because you are preparing the slide window to create the logo, perform the step on the next page to display the guides.

Steps To Display Guides

1 **Right-click anywhere on the blank slide and then click Guides on the shortcut menu.**

The horizontal and vertical guides intersect in the middle of the slide window (Figure 4-19). The vertical guide aligns with the 0 tick mark on the horizontal ruler. The horizontal guide aligns with the 0 tick mark on the vertical ruler.

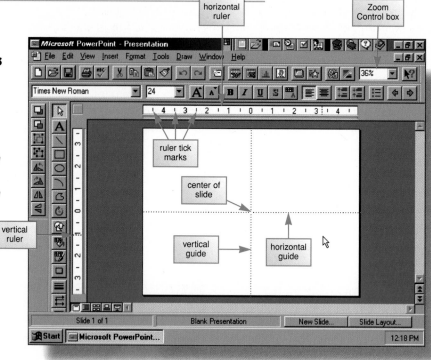

FIGURE 4-19

OtherWays

1. On View menu click Guides
2. Press ALT+V, press G

In the shortcut menu illustrated in Step 1, a check mark displayed in front of the Ruler command because you activated it in the previous section. Recall that a check mark displays when a command is active, or turned on. In the same manner, when the Guides command is active, a check mark displays in front of the Guides command on both the shortcut menu and the View menu.

When you no longer want the guides to display on the screen or want to control the exact placement of objects, you hide the guides. To hide the guides, right-click anywhere in the PowerPoint window except on an object, and click Guides.

Increasing Zoom Control

More *About* **Guides**

PowerPoint allows you to display multiple guides. To display an additional guide, press and hold down the CTRL key and then drag one of the guides. When the new guide displays, drag it to the position at which you want to place an object.

Increasing Zoom Control reduces the editing view of a slide in Slide view, but increases the editing view of individual objects. You increase Zoom Control to make working with detailed objects or small objects easier. In this project, you increase Zoom Control to 100% because it allows you to work with the two logo objects more easily. The following steps summarize how to increase Zoom Control.

TO INCREASE ZOOM CONTROL

Step 1: Click the Zoom Control box arrow.
Step 2: Click 100%.

Zoom Control changes to 100% (Figure 4-20). When you compare Figure 4-19 to Figure 4-20 you see that the ruler tick marks display 1/8" increments.

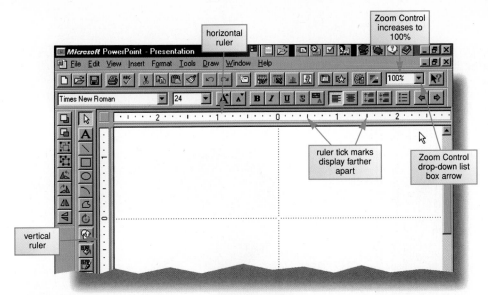

FIGURE 4-20

Drawing a Circle

The next step in creating the Executive Training Tours logo is drawing a circle. A **circle** is a plane curved everywhere at an equal distance from a given fixed point — the center. You draw a circle with the Ellipse Tool on the Drawing toolbar. Because a circle tool is not available, you constrain the shape of the object drawn with the Ellipse tool. To draw a circle, press and hold down the CTRL key and the SHIFT key, and then drag the pointer as shown in the following steps.

 Steps **To Draw a Circle**

---

1 **Click the Ellipse Tool button on the Drawing toolbar. Press and hold down the CTRL key and the SHIFT key. Then position the cross-hair pointer at the intersection of the horizontal and vertical guides.**

The Ellipse Tool button displays recessed, which indicates it is selected (Figure 4-21).

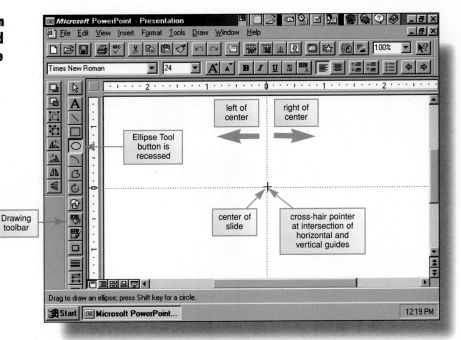

FIGURE 4-21

2 While holding the CTRL and SHIFT keys, drag the cross-hair pointer to the right of center until the pointer indicates on the horizontal ruler is on the 1-inch mark. Release the left mouse button. Then release the CTRL and SHIFT keys.

A circle displays the default attributes of the Default Design Template: green fill color and black lines (Figure 4-22). A selection rectangle around the circle indicates it is selected. The SHIFT key constrains the shape of the ellipse to draw a circle. The CTRL key constrains the size of the circle about center.

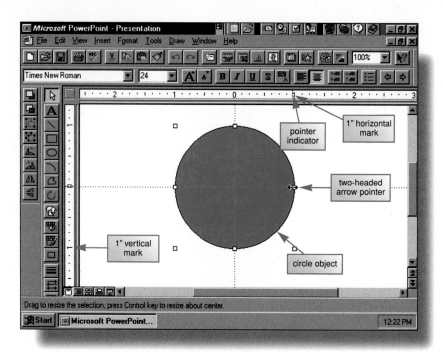

FIGURE 4-22

Adding a Border to a Logo

The next step in drawing the Executive Training Tours logo is to add a border to the circle object. Recall a border is the visible line around the edge of an object and is composed of three attributes: line style, line color, and fill color. The circle shown in Figure 4-22 has a single line border. Perform the steps below to add a thicker border.

TO ADD A BORDER

Step 1: With the circle object selected, click the Line Style button on the Drawing toolbar.

Step 2: Click the second line style from the top of the Line Style menu.

The new border displays around the circle object (Figure 4-23).

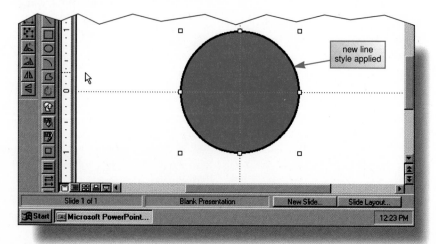

FIGURE 4-23

Creating a Graphic Object with Text

The Executive Training Tours logo contains text that has been manipulated into a graphic object using Microsoft WordArt. **Microsoft WordArt**, a supplementary application that comes with PowerPoint, allows you to create graphic objects with text. Because Microsoft WordArt is an object linking and embedding application, its menu bar and toolbar display in the PowerPoint window when you open WordArt. The next several sections explain how to use Microsoft WordArt to create the graphic text object shown inside the circle in Figure 4-16 on page PP 4.16.

Opening WordArt

To create the graphic text object in the Executive Training Tours logo, you first must open WordArt. Object linking and embedding brings this supplementary application on the PowerPoint screen and makes the menus, buttons, and toolbar in WordArt available. Table 4-2 explains the purpose of each button on the WordArt toolbar.

Table 4-2

BUTTON	NAME	FUNCTION
([— Plain Text ▼])	Shape box	A list from which you choose a shape
([Arial ▼])	Font box	A list from which you choose a font
([Best Fit ▼])	Font Size box	A list from which you choose a font size
([B])	Bold button	To make WordArt text thick
([I])	Italic button	To add a slight slant to WordArt letters
([Ee])	Even Height button	To make all letters the same height regardless of case
([◁])	Flip button	To turn WordArt on its side
([⬚])	Stretch button	To stretch out text both horizontally and vertically
([≣])	Alignment button	Left justify, right justify, centers, stretch justify, word justify, or letter justify WordArt text
([AV])	Character Spacing button	To display options for adjusting spacing between WordArt text
([C])	Special Effects button	To display options for turning WordArt text
([⬚])	Shading button	To change color and shading of WordArt text
([▢])	Shadow button	To display options for adding shadow to WordArt text
([≣])	Line Thickness button	To display options for choosing a border thickness for WordArt text

Once open, WordArt displays a window on the PowerPoint screen as explained in the steps below.

Steps **To Open WordArt**

1 **Click Insert on the menu bar and then click Object. When the Insert Object dialog box displays, scroll down the Object Type list until Microsoft WordArt 2.0 displays. Point to Microsoft WordArt 2.0.**

The Insert Object dialog box displays (Figure 4-24). By default, Create New is selected.

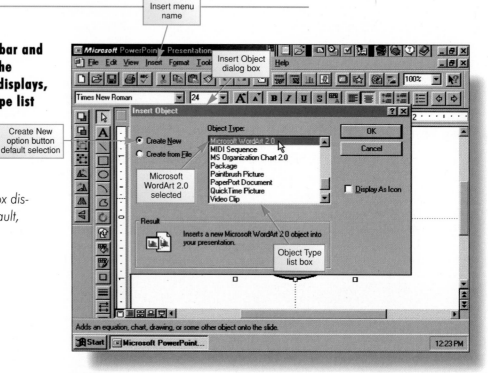

FIGURE 4-24

2 **Double-click Microsoft WordArt 2.0.**

Microsoft WordArt opens and displays its menu bar and toolbar (Figure 4-25). The Enter Your Text Here dialog box displays. The default text inside the Enter Your Text Here dialog box displays in the WordArt window.

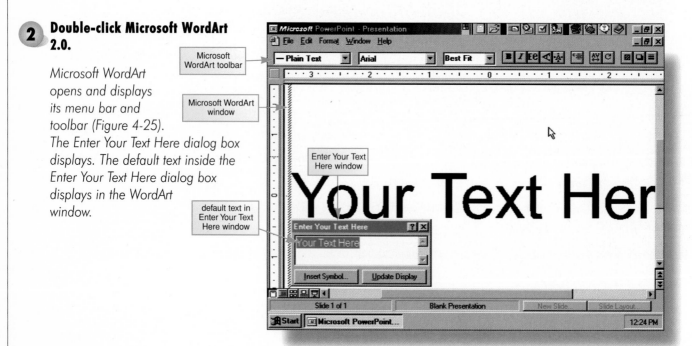

FIGURE 4-25

Entering WordArt Text

When you create a graphic object in WordArt, you enter the text in the Enter Your Text Here dialog box. By default, WordArt highlights the words, Your Text Here, in the Enter Your Text Here window. When you type the text for your graphic object, it replaces the highlighted text. When you want to start a new line, press the ENTER key. Perform the following step to enter the text for the graphic text object for the Executive Training Tours logo.

Steps To Enter WordArt Text

More *About* **WordArt Text**

The WordArt toolbar does not have Copy or Paste buttons. Nor, does the Edit menu contain Copy or Paste commands. To use WordArt to create a graphic object with text created in an application that supports the Copy command, copy the text in the original application and then paste it into the Enter Your Text Here box by pressing the CTRL+V keys.

1 **With the text in the Enter Your Text Here window selected, type** Executive **and press the** ENTER **key. Type** Training **and press the** ENTER **key. Type** Tours **but do not press the** ENTER **key.**

Two of the three text lines display in the Enter Your Text Here window: Training and Tours (Figure 4-26). WordArt updates the text in the WordArt window when you click the Update Display button in the Enter Your Text Here window, click one of the buttons on the WordArt toolbar, or click a menu name.

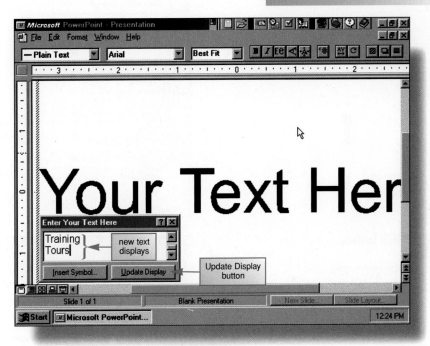

FIGURE 4-26

The next section explains how to shape WordArt text.

Shaping WordArt Text

After you enter text in the Enter Your Text Here window, you want to choose the basic shape of the WordArt text. The text in the Executive Training Tours logo in Figure 4-16 on PP 4.16 displays inflated in the center and tapered at both ends. Perform the steps on the next page to choose a shape for the logo text object.

Steps **To Shape WordArt Text**

1 **Click the Shape box arrow on the WordArt toolbar. When the Shape list displays, point to Inflate (column 1, row 5).**

The Shape drop-down list box displays (Figure 4-27). By default, Plain Text is the selected shape. The WordArt window now displays the Enter Your Text Here window because you clicked the Shape drop-down list box arrow.

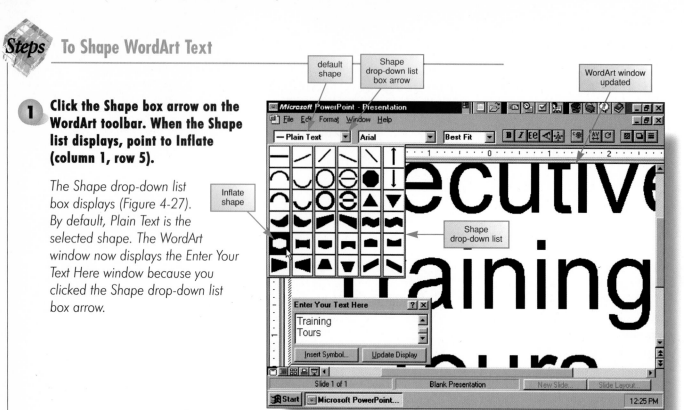

FIGURE 4-27

2 **Click Inflate.**

WordArt applies the Inflate shape to the text in the WordArt window (Figure 4-28). Inflate displays in the Shape box.

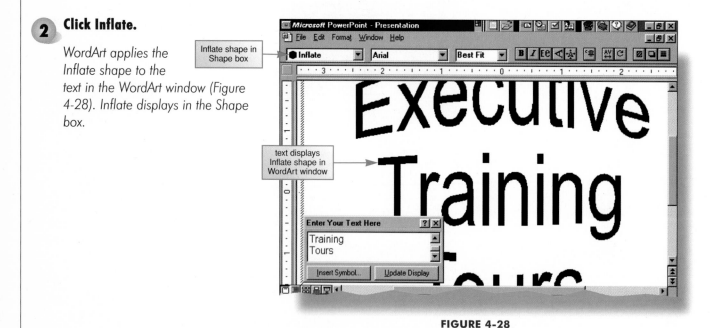

FIGURE 4-28

Changing the WordArt Font Color

WordArt has a Shading command to give you options for adding color and patterns to WordArt text. The Shading dialog box contains three boxes: a Style box, a Color box, and the Sample box. The **Style box** displays twenty-four pattern styles. The **Color box** contains a drop-down list box for the text foreground color and another drop-down list box for the text background color. You select a new foreground color by clicking the box arrow in the Foreground box. You select a new background color by clicking the box arrow in the Background box. The **Sample box** displays a preview of the selected pattern and colors.

In this project, you change the WordArt text to solid blue. Follow the steps below to change the WordArt font color.

 Steps To Change the WordArt Font Color

1 **Click the Shading button on the WordArt toolbar.**

The Shading dialog box displays (Figure 4-29). The default shading style is solid. The default foreground color is black. The Sample box displays the defaults.

FIGURE 4-29

2 **Click the Foreground drop-down list box arrow in the Color area. When the list of colors displays, point to Blue.**

The Foreground drop-down list box displays the available colors (Figure 4-30).

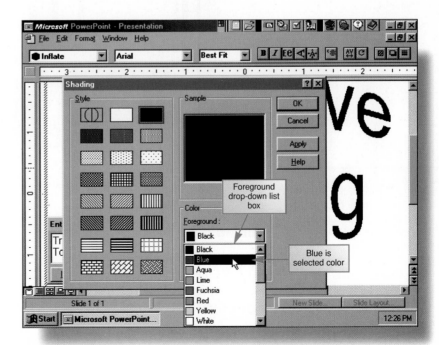

FIGURE 4-30

3 Click Blue.

The Sample box displays the solid style and the blue foreground color (Figure 4-31). The background color is not visible because the style is solid.

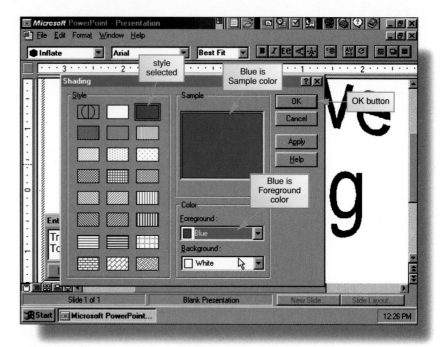

FIGURE 4-31

4 Click the OK button.

WordArt applies the solid style and blue foreground color to the text in the WordArt window (Figure 4-32).

FIGURE 4-32

Adding a Border to WordArt Text

The text in the Executive Training Tours logo has a thin black border. Clicking the Line Thickness button on the WordArt toolbar opens the Border dialog box. You select the border thickness and border color in the Border dialog box. Perform the following steps to add a border to the WordArt text.

Steps To Add a Border to the WordArt Text

1 **Click the Line Thickness button on the WordArt toolbar.**

The Border dialog box displays (Figure 4-33).

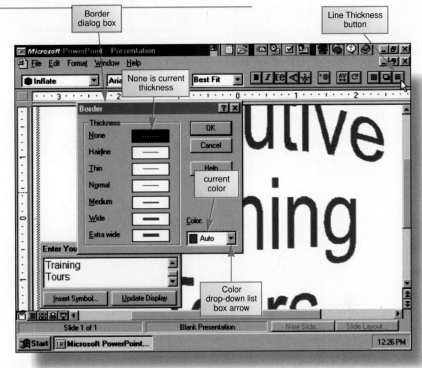

FIGURE 4-33

2 **Click the Color drop-down list box arrow and then point to Black (Figure 4-34).**

FIGURE 4-34

3 **Click Black, and then click the Thin box in the Thickness area.**

The Thin box is highlighted (Figure 4-35). Black displays in the Color box.

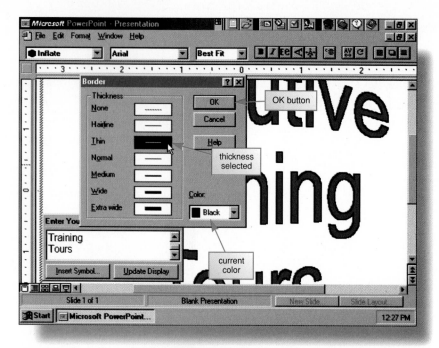

FIGURE 4-35

4 **Click the OK button.**

WordArt applies a thin black border to the blue text in the WordArt window (Figure 4-36).

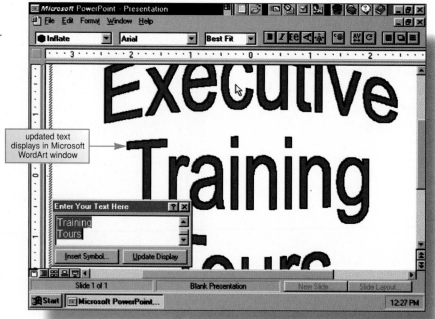

FIGURE 4-36

*Other*Ways

1. On Format menu click Border, click Color box down arrow, click new color, click new thickness, click OK

2. Press ALT+T, press E, press ARROW keys to select thickness, press TAB, press ARROW keys to select new color, press ENTER

Exiting WordArt

The graphic text object is complete. Next, you exit WordArt and update the presentation in which you created the circle object. Perform the following steps to exit WordArt and return to the Office 95 Workshop Phoenix presentation.

Steps **To Exit WordArt**

1 Click the vertical scroll bar down arrow until the WordArt window border is visible (Figure 4-37).

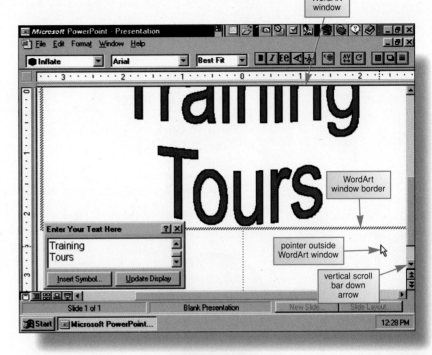

FIGURE 4-37

2 Click anywhere on the PowerPoint slide outside the WordArt window to return to the PowerPoint window.

The PowerPoint window displays the WordArt object centered over the circle object (Figure 4-38). The PowerPoint toolbar and menu bar display.

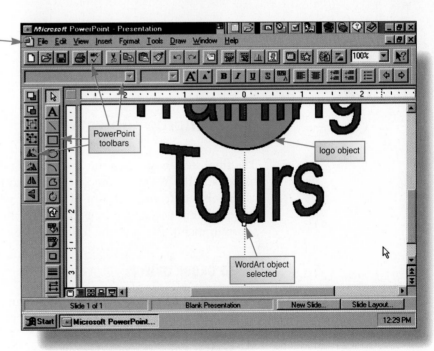

FIGURE 4-38

Scaling an Object

The WordArt object is too large to fit inside the circle object. To reduce the size of the WordArt object, scale it to 30% of its original size. Perform the following steps to scale an object.

TO SCALE AN OBJECT

Step 1: Click the WordArt object.
Step 2: Click Draw on the menu bar and then click Scale.
Step 3: Type 30 in the Scale To box. Click the OK button.

The WordArt object is scaled to 30% (Figure 4-39).

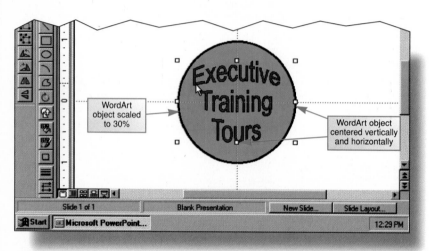

Recall from Project 2 that if you do not know the number to type in the Scale To box, you can type a number and then click the Preview button. This allows you to see if you need to increase the number to increase the size of the object or decrease the number to decrease the size of the object. You can continue to change the number in the Scale To box and click the Preview button until the object displays at the proper scale. An alternative to scaling the WordArt object is to resize the object about center.

FIGURE 4-39

Grouping Objects

The final step in creating the Executive Training Tours logo is to group the circle object and the WordArt object together to form one object. This prevents one of the objects from being out of position when the logo is moved. Recall from Project 3 that you group objects together with the Group command on the shortcut menu. Perform the following steps to group the two logo objects.

TO GROUP OBJECTS

Step 1: Click Edit on the menu bar and then click Select All.
Step 2: Right-click the selected objects and then click Group on the shortcut menu.
Step 3: Click the Save button. Type ETT Logo in the File name box. Click the Save button on the Standard toolbar.

The logo objects are grouped into one object (Figure 4-40). A selection rectangle displays around the grouped object. The logo is saved to a floppy disk.

Grouping the text object with the circle object converts the WordArt object into a PowerPoint object. The link is lost between the WordArt object and the WordArt application, so that if you double-click the WordArt object, the WordArt application will not automatically start. If you ungroup the logo, however, you can once again double-click the WordArt object and automatically start WordArt.

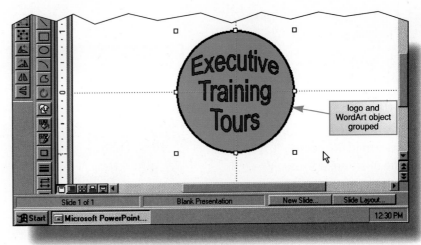

FIGURE 4-40

A dding an Object to the Slide Master

Once a logo is created, it can be added to any new or existing presentation. You add a logo by copying a logo object from its presentation and then pasting it in the presentation in which you want it to display. For example, in this project you copy the Executive Training Tours logo object from the ETT Logo presentation and paste it in the Office 95 Workshop Phoenix presentation. If you want the logo to display on every slide, you paste it in the Slide Master.

Perform the following steps to add the Executive Training Tours logo to the Slide Master.

Steps To Add an Object to the Slide Master

1 **Right-click the Executive Training Tours logo and then click Copy on the shortcut menu.**

A copy of the Executive Training Tours logo is placed onto the Clipboard.

2 **Click Window on the menu bar and then point to 1 Office 95 Workshop Phoenix (Figure 4-41).**

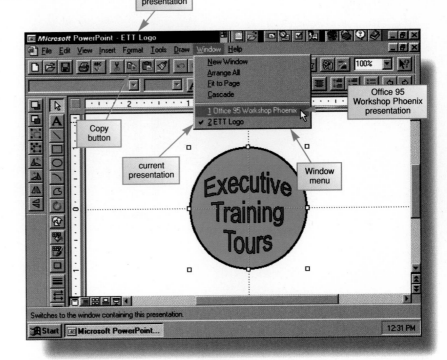

FIGURE 4-41

3 **Click 1 Office 95 Workshop Phoenix.**

PowerPoint displays the Office 95 Workshop Phoenix presentation (Figure 4-42). The ETT Logo presentation is still open but does not display. Zoom Control is 36% instead of the default 40% because the rulers are active.

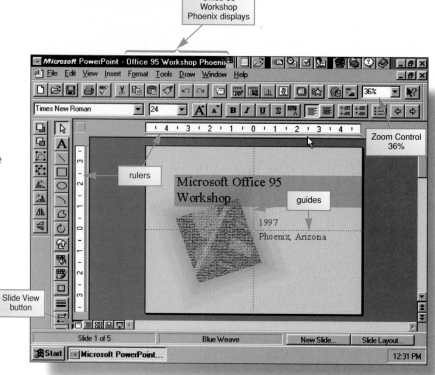

FIGURE 4-42

4 **Press and hold down the SHIFT key and then click the Slide View button. Release the SHIFT key. Then drag the elevator to the top of the vertical scroll bar to display the Slide Master.**

PowerPoint displays the Slide Master for Office 95 Workshop Phoenix (Figure 4-43).

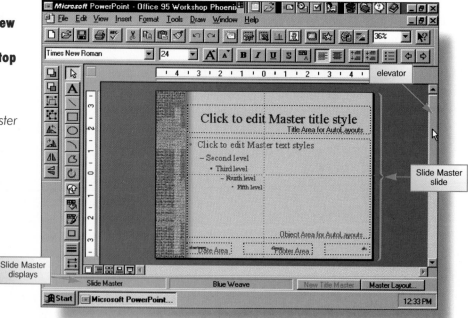

FIGURE 4-43

5 **Right-click anywhere on the Slide Master. Then click Paste on the shortcut menu.**

The logo object displays in the center of the Slide Master (Figure 4-44).

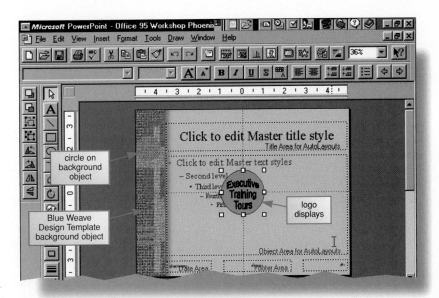

FIGURE 4-44

6 **Drag the logo object to the upper left corner of the Slide Master so it covers the circle on the left side of the Blue Weave Design Template background object.**

The logo displays in the upper left corner of the Slide Master (Figure 4-45).

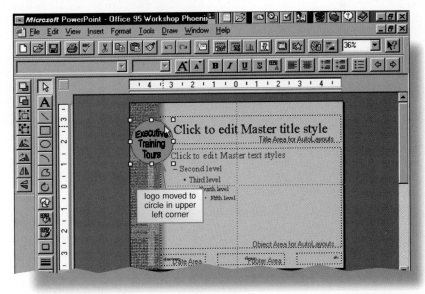

FIGURE 4-45

The rulers and guides stayed active when you changed presentation windows in Step 3. The Ruler command and the Guides command are PowerPoint settings, not slide attributes. Therefore, the rulers and guides display on the PowerPoint window whenever they are active, regardless of the presentation.

Adjusting the Size and Placement of an Object

To position the logo in the middle of the circle in the upper left corner of the Slide Master, you first must scale the logo and then drag it to the center of the circle. Recall that scaling changes the size of an object while maintaining the proportions of the object. Perform the steps on the next page to scale and position the logo.

More *About*
Positioning an Object

To help position objects, PowerPoint uses guides and a grid. The grid is a series of invisible, crisscrossing lines, called gridlines, which are spaced about one-twelfth of an inch apart. When an object moves close to one of the gridlines, it jumps to it as though it were a magnet. To turn off the grid, click Snap to Grid on the Draw menu.

TO ADJUST THE SIZE AND PLACEMENT OF AN OBJECT

Step 1: With the logo object selected, click Draw on the menu bar and then click Scale.

Step 2: Type 60 in the Scale To box and click the OK button.

Step 3: Drag the logo to center it vertically and horizontally over the circle in the upper left corner of the Slide Master.

The logo covers the circle in the upper left corner of the Slide Master (Figure 4-46).

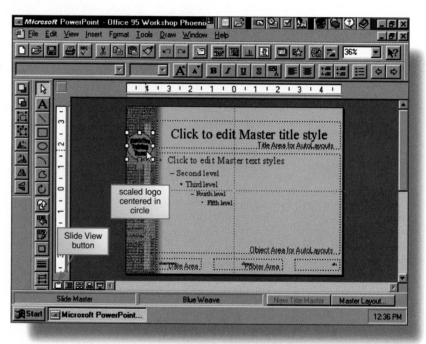

FIGURE 4-46

If you want to make small adjustments in the position of an object, select the object and press the arrow keys on the keyboard that correspond to the direction in which you want to move.

To inspect the logo and color scheme, click the Slide Show button. Notice the logo does not display on the title slide because the logo was pasted on the Slide Master, not the Title Master. Also notice the logo uses the color scheme of the slide. The next section explains how to paste the logo on the title slide.

Pasting an Object on a Slide

Because the organizing team wants the Executive Training Tours logo to display on every slide, you also must paste it on the title slide. Later in this project, you will animate the logo so it flies across the title slide from the right. Perform the following steps to paste the logo on the title slide.

Steps To Paste an Object on a Slide

1 Right-click the logo object and then click Copy on the shortcut menu.

2 Click the Slide View button on the View button bar. Right-click the title slide and then click Paste on the shortcut menu.

The logo displays on the title slide in the same location as it was copied on the Slide Master (Figure 4-47).

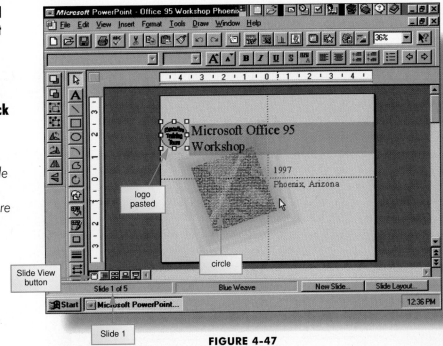

FIGURE 4-47

3 Drag the logo to cover the circle on the background graphic near the center of the title slide (Figure 4-48).

4 Click the Save button on the Standard toolbar.

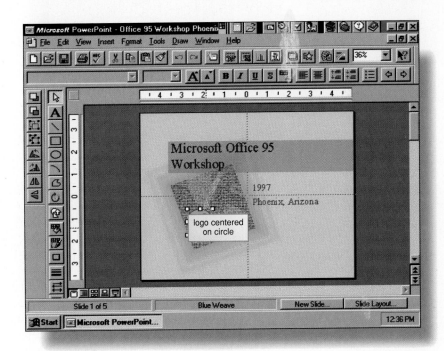

FIGURE 4-48

Creating an Interactive Document

The next step in customizing the Office 95 Workshop Phoenix presentation is to add a slide to demonstrate the four Microsoft Office 95 applications featured in the workshop. You add the new slide after Slide 2. Figure 4-49 illustrates the new Slide 3, which contains four icon objects to reference the four Microsoft Office applications presented at the Office 95 Workshop. An **icon** is a graphic representation of a command. For example, the picture on the face of the Copy button on the Standard toolbar is an icon. When you click the button, you actually execute the Copy command.

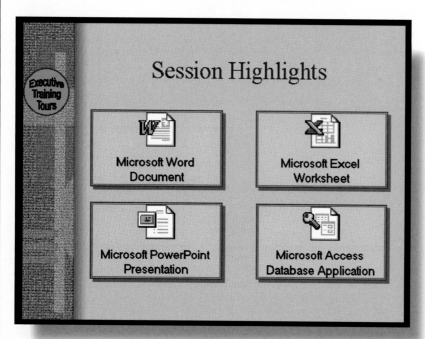

FIGURE 4- 49

In this project, an icon represents an interactive document. An interactive document is a file created in an object linking and embedding (OLE) application, such as Microsoft Word or Microsoft Excel. When you run the Office 95 Workshop Phoenix presentation and click one of the icon objects, PowerPoint starts the associated application and loads the designated file. For example, if you click the Word icon object on Slide 3, PowerPoint opens the Microsoft Word application and loads the Word document, Phantom Announcement. For an interactive document to function properly, the application used to create the OLE object must be installed on the computer used to run the presentation. The applications required for Slide 3 are Microsoft Word 7, Excel 7, PowerPoint 7, and Access 7.

Interactive documents give you the capability to run an application during a slide show without leaving PowerPoint. Once an interactive document displays, you can make changes to the source document. A **source document** is the file or document in which a linked object is created. A **linked object** is similar to an embedded object in that it is created in another application. The difference between a linked object and an embedded object is that the linked object maintains a connection to its source. Whenever the original object changes, the linked object also changes. A linked object is stored in its source document. The PowerPoint presentation stores a representation of the original document and information about its location. PowerPoint is a container document for the linked object. A **container document** is the receiver of a linked object.

When you create an interactive document, you can display either the document object or an icon that represents the document object. With either choice, you click the document object or the icon object to activate the source document when running the slide show.

Creating the slide shown in Figure 4-49 requires several steps. First, you add a new slide to your presentation. Next, you create an interactive document for each of the four applications featured in the workshop by linking and embedding source documents. Then you scale the icon objects that represent the interactive documents. Next, you add fill color, shading, and borders. Finally, you designate the action to be taken when the interactive document is activated. The next several sections explain how to create Slide 3.

Adding a New Slide

The first step in creating Slide 3 in this project is to add a new slide. Perform the following steps to add a new slide.

TO ADD A NEW SLIDE

Step 1: Click the Next Slide button to display Slide 2.
Step 2: Click the New Slide button on the status bar.
Step 3: When the New Slide dialog box displays, click the 4 Objects AutoLayout.
Step 4: Click the OK button.

The new Slide 3 displays the 4 Objects AutoLayout (Figure 4-50). PowerPoint automatically renumbers the original Slide 3, Slide 4, and Slide 5 as Slide 4, Slide 5, and Slide 6, respectively.

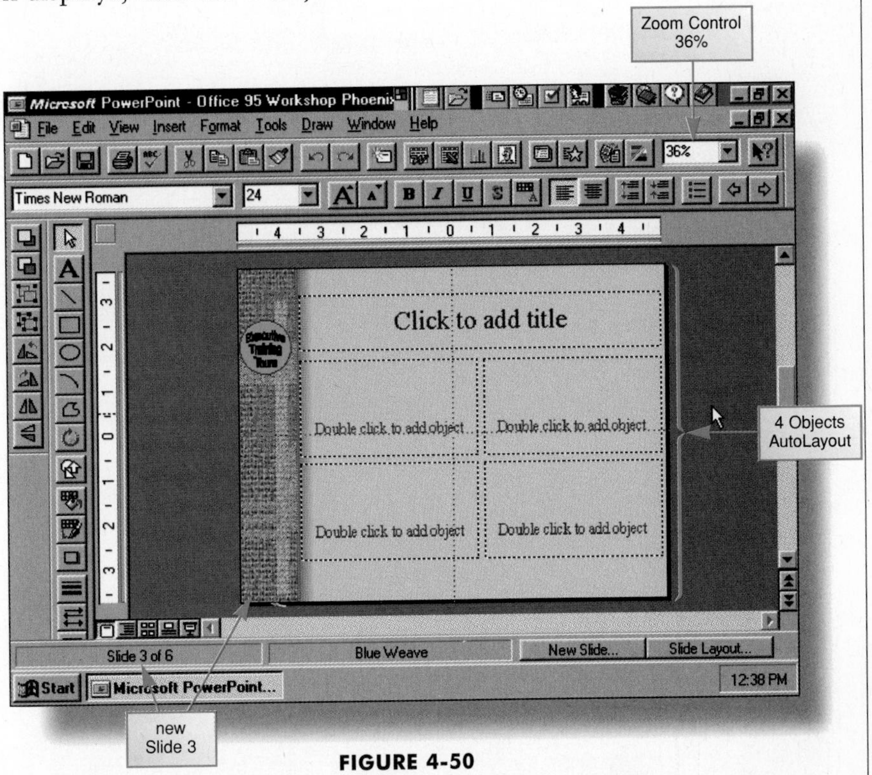

The title for Slide 3 is Session Highlights. Perform the following step to add a slide title to Slide 3.

TO ADD A TITLE TO A SLIDE

Step 1: Type `Session Highlights` in the slide title placeholder.

Session Highlights displays in the title placeholder on Slide 3.

Because you no longer need the rulers or guides, you want to hide them. Recall that a check mark displays in front of the Ruler command and Guides command on the shortcut menu and View menu when the commands are active. Perform the following steps to remove the check mark and deactivate, or hide, the rulers and guides.

FIGURE 4-50

TO HIDE RULERS AND GUIDES

Step 1: Right-click Slide 3 anywhere except the slide title placeholder or an object placeholder.
Step 2: Click Ruler on the shortcut menu.
Step 3: Right-click Slide 3 anywhere except the slide title or object placeholders.
Step 4: Click Guides on the shortcut menu.

The rulers and guides no longer display (Figure 4-51 on the next page). The four object placeholders now display a graphic because Zoom Control returns to 40% when the rulers are not active.

Inserting and Linking a Word Document to a PowerPoint Presentation

Slide 3 (Figure 4-49 on the previous page) contains four interactive documents. The first interactive document you create illustrates a Microsoft Word announcement. To be certain that you display the most current version of this announcement when you run the presentation, you link the source document, Phantom Announcement. The next section explains how to insert and link a Word document.

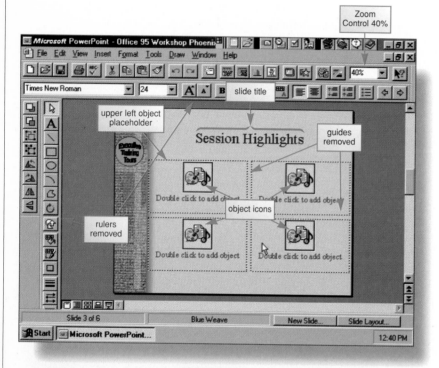

FIGURE 4-51

TO INSERT AND LINK A WORD DOCUMENT TO A POWERPOINT PRESENTATION

Step 1: Insert the floppy disk with the Project 4 files into drive A.

Step 2: Double-click the upper left object placeholder.

Step 3: When the Insert Object dialog box displays, click Create from File. Then click the Browse button.

Step 4: When the Browse dialog box displays, click the Look in box arrow. Click 3½ Floppy [A:] and then double-click the PowerPoint folder.

Step 5: Double-click Phantom Announcement.

Step 6: When the Insert Object dialog box displays, click Link. Click Display As Icon. Then click the OK button.

The Microsoft Word Document icon displays in the upper left object placeholder (Figure 4-52).

If you wish to select a different icon for the interactive document, click the Change Icon button in the Insert Object dialog box. When the Change Icon dialog box displays, choose a new icon from the Icon box. You can change the icon label by typing a new label name in the Caption box in the Change Icon dialog box. After making icon changes, click the OK button. When the Insert Object dialog box displays, click the OK button.

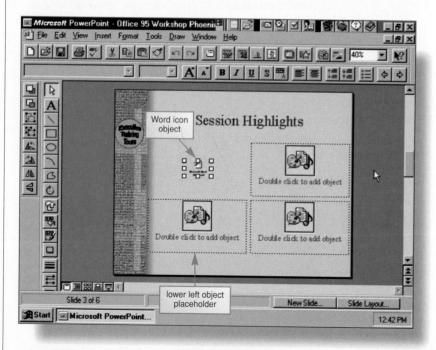

FIGURE 4-52

Linking a PowerPoint Presentation to Another PowerPoint Presentation

Linking a PowerPoint presentation is the same as linking any other interactive document. The difference between all other linked documents and a linked PowerPoint presentation is obvious only when you run the presentation. When you activate any other interactive document, the application window associated with the document displays so you can edit the source document. When you activate a linked presentation, the PowerPoint window does not display. Instead, the linked presentation runs in Slide Show view.

The process for linking a PowerPoint presentation is the same as for creating a linked document. The source file, however, is a PowerPoint presentation. Perform the following steps to link a PowerPoint presentation.

TO LINK A POWERPOINT PRESENTATION TO ANOTHER POWERPOINT PRESENTATION

Step 1: Double-click the lower left object placeholder on Slide 3.
Step 2: When the Insert Object dialog box displays, click Create from File. Then click the Browse button.
Step 3: Double-click Rally.
Step 4: When the Insert Object dialog box displays, click Link. Click Display As Icon. Then click the OK button.

The Microsoft PowerPoint Presentation icon displays in the lower left object placeholder (Figure 4-53).

Linking a Worksheet and Chart to a PowerPoint Presentation

Because Microsoft Excel is an OLE application, it too, can be linked to the presentation as an interactive document. When the slide show is running, you can activate the Excel application and edit the worksheet and chart. The following steps summarize how to add an Excel worksheet and chart to a presentation.

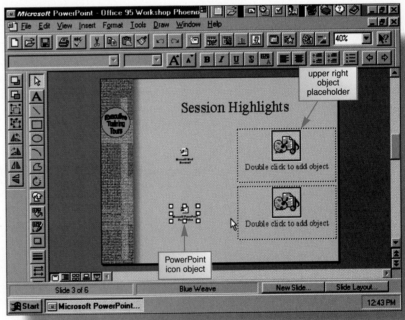

FIGURE 4-53

TO LINK A WORKSHEET AND CHART TO A POWERPOINT PRESENTATION

Step 1: Double-click the upper right object placeholder on Slide 3.
Step 2: When the Insert Object dialog box displays, click Create from File. Then click the Browse button.
Step 3: Double-click Weekly Sales Summary.
Step 4: When the Insert Object dialog box displays, click Link. Click Display As Icon. Then click the OK button.

The Microsoft Excel Worksheet icon displays in the upper right object placeholder (Figure 4-54 on the next page).

Embedding an Access Database to a PowerPoint Presentation

There may be times when you do not want to maintain the links to the source documents, such as when you are the only user of the source documents, or the source documents do not change frequently. In these cases, you choose to embed, instead of link, your interactive document. Recall that an embedded object is created in another application and a copy of that object is inserted into your presentation. Changes made to the original object, the source document, are not reflected in the embedded object. In other words, the embedded object is static; it does not change. In this project, an Access database is embedded into the presentation. The process for embedding an interactive document is the same as creating a linked interactive document except you do not click the Link check box in the Insert Object dialog box. Perform the following steps to embed an Access database.

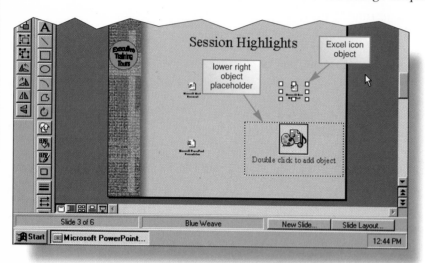

FIGURE 4-54

TO EMBED AN ACCESS DATABASE TO A POWERPOINT PRESENTATION

Step 1: Double-click the lower right object placeholder on Slide 3.
Step 2: When the Insert Object dialog box displays, click Create from File. Then click the Browse button.
Step 3: Double-click Extra Hands.
Step 4: When the Insert Object dialog box displays, click Display As Icon. Then click the OK button.

The Microsoft Access Database Application icon displays in the lower right object placeholder (Figure 4-55).

Scaling Objects

The icon objects on Slide 3 are too small for the audience to see (Figure 4-55). The icon label font size is approximately six points. Because the icon label is part of the icon, scale the four icon objects to 300% to increase the size of each icon three times. Consequently, you increase the label font size to approximately 18 points. Perform the following steps to scale the four icon objects simultaneously.

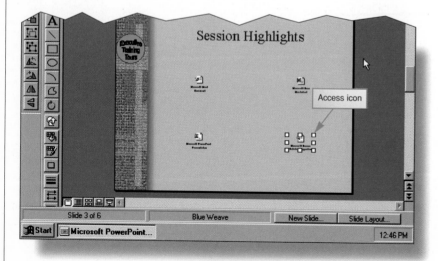

FIGURE 4-55

TO SCALE OBJECTS

Step 1: Press and hold down the SHIFT key and then click the Microsoft Excel Worksheet icon, the Microsoft Word Document icon, and the Microsoft PowerPoint Presentation icon. Release the SHIFT key.

Step 2: Click Draw on the menu bar and then click Scale. When the Scale dialog box displays, type 300 in the Scale To box.

Step 3: Click the OK button.

All four icon objects are resized (Figure 4-56). Scaling the icon objects to 300% increases the icon size to three times their original size.

Adding Fill Color to an Object

To better identify the icon objects from the slide background, you add fill color. Recall that fill color is the interior color of a selected object. Perform the following steps to add fill color to the icon objects on Slide 3.

TO ADD FILL COLOR TO AN OBJECT

Step 1: With the four icon objects selected, click the Fill Color button on the Drawing toolbar.

Step 2: Click the yellow-orange color box (column 4, row 2) on the Fill Color menu.

PowerPoint adds the yellow-orange color of the Blue Weave color scheme to the four icon objects (Figure 4-57).

Adding Shadow to an Object

To add depth to an object, you **shadow** it by clicking the Shadow On/Off button on the Drawing toolbar. The Shadow On/Off button is a toggle. Shadow is on when the button is recessed. Shadow is off when the button is not recessed. Perform the step on the next page to add the default shadow color to the four icon objects on Slide 3.

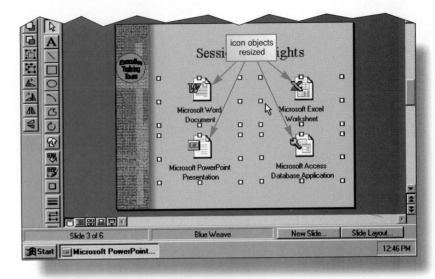

FIGURE 4-56

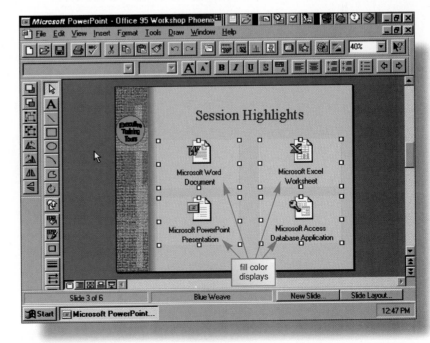

FIGURE 4-57

Steps To Add Shadow to an Object

1 Click the Shadow On/Off button on the Drawing toolbar.

PowerPoint adds the default shadow color to the four icon objects (Figure 4-58).

Shadow On/Off button

FIGURE 4-58

Adding a Border to an Object

To give the icon objects added depth, you define their edges by adding a border. Perform the following steps to add a border.

TO ADD A BORDER TO AN OBJECT

Step 1: With the four icon objects still selected, click the Line Color button on the Drawing toolbar.
Step 2: Click Automatic on the Line Color menu.

PowerPoint adds a border to the icon objects (Figure 4-59). Automatic is the Text and Lines color as defined by the color scheme.

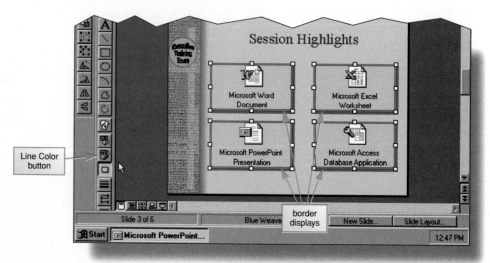

FIGURE 4-59

Setting Up an Application to Open During a Slide Show

Before an interactive document can function properly during a slide show, you must assign an action for the document to perform. The **Interactive Settings** command uses the OLE capability of Windows 95 to start the application in which the interactive document was created and then perform the action specified for the file. The contents of the file display as though you were running the application outside of PowerPoint.

The Interactive dialog box contains five actions from which to choose to establish the action the interactive document takes during a slide show. The purpose of the interactive documents in the Office 95 Workshop Phoenix presentation is to demonstrate to the audience the four Office 95 applications featured in this workshop. You set the action for each icon object on Slide 3 based on its corresponding application. For example, when you click the Microsoft Word Document icon object during a slide show, you want Word to start and open the Phantom Announcement for editing. Therefore, in the Interactive Settings dialog box, you set the action for the Microsoft Word Document to Edit. You set the same object action for the Microsoft Excel icon object. Because you want the Rally presentation to run in Slide Show view when you click the Microsoft PowerPoint presentation icon object, you set the object action to Show. Because you want to demonstrate the various features of Microsoft Access such as forms, reports, and queries, you set the object action to Activate Contents. The action selected in the Object Action dialog box determines how the interactive document performs when activated during a slide show.

Perform the following steps to establish the interactive settings for each interactive document on Slide 3.

 Steps To Set Word to Open During a Slide Show

1 Click the slide background to deselect the four icons.

2 Click the Microsoft Word Document icon object on Slide 3. Click Tools on the menu bar and then point to Interactive Settings.

The Tools menu displays (Figure 4-60). Interactive Settings is highlighted.

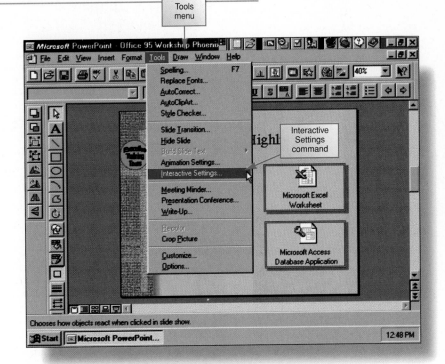

FIGURE 4-60

3 **Click Interactive Settings. When the Interactive Settings dialog box displays, click Object Action.**

The Interactive Settings dialog box displays (Figure 4-61). By default, Edit displays in the Object Action box.

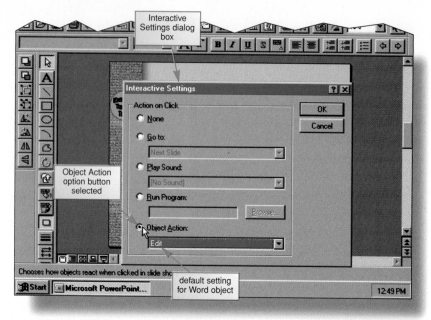

FIGURE 4-61

4 **Click the OK button.**

Slide 3 displays (Figure 4-62). The Interactive Settings for the interactive Word document is complete.

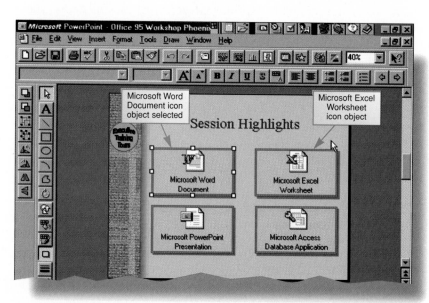

FIGURE 4-62

The interactive settings for the three remaining interactive documents must be established before running the slide show. Perform the following steps to set the interactive settings for Excel, PowerPoint, and Access.

TO SET EXCEL TO OPEN DURING A SLIDE SHOW

Step 1: Click the Microsoft Excel Document icon object on Slide 3.
Step 2: Click Tools on the menu bar and then click Interactive Settings. When the Interactive Settings dialog box displays, click Object Action.
Step 3: Click the OK button.

Slide 3 displays. The Interactive Settings specification for the interactive Excel document is Edit.

TO SET POWERPOINT TO RUN DURING A SLIDE SHOW

Step 1: Click the Microsoft PowerPoint Document icon object on Slide 3.
Step 2: Click Tools on the menu bar and then click Interactive Settings. When the Interactive Settings dialog box displays, click Object Action.
Step 3: Click the OK button.

Slide 3 displays. The Interactive Settings specification for the interactive PowerPoint document is Show.

TO SET ACCESS TO OPEN DURING A SLIDE SHOW

Step 1: Click the Microsoft Access Document icon object on Slide 3.
Step 2: Click Tools on the menu bar and then click Interactive Settings. When the Interactive Settings dialog box displays, click Object Action.
Step 3: Click the OK button.

Slide 3 displays. The Interactive Settings specification for the interactive Access document is Activate Contents. All Interactive Settings are now set.

Replacing a Picture

Recall from Project 3, that the Leisure Time Activities slide, Slide 5, encourages prospective seminar attendees to integrate the educational activities with the recreational activities. Because this presentation is being customized for the Phoenix Arizona workshop, you will replace the picture of the breeching whale with the picture of a Phoenix area golf course (Figure 4-63). To replace a picture, delete the existing picture, insert the new picture, scale the picture, position and resize the picture to fit the slide, and then reapply the border. The next several sections explain how to replace the picture on Slide 5.

Deleting an Object

A picture is an object. To delete any object in PowerPoint, you select the object and then press the DELETE key. Perform the steps on the next page to delete the breeching whale picture on Slide 5.

FIGURE 4-63

Steps **To Delete an Object**

1 **Click the Next Slide button two times. When Slide 5 displays, click the picture of the breeching whale.**

Slide 5 displays (Figure 4-64). The picture is selected.

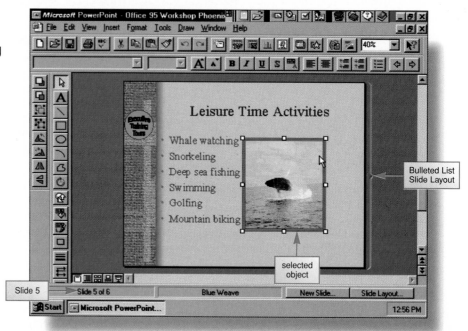

FIGURE 4-64

2 **Press the DELETE key.**

The picture is deleted (Figure 4-65).

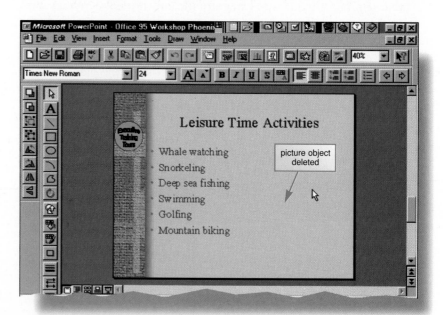

FIGURE 4-65

Editing a Bulleted List

Because the leisure time activities for the Phoenix workshop are different from those for the Maui workshop, you edit the bulleted list. Recall that you select text before editing it. Drag through the text in the bulleted list to select it. Then type the replacement text. Perform the following steps to edit the bulleted list on Slide 5.

TO EDIT A BULLETED LIST

Step 1: Drag to select the bulleted list on Slide 5.

Step 2: Type Golf and then press the ENTER key. Type Hike and then press the ENTER key. Type Rodeo then press the ENTER key. Type Shop then press the ENTER key. Type Swim and then press the ENTER key. Type Tennis but do not press the ENTER key.

Slide 5 displays the edited bulleted list (Figure 4-66).

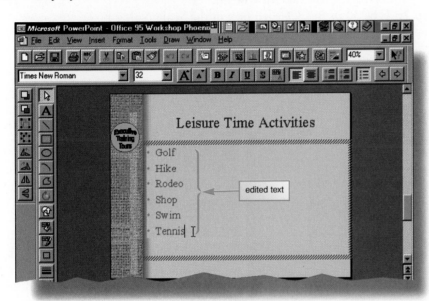

FIGURE 4-66

Inserting a Picture

The Office 95 Workshop Phoenix presentation displays a picture of a golf course to enhance the Leisure Time Activities slide. Perform the following steps to insert a picture on Slide 5.

TO INSERT A PICTURE

Step 1: Click Insert on the menu bar and then click Picture on the Insert menu.

Step 2: Click the Look in box arrow and then click 3½ Floppy [A:]. Double-click the PowerPoint folder.

Step 3: Double-click Golf in the Name box.

The Golf picture displays in the center of the slide (Figure 4-67).

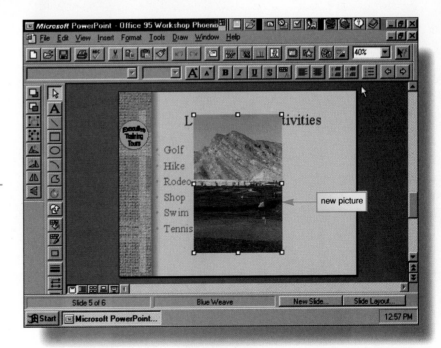

FIGURE 4-67

Scaling an Object

To reduce the size of an object, you scale it using the Scale command on the Draw menu. Perform the following steps to scale the Golf picture to 60%.

TO SCALE AN OBJECT

Step 1: With the Golf picture selected, click Draw on the menu bar. Then click Scale on the Draw menu.
Step 2: Type 60 in the Scale To box in the Scale dialog box.
Step 3: Click the OK button.

PowerPoint scales the picture to 60 percent of its original size (Figure 4-68).

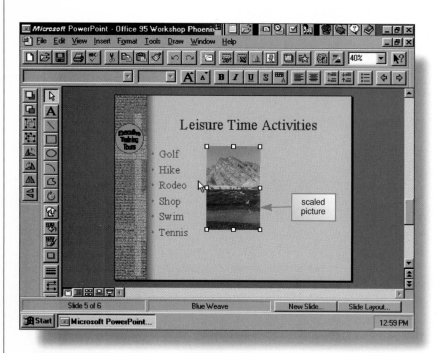

FIGURE 4-68

Displaying and Positioning Guides

Recall that the guides assist you in placing objects at specific locations on the slide. In this project, you use the guides to help position and resize the picture on Slide 5. You position a guide by dragging it to a new location. The center of a slide is 0.00 on both the vertical and the horizontal guides. When you point to a guide and then press and hold down the left mouse button, PowerPoint displays a box containing the exact position of the guide on the slide in inches. An arrow displays under the guide position to indicate the vertical guide is either left or right of center. An arrow displays to the right of the guide position to indicate the horizontal guide is either above or below center. Perform the following steps to display and position the guides.

TO DISPLAY AND POSITION GUIDES

Step 1: Right-click Slide 5 anywhere except on an object placeholder.
Step 2: Click Guides on the shortcut menu.
Step 3: Drag the guides, if necessary, to the center of the slide — position 0.00.

The horizontal and vertical guides display at the center of Slide 5 (Figure 4-69).

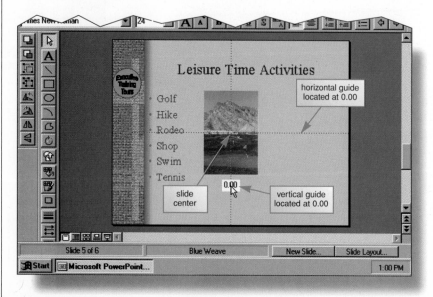

FIGURE 4-69

Positioning and Resizing an Object

To create the picture in Figure 4-63 on page PP 4.45, you resized the picture about center; but because this slide also has a bulleted list, resizing about center results in a picture that covers the bulleted list. Therefore, you move the picture to the right before resizing it. Recall that when an object is close to a guide, it jumps to the guide. In this project, use the vertical guide to align the picture before you resize it. Then move the guides to help resize the picture to fit the slide. Finally, you resize the picture about center. Perform the following steps to position and resize the golf picture.

 Steps To Position and Resize an Object

1 **Drag the picture to the right until it snaps to the vertical guide.**

The left side of the picture aligns with the vertical guide (Figure 4-70).

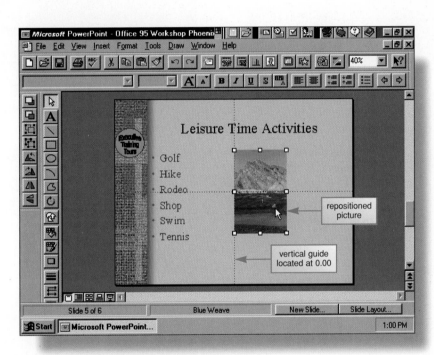

FIGURE 4-70

2 **Drag the vertical guide to 1.25 inches left of center (Figure 4-71).**

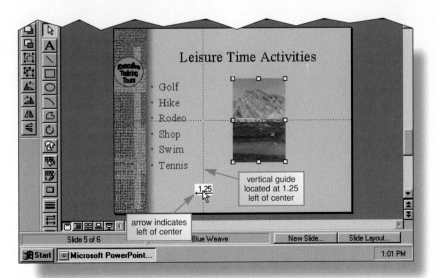

FIGURE 4-71

3 Drag the horizontal guide to 1.50 inches above center (Figure 4-72).

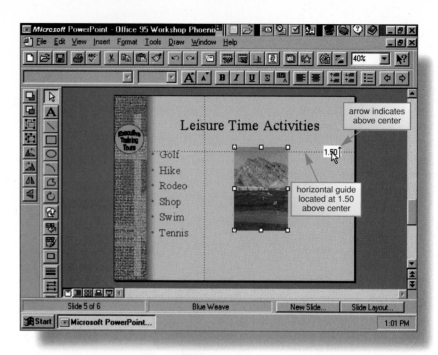

FIGURE 4-72

4 Press and hold down the CTRL key. Then drag the right resize handle of the picture until the left side of the picture jumps to the vertical guide. Release the CTRL key.

The picture is resized about center (Figure 4-73). The left side of the picture aligns with the vertical guide.

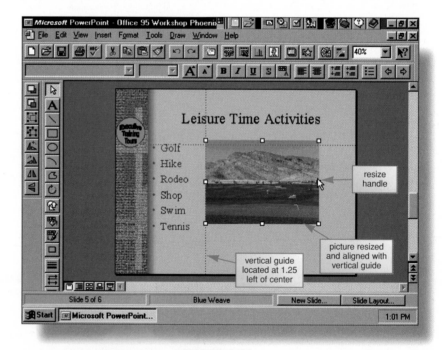

FIGURE 4-73

5 Drag the picture down until the top of the picture jumps to the horizontal guide (Figure 4-74).

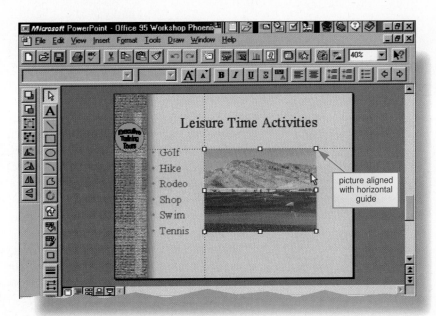

FIGURE 4-74

Adding a Border

The final step in replacing the picture on Slide 5 is to reapply the three lines border. Recall that the Text and Lines color in the Blue Weave Design Template color scheme is a purple color. When you apply a line style, PowerPoint applies the Text and Lines color automatically. Perform the following steps to apply the three line border to the golf picture on Slide 5.

TO ADD A BORDER

Step 1: Click the picture, if not already selected.
Step 2: Click the Line Style button on the Drawing toolbar.
Step 3: When the Line Style menu displays, click the bottom line style (three lines).

A border displays around the picture of the golf course (Figure 4-75).

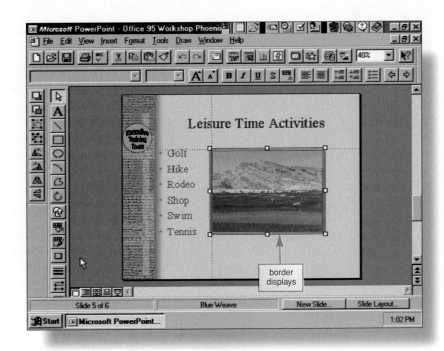

FIGURE 4-75

Ending a Presentation with a Black Slide

When you end a slide show, PowerPoint returns to the PowerPoint window. Recall that a closing slide allows you to gracefully end a slide show so the audience never sees the PowerPoint window. The Office 95 Workshop Phoenix presentation currently uses Slide 6 for a closing slide. Recall that in Project 3, you added a slide and applied the Blank AutoLayout to end the presentation with the Bay View picture background. This blank closing slide was designed to end the presentation and to entice the audience to attend the workshop. But now that the Blue Weave Design Template displays in the background, you want to end the presentation with a black closing slide. A blank closing slide is no longer appropriate for this presentation.

PowerPoint has an option setting that, when activated, displays a black slide at the end of a slide show. You activate the black slide option by clicking the **End with Black Slide** check box on the View sheet in the Options dialog box. A black slide displays only when the slide show is running. A black slide ends all slide shows until the option setting is deactivated.

Before activating the black closing slide option setting, you want to delete Slide 6, the blank slide. Perform the following step to delete Slide 6.

TO DELETE A SLIDE

Step 1: Click the Slide Sorter View button.
Step 2: Click Slide 6.
Step 3: Press the DELETE key.

Slides 1 through 5 display in Slide Sorter view (Figure 4-76). The placement indicator displays after Slide 5.

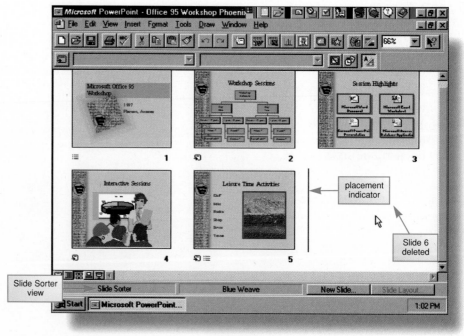

FIGURE 4-76

Ending with a Black Slide

You are now ready to activate the End with Black Slide option to display a black slide at the end of a slide show as described in the following steps.

 Steps ## To End with a Black Slide

1 **Click Tools on the menu bar and then click Options on the Tools menu. Click the View tab, if necessary. Then click End with Black Slide.**

The View sheet displays in the Options dialog box (Figure 4-77). A check mark displays in the End with Black Slide check box.

2 **Click the OK button.**

The Options dialog box closes. The End with Black Slide option is activated.

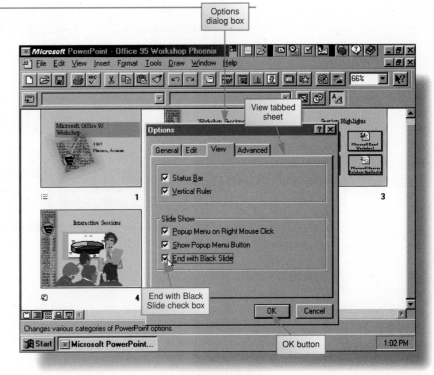

FIGURE 4-77

Applying Slide Transition Effects

Slide 3 was added to the presentation and therefore does not have slide transition effects applied. Recall from Project 3 that the Dissolve slide transition effect was applied to all slides except Slide 1. To keep Slide 3 consistent with the other slides in the presentation, apply the Dissolve slide transition effect as described in the following steps.

TO APPLY SLIDE TRANSITION EFFECTS

Step 1: Click Slide 3.
Step 2: Click the Slide Transition Effects down arrow. Scroll the Slide Transition Effects list to display Dissolve.
Step 3: Click Dissolve.

PowerPoint applies the Dissolve slide transition effect to Slide 3. An icon displays below Slide 3 indicating a slide transition effect is applied (Figure 4-78 on the next page).

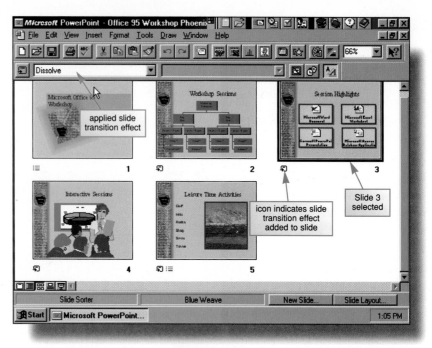

FIGURE 4-78

Hiding Slides

A **supporting slide** provides detailed information to supplement another slide in
the presentation. For example, in a presentation to department chairpersons
about the increase in student enrollment, one slide displays a graph representing
the current year's and the previous three years' enrollments. The supporting slide
for the slide with the graph displays a departmental student enrollment table for
each year in the graph.

When running a slide show, you do not always want to display the supporting
slide. You display the supporting slide when you want to show the audience more
detail about a topic. The supporting slide is inserted after the slide you anticipate
may warrant more detail. Then, you use the Hide Slide command to hide the
supporting slide. The **Hide Slide command** hides the supporting slide from the
audience during the normal running of a slide show. When you want to display
the supporting hidden slide, press the H key. There is no visible indicator on any
slide in the slide show that a hidden slide exists. It is up to the person delivering
the presentation to know the content of the presentation.

Hiding a Slide

Slide 3 is a slide that supports the session information discussed in Slide 2. If
time permits, or if the audience requires more information, you can display Slide 3.
As the presenter, you decide to show, or not to show, Slide 3. You hide a slide in
Slide Sorter view so you can see the slashed square that surrounds the slide number that indicates the slide is hidden. Perform the following step to hide Slide 3.

 **To Hide a Slide**

1 **Right-click Slide 3. Then click Hide Slide on the shortcut menu.**

A square with a slash surrounds the slide number to indicate Slide 3 is a hidden slide (Figure 4-79). The Hide Slide button is recessed on the Slide Sorter toolbar.

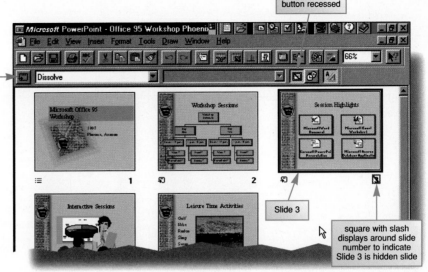

FIGURE 4-79

Other Ways
1. Click Hide Slide button on Slide Sorter toolbar
2. On Tools menu click Hide Slide
3. Press ALT+T, press H

The Hide Slide button is a toggle: it either hides or displays a slide. It also applies or removes a square with a slash surrounding the slide number. When you no longer want to hide a slide, change views to Slide Sorter view, right-click the slide, and then click Hide Slide on the shortcut menu. This removes the square with a slash surrounding the slide number.

An alternative to hiding a slide in Slide Sorter view is to hide a slide in Slide view, Outline view, or Notes view. In these views, however, there is no visible indication that a slide is hidden. To hide a slide in Slide view or Notes view, display the slide you want to hide, select Tools on the menu bar, and then click Hide Slide. To hide a slide in Outline view, select the slide icon of the slide you want to hide, click Tools on the menu bar, and then click Hide Slide. A check mark displays in front of the Hide Slide command on the Tools menu. You also can choose not to hide a slide in Slide view, Notes view, and Outline view by clicking Hide Slide on the Tools menu. The slide then displays like all the other slides in the presentation.

When you run your presentation, the hidden slide does not display unless you press the H key when the slide preceding the hidden slide is displaying. For example, Slide 3 does not display unless you press the H key when Slide 2 displays in Slide Show view. You continue your presentation by clicking the mouse or pressing any of the keys associated with running a slide show. You skip the hidden slide by clicking the mouse and advancing to the next slide.

Animating an Object

The Office 95 Workshop Phoenix organizing team wants the Executive Training Tours logo to fly across the slide before it displays on the title slide. PowerPoint allows you to animate individual objects on a slide. The animation settings for objects are the same as those used for text build effects. Perform the steps on the next page to animate the Executive Training Tours logo on Slide 1.

More *About*
Animating Objects

Used sparingly, animated objects add interest to a presentation. Overused, animated objects are distracting and minimize the message of the presentation.

Steps To Animate an Object

---

1 **Double-click Slide 1. Then click the logo object.**

Slide 1 displays in Slide view (Figure 4-80). The logo object is selected.

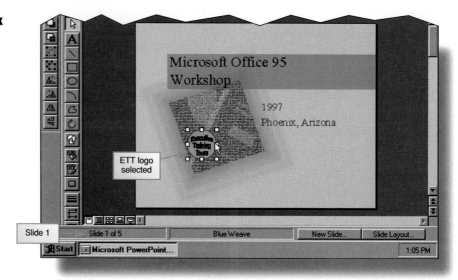

FIGURE 4-80

2 **Right-click the logo object and then click Animation Settings on the shortcut menu. When the Animation Settings dialog box displays, click the Build Options box arrow and then click Build. Click Start when previous build ends. Click the Effects box arrow and then click Fly From Right. Click the Build this object box arrow and then click First.**

The Animation Settings dialog box displays (Figure 4-81). Build displays in the Build Options box. A check mark displays in the Start when previous build ends check box so the animation occurs automatically. Fly From Right displays in the Effects box. First displays in the Build this object box so that the animation effect begins as soon as the slide title displays.

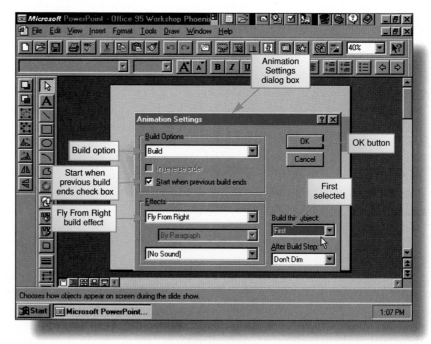

FIGURE 4-81

3 **Click the OK button.**

PowerPoint applies the Animation Settings and closes the dialog box.

*Other***Ways**

1. On Tools menu click Animation Settings, click Build Options box arrow, click Build, click Start when previous build ends, click Effects box arrow, click an effect, click Build this object box arrow, click option of choice, click OK

2. Press ALT+T, press N, press DOWN ARROW key two times, press TAB, press SPACEBAR, press TAB, press ARROW keys to choose option, press ENTER, press TAB two times, press ARROW keys to choose option, press ENTER two times

Animating Text

To seize the attention of the audience, the Office 95 Workshop Phoenix organization committee wants to animate the subtitle text on Slide 1 so the text automatically displays after the logo object flies across the slide. Perform the following steps to animate the text.

 Steps **To Animate Text**

1 **Right-click the subtitle placeholder on Slide 1 and then click Animation Settings on the shortcut menu. When the Animation Settings dialog box displays, click Start when previous build ends.**

The Animation Settings dialog box displays (Figure 4-82). All at Once displays in the Build Options box because the subtitle placeholder was selected, instead of the text as you did when you applied text build effects. A check mark displays in the Start when previous build ends check box so the animation occurs automatically. Split Horizontal Out displays in the Effects box because that was the text build effect applied in Project 3. Second displays in the Build this object box so the animation effect begins as soon as the logo object flies across the slide.

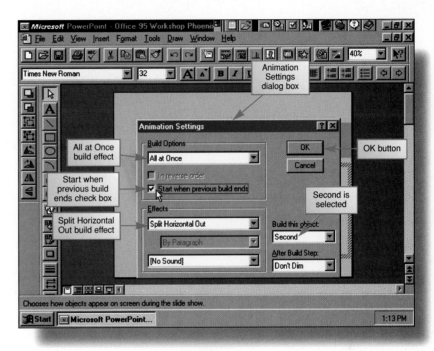

FIGURE 4-82

2 **Click the OK button.**

PowerPoint applies the animation settings to the subtitle text and closes the dialog box.

Spell Check and Save the Presentation

The presentation is complete. You now should spell check the presentation and save it again.

Other Ways

1. On Tools menu click Animation Settings, click Build Options box arrow, click option of choice, click Start when previous build ends, click Effects box arrow, click effect, click Build this object box arrow, click option of choice, click OK

2. Press ALT+T, press N, press DOWN ARROW to choose option, press TAB, press SPACEBAR, press TAB, press ARROW keys to choose option, press ENTER, press TAB two times, press ARROW keys to choose option, press ENTER two times

More *About*
Electronic Slide Shows

Install and run your slide show on the computer you will be using *before* presenting it to an audience. This gives you the opportunity to correct any problems so your presentation runs without any surprises.

More *About*
Electronic Slide Shows

PowerPoint comes with an application called PowerPoint Viewer that allows you to run an electronic slide show without installing PowerPoint. Microsoft has licensed PowerPoint Viewer to be distributed freely because PowerPoint Viewer runs only existing presentations and does not allow you to create or edit presentations. PowerPoint Viewer does not support all PowerPoint features such as animated builds and interactive document branching.

Running a Slide Show with a Hidden Slide and Interactive Documents

Running a slide show that contains hidden slides or interactive documents is basically the same as running any other slide show. You must, however, know where slides are hidden. When a slide contains interactive documents, you activate them by clicking the icon object that represents the document. When you are finished displaying or editing the interactive document and wish to return to the presentation, click the Close button on the title bar of the interactive document. Perform the following steps to run the Office 95 Workshop Phoenix presentation.

TO RUN A SLIDE SHOW WITH A HIDDEN SLIDE AND INTERACTIVE DOCUMENTS

Step 1: Insert the floppy disk with the Project 4 files into drive A.

Step 2: Go to Slide 1, if necessary. Click the Slide Show button.

Step 3: After the subtitle text displays, click Slide 1 to display Slide 2. Then press the H key to display the hidden slide, Slide 3.

Step 4: When Slide 3 displays, click the Microsoft Word Document icon object. When the Phantom Announcement document displays, maximize the Microsoft Word window. Click the Close button on the Word title bar.

Step 5: Click the Microsoft PowerPoint Presentation icon object. When Slide 1 of the linked slide show displays, titled S.C.C.A. Spring Road Rally, click it to display the second slide. When Slide 2 of the linked slide show displays, click it to return to Slide 3 of the Office 95 Workshop Phoenix presentation.

Step 6: Click the Microsoft Excel Worksheet icon object. Maximize the Excel window. Scroll the Excel window to display the worksheet. Click the Close button on the Microsoft Excel title bar. When the Microsoft Excel dialog box displays, click the No button.

Step 7: Click the Microsoft Access Database Application icon object. Click the Open button in the Database window. Maximize both the Microsoft Access window and the Client: Table window. Click the Close button on the Microsoft Access title bar.

Step 8: Click the background of Slide 3 to display Slide 4. Click Slide 4 to display Slide 5.

Step 9: Click Slide 5 six times to display the bulleted list.

Step 10: Click Slide 5 to display the black slide that ends the slide show. Click the black slide to return to the PowerPoint window.

Step 11: Click the Save button on the Standard toolbar.

Step 12: Click the Close button on the title bar.

Slide 1 displays in Slide view. Then control returns to the desktop.

When running a presentation with interactive documents, you must supply the source documents in the same directories in which they were created. Recall that when you run a presentation containing linked documents, PowerPoint loads the source document. Therefore, you must place the source document exactly where you told PowerPoint to find it. For more information, refer to the section, Creating an Interactive Document, on page PP 4.36.

Project Summary

Project 4 customized the Office 95 Workshop presentation created in Project 3. The first step was to save the presentation with a new name to preserve the Project 3 presentation. You then changed Design Templates. Because the colors in the new Design Template did not satisfy Executive Training Tours standards, you selected and modified a new color scheme. Next, you used the drawing tools to create a company logo. After drawing the logo, you created a graphic object from text using Microsoft WordArt. Then, you grouped the graphic object with the logo to create a single logo object. The logo object was pasted on the Slide Master of the Office 95 Workshop Phoenix presentation so it would display on every slide in the presentation. Then you pasted the logo object on the title slide. Next, you created a slide containing interactive documents to demonstrate the four Microsoft Office applications featured in the workshop. Then, you replaced a picture. After replacing the picture, you deleted the blank closing slide and activated the option to end every presentation with a black slide. You added slide transition effects to the slide added in this project. Next, you hid the new slide because you will display it during the slide show only if time permits. Then, you added animation effects to objects on the title slide. You ran the slide show to display the hidden slide and interactive documents. Finally, you closed both presentations and PowerPoint.

What You Should Know

Having completed this project, you now should be able to perform the following tasks:

▶ Add a Border *(PP 4.20, PP 4.51)*
▶ Add a Border to an Object *(PP 4.42)*
▶ Add a Border to the WordArt Text *(PP 4.27)*
▶ Add a New Slide *(PP 4.37)*
▶ Add an Object to the Slide Master *(PP 4.31)*
▶ Add a Title to a Slide *(PP 4.37)*
▶ Add Fill Color to an Object *(PP 4.41)*
▶ Add Shadow to an Object *(PP 4.42)*
▶ Adjust the Size and Placement of an Object *(PP 4.34)*
▶ Animate an Object *(PP 4.56)*
▶ Animate Text *(PP 4.57)*
▶ Apply Slide Transition Effects *(PP 4.53)*
▶ Change Text *(PP 4.8)*
▶ Change the Design Template *(PP 4.8)*
▶ Change the WordArt Font Color *(PP 4.25)*
▶ Delete an Object *(PP 4.46)*
▶ Delete a Slide *(PP 4.52)*
▶ Display and Position Guides *(PP 4.48)*
▶ Display Background Graphics on the Masters *(PP 4.19)*
▶ Display Guides *(PP 4.18)*
▶ Display Rulers *(PP 4.17)*
▶ Draw a Circle *(PP 4.19)*
▶ Edit a Bulleted List *(PP 4.47)*
▶ Embed an Access Database to a PowerPoint Presentation *(PP 4.40)*
▶ End with a Black Slide *(PP 4.53)*
▶ Enter WordArt Text *(PP 4.23)*
▶ Exit WordArt *(PP 4.29)*

▶ Group Objects *(PP 4.30)*
▶ Hide a Slide *(PP 4.55)*
▶ Hide Rulers and Guides *(PP 4.37)*
▶ Increase Zoom Control *(PP 4.18)*
▶ Insert a Picture *(PP 4.47)*
▶ Insert and Link a Word Document to a PowerPoint Presentation *(PP 4.38)*
▶ Link a PowerPoint Presentation to Another PowerPoint Presentation *(PP 4.39)*
▶ Link a Worksheet and Chart to a PowerPoint Presentation *(PP 4.39)*
▶ Modify a Color Scheme *(PP 4.12)*
▶ Open a New Presentation *(PP 4.16)*
▶ Open a Presentation and Save it with a New Filename *(PP 4.7)*
▶ Open WordArt *(PP 4.22)*
▶ Paste an Object on a Slide *(PP 4.35)*
▶ Position and Resize an Object *(PP 4.49)*
▶ Run a Slide Show with a Hidden Slide and Interactive Documents *(PP 4.58)*
▶ Select a Color Scheme *(PP 4.10)*
▶ Scale an Object *(PP 4.30, PP 4.48)*
▶ Scale Objects *(PP 4.41)*
▶ Set Access to Open During a Slide Show *(PP 4.45)*
▶ Set Excel to Open During a Slide Show *(PP 4.44)*
▶ Set PowerPoint to Run During a Slide Show *(PP 4.45)*
▶ Set Word to Open During a Slide Show *(PP 4.43)*
▶ Shape WordArt Text *(PP 4.24)*

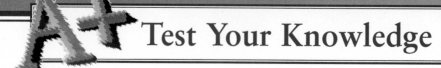

Test Your Knowledge

1 True/False

Instructions: Circle T if the statement is true or F if the statement is false.

T F 1. A color scheme is a set of eight colors assigned to a slide.

T F 2. PowerPoint provides two rulers: one horizontal and one vertical.

T F 3. An interactive document is a file created in an OLE application.

T F 4. A slide can be hidden in any PowerPoint view except Slide Show.

T F 5. The guides are two straight dotted lines — one horizontal and one vertical — used for aligning objects.

T F 6. PowerPoint does not allow changes to a color scheme color.

T F 7. Marks indicating segments on the rulers are identified as tick marks.

T F 8. The file in which a linked object is created is the container document.

T F 9. The difference between a linked object and an embedded object is that the linked object maintains a connection to its source.

T F 10. PowerPoint uses the OLE capability of Windows to open an application in which an interactive document was created and then perform a specific action on the file.

2 Multiple Choice

Instructions: Circle the correct response.

1. A _____ also is created in another application like an embedded object but maintains a connection to its source.
   a. pasted object
   b. linked object
   c. copied object
   d. all of the above

2. When running a slide show and the slide before a hidden slide displays, _____ to display the hidden slide.
   a. click
   b. right-click
   c. press H
   d. press ENTER

3. In the Insert Object dialog box, clicking the _____ inserts the object as a linked object.
   a. Create New option button
   b. Link check box
   c. Display As Icon check box
   d. Create from File option button

4. The fundamental color of a PowerPoint slide is _____.
   a. text and lines color
   b. accent color
   c. background color
   d. fill color

5. A set of eight colors assigned to a slide is called a _____.
   a. color layout
   b. background color
   c. color scheme
   d. slide color

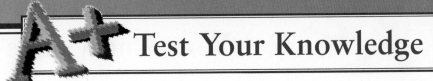

Test Your Knowledge

6. The two _____, straightedges — one horizontal and one vertical — are used for aligning objects.
   a. grids
   b. indicators
   c. rulers
   d. guides

7. To exit WordArt and return to the PowerPoint window, _____.
   a. click the Close button on the WordArt title bar
   b. click Exit on the File menu
   c. right-click the WordArt window and click Exit on the shortcut menu
   d. click outside of the WordArt window in the PowerPoint window

8. Tick Marks on the rulers identify _____.
   a. 1-inch segments
   b. 1/8-inch segments
   c. 1/4-inch segments
   d. 1/64-inch segments

9. A border is composed of _____.
   a. line style
   b. line color
   c. fill color
   d. all of the above

10. When you do not want to maintain the link to a source document, you _____ the interactive document.
    a. embed
    b. insert
    c. place
    d. all of the above

3 Understanding the WordArt Shading Dialog Box

Instructions: Arrows in Figure 4-83 point to the major components of the WordArt Shading dialog box. Identify the various parts of the window in the spaces provided.

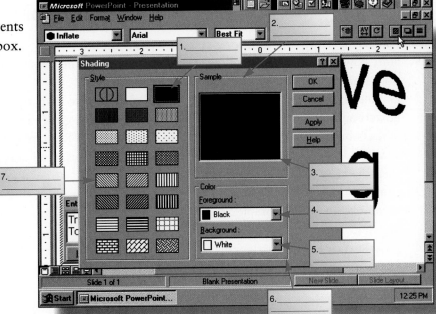

FIGURE 4-83

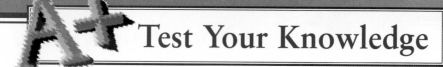

4 Understanding a Color Scheme

Instructions: Answer the following questions using a separate piece of paper.
1. What is a color scheme?
2. What are the eight components of a color scheme?
3. What is a background color?
4. What color scheme component is used for graphs and charts and contrasts with both the background color and text and lines color?
5. What color scheme component is applied when you shadow an object?
6. How does text and lines color work together with background color?
7. How many accent colors are in a color scheme?
8. What color scheme component is applied to the title text?
9. What happens when you click the Apply to All button in the Slide Color Scheme dialog box?
10. What color scheme component is designed for secondary features on a slide?

1 Learning More About PowerPoint Drawing Tools

Instructions: Perform the following tasks using a computer:
1. Start PowerPoint. When the PowerPoint startup dialog box displays, double-click Blank Presentation. Then double-click the Blank AutoLayout.
2. Double-click the Help button on the Standard toolbar to display the Help Topics: Microsoft PowerPoint dialog box. Click the Contents tab. Double-click the Drawing and Working With Objects book. Double-click the Drawing, Resizing, and Reshaping Objects book. Double-click adding a logo. When the Adding a logo window displays, read and print the information. Then click the Help Topics button.
3. Double-click Creating cylinders, pyramids, and other complex shapes. When the Creating cylinders, pyramids, and other complex shapes window displays, read and print the information. Then click the Help Topics button.
4. Double-click Using Overlapping objects to create donuts, crescents, and so on. When the Using Overlapping objects to create donuts, crescents, and so on window displays, read and print the information. Then click the Help Topics button.
5. Double-click Reuse a drawing tool without reselecting it. When the Reuse a drawing tool without reselecting it window displays, read and print the information. Then click the Close button to exit Help. Submit the printouts to your instructor.

Use Help

2 Expanding on the Basics

Instructions: Use PowerPoint's online Help to better understand the topics listed below. Begin each of the following by double-clicking the Help button on the Standard toolbar. If you cannot print the help information, answer the questions on a separate piece of paper.

1. When running a slide show with a hidden slide, how do you display the hidden slide without pressing H?
2. How do you create your own personal color scheme and add it as a standard scheme?
3. How do you apply the color scheme of one presentation to another?
4. How do you combine color schemes?
5. How do you branch to another slide in a presentation without using a hidden slide?

Apply Your Knowledge

1 Editing a WordArt Object and Changing a Color Scheme

Instructions: Start PowerPoint. Open the Executive Training Tours logo that you created in Project 4 and saved with the filename, ETT Logo. If you did not create the Executive Training Tours logo in Project 4, ask your instructor for a copy. Perform the following tasks to modify the logo to look like Figure 4-84:

1. Click the File menu and then click Save As. Save the presentation with the filename, Student Logo.
2. Right-click the logo object and then click Ungroup on the shortcut menu. Click outside the logo object to deselect the ungrouped objects.

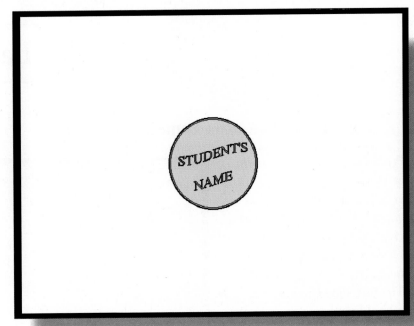

FIGURE 4-84

(continued)

Apply Your Knowledge

Editing a WordArt Object and Changing a Color Scheme *(continued)*

3. Click the border around the circle. Click the Line Style button on the Drawing toolbar. Click the second line style from the bottom of the list on the Line Style menu.

4. Press the TAB key to select the WordArt object. Double-click the WordArt object to open WordArt. Select the text in the Enter Your Text Here window, if necessary. Type your first name, press the ENTER key two times, and then type your last name.

5. Click the Shapes box arrow. Then click the Wave 2 shape (column 6, row 4).

6. Click the Font box arrow. Scroll down the list of fonts and then click Times New Roman.

7. Click the Shading button. Click the Foreground box arrow, click Red and then click the OK button.

8. Click outside the logo object to return to the PowerPoint window. Resize the circle object about center so your name fits inside, if necessary. Click Edit on the menu bar and then click Select All. Right-click the selected objects and then click Group on the shortcut menu.

9. Right-click the slide background and then click Slide Color Scheme on the shortcut menu. When the Color Scheme dialog box displays, click the color scheme in column 2, row 2 in the Color Schemes area on the Standard sheet. Click the Custom tab. Click the Fills color box. Click the Change Color button. When the Fill Color dialog box displays, double-click the color immediately to the left of the current color. Click the Apply to All button.

10. Save the logo object again by clicking the Save button on the Standard toolbar.

11. Print the logo slide using the Black & White and Scale to Fit Paper options.

In the Lab

1 Creating a Title Slide Containing a Logo

Problem: You are a student at Hammond University enrolled in a computer literacy course. Your assignment is to create the title slide for the Hammond University Freshman Orientation presentation. The title slide contains the school logo using the school colors (purple and gold), the school's name, a border, and a graphic. You create the title slide shown in Figure 4-85.

FIGURE 4-85

In the Lab

1. Open a blank presentation, apply the Title Slide AutoLayout, and then apply the Double Lines Design Template. Change the color scheme to the middle color scheme, which has a light yellow background. Type the text for the title slide as shown in Figure 4-85.
2. Save the presentation with the filename, Freshman Orientation.
3. Open a new presentation and apply the Blank AutoLayout. Insert the diploma clip art picture that has the description, Reward Accomplishment.
4. Use WordArt to create the logo text. Type Hammond University on two lines. Use the Button [Curve] shape. Change the WordArt text color to purple. Then apply a black, hairline border to the WordArt text. Scale the WordArt object to 35% and then center it on the diploma picture. Group the WordArt text and the diploma picture. Save the Hammond University WordArt logo with the filename, Hammond U Logo.
5. Paste a copy of the Hammond University Logo on the Freshman Orientation title slide. Scale the logo to 45%. Drag the logo to the upper left corner of the slide.
6. Save the Freshman Orientation presentation. Print the title slide using the Black & White and Scale to Fit Paper options. Close both presentations and PowerPoint.

2 Drawing a Company Logo

Problem: You are the national sales manager of a new company called Good Golf Wear, a golfing apparel manufacturer. Every employee has been asked to submit an idea for the company logo. You create the logo shown in Figure 4-86. *Hint*: Use Help to solve this problem.

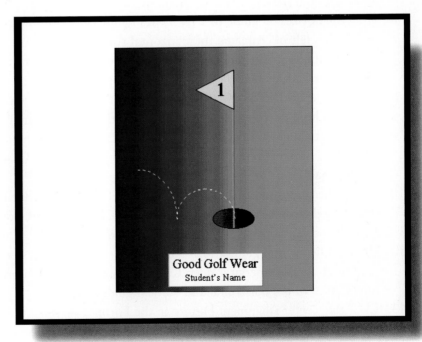

FIGURE 4-86

1. Open a blank presentation and apply the Blank Auto-Layout. Display the guides and rulers.
2. At the intersection of the vertical and horizontal guides, draw a rectangle about center, constraining the Rectangle Tool, so that it is five-inches wide and six-inches high. Apply shaded fill color to the rectangle using the Vertical Shade Style and the upper right variant in the Variants box.

(continued)

In the Lab

Drawing a Company Logo *(continued)*

3. Increase Zoom Control to 50%. Drag the vertical guide to .5 inch right of center on the horizontal ruler. Drag the horizontal guide to 1.25 inches below center on the vertical ruler. At the intersection of the vertical and horizontal guides, draw an ellipse about center that is 1-inch wide and .5-inch high. Change the fill color of the ellipse to shaded fill using the Vertical Shade Style, and then change the color to dark gray.

4. Draw a straight line down the vertical guide by constraining the Line Tool and then dragging the mouse pointer from a point 2.5 inches above center on the vertical ruler to a point at the bottom of the ellipse.

5. Change the line style of the straight line by choosing the third line style from the top of the list in the Line Style list box. Change the color of the straight line to red.

6. Drag the horizontal guide to 1.5 inches above center. Draw the flag object by clicking the AutoShapes button on the Drawing toolbar, clicking the Isosceles Triangle Tool button. Drag the mouse pointer from the intersection of the horizontal and vertical guides to 2.5 inches above center on the vertical ruler, and .5 inch left of center on the horizontal ruler.

7. Rotate the triangle 90° to the left so that it looks like the flag shown in Figure 4-86. Change the flag fill color to yellow. Type 1 but do not press the ENTER key. Increase the font size to 36 points and then bold the number 1. Hide the AutoShapes toolbar.

8. Drag the horizontal guide to 1.25 inches below center on the vertical ruler. Drag the vertical guide to 2 inches left of center on the horizontal ruler. Click the Arc Tool button on the Drawing toolbar. Drag the mouse pointer to the horizontal guide from the zero mark of the vertical guide to the 1-inch mark left of center on the horizontal ruler.

9. Drag the vertical guide to .25 inch left of center on the horizontal ruler. Click the Arc Tool button. Press and hold down the SHIFT key and drag the mouse pointer from the .5-inch below center mark on the vertical guide to the red straight line. Click the Edit menu and click the Duplicate command. Click the Flip Horizontal button on the Drawing+ toolbar. Drag the duplicated arc to the left to create a half-circle as shown in Figure 4-86.

10. Group the three arcs as shown in Figure 4-86. Change the line style of the arcs to the third dashed line from the top of the Dashed Lines menu. Change the arc color to white.

11. Save the presentation with the filename, Good Golf Wear.

12. Drag the horizontal guide to 2.5 inches below center on the vertical ruler. Drag the vertical guide to the center of the horizontal ruler. Click the Text Tool button on the Drawing toolbar. Click the intersection of the horizontal and vertical guides.

13. Click the Center Alignment button on the Formatting toolbar. Type Good Golf Wear and press the ENTER key. Type your name in place of the Student's Name shown in Figure 4-86.

14. Decrease the font size of your name to 18 points. Add a red border to the name box. Change the name box fill color to white.

15. Save the presentation again. Print the slide using the Black & White and Scale to Fit Paper options. Exit PowerPoint.

In the Lab

3 Linking PowerPoint Presentations

Problem: The state organ procurement organization has requested all hospitals to educate the community about the need for organ and tissue donors. Because of the difficulty in speaking to family members about organ and tissue donations when a loved one is dying, the nursing staff suggests that someone create an interactive presentation. This presentation would educate family members about organ donation. As a volunteer at the local hospital, you offer to develop the presentations shown in Figures 4-87 through 4-92 on page PP 4.67 through PP 4.70.

Instructions Part 1: Perform the following tasks to create the presentation in Figures 4-87 and 4-88:

1. Open a blank presentation and apply the Bulleted List AutoLayout. Apply the Side Fade Design Template. Type and center the slide title and bulleted list shown in Figure 4-87. Insert the clip art picture with the description, Leadership.

2. Create the bulleted list slide shown in Figure 4-88. Increase the line spacing after the demoted paragraph to .75 of a line after the paragraph. Apply the Blinds Vertical Slide Transition effect to both slides. Apply the Fly From Left Text Build effect to Slide 2. Save the presentation with the filename, Who Can Donate. Print the presentation using the Black & White option. Close the presentation.

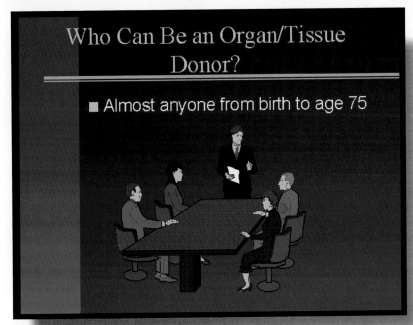

FIGURE 4-87

FIGURE 4-88

(continued)

In the Lab

Linking PowerPoint Presentations *(continued)*

3. Open a new presentation, apply the 2 Column Text AutoLayout, and then apply the Side Fade Design Template. Create the slide shown in Figure 4-89. Increase line spacing to .5 lines after each paragraph. Apply the Blinds Vertical Slide Transition effect. Save the presentation with the filename, What Can Be Donated. Print the presentation slides using the Black & White option. Close the presentation.

4. Open a new presentation, apply the Bulleted List AutoLayout, and then apply the Side Fade Design Template. Create the slide shown in Figure 4-90. Increase line spacing to .5 lines after each paragraph. Apply the Blinds Vertical Slide Transition effect. Save the presentation with the filename, Can I Sell My Organs. Print the presentation slides using the Black & White option. Close the presentation.

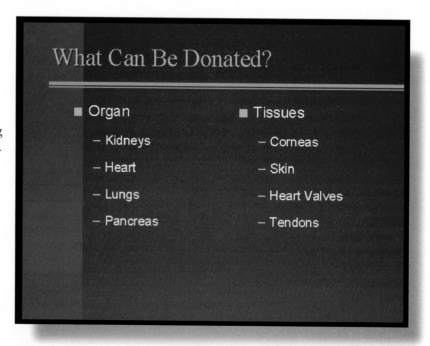

FIGURE 4-89

FIGURE 4-90

In the Lab

5. Open a new presentation, apply the Bulleted List AutoLayout, and then apply the Side Fade Design Template. Create the slide shown in Figure 4-91. Increase the line spacing for both paragraphs to .5 lines after each paragraph. Apply the Blinds Vertical Slide Transition effect. Apply the Fly From Left text build effect. Save the presentation with the filename, How Do I Become a Donor. Print the presentation slides using the Black & White option. Close the presentation.

How Do I Become a Donor?

- Discuss your wishes with your immediate family members. At the time of death, the family is asked to give permission for your donation.

- Complete and sign a donor card or complete the donor card on the back of your driver's license.

FIGURE 4-91

Instructions Part 2: Perform the following tasks to create the presentation shown in Figure 4-92:

1. Open a new presentation, apply the 4 Objects AutoLayout, and then apply the Side Fade Design Template. Create the slide title shown in Figure 4-92.

2. Link the Who Can Donate presentation, created in Part 1, to the upper left object placeholder. Change the icon caption by typing Who Can Donate? in the Caption box in the Change Icon dialog box. Set Interactive Settings to Show.

3. Link the What Can Be Donated presentation to the lower left object placeholder. Change the icon caption by typing What Can Be Donated? in the Caption box. Set Interactive Settings to Show.

4. Link the Can I Sell My Organs presentation in the upper right object placeholder. Change the icon caption by typing Can I Sell My Organs? in the Caption box. Set Interactive Settings to Show.

5. Link the How Do I Become a Donor presentation to the lower right object placeholder. Change the icon caption by typing How Do I Become a Donor? in the Caption box. Set Interactive Settings to Show.

6. Scale the four icon objects to 300%. Using the color scheme colors, add a yellow fill color (column 2, row 2) and orange borders (column 4, row 1) to the icon objects. Change the border line style to the second line style from the bottom of the Line Style menu.

7. Apply the Blinds Vertical slide transition effect. End the presentation with a black slide. Save the presentation with the filename, Commonly Asked Questions. Print the presentation slides using the Black & White option.

(continued)

In the Lab

Linking PowerPoint Presentations *(continued)*

8. Run the slide show. Click the Who Can Donate? icon object to display the linked presentation. Display both slides. When the Commonly Asked Questions presentation returns, click the What Can I Donate? icon object. When the Commonly Asked Questions presentation returns, click the Can I Sell My Organs? icon object. When the Commonly Asked Questions presentation returns, click the How Can I Be a Donor? icon object. When the Commonly Asked Questions presentation returns, click to display the black closing slide. End the slide show and close PowerPoint.

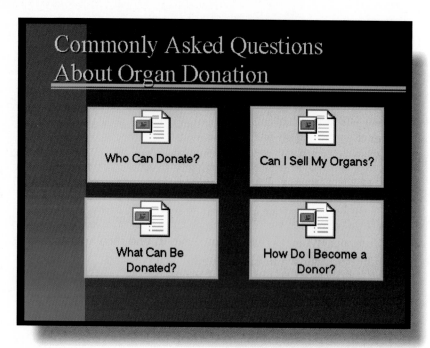

FIGURE 4-92

Cases and Places

The difficulty of these case studies varies:

▶ Case studies preceded by a single half moon are the least difficult. You are asked to create the required presentation based on information that has already been placed in an organized form.

▶▶ Case studies preceded by two half moons are more difficult. You must organize the information presented before using it to create the required presentation.

▶▶▶ Case studies preceded by three half moons are the most difficult. You must decide on a specific topic, and then obtain and organize the necessary information before using it to create the required presentation.

1 ▶ Hill & Dale Bike Works sells, rents, and repairs mountain bicycles. They are a small company in a Colorado resort area and are seeking growth. They want to open another bike shop in a nearby resort area, but need to borrow money for start-up costs. The anticipated start-up costs are $80,000 for inventory, repair equipment, building improvements, and rent. The bank wants more information about the proposed expansion and Hill & Dale Bike Works' budget. Its current annual sales income is $82,000, rental income is $150,000, and repair income is $40,000. Its current annual expense for cost of goods sold is $42,000, expense for parts is $27,000, expense for miscellaneous supplies is $8,000, building rent is $10,200, utility expense is $2,400, and salary expense is $120,000, which includes taxes. Create a current budget for Hill & Dale Bike Works using Microsoft Excel. Also create a pie chart for the current budget. Create a second worksheet and chart that include repayment of a one-year $80,000 loan at the current commercial loan rate. Also adjust for a projected sixty-percent increase in sales and a forty-percent increase in expenses. Using the techniques introduced in this project, create a short presentation stating Hill & Dale Bike Works current objectives and what they are proposing. Include both Excel worksheets as interactive documents. Run the presentation and activate the interactive documents.

2 ▶▶ Diver Dan's Dive Shop sells equipment for SCUBA divers. SCUBA is the acronym for Self Contained Underwater Breathing Apparatus. Dan, the store's owner, is frequently asked for information about three SCUBA certification programs, PATI, NAUI, and YMCA. Each program has different teaching approaches and certification standards. Dan wants a presentation that compares and contrasts the three programs. He also wants the presentation to have buttons or icons that will activate another slide to provide names and telephone numbers of each of the local certification programs. Research the three certification programs and then use the concepts and techniques introduced in this project to create the presentation.

3 ▶▶ You are working part-time at Logo Artisans, a company that specializes in the creation of company logos. You have been awarded the logo design for a new client, Kool Down Water Park. Kool Down Water Park has swimming pools, wave pools, and water slides. They want a logo that people will associate with the fun spirit of the water park. Use PowerPoint's drawing tools and WordArt to create a logo for Kool Down Water Park. Then create a short presentation to present the logo to Kool Down Water Park executives. Explain your design and thoughts behind the logo component objects.

Cases and Places

4 ▶▶ Studies show that home-based businesses are the largest portion of all new business starts. These include daycare providers, consultants, computer repair companies, and telephone sales. Investigate a business that interests you that can be operated from your home. Interview a person operating this type of home-based business. Identify start-up costs, potential earnings, continuing education and training costs, insurance requirements, government regulations, licensing requirements, and any other industry-specific requirement you discover. Prepare a presentation to report your findings. Include at least one additional slide to display if time permits.

5 ▶▶ Universities and colleges periodically conduct seminars to explain their educational programs to prospective students and their families. Research your school's seminar by interviewing the person responsible for the seminar. Gather information about the purpose of the seminar and the type of information dispersed. Discuss how an interactive electronic presentation might enhance the seminar. Take your findings and create an interactive presentation. Enhance the presentation by including your school's logo and a modified color scheme. Deliver your final presentation to the person with whom you spoke to collect your information.

6 ▶▶▶ As an employee of Trainers Unlimited, you are responsible for developing training presentations. Your current project is to create an introductory presentation for Microsoft Word. This presentation provides an overview of the many features of Word. Research Microsoft Word. Using this information and the techniques introduced in this project, create a ten-minute presentation that explains what a word processing application is, how Word increases productivity, and discuss some of the features included in Word. Include at least one interactive document that demonstrates a Word feature, such as checking for spelling errors. Create and then display a company logo on every slide. Enhance the presentation by modifying a Design Template color scheme and adding the appropriate graphics. Submit all files on a floppy disk to your instructor.

7 ▶▶▶ Administrators depend on budgets to plan their organization's future. They take the current year's budget, compare it to the current year's actual income and expenses, and then forecast next year's budget. When forecasting the next budget, they project next year's income based on industry trends. They then determine how they can reduce expenses, or if a major expense is predicted, they allow for an increase in expenses. You too will work with a budget most of your life. You determine your monthly income and total your monthly expenses. Any overages are allocated to savings or miscellaneous expenses. Without some type of budget, you can quickly get into financial trouble. Prepare an Excel worksheet and pie chart of your current, or projected, budget. Allow for savings and/or investments. Research and then prepare a presentation about the importance of maintaining a personal budget. Link your worksheet and pie chart to the presentation as an interactive document. Create a personal logo to display on all slides. Enhance the presentation by modifying a Design Template color scheme and including appropriate graphics. Run your presentation and perform a *what-if* scenario by increasing your income by ten percent. Submit all files on a floppy disk to your instructor.

Embedding a Word Table into a PowerPoint Presentation

Case Perspective

You are the public relations officer for Metropolitan Transportation. Your company recently re-evaluated all of its service areas. To improve community relations, the company is implementing new discounts and increasing the number of busses and bus routes. To promote the new services, you requested time to speak at the next town meeting. The town leaders granted you ten minutes for your presentation. Because of the time constraint, you decide to add a table to summarize the details of the new bus schedule.

Introduction

This Integration Feature uses the Object Linking and Embedding (OLE) feature of Microsoft Office to insert a Word table into a PowerPoint slide. Recall that OLE allows you to incorporate parts of documents or entire documents from one application into another. OLE also allows you to create an object without leaving PowerPoint by opening the source document application on the PowerPoint screen. For example, when viewing a slide in Slide view, you can insert a Microsoft Word table on a slide, have the Word toolbars and menu bar available, and never leave PowerPoint. PowerPoint also allows you to insert a Microsoft Excel worksheet and chart using the same OLE feature.

In this section, you will open an existing presentation, Metropolitan Transportation, insert a new slide, and embed the Word table shown in Figure 1 and Figure 2.

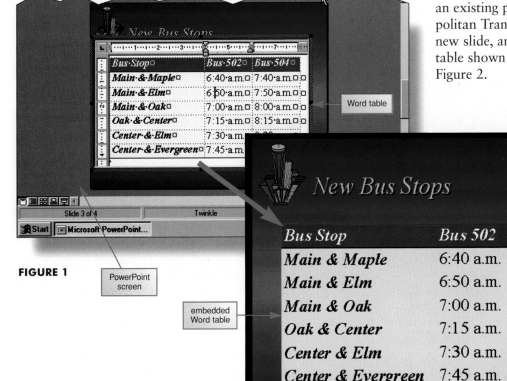

FIGURE 1

FIGURE 2

Opening an Existing Presentation and Saving It with a New Filename

The Metropolitan Transportation presentation was partially complete when saved. Because you are inserting a table into the existing presentation, the first step is to open it. To ensure the original presentation remains intact, you will save the presentation with a new name, New Metropolitan Transportation. Perform the following steps to open the Metropolitan Transportation presentation.

TO OPEN AN EXISTING PRESENTATION

Step 1: Insert the floppy disk with the Integration Feature files into drive A.
Step 2: Click the Start button on the taskbar. On the Start menu, click Open Office Document. Click 3½ Floppy [A:] in the Look in box.
Step 3: Double-click the PowerPoint folder.
Step 4: Double-click Metropolitan Transportation.

PowerPoint opens and displays the Metropolitan Transportation presentation in Slide view.

To preserve the original Metropolitan Transportation presentation, you save the open presentation with a new filename. Then you make changes to the new presentation. Perform the following steps to save the Metropolitan Transportation presentation with a new filename using the Save As command.

TO SAVE A PRESENTATION WITH A NEW FILENAME

Step 1: Click File on the menu bar and then click Save As.
Step 2: Type New Metropolitan Transportation in the File name box.
Step 3: Click the Save button.

The Metropolitan Transportation presentation is saved with the filename New Metropolitan Transportation. The new filename displays in the title bar (see Figure 3).

Adding a Word Table to a PowerPoint Presentation

A **table** is a collection of columns and rows. The intersection of a column and a row is called a **cell**. A cell contains data. When the data within a cell exceeds the width of the cell, Word wraps the data to a new line in the cell, just as Word wraps text in a Word document. In PowerPoint, a table is an embedded object that is created in Microsoft Word. When you instruct PowerPoint to insert a table on a slide, Microsoft Word opens and its menu bar, buttons, and toolbars are available to you directly on the PowerPoint screen. A table provides a convenient way to create side-by-side paragraphs, or to display a graphic next to text. For example, Table 4-2 on page PP 4.21, is a table that contains a graphic of each WordArt button, a paragraph that identifies the button, and another paragraph that describes the function of the button.

The third slide in this presentation contains a table that shows the newly added bus stops (Figure 2 on the previous page). The columns in the table display the bus stop locations and the arrival times for each new bus. The rows in the table display the arrival times for each bus stop location.

More *About* **Embedded Tables**

You can create and format a table in Microsoft Word, Microsoft Excel, or Microsoft Access. Use Word to create a table that is easy to insert into a PowerPoint presentation or that requires special formatting such as bulleted lists, custom tabs, numbering, or hanging indents.

Creating a table requires several steps. First, you add a new slide and apply the Table layout. Next, you open the Word application into PowerPoint. Then, you enter column headings and data into the table. Finally, you format the table.

Inserting a New Slide with the Table AutoLayout

The slide containing the Word table displays after Slide 2, Improved Services. Perform the following steps to insert a new slide with the Table AutoLayout.

TO INSERT A NEW SLIDE WITH THE TABLE AUTOLAYOUT

Step 1: Click the Next Slide button to display Slide 2.

Step 2: Click the New Slide button on the status bar.

Step 3: Double-click the Table Auto-Layout in the New Slide dialog box.

Slide 3 displays the table placeholder (Figure 3).

Opening Word and Inserting a Table

To create the table on Slide 3, you must type a slide title and then open Word into PowerPoint. Perform the following steps to insert a Word table.

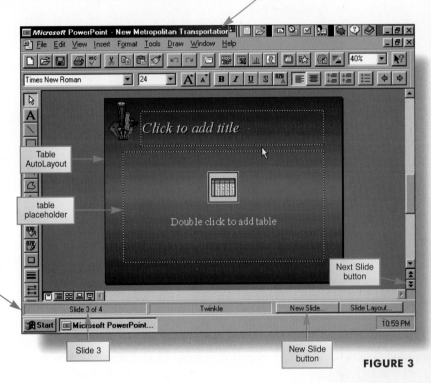

FIGURE 3

  Steps To Open Word and Insert a Table

1 **Type** New Bus Stops **in the title placeholder on Slide 3. Double-click the table placeholder in the Table AutoLayout. Click the Number of Columns box up arrow once to display 3. Click the Number of Rows box up arrow five times to display 7.**

Word displays the Insert Word Table dialog box on the PowerPoint screen (Figure 4).

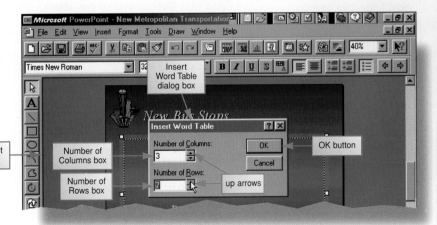

FIGURE 4

2 Click the OK button.

Word inserts an empty table containing three columns of equal width and seven rows of equal height (Figure 5). The insertion point is in the first cell (column 1, row 1) of the table. The PowerPoint toolbars and menu bar have been replaced with the Word toolbars and menu bar.

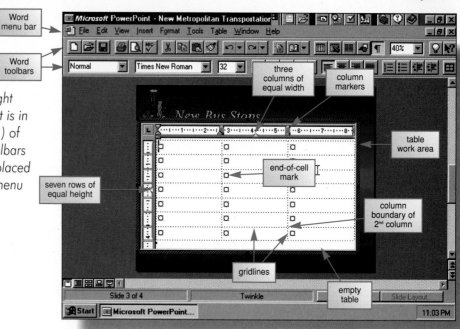

FIGURE 5

*Other*Ways

1. Right-click table placeholder, click Edit Placeholder Object, click Number of Columns box arrows to set columns, click Number of Rows box arrows to set rows, click OK button

2. Click Insert Word Table button on Standard toolbar, drag to select number of columns and number of rows

3. On Insert menu click Insert Word Table, click Number of Columns box arrows to set columns, click Number of Rows box arrows to set rows, click OK button

4. Press ALT+I, press W, press arrow keys to set columns, press TAB, press arrow keys to set rows, press TAB, press ENTER

The table displays on the screen with dotted **gridlines**. If your table does not have gridlines, click Table on the menu bar and then click Gridlines. Word does not print the table with gridlines; instead the gridlines display to help you identify in which column and row you are working.

The vertical gridline immediately to the right of a column is called the **column boundary.** You may decrease the width of a column by dragging the column boundary to the left. You may increase the width of the column by dragging the column boundary to the right. You can also change column widths by dragging the **column markers** on the horizontal ruler.

Each cell has an **end-of-cell mark,** which is used to select a cell. That is, you click the end-of-cell mark to select a cell. The end-of-cell marks are, in the table in Figure 5, currently left-aligned within each cell, indicating the data will be left-aligned. You use the alignment buttons on the Formatting toolbar to change the alignment of a cell's contents.

To advance from one cell to the next, press the TAB key. To advance from one row to the next, also press the TAB key or click the cell; do not press the ENTER key. The ENTER key is used to begin new paragraphs within a cell.

Adding Column Headings

Each column containing data should be identified with a **column heading.** Perform the following step to add column headings to the table.

Steps **To Add Column Headings**

1 **Click the cell at the intersection of column 1, row 1, if necessary. Type** Bus Stop **in the cell. Press the TAB key. Type** Bus 502 **and then press the TAB key. Type** Bus 504 **and then press the TAB key.**

The table displays three column headings (Figure 6). Cell contents are left-aligned. The insertion point is in the cell located at the intersection of column 1, row 2.

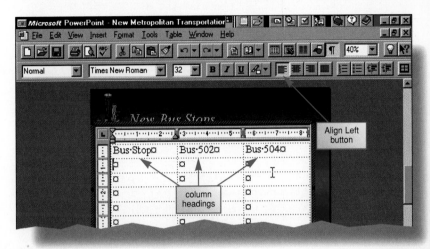

FIGURE 6

The column headings are complete. The next step is to enter data in the rows of the table.

Entering Data into Rows in a Table

As you enter data into a table, label the first cell of each row with a **row heading**. Then, complete the row with data in the appropriate columns. Follow the steps below to fill in the rows for the table on Slide 3.

TO ENTER DATA INTO ROWS OF A TABLE

Step 1: Type Main & Maple and press the TAB key. Type 6:40 a.m. and press the TAB key. Type 7:40 a.m. and press the TAB key.

Step 2: Type Main & Elm and press the TAB key. Type 6:50 a.m. and press the TAB key. Type 7:50 a.m. and press the TAB key.

Step 3: Type Main & Oak and press the TAB key. Type 7:00 a.m. and press the TAB key. Type 8:00 a.m. and press the TAB key.

Step 4: Type Oak & Center and press the TAB key. Type 7:15 a.m. and press the TAB key. Type 8:15 a.m. and press the TAB key.

Step 5: Type Center & Elm and press the TAB key. Type 7:30 a.m. and press the TAB key. Type 8:30 a.m. and press the TAB key.

Step 6: Type Center & Evergreen and press the TAB key. Type 7:45 a.m. and press the TAB key. Type 8:45 a.m. but do not press the TAB key.

The table is complete (Figure 7). The first column in the table contains the row headings.

More *About* **Table Column Headings**

Use meaningful column heading names for your tables. The audience will quickly understand the table if they know what table columns represent.

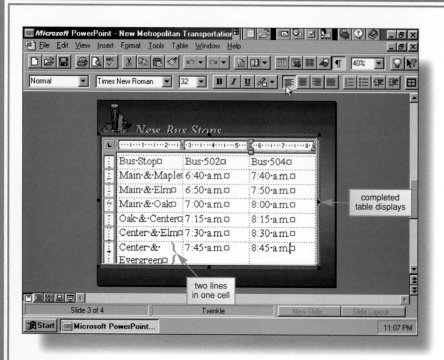

FIGURE 7

Notice that the row heading Center & Evergreen wrapped because the heading is too long to fit on one line in the cell. When you format the table in the next section, the row heading will no longer wrap.

Formatting a Word Table in PowerPoint

Because PowerPoint creates tables using Microsoft Word, you format the table using Word's Table AutoFormat command, which provides thirty-eight predefined table formats. Predefined formats vary the borders, shading, colors, and fonts for the cells within a table. Perform the following steps to format a table using Table AutoFormat.

Steps To Format a Table Using Table AutoFormat

1 **Right-click the table. Click Table AutoFormat on the shortcut menu. Click Colorful 2 in the Formats box. Click Color in the Formats to Apply area.**

The Table AutoFormat dialog box displays (Figure 8). Word displays a preview of the Colorful 2 format in the Preview area. The table displays in color because the Color check box is selected.

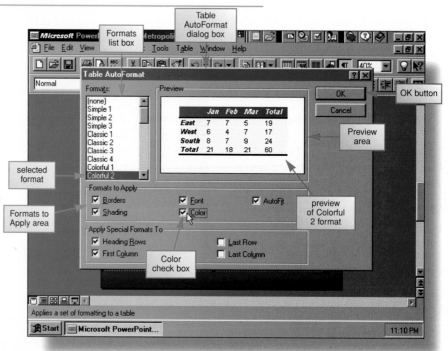

FIGURE 8

More *About*
More About
Formatting a Table

Keep the audience in mind when selecting one of Word's predefined table formats. Choose one that maintains a sharp contrast between the table background and the contents of the table cells.

2 **Click the OK button.**

The Table AutoFormat dialog box closes and the table displays with the Colorful 2 format (Figure 9). Center & Evergreen no longer wraps. Word redefines column widths based on the cell containing the longest data item because AutoFit was selected in the Table AutoFormat dialog box.

FIGURE 9

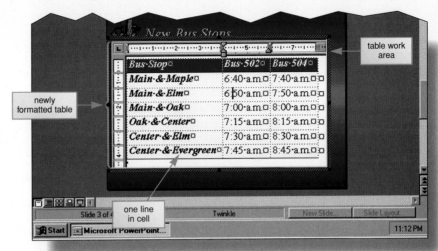

3 **Click outside the table work area.**

Word closes, the PowerPoint toolbars and menu bar redisplay, and the table displays on Slide 3 in PowerPoint (Figure 10). Because the table does not fill the table placeholder, it displays left-aligned in the table placeholder.

FIGURE 10

To edit the table, double-click it to open Word. When you complete your edits, click outside the table placeholder to return to PowerPoint.

Saving and Printing an Embedded Presentation

Perform the following steps to save and then print the New Metropolitan Transportation presentation.

TO SAVE AND PRINT A LINKED PRESENTATION

Step 1: Click the Save button on the Standard toolbar.
Step 2: Click the Black & White View button on the Standard toolbar.
Step 3: Click the Print button on the Standard toolbar.

PowerPoint saves and then prints the presentation in black and white.

> **Other Ways**
>
> 1. On Table menu click Table AutoFormat, click a format, click OK button
> 2. Press ALT+A, press F, press T, press arrow keys to select format, press TAB to select OK button, press ENTER

Summary

This Integration Feature introduced you to embedding a Microsoft Word table into a PowerPoint presentation. First, you opened an existing presentation, saved it with a new name, and inserted a new slide into which a blank Word table was embedded. Then, you entered data into the table. Next, you formatted the table using Word's Table AutoFormat command. Finally, you saved and printed the presentation.

1 Using Help

Instructions: Perform the following tasks using a computer.

1. Start PowerPoint. Double-click the Help button on the Standard toolbar to display the Help Topics: Microsoft PowerPoint dialog box.
2. Click the Index tab. Type table in box 1 and then click the Display button. Double-click Deciding which Office application to use to create a table, in the Topics Found dialog box. Read and print the Help information. Click the Help Topics button.
3. Double-click editing in box 2 of the Index sheet. Read and print the Help information. Click the Help Topics button.
4. Double-click inserting in box 2 of the Index sheet. Read and print the Help information. Click the Help Topics button.
5. Type embed in box 1. Click the Display button. Double-click Embed a new object in the Topics Found dialog box. Read and print the Help information. Click the Close button.
6. Label each printout with your name. Submit the printouts to your instructor.

2 Adding a Table to a Presentation

Problem: You created a presentation for your car club's road rally, but realize you must insert a table to define the awards.

Instructions: Start PowerPoint. Open the Rally presentation from the floppy disk with the Integration Feature files. Perform the following tasks. *Hint*: Use Help to solve this problem.

1. Insert a new slide after Slide 2 using the Table AutoLayout.
2. Type Awards for the slide title.
3. Insert a table with two columns and five rows.
4. Type Category in the first cell (1,1) and press the TAB key. Type Award and press the TAB key. Type Best Overall and press the TAB key. Type $100 gift certificate and press the TAB key. Type Best Time and press the TAB key. Type $25 gift certificate and press the TAB key. Type Best Speed and press the TAB

In the Lab

key. Type $25 gift certificate and press the TAB key. Type Best Distance and press the TAB key. Type $25 gift certificate in the last cell.

5. AutoFormat the table using the Simple 2 format. Change the table text color to white.
6. Resize the Word work area to 7 inches on the horizontal ruler.
7. Display and center the table on Slide 3.
8. Save the presentation with the filename Rally Table.
9. Print the presentation. Then, close PowerPoint.

3 Embedding and Formatting a Word Table

Problem: You are the Director of Safety for Intergalactic Pipeline. You are presenting the annual safety review to all department managers tomorrow afternoon. After reviewing accident statistics, you decide a table would best summarize the previous five year accident history.

Instructions:

1. Create a presentation using the outline in Figure 11 substituting your name for J. L. Jones on the title slide. Apply the Tridots Design Template.
2. Insert an appropriate clip art picture on Slide 2 using the Object over Text AutoLayout.
3. Embed a table on Slide 3 using the data in Figure 12. Format the table with the Columns 3 Auto-Format. Center the table on the slide.
4. Insert an appropriate clip art picture on Slide 4 using the Text and Clip Art AutoLayout.
5. Add slide transition and text build effects.
6. Save the presentation with the filename Safety Review.
7. Print the presentation.
8. Close PowerPoint.

I. **Annual Safety Review**
   A.   J. L. Jones
   B.   Director of Safety
   C.   Intergalactic Pipeline

II. **Agenda**
   A.   Accident history
   B.   Safety goal & objectives
   C.   Plan of action

III. **Accident History**

IV. **Safety Goals & Objectives**
   A.   Goals
       1.   Accident-free workplace
   B.   Objectives
       1.   Reduce accidents by 20% per year
       2.   Eliminate preventable accidents

V. **Plan of Action**
   A.   Pre-plan every job
       1.   Job safety analysis sheet
       2.   Material safety data sheet
   B.   Train employees
       1.   Proper use of tools and equipment
   C.   Inspect equipment
       1.   Repair or replace damaged equipment

FIGURE 11

YEAR	TOTAL ACCIDENTS	CHARGEABLE	NON-CHARGEABLE
1992	399	187	214
1993	357	148	209
1994	323	153	170
1995	306	106	200
1996	300	89	211

FIGURE 12

Index

Academic clip art, PP 2.26
Access database, embedding in presentation, PP 4.40
Active application, PP 1.40
Alignment, PP 3.56, PP 4.17-18
All Outlines option, importing file and, PP 3.8, PP 3.11
Animation effects
   object and, PP 4.55-56
   running slide show with, PP 2.46-47
   slide transition, PP 2.39-42
   text build, PP 2.39, PP 2.43-45, PP 4.57
Animation Settings command (shortcut menu), PP 4.56, PP 4.57
Applications
   active, PP 1.40
   importing outlines from other, PP 3.8-11
   opening during slide show, PP 4.43-45
   switching between, PP 1.40
Arrow keys, positioning object using, PP 4.34
Aspect ratio, object, **PP 2.33**
Attribute(s), PP 1.13, PP 2.8, PP 2.13
Attribute buttons, Formatting toolbar, **PP 1.16**
Audience handouts, PP 2.36-38
   printing, PP 2.53, PP 3.61-62
AutoClipArt feature, **PP 1.8**
AutoContent Wizard, **PP 1.8**
AutoLayout(s)
   adding clip art using, PP 2.27
   adding new slide with same, PP 1.30-31
   types of, PP 1.24
AutoLayout object area, **PP 1.14**
AutoLayouts Bulleted List, PP 1.25
Automatic slide show, PP 4.36

Background, Design Templates, PP 1.13
   creating custom, PP 3.14-19
   fill area and, PP 3.17-18
   graphics, PP 4.9
Background, sending object to, PP 3.51-52
Background Fill area, PP 3.17-18
Background object, **PP 3.49**
Balance, on slide, **PP 3.55**
B&W View button, **PP 1.49-50**
Bit-mapped graphic, **PP 3.15-16**
Black and white, displaying presentation in, PP 1.49-50
Black slide, ending presentation with, PP 4.52-53
Blank line, adding for white space, PP 2.20-23
Blank slide, ending presentation with, PP 3.60
Body text, Outline view and, PP 2.8
Bold button, **PP 1.16**
Border
   deleting from around object, PP 3.58
   fill color, PP 3.57, PP 3.58-59
   icon object, PP 4.42
   line color, PP 3.57, PP 4.42
   line style, PP 3.57, PP 3.58, PP 4.20, PP 4.51
   logo, PP 4.20
   organization chart, PP 3.35-36
   picture, PP 3.57-58
   WordArt text, PP 4.26-27
Branch, organization chart, **PP 3.30-32**
Branch, organization chart, **PP 3.30-32**
Buffer, **PP 2.60**
Build, animation settings and, PP 2.44, PP 4.56

Build Slide Text command (shortcut menu), PP 2.44
Bullet(s), **PP 1.8**
   Outline levels and, PP 2.8
   removing when creating blank line, PP 2.20, PP 2.23
   Style Checker and, PP 2.16
Bulleted list, PP 1.8, PP 4.46-47
Bulleted List AutoLayout, PP 1.25-26, PP 3.11
Bulleted list slide, **PP 1.24**
   adding in Outline view, PP 2.13-14, PP 3.11
   adding using Bulleted List AutoLayout, PP 1.25-26, PP 3.11
   moving text and, PP 2.25-26
   multi-level, PP 1.24-32, PP 2.13-14
   text build effects and, PP 2.43-45

Bulletin board system, clip art and, **PP 2.31**
Bullet On/Off button, **PP 1.16**, PP 2.22-23

Cartoons clip art, PP 2.26
Cell, Word table, **PPI 2.2**
Center, resizing about, PP 3.55-57
Centered title, PP 1.17
Change Color button, color scheme and, PP 4.12-13
Chart
   Excel, PP 3.38, PP 3.44, PP 3.45-47
   hierarchy, PP 3.20
Circle, drawing for logo, **PP 4.19**-20
Clip art, **PP 1.8**, **PP 2.26-35**, PP 3.6
   AutoLayout and, PP 2.27, PP 3.21
   converting to PowerPoint object, PP 3.41-43
   creating object, PP 3.38-48
   deselecting, PP 3.43-44
   disassembling, PP 3.38, PP 3.41-43
   inserting into clip art placeholder, PP 2.28-31, PP 3.39
   inserting without clip art placeholder, PP 2.32
   modifying using Drawing+ toolbar, PP 3.40-41
   moving, PP 2.33, PP 3.44-45
   regrouping, PP 3.43
   resizing using Scale command, PP 2.33-35
   scaling, PP 3.39
Clip Art & Text AutoLayout, PP 2.27-28, PP 3.21
Clip Art command (Insert menu), PP 2.31, PP 2.32
Clip art placeholders, PP 2.27
   inserting clip art and, PP 2.28-31, PP 3.39
   text in, PP 3.21
Closing PowerPoint, PP 1.37-38, PP 1.61
Closing slide, creating, **PP 2.17-18**, PP 3.60
Color
   bit mapped objects and, PP 3.15
   border line, PP 3.57, PP 4.42
   Design Templates, PP 1.13, PP 4.10-15
   dimmed, PP 2.43
   WordArt text, PP 4.24-26
Color box, WordArt text and, **PP 4.24-25**
Color scheme, Design Template and, **PP 4.10-15**
Column(s), Word table, PPI 2.2, PPI 2.4-5
Column boundary, table and, **PPI 2.4**
Column headings, adding to table, **PPI 2.4-5**
Column markers, PPI 2.4
Constrain resizing an object from center, **PP 3.55-56**
Container document, **PP 4.36**
Copy command (shortcut menu)
   adding object to Slide Master and, PP 4.31
   branch of organization chart and, PP 3.31
   slides and, PP 2.58
Copying
   branch of organization chart, PP 3.30-31
   slide in Slide Sorter view, PP 2.58
Create from File option, embedding Excel chart and, PP 3.46, PP 3.47
Custom background, PP 3.14-19, PP 4.9
Custom Background command (shortcut menu), PP 3.17, PP 4.9
Custom dictionary, **PP 1.41**
Customizing
   background, PP 3.14-19, PP 4.9
   existing presentation, PP 4.6-58
Cut command (shortcut menu), PP 2.26

Data, entering into table, PPI 2.5
Date, Notes and Handouts sheet and, PP 2.37
Decrease Font Size button, **PP 1.20**
Default setting, **PP 1.13**
DELETE key, PP 1.44, PP 4.45-46
Deleting
   border around object, PP 3.58
   object, PP 4.45-46
   paragraph, PP 1.44
   subordinate boxes, PP 3.24

text, PP 1.44
Demoted paragraph, **PP 1.26**
Demote (Indent more) button, PP 1.26, PP 1.28-29, PP 2.11-12, PP 2.13-14
Deselecting clip art objects, **PP 3.43-44**
Design Templates, **PP 1.9**
   background, PP 1.13, PP 4.9
   border fill color, PP 3.58-59
   changing, PP 2.7, PP 3.11-13, PP 4.8
   color scheme, PP 4.10-15
   color versus background and, PP 1.13
   displaying background graphics on, PP 4.9
   identifier, PP 1.14
   Slide Master and, PP 1.45
   text attributes and, PP 1.19
   types of, PP 1.11
Digitized signal, **PP 3.16**
Digitizing, **PP 3.16**
Disassemble Picture button, PP 3.40, PP 3.41-43
Disassembling clip art, **PP 3.38**, PP 3.41-43
Dissolve slide transition effect, PP 3.60-61, PP 4.53
Document
   container, PP 4.36
   source, PP 4.36
Drag and drop, **PP 2.9**
Dragging
   changing slide order by, PP 2.54-55
   clip art to move, PP 2.33
   clip art to size, PP 2.35, PP 4.49-50
   elevator, PP 1.33
   modified object, PP 3.51
   moving PowerPoint object by, PP 3.44-45, PP 4.34
   resizing picture by, PP 4.49-50
Drawing, **PP 1.8**
   circle, PP 4.19-20
   logo, PP 4.16
Drawing toolbar, PP 1.15, **PP 1.16**
   border fill color and, PP 3.58-59
   border line style and, PP 3.58, PP 4.51
   circles and, PP 4.19
   shadow and, PP 4.41
Drawing+ command (shortcut menu), PP 3.40
Drawing+ toolbar, **PP 3.40**
   grouping objects and, PP 3.48, PP 3.53
   using View menu to display, PP 3.40-41
Draw menu
   Bring Forward command, PP 3.52
   Bring to Front command, PP 3.52
   Regroup command, PP 3.43
   Scale command, clip art and, PP 3.39

Scale command, Excel chart and, PP 3.47-48
Scale command, icon objects and, PP 4.41
Scale command, logo object and, PP 4.34
Scale command, organization chart object and, PP 3.37
Scale command, picture and, PP 2.34, PP 4.48
Scale command, restoring scaled object and, PP 3.57
Scale command, WordArt object and, PP 4.30
Send Backward command, PP 3.52
Send to Back command, PP 3.51

Edit Bitmap Image Object command (shortcut menu), color and, PP 3.15
Editing
   bulleted list, PP 4.46-47
   changing slide order in Outline view, PP 2.54-55
   changing slide order in Slide Sorter view, PP 2.56-58
   clip art, PP 2.31
   copying and pasting slide, PP 2.58-60
   displaying slide titles in Outline view, PP 2.53-54
   error correction and, PP 1.44-45
   organization chart, PP 3.32-33
   reversing using Undo button, PP 2.60
   text, PP 4.7-8
Edit menu
   Copy command, PP 2.58

Cut command, PP 2.26
Paste command, PP 2.26, PP 2.58
Select All command, objects and, PP 3.52, PP 4.30
Select command, all boxes in organization chart, PP 3.33-34
Undo command, PP 2.60
Undo Typing command, PP 1.17
Edit Placeholder Object command (shortcut menu), PP 2.31
Electronic presentations, PP 1.8
Elevator, scrolling and, **PP 1.33**
Ellipse Tool, PP 4.19
Embedded visuals, PP 3.3-63
Embedding
   Access database in presentation, PP 4.40
   Excel chart, PP 3.38, PP 3.44, PP 3.45-47
   organization chart, PP 3.20-37
   picture into a slide, PP 3.54-59
   scaling object, PP 3.47-48
   Word table into presentation, PPI 2.1-8
End Show command (shortcut menu), **PP 1.36**
End-of-cell mark, **PPI 2.4**
ENTER key, creating new paragraph using, PP 1.17, PP 1.28, PP 1.29
Error correction
   editing and, PP 1.44-45
   Style Checker and, PP 1.40-43
ESC key, displaying last slide using, PP 1.37
Excel, opening during slide show, PP 4.44
Excel chart
   embedding, PP 3.38, PP 3.44, PP 3.45-47
   linking to, PP 4.39
   overlaying on screen object, PP 3.49
   scaling, PP 3.47-48
Excel worksheet, linking to presentation, PP 4.39

File(s)
   bit-mapped, PP 3.15-16
   embedding Excel chart from list of, PP 3.46
   graphic, PP 3.8
   linked object and, PP 3.47
   picture, PP 2.32, PP 3.55
   plain text, PP 3.11
   RTF, PP 2.9, PP 3.8
   TXT, PP 3.8
   vector graphic, PP 3.16
File menu
   Exit command, PP 1.38
   Open command, importing outline and, PP 3.11
   Print command, handouts and, PP 3.61
   Print command, hard copies and, PP 1.52
   Print command, printing in Outline view and, PP 2.47, PP 2.49-53
   Save As command, PP 1.22, PP 4.7
   Save command, PP 1.24
Filename
   clip art, PP 2.30-31
   saving presentation with new, PP 1.22, PP 4.7
   saving presentation with same, PP 1.32
Fill color, PP 1.16
   border, PP 3.57, PP 3.58-59
   custom background, PP 3.17-18
   icon object, PP 4.41
Fill Color button, **PP 1.16**, PP 3.58-59
Fill Color menu, Picture command, PP 3.18
Filters, graphic, PP 3.16
Finding clip art, PP 2.30-31, PP 2.32, PP 3.39
Fly From Right animation setting, PP 4.56
Font
   bullet, PP 1.26
   Outline view slides, PP 2.11, PP 2.12, PP 2.13
Font color, WordArt text and, PP 4.24-26
Font (shortcut menu), PP 1.21
Font size
   Outline view slides, PP 2.11, PP 2.12
   title slide, PP 1.19-21
Font Size box, **PP 1.21**

Font style, PP 1.21, PP 2.11, PP 2.12, PP 2.13
Footer, adding to audience handout outline, PP 2.36-38
Foreground objects, PP 3.49
Format(s)
  Design Templates, PP 3.13
  graphics, PP 3.15-16
Format menu
  Color and Lines command, border and, PP 3.58, PP 3.59
  Custom Background command, PP 3.19
  Font command, PP 1.21
  Line Spacing command, PP 1.47
  Shading command, WordArt text and, PP 4.26
  Slide Color Scheme command, PP 4.11
  Slide Layout command, PP 2.25, PP 2.28
Formatting, PP 1.45-50
  organization chart, PP 3.33-34
  Slide Master and, PP 1.45
  text attributes and, PP 1.19-22
  title slide, PP 1.19-22
  Word table in PowerPoint, PPI 2.6-7
Formatting toolbar, PP 1.15, PP 1.16
  font size and, PP 1.21
  paragraph levels and, PP 1.26
Free Rotate Tool button, PP 1.16

Go To command (shortcut menu), PP 1.35
Graphic(s), PP 1.8, PP 3.6
  Outline view and, PP 2.8
Graphic filters, PP 3.16
Graphic formats, PP 3.15-16
Gridlines, table and, PPI 2.4
Group button, regrouping object using, PP 3.43
Group command (shortcut menu), PP 3.50, PP 3.53
Grouping objects, PP 3.48-53
  layered objects into one modified screen object, PP 3.50
  objects for logo, PP 4.30-31
  selected objects, PP 3.53
Group Objects button (Drawing+ toolbar), PP 3.48, PP 3.53
Guides, PP 4.17-18
  displaying and positioning, PP 4.48
  hiding, PP 4.37
Guides command (shortcut menu), PP 4.18, PP 4.48

Hard copy, presentation, PP 1.50
Header, adding to audience handout outline, PP 2.36-38
Header and Footer command (PowerPoint View command), PP 2.36-37
Hide Slide button, PP 4.55
Hide Slide command (shortcut menu), PP 4.54-55
Hiding
  rulers and guides, PP 4.37
  slides, PP 4.54-55
Hierarchy chart, PP 3.20
Horizontal ruler, PP 4.17
Horizontal scroll bar, PP 1.14

Icon objects, PP 4.36, PP 4.38
Importing
  outlines, PP 3.8-11
  picture, PP 3.54-55
Indents
  Outline levels and, PP 2.8
  paragraph levels and, PP 1.26
Inflate shape, WordArt text and, PP 4.24
Insert Clip Art button, PP 2.31, PP 2.32, PP 3.39, PP 3.42
Inserting
  clip art, PP 2.26-32, PP 3.39, PP 3.42
  Excel chart, PP 3.45
  new slide, PP 1.25
  picture for customized background, PP 3.14-19
  picture into slide, PP 3.54-55, PP 4.47
  slide with Table AutoLayout, PPI 2.3
  text, PP 1.44, PP 1.45
  WordArt object, PP 4.22
  Word document into presentation, PP 4.38
Insert menu
  Clip Art command, PP 2.31, PP 2.32, PP 3.42
  New Slide command, PP 1.25

Object command, Excel chart and, PP 3.45
Object command, WordArt and, PP 4.22
Picture command, PP 4.47
WordArt and, PP 4.22
Integrating applications, embedding Word table into presentation, PPI 2.1-8
Interactive documents, PP 4.4, PP 4.36-45
Italic button, PP 1.16, PP 1.21

Landscape orientation, PP 1.13
Layered objects, PP 3.49
  grouping into one modified screen object, PP 3.50
  selecting object from, PP 3.52
Levels, PP 1.26, PP 2.8-9, PP 3.11
Line, adding blank, PP 2.20-23
Line color, border, PP 3.57-58, PP 4.42
Line Color menu, PP 3.58, PP 4.42
Line style, border, PP 3.57, PP 3.58, PP 4.20, PP 4.51
Line Style button (Drawing toolbar), PP 3.58, PP 4.51
Line Style menu, PP 3.58
Line Thickness button (WordArt toolbar), PP 4.27
Line wrap text, PP 1.17
Link/linked object, PP 3.47, PP 4.36
  Excel worksheet and chart to presentation, PP 4.39
  losing when importing clip art, PP 3.38, PP 3.42
  presentation to another presentation, PP 4.39
  Word document to presentation, PP 4.38
Logo
  adding to Slide Master, PP 4.31-35
  animating, PP 4.55-57
  creating, PP 4.15-20
  grouping objects, PP 4.30-31
  scaling, PP 4.30
  text for, PP 4.21-29

Manager box, PP 3.22
Menu bar, PP 1.14
Microsoft ClipArt Gallery 2.0, PP 2.26, PP 2.29, PP 2.32, PP 3.6, PP 3.16, PP 3.38, PP 3.39
Microsoft Organization Chart, PP 3.20-37
Microsoft Windows Paintbrush, PP 3.16
Mouse pointer, PP 1.15, PP 1.35
Moving
  to another slide in Slide view, PP 1.33
  clip art, PP 2.33
  manually through slides, PP 1.35
  object, PP 3.44-45
  slide order in Outline view, PP 2.54
  slides, PP 2.53
  text on slide, PP 2.25-26
Multi-level bulleted list slides, PP 1.26-32
  creating in Outline view, PP 2.13-14
Multimedia effects, PP 1.8
Multiple text objects, creating slide with in Outline view, PP 2.16-17

New Slide button, PP 1.14
  bulleted list slide, PP 1.24-25, PP 2.13
  Table AutoLayout and, PPI 2.3
Next command (shortcut menu), PP 1.35
Next Slide button, PP 1.14, PP 1.33
Notes Pages view, PP 1.13, PP 2.35
Notes view, hiding slide in, PP 4.55

Object(s), PP 1.13
  adding to Slide Master, PP 4.31-35
  aligning with guides, PP 4.17-18
  animating, PP 4.55-56
  aspect ratio, PP 2.33
  attributes, PP 1.13
  background, PP 3.49
  border around, PP 3.57-58, PP 4.42
  constraining resizing from center, PP 3.55-56
  creating slide with multiple text, PP 2.16-17
  deleting, PP 4.45-46
  deleting border around, PP 3.58
  dragging modified, PP 3.51
  fill color, PP 4.41
  foreground, PP 3.49
  grouping, PP 3.48-53
  grouping layered into one modified screen object, PP 3.50
  grouping logo, PP 4.30-31
  grouping selected, PP 3.53

icon, PP 4.36
layered, PP 3.49
linked, PP 3.47, PP 4.36
logo, PP 4.15-35
organization chart, PP 3.20-37
overlaying, PP 3.49
pasting on slide, PP 4.34-35
placeholders, PP 1.14
position of, PP 3.51, PP 4.33, PP 4.49-51
regrouping, PP 3.43
resizing, PP 4.49-51
scaling icon, PP 4.40-41
scaling logo, PP 4.30
selecting using Select All command, PP 3.52
semi-transparent, PP 3.59
sending to background, PP 3.51-52
shadow, PP 4.41-42
size of, PP 4.33
text for logo, PP 4.21-29
title, PP 1.15
vector graphic, PP 3.16
Object AutoLayout, inserting clip art and, PP 3.39
Object linking and embedding (OLE)
  embedding Word table into presentation and, PPI 2.1-8
  Microsoft Organization Chart and, PP 3.20
  opening application during slide show and, PP 4.43-45
  presentation containing interactive documents and, PP 4.4, PP 4.36-45
  WordArt and, PP 4.21-22
Object-oriented pictures, PP 3.16
Online Help, PP 1.53-61
Opening
  application during slide show, PP 4.43-45
  existing presentation, PP 1.38-40, PP 3.9
  existing presentation and saving with new filename, PP 4.7
  new presentation, PP 1.9
Organization chart, PP 3.20
  adding subordinate boxes, PP 3.25-27
  border styles in, PP 3.35-36
  closing, PP 3.36-37
  copying and pasting branch of, PP 3.30-32
  deleting subordinate boxes, PP 3.24
  editing, PP 3.32-33
  embedding, PP 3.20-37
  formatting, PP 3.33-34
  manager box, PP 3.22
  names for subordinate boxes and, PP 3.27-28
  root manager box, PP 3.22, PP 3.23
  scaling object, PP 3.37
  shadow effects for boxes, PP 3.34-35
  styles, PP 3.28-30
  subordinate boxes, PP 3.22
Organization Chart layout, PP 3.21
Organization Chart window, maximizing, PP 3.22
Outline/outlining, PP 1.7, PP 2.7
  changing Slide layout to Title Slide and, PP 3.14-15
  creating presentation from, PP 2.4-18
  importing, PP 3.8-11
Outline for audience, adding header and footer to, PP 2.36-38
Outline levels, PP 3.11
  one, PP 2.8, PP 2.11
  two, PP 2.8, PP 2.12
  three, PP 2.8, PP 2.14
  four, PP 2.8
  five, PP 2.8
  six, PP 2.8
Outline view, PP 1.13, PP 2.4, PP 2.7-18
  changing slide order in, PP 2.54-55
  creating closing slide in, PP 2.17-18
  displaying all text in, PP 2.55
  displaying slide titles in, PP 2.53-54
  printing in, PP 2.47-53
  slide with multiple text objects and, PP 2.16-17
  using, PP 2.7-10
Outline View button, PP 2.8-9
Outline View window, PP 2.9
Outlining toolbar, PP 2.10
  displaying all text and, PP 2.56
  displaying slide titles and, PP 2.53-54
Overhead transparencies, PP 1.7, PP 1.53
Overlayering objects, PP 3.49

Pack And Go Wizard, PP 1.8
Paint programs, bit-mapped graphics created in, PP 3.16
Paragraph(s), PP 1.17
  blank line between, PP 2.20-23
  creating new, PP 1.17, PP 1.28
  deleting, PP 1.44
  demoted, PP 1.26, PP 1.28-29
  levels of, PP 1.26, PP 2.13
  line spacing and, PP 1.47
  promoting, PP 1.26, PP 1.29-30
Paste Boxes command (shortcut menu), branch of organization chart and, PP 3.31-32
Paste command (shortcut menu)
  logo object and, PP 4.35
  slide and, PP 2.59
  text and, PP 2.26
Pasting
  branch of organization chart, PP 3.31-32
  logo object, PP 4.35
  object on slide, PP 4.34-35
  slide, PP 2.58-59
  text, PP 2.26
PCS file extension, PP 3.16
Pen command (shortcut menu), PP 1.35
Percentage
  changing size of clip art by exact, PP 2.33
  clip art scale and, PP 3.39, PP 3.48
  Zoom Control and, PP 4.17, PP 4.18
Photographs, PP 2.32
Picture(s), PP 2.32, PP 3.6, PP 3.15
  border, PP 3.57-58
  embedding into a slide, PP 3.54-59
  inserting, PP 3.54-55, PP 4.47
  inserting for customized background, PP 3.14-19
  object-oriented, PP 3.16
  replacing, PP 4.45-51
  resizing, PP 3.55-57
  resizing about center, PP 3.55-57
  scaling, PP 4.48
  scanned, PP 3.16
Picture element (pixel), PP 3.15
Placeholders, PP 1.14
  changing slide layout and, PP 2.23
  clip art, PP 2.27, PP 2.28-31, PP 3.21, PP 3.39
  nontext object, PP 2.23
  sub-title, PP 1.15, PP 1.18
  text, PP 3.21
  title, PP 1.15, PP 1.17
Plain text files, PP 3.11
Pointer indicator, PP 4.17
Popup menu, Slide Show view and, PP 1.35-37
Popup Menu button, PP 1.36
Portrait orientation, PP 1.13
Positioning
  guides, PP 4.48
  object, PP 4.33, PP 4.49-51
PowerPoint, PP 1.6
  closing, PP 1.37-38, PP 1.61
  online Help and, PP 1.53-61
  views, PP 1.13
PowerPoint object, PP 3.38
  converting clip art object to, PP 3.38, PP 3.41-43
  converting WordArt object into, PP 4.31
  moving, PP 3.44-45
  returning modified screen object to, PP 3.51
PowerPoint window
  in Outline view, PP 2.9-10
  in Slide view, PP 1.13-16
PPT extension, PP 1.24
Presentation
  adding new slide to, PP 1.24-32
  animation effects, PP 2.39-47
  audience handouts, PP 2.36-38
  closing slide in, PP 2.17-18, PP 3.60-62
  color scheme, PP 4.10-15
  copying and pasting slides in, PP 2.58-59
  creating from Outline view, PP 2.4-18
  customizing existing, PP 4.6-58
  design, PP 1.8, PP 1.14, PP 1.15
  displaying in black and white, PP 1.49-50
  editing, PP 2.53-60
  embedded visuals and, PP 3.3-63
  embedding Access database in, PP 4.40
  embedding Word table into, PPI 2.1-8
  ending with black slide, PP 4.52-53
  error correction, PP 1.40-45

inserting and linking Word document to, PP 4.38
interactive OLE documents and, PP 4.4, PP 4.36-45
line spacing, PP 1.47-49
linking Excel worksheet and chart to, PP 4.39
linking to another presentation, PP 4.39
logo and, PP 4.15-35
opening existing, PP 1.38-40, PP 3.9
opening new, PP 1.9
printing, PP 1.50-53
printing in Outline view, PP 2.47-53
saving to floppy disk, PP 1.22-24
saving with new filename, PP 4.7
slide layout, PP 2.23-26
slide order in Outline view, PP 2.54-55
slide order in Slide Sorter view, PP 2.56-58
Slide Sorter view and, PP 2.19-20
spell checking, PP 1.40-43, PP 2.38-39
starting new, PP 1.9-16
style checking, PP 1.40-43, PP 2.38-39
subordinate slides and, PP 2.15-16
subtitle, PP 1.18-19
title slide, PP 1.16-22
viewing using Slide Show, PP 1.34-37
white space and, PP 2.20-23
Presentation Designs sheet, PP 1.11
Presentation management, **PP 1.8**
Previewing
  Design Template, PP 3.12
  picture, PP 3.55
  scaled clip art, PP 3.48
  slide transition effects, PP 2.42
Previous command (shortcut menu), **PP 1.35**
Previous points, dimmed, PP 2.43
Previous Slide button, **PP 1.14**, PP 1.33
Print button, **PP 1.51**
Printing/printout, **PP 1.50**
  handouts, PP 2.53
  in Outline view, PP 2.47-53
  presentation, PP 1.50-53
  presentation outline, PP 2.36-38
  slides as handouts, PP 3.61-62
  transparencies, PP 1.53
Promote a paragraph, **PP 1.26**
Promote (Indent less) button, **PP 1.26**, PP 1.29-30
  Outline view and, PP 2.12-13
Punctuation errors, PP 1.43

Raster images, **PP 3.16**
Regroup command (shortcut menu), PP 3.43
Regroup object, **PP 3.43**
Resize handle
  clip art and, PP 2.35
  picture about center and, PP 3.56
Resizing
  clip art, PP 2.35
  object, PP 4.49-51
  picture about center, **PP 3.55-57**
Root manager box, **PP 3.22**, PP 3.23
Rotating object, PP 1.16
Rough draft, **PP 1.50**
Row heading, table and, **PPI 2.5**
RTF (Rich Text Format) file, **PP 2.9**, PP 3.8
Ruler(s), **PP 4.17**, PP 4.37
Ruler command (shortcut menu), PP 4.17

Save button, PP 1.22-24, PP 1.32
Saving
  before printing, PP 1.51
  presentation to floppy disk, PP 1.22-24
  presentation with new filename, PP 4.7
  presentation with same filename, PP 1.32
Scaling
  clip art, PPP 2.33-35, P 3.39
  Excel chart, PP 3.47-48
  icon objects, PP 4.40-41
  logo object, PP 4.30
  organization chart object, PP 3.37
  picture object, PP 4.48
Scanned pictures, **PP 3.16**
Scanner, **PP 3.16**
Selected objects, grouping, PP 3.53
Selecting
  all boxes in organization chart, PP 3.33-34
  bulleted list text, PP 4.46-47
  moving clip art and, PP 2.33
  multiple slides using SHIFT+click technique, PP 2.40-41

objects using Select All command, PP 3.52, PP 4.30
slide before applying transition effects, PP 2.40
text on slide and moving, PP 2.25-26
text placeholder, PP 1.27
Selection box/rectangle, **PP 1.17**
  disassembled objects and, PP 3.42
  grouping layered objects into one object and, PP 3.50
  moving PowerPoint object and, PP 3.44
  removing, PP 3.43-44
Semi-transparent objects, PP 3.59
Sending object to background, PP 3.51-52
Shading command, WordArt and, PP 4.24-25, PP 4.26
Shadow
  for boxes in organization chart, PP 3.34-35
  icon object, **PP 4.41-42**
  text, PP 1.16
Shadow On/Off button (Drawing toolbar), PP 4.41
Shaping WordArt text, PP 4.23-24
SHIFT+click technique, **PP 2.40-41**
  adding multiple subordinate boxes using, PP 3.25-26
  copying organization chart branch using, PP 3.30
  grouping layered objects using, PP 3.50
  selecting multiple slides using, **PP 2.40-41**
Show All button, PP 2.56
Show Titles button, PP 2.53, PP 2.54
Slide(s), **PP 1.13**
  adding in Outline view, PP 2.12-13
  adding new, PP 1.24-32
  adding new with same AutoLayout, PP 1.30-31
  AutoLayout types, PP 1.24
  balance on, PP 3.55
  changing order of, in Outline view, PP 2.54-55
  changing order of, in Slide Sorter view, PP 2.56-58
  clip art on, PP 2.26-35
  closing, PP 2.17-18, PP 3.60
  copying in Slide Sorter view, PP 2.58
  current, PP 1.12, PP 1.14
  custom background for, PP 3.14-19
  editing, PP 2.53-60
  embedding picture into, PP 3.54-59
  hiding, PP 4.54-55
  inserting with Table AutoLayout, PPI 2.3
  layout of, PP 2.23-26
  line spacing on, PP 1.47-49
  moving, PP 2.53
  moving text on, PP 2.25-26
  moving through manually, PP 1.35
  moving to another in Slide view, PP 1.33
  multi-level bulleted list, PP 1.26, PP 2.13-14
  multiple text objects and, PP 2.16-17
  number, PP 1.12, PP 1.14
  objects and, PP 1.13
  pasting, PP 2.59
  pasting object on, PP 4.34-35
  selecting multiple, using SHIFT+click technique, PP 2.40-41
  subordinate, PP 2.15-16
  supporting, PP 4.54
  35mm, PP 1.8
  three-dimensional, PP 3.49
  title, PP 1.8, PP 1.12, PP 1.17-22
  white space on, PP 1.49
Slide Color Scheme command (shortcut menu), PP 4.10-11, PP 4.12
Slide indicator, **PP 1.33**
Slide layout, **PP 1.13**
  bulleted list slide, PP 2.23-24
  changing to Title Slide, for imported outline, PP 3.14-15
  clip art and, PP 2.28, PP 2.33, PP 3.39
  Organization Chart, PP 3.21
Slide Layout button, **PP 1.14**, **PP 2.23**
  bulleted list slide, PP 2.23-24
  changing slide layout using, PP 2.23
  clip art and, PP 2.28, PP 2.33
  imported outline and, PP 3.14
Slide Layout command (shortcut menu), PP 2.25
Slide Master, **PP 1.45**
  adding logo object to, PP 4.31-35
  displaying, PP 1.46-47
  displaying background graphics on, PP 4.9

line spacing and, PP 1.47-49
omitting bit-mapped graphics and, PP 3.16-19
Slide show
  automatic, PP 4.36
  blank slide ending, PP 3.60
  hidden slide and, PP 4.58
  interactive documents and, PP 4.58
  opening application during, PP 4.43-45
  running with animation effects, PP 2.46-47
Slide Show button, **PP 1.34**
  animation effects and, PP 2.46-47
Slide Show view, **PP 1.13**
  exiting, PP 1.36
  Popup menu and, PP 1.35-37
  viewing presentation in, PP 1.34-37
Slide Sorter toolbar
  text build effects and, PP 2.45
  transition effects and, PP 2.40, PP 2.43
Slide Sorter view, **PP 1.13**
  changing slide order in, PP 2.56-58
  copying slide in, PP 2.58
  hiding slide in, PP 4.54-55
  reviewing presentation in, PP 2.19-20
  transition effects and, PP 2.40, PP 2.42, PP 3.60
Slide Sorter View button, PP 2.19, PP 2.57
Slide title
  displaying in Outline view, PP 2.53-54
  entering, PP 1.26-27
Slide Transition button, PP 2.42
Slide transition effects, **PP 2.39-42**, PP 2.43-54, PP 3.60-61, PP 4.53
Slide view, **PP 1.13**
  changing slide layout in, PP 3.14-15
  changing to, PP 2.21
  editing text in, PP 4.7-8
  hiding slide in, PP 4.55
  moving to another slide in, PP 1.33
  PowerPoint window in, PP 1.13-16
  Scale command and, PP 2.35
Slide View button, PP 2.21, PP 3.14
Snap to guides, PP 4.17, PP 4.49
Source document, **PP 4.36**
Source file, linked object and, PP 3.47
Spell checking, PP 1.40-43, PP 2.38-39
Standard toolbar, **PP 1.15**
Start button, PP 1.9
Start menu, PP 1.9
Status bar, PP 1.12, **PP 1.14**
Style Checker, PP 1.40-43, PP 2.38-39
  bullets and, PP 2.16
Subordinate boxes, **PP 3.22**
  adding, PP 3.25-27
  adding another level of, PP 3.27
  deleting, PP 3.24
  names for, PP 3.27-28
  title, PP 3.25, PP 3.32-33
Subordinate box tool button, PP 3.25
Supporting slide, **PP 4.54**

Table, Word, **PPI 2.2**
  embedding into presentation, PPI 2.1-8
Table AutoFormat (Word shortcut menu), PPI 2.6
Table AutoLayout, inserting new slide with, PPI 2.3
Tabs at beginning of paragraphs, defining outline structure and, PP 3.11
Text
  animating, PP 4.57
  editing, PP 4.7-8
  graphic object with, PP 4.21-29
  moving, PP 2.25-26
  organization chart, PP 3.32-33
  Outline view and, PP 2.8
  replacing, PP 1.44
  title slide, PP 1.17
  WordArt, PP 4.23-24
Text attribute, **PP 1.19-22**
Text box, **PP 1.17**
Text build effects, **PP 2.39**, PP 2.43-45, PP 3.60-61
Text Shadow button, **PP 1.16**
Text Tool button, **PP 1.16**
Three-dimensional slides, PP 3.49
Tick marks, on rulers, **PP 4.17**
TIF file, PP 3.55
Title
  for bulleted list slide, PP 1.26-27
  outline, PP 2.5
  root manager box, PP 3.23
  subordinate boxes, PP 3.25, PP 3.32-33
Title bar, **PP 1.14**
Title Master, **PP 1.45**

displaying background graphics on, PP 4.9
omitting bit-mapped graphics and, PP 3.16-19
Title object, **PP 1.15**
Title slide, **PP 1.8**
  changing slide layout to, for imported outline, PP 3.14-15
  creating, PP 1.16-19
  formatting, PP 1.19-22
  Master, PP 1.45
  Outline view, PP 2.10-12
Title Slide AutoLayout, PP 1.12
Title text, Outline view and, PP 2.8
Toolbars, **PP 1.15**
  Drawing+, PP 3.40-41, PP 3.48, PP 3.53
  Formatting, PP 1.15, PP 1.16, PP 1.21, PP 1.26
  Outlining, PP 2.9-10, PP 2.53-54, PP 2.56
  Slide Sorter, PP 2.40, PP 2.43, PP 2.45
  Standard, PP 1.15
  WordArt, PP 4.21
Toolbars command (shortcut menu), displaying Drawing+ toolbar and, PP 3.41
Tools menu
  Animation Settings command, PP 2.45, PP 4.56, PP 4.57
  Hide Slide command, PP 4.55
  Interactive Settings command, PP 4.43-44
  Options command, Slide Show view Popup menu and, PP 1.36
  Slide Transition command, PP 2.42
  Style Checker command, PP 1.41-42, PP 2.39
Triple-clicking, **PP 1.9**
TXT files, PP 3.8

Underline button, **PP 1.16**
Undo button
  grouping layered objects and, PP 3.50
  resizing picture about center and, PP 3.57
  reversing changes with, PP 1.17
  reversing last edit with, PP 2.60
Ungrouping clip art object, **PP 3.38**

Variables, default setting, PP 1.13
Vector graphic, **PP 3.16**
Vertical organization chart style, PP 3.29-30
Vertical ruler, **PP 4.17**
Vertical scroll box, PP 1.33
View(s), **PP 1.13**
  B&W, PP 1.49-50
  Notes Pages, PP 2.35
  Slide Master for, PP 1.46
View Button Bar, **PP 1.13**, PP 1.34
View menu
  Black and White command, PP 1.50
  Guides command, PP 4.18
  Header and Footer command, PP 2.36-37
  Outline command, PP 2.9
  Ruler command, PP 4.17
  Slides command, PP 2.21
  Slide Sorter command, PP 2.20
  Toolbars command, PP 3.41
Visual Clarity, Style Checker and, PP 1.43

White space, **PP 1.49**, PP 2.20-23
Window(s), PP 1.13-16, PP 2.9
Wizards, **PP 1.8**
WMF file extension, PP 3.16
Word, opening during slide show, PP 4.43-44
WordArt, **PP 4.21-29**
WordArt text
  border, PP 4.26-27
  entering, PP 4.23
  font color, PP 4.24-26
  shaping, PP 4.23-24
WordArt toolbar, PP 4.21
Word document
  importing outline from, PP 3.8-11
  inserting and linking to presentation, PP 4.38
Word processing, PowerPoint and, PP 1.7
Word table, embedding into presentation, PPI 2.1-8

Zoom, Outline view and, PP 2.11
Zoom Control, **PP 1.14**, PP 4.18-19